# 1000
## SLOVAKIAN
## SIGHTS AND MONUMENTS

# 1000
# SLOVAKIAN
# SIGHTS AND MONUMENTS

## JÁN LACIKA

### PHOTOGRAPHS BY:

JÁN LACIKA

KAROL DEMUTH | JOZEF LOMNICKÝ | KAROL KÁLLAY

MICHAL RENGEVIČ | LADISLAV STERNMÜLLER

**IKAR**

From the Slovakian original by Ján Lacika: 1000 zaujímavostí Slovenska translated by Alena Byrne.
Photographs: Ján Lacika, Jozef Lomnický, Karol Demuth, Michal Rengevič, Karol Kállay, Ladislav Sternmüller
Graphic Design: Viera Fabianová
Editor: Jessica Kendall Williamson
Layout: PRO 2, s. r. o., Bratislava
Published by Ikar, a. s., Bratislava in 2008 as its publication number 2597.
Printed by: Tlačiarne BB, Banská Bystrica.

ISBN 978-80-551-1783-6

# INTRODUCTION

It is said that beauty is diversity. Indeed, the Slovakian landscape is a beauty. An especially colourful mosaic of landscape pieces together this rather smallish country in the heart of Europe, including numerous natural formations as well as creations made by the work and skill of man. In some places, one can drive hundreds of kilometres, yet the surrounding countryside remains monotonous and unchanging. Many travellers do appreciate the charm of such lands, and there is nothing wrong with this. However, more people are fascinated by diversity and in this case, Slovakia has a lot to offer. Just take a bike and in several hours, you will ride through very different landscapes. Starting in Vranov nad Topľou in the morning and finishing in Tatranská Lomnica in the evening, you will be enchanted by the lowlands and valleys and admire the low mountain ranges as well as the sharp looming peaks of the Tatras Mountains. The Footprints of history and monuments of sacral and secular architecture are less colourful. It cannot be otherwise in a landscape, which lies in the heart of Europe. Thus, the task to find and describe a thousand remarkable Slovakian features does not strike us as difficult, as the offer is indeed both interesting and rich. However, after listing all the features that should be included in this book, we ended up with many more, greatly exceeding the set number of one thousand; To decide what to keep and what to leave out was no easy task. In many cases the aesthetic criterion was applied, as each feature has its own photo in this publication, which made some monuments, even the important ones (such as chateaus and sacral buildings), unsuitable to be included due to their bad technical state. Furthermore, we also have features in Slovakia which are extremely difficult to take a picture of, and these are indeed also missing from this publication. Just to mention a few, there is the Špaňdolinský Vodovod (Aqueduct) an the hills Starohorské vrchy, the prehistoric town on the Myšia Hôrka mountain near the village of Spišský Štvrtok and the mysterious mound in the Štiavnické vrchy Hills nicknamed the "Slovakian Wall of China". The one thousand remarkable features of Slovakia are listed according to their regions. For this purpose, we have divided Slovakia into five main areas: Bratislava, western Slovakia, north-central Slovakia, South-central Slovakia and eastern Slovakia. The sights within these areas are grouped according to the local regions and areas, such as Kysuce, Liptov and Košice and the surroundings. The palette of the localities is very colourful and varied. Amongst the natural phenomena are dominant mountains, valleys, rock formations, caves, bogs and moors, marshlands and virgin forests. As for the significant man-made creations, the book presents castles, chateaus and mansions, ruins, churches and chapels, monasteries, Marian poles, city palaces, burgher houses, town halls, outlook-towers, technical monuments, open-air museums, rustic and peasant houses, spas, thermal spas and swimming pools, reservoirs and lakes, and also several brilliant modern buildings. We do apologise in advance to those readers who will not find all they expected in this book – one thousand has proved to be a very low number indeed.

JÁN LACIKA

# CONTENTS

# BRATISLAVA

Bratislava is referred to as a small metropolis. One of the smallest European cities, it offers a thriving city life as well as an intimate atmosphere typical for quiet middle-sized towns. Bratislava has a splendid location, sprawling on both banks of the Danube River, and it lies relatively close to two large central European cities, Vienna and Budapest. It is a city that boasts scores of monuments dating from the times of the Bratislava Celtic oppidum up to the current modern times. A great jewel of this Slovakian metropolis is the stately Bratislava Castle. The historical centre of Bratislava is a tangle of picturesque lines and tiny squares confined to a small area dotted with scores of historical monuments. Many of them remember the times when Bratislava was the capital city of Hungary. Yet, charming places can also be found in the suburbs of Bratislava. One of them is Devín Castle, perched on a high romantic rock above the confluence of the Danube and Morava rivers.

## BRATISLAVA CASTLE (1)

The surface of the Danube River has reflected the silhouette of Bratislava Castle for over eight centuries. Originally, a Great Moravian hill-fort with a stone church occupied the site. It was a strong Romanian castle of the Arpád movement as well as a stronghold of the Hungarian boarders of the king Sigismund of Luxemburg. The present-day appearance of the castle is a result of development that started in the 16th century. After years of prime times under the reign of Maria Theresa, worse times fell upon the castle towards the end of the 18th century, when the building was turned into a cleric seminary. A fire damaged Bratislava Castle in 1911. For many years after the fire, the castle was a ruin and created the typical silhouette of the town. Fortunately, a reconstruction was initiated in 1953 and today Bratislava Castle is the pride of Bratislava as well as Slovakia. It houses valuable collections of the Slovakian National Museum.

### GREAT MORAVIAN BASILICA AT BRATISLAVA CASTLE (2)

A Great Moravian hill-fort existed on the hill of Bratislava Castle. It is mentioned in the Salzburg's Chronicle from 907 in connection with a memorable battle between the Bavarians and Magyars (Hungarians). It is described as a significant fortification point that was built towards the end of the existence of the Great Moravian Empire. The hill-fort had a three-nave basilica. We have some idea about its proportions as fragments up to the foundation level were successfully preserved on the eastern side. The brown quarry stones outline the ground-plan of the 9th-century basilica while the white coloured stones illustrate somewhat younger buildings from the post Great-Moravian period, built between the 10th and 12th centuries. The archaeological excavations confirmed that burials once took place near the church.

### ŽIGMUNDOVA GATE (3)

The Ottoman threat was behind a reconstruction of the Bratislava Castle in the Renaissance style in the second half of the 17th century. Only part of the project, which was to turn the Castle into a safe fortress with massive bastions, was realised. Thus, some of the older parts built in the 15th century by the Holy Roman emperor Sigismund of Luxemburg have been preserved. Thanks to this, we can admire a splendid Gothic monument – Žigmundova Gate, built between 1431 and 1434. It is also called Korvínova Gate, as at one point it was believed to have been built during the reign of the king Matthias Corvinus (Matej Korvín). This beautiful Gothic square building with rich stone decorations allowed access to the castle from the east. It created a short-cut to the ford across the Danube near the Vodná Tower. A castle moat was also part of the fortification system.

### DEVÍN CASTLE (4)

Perched on a high rock above the confluence of the Morava and Danube rivers, Devín Castle occupies an especially romantic spot. In the past, the Celts left their footprints and the Romans built an army seat in this place, which was predestined to play a part in history. Famous chapters from the Slovakian national history were written in this place during the existence of the Great-Moravian Empire in the 9th century. A Dowina fortress was first mentioned in the Fuldské Chronicles from 864. Then a Medieval castle appeared on the rock in the 13th century. It guarded the western border of Hungary and survived until 1809 when it was blown up by Napoleon's soldiers. Members of the Štúrovské Movement visited Devín to venerate the roots of the Slovakian nation in the middle of the 19th century. The castle is one of the most favourite tourist destinations in Bratislava.

MAIN SQUARE
HLAVNÉ NÁMESTIE

## MICHALSKÁ TOWER (1)

When the medieval fortification walls prevented Bratislava to spread on a larger territory, Maria Teresa had them demolished in 1775. Only fragments now remain from the fortification system. The best-preserved fortification monument in Bratislava is the Michalská Tower. It is one of the original four city gates that led inside the city. It was built in the 14th century and has undergone a complicated building development. On the outside of the Michalská Tower are buildings that once served as a stronghold of the barbican type. Before entering the gate, you must walk across a bridge over the former moat. The Michalská Tower houses weaponry and city fortifications exhibitions.

## VODNÁ TOWER (2)

The remains of a medieval sentry tower, which once protected a significant ford across the Danube, were discovered only after the demolition of old Vydrica Street, built on the site of a former village, due to the construction of the Nový (New) Bridge over the Danube. The tower was demolished in 1620 and it is one of Bratislava's oldest monuments, with history going back minimally as far as the 13th century.

## VILLA RUSTICA NEAR DÚBRAVKA (3)

The Romans also left their monuments on the left bank of Bratislava (in the Old Town as well as in the suburbs), even though it was not part of the Roman Empire. One of such monuments is an ancient building called Villa Rustica, dating from the 3rd century AD. It was discovered in 1982 in the north foothills of the mountain Devínska Kobyla on the present-day territory of the town quarter Dúbravka. It is believed to be an estate of a German aristocrat related to the Romans. Part of the building served as classical heated Roman baths.

## GERULATA (4)

The site of today's Bratislava was on the northern border of the Roman Empire in Roman times. A fortification system (Limes Romanus) followed the right bank of the Danube River. The present-day city was outside this border; only the part of the city on the other side of the river belonged to the empire. Archaeologists discovered remains of a Roman army camp in the Rusovce area (now Bratislava's quarter) in 1965. It was the long-sought Gerulata Fort depicted on a contemporary map called Itinerarioum Antonini. The almost two thousand year-old precious monument is currently open to the public as the Antique Gerulata Museum.

## ST. MARTIN'S CATHEDRAL (1)

The largest sacral building in Bratislava is the Cathedral of St. Martin. Its construction started in 1221 and the cathedral was finished in 1452. As the city spread out, the cathedral ended in its western part and thus was included in the fortification walls. The cathedral was built in the Gothic style and reconstructed in the Baroque style in the 18th century. Yet another Neo-Gothic reconstruction in the 19th century gave it back some of its original look. The monumental lead equestrian statue of St. Martin inside the cathedral is an artistic jewel. It was made by the famous Baroque sculptor Georg Rafael Donner. A replica of a gold-plated Hungarian crown is reminiscent of the times when the St. Martin's Cathedral served as the coronation church. The main coronation ceremony was held here between 1563 and 1830; the modern replica commemorates these times.

## CHAPEL OF ST. JOHN ALMUŽNÍK (2)

Of the four chapels of St. Martin's Cathedral, the 1734-built Baroque chapel is especially significant. This chapel in the shape of the Greek cross was added to the northern side of the cathedral as a dignified area for the placing of the remains of St. John Almužník, a saint from Cyprus. They were a present to the Hungarian King Matthias Corvinus from a Turkish Sultan and were brought to Bratislava in 1541. St. John Almužník's Chapel is also the tomb of Imrich Esterházi (Eszterházy), the archbishop and Hungarian primate called also the Hungarian Medici for his generous support of the arts. The interior of the chapel is richly decorated with sculptures by the famous sculptor George Rafael Donner (1693 – 1741).

## FRANCISCAN CHURCH
## AND MONASTERY (3)

In the upper part of the quiet Františkánske Square is one of Bratislava's oldest churches. It was ceremoniously consecrated on 25th March 1297 in the presence of the Hungarian King Ondrej III. The Baroque faćade of the church houses a splendid interior with a Gothic vault and rich, mostly Baroque decorations. The church became one of the stops of the coronation procession in the 16th century, where the newly crowned king dubbed aristocrats of the Golden Spur Order. One of the three chapels, the two-story St. John the Evangelist's Chapel from the 14th century, is one of the most valuable Gothic monuments in Slovakia. It is a splendid family tomb of Bratislava's reeve Jakubovci dynasty.

## ORDER OF ST. CLARA (4)

According to an old legend, a young knight called Kristian built the slim spire of the Gothic Church of St. Clara, which dates from the 14th century. For this deed, he was supposed to win the heart of one of the nuns, Matilda. Allegedly, he did not get his reward, however the city obtained its most beautiful tower. Originally, it was boldly added to the south wall of the church nave and only received its supporting pillar after it was damaged by an earthquake in 1700. It had a Baroque appearance in the 18th century, however it received its elegant Gothic features back in the following century. There is no worship service in the Church of St. Clara these days; it is used for concerts because of the magnificent acoustics of the nave. The adjacent Renaissance building of the former monastery of the Order of St. Clara is currently used by the University Library.

## JESUIT CHURCH, ENTRY PORTAL (5)

The Catholic church with a small spire near the Old Town House in the lower part of Františkánske Square gives an austere, puritan impression. It was built in 1636 by Bratislava's Protestants and the simplicity of the building fulfilled the rules of the so-called Sopron Council Articulas, which prescribed the appearance of Protestant churches. Following the victory of the Habsburg-supported Reformation Movement, the church was confiscated and given to the Jesuits in 1672.

## COLUMN OF THE VIRGIN
## MARY THE VICTORIOUS (6)

The Baroque column outside the Jesuit Church on Františkánske Square was built in 1675. It was to commemorate the victory over the Turks at St. Gotthard in 1664 and the successful suppression of the Estates Uprising in 1671. A column celebrating the victorious Virgin Mary well suited the anti-reformation efforts of the Catholic Habsburgs.

### CHURCH OF THE TRINITY (1)

The architecture of the 1727-built Church of the Trinity on the Hurbanovo Square in Bratislava much resembles the Church of St. Peter in Vienna. Architects of the churches were charmed by the oval curved composition of the front façade and an oval ground plan of the church nave. An artistic jewel of the interior is the illusive painting in the dome-shaped vault, hidden from the outside by a saddle roof by the Baroque painter A. Galli-Bibienu. Above the main altar is a large painting by F.X. Palko depicting the founders of the Order of the Trinity, St. Felix of Valoa and St. John of Matha buying back Christians from a Muslim capture. The adjacent building was a monastery of the Trinity Order and was turned into a hospital following the extinction of the order. The building was reconstructed as the County Council of Bratislava in 1844 (edge is visible). It was the seat of the National Council of the Slovakian Republic until 1994.

### CHURCH AND MONASTERY OF THE ORDER OF ST. ELIZABETH (2)

There is a reason behind Bratislava having two churches consecrated to St. Elizabeth of Hungary. This saint was born at Bratislava Castle in 1207 as the daughter of the Hungarian King Andrew II. She dedicated her life to charity, founding a hospice and an alms-house in 1229. Her work was continued in 1566 by the Order of St. Elizabeth, invited to Bratislava by the archbishop Imrich Esterházy. The 1743-built Church of St. Elizabeth is a prime Baroque building designed by a top Viennese architect, A. Pilgram. The façade is impressively decorated with sculptures of St. Elizabeth, St. Ladislaus and St. Stephen by Ľudovít Gode. The most significant work in the richly decorated interior of church is the Vision of St. Elizabeth painting in the vault by a prominent Baroque painter, Paul Troger. The adjacent building of St. Elizabeth's monastery is still a hospital.

### MODRÝ KOSTOLÍK (3)

The Church of St. Elizabeth of Hungary on Bezručova Street is called the Modrý (Blue) Church due to its blue-coloured facade. It is the work of a Budapest-born architect named E. Lechner. Countess Gabriela M. Szapáryová played a large role in the building of the church. The countess organised the moving of the relics of the popular Bratislava-born Hungarian patroness from Vienna to Bratislava and their placement into the newly built and ceremoniously consecrated (on 11th October 1913) church. St. Elizabeth's theme is ever-present here. The Italian mosaic above the entry depicts a motif of the well-knowned legend about St. Elizabeth with roses (about the miraculous metamorphosis of bread for the poor). The nearby architectonically matching rectory houses a valuable marble relief by a Bratislava citizen, Alojz Rigel, which once again portraits the Hungarian Queen Elizabeth, the famous empress Sisi.

## BLUMENTÁLSKY CHURCH (4)

A new parish building was built in 1770 on the site of the former Blumental settlement for citizens of the new quarters of Bratislava, and a new church was added in 1784. However, it failed to reach the requirements of the growing community so a new, much larger church was built nearby. The monumental Neo-Romanesque church designed by Viennese architect F. Rumpelmayer was ceremoniously consecrated in 1888. Despite being devoted to the Assumption of the Virgin Mary, the church is still called the Blumentálsky Church. Its 76-metre high tower is the second highest in the city after the tower of St. Martin's Cathedral. The most valuable artistic work of the interior is the famous sculpture of the Crucified from 1892; created by a Bratislava citizen, Ján Fadrusz, during his sculpture studies in Vienna. The Baroque Column of St. Florian outside the church was moved from its original place outside the Laurinská Gate.

## EVANGELIC CHURCHES (5)

Bratislava's Evangelic community settled in the northern suburbs of the town near the Suché Mýto Gate in the outside palisade town fortification in the middle of the 17th century. When the 1682-built wooden church was no longer sufficient for the needs of the Evangelists, they used the favourable environment of the reign of Joseph II and his tolerance period and set about building two new churches on Panenská Street. Both churches were designed by Matej Walch. Initially, they opened the Veľký (Large) Evangelic Church in 1777 (picture) similar to the Jesuit Church that was confiscated to the Evangelists. However, as it served the German speaking worshipers, another church was needed. A year later, the Malý (Small) Evangelic Church appeared on the site of the above-mentioned wooden church north of the Veľký Evangelic Church and served the Hungarian and Slovakian speaking Evangelists.

17

## ST. NICHOLAS CHURCH (1)

The settlement around Bratislava Castle called Podhradie was an independent town that only became part of the free royal city of Bratislava in 1851. It belonged to the lords of Bratislava Castle. The citizens of Podhradie had a Gothic church devoted to St. Nicholas, the patron of merchants and sailors. However, it was demolished because of the Turkish threat in 1531. The widow of count Pavel Pálfi (Pálffy) initiated the building of a Baroque church in 1661. The church has been used by Orthodox worshipers since 1950. Next to the church used to be a cemetery with the tomb of the famous Baroque sculptor František Xaver Messerschmidt (1736-1783). The cemetery vanished just as did a nearby Romanesque rotunda from the 11th century, the remains of which have been recently uncovered.

## CAPUCHIN CHURCH (2)

The Capuchin Church, with a monastery on the Župné Square, did not come into existence on a lucky day. Cracks appeared on its walls soon after its consecration, due to the movement of liquid sand in the foundations, so part of the church was demolished in 1735 and the whole complex was reconstructed. The austere appearance of the Capuchin Church consecrated to St. Stephen of Hungary fulfils the Puritan requirements of the Order of Capuchins. The only ornament on the exterior is a statue of a patron in a niche above the main entry portal. It was not placed there until a reconstruction of the front faćade carried out by Ignác Feigler jr. in 1861. The interior is slightly more decorated, as the Capuchins enjoyed the support of the court and aristocracy. Francis of Lorraine and the primate Imrich Esterházi (Esterházy) donated generously to the Baroque altars. The altarpiece by a Capuchin called Udalrik is interesting, for it depicts Bratislava Castle. Today, monks once again use the monastery behind the church. A Baroque Column of Immaculata from 1723 adorns the space outside the church.

## COLUMN OF THE TRINITY ON RYBNÉ SQUARE (3)

The ceremonious coronation of King Karol III in May 1712 linked to a session of the Parliament had a dreadful follow up. Some people who visited Bratislava developed symptoms of the Black Death and soon the plague was spreading. Numerous white crosses were painted on the doors of houses in Bratislava, which were affected by the illness. The plague spread terribly and did not start to recede until October 1713. A report by the main Viennese doctor states that as many as 3,422 people succumbed to the Black Death in the city and its suburbs. To express the gratefulness for the end of the plague, a column with a sculpture of the Trinity was erected on Rybné Square. Archbishop Christian August of Saxony, who personally helped to eradicate the plague, contributed to its construction. Apart from the central sculpture of the Trinity, three other sculptures, traditional protectors against the Black Death, St Rochus, St Andrew and St Karol of Bartolomew, adorn the column as well as other statues and relieves added around 1780.

## SCULPTURE OF ST. ELIZABETH
## OUTSIDE PREPOŠTSKÝ PALACE (4)

Kapitulská Street has been the centre of religious life in Bratislava since the Middle Ages. Several institutions connected with the Catholic Church are concentrated on this quiet street stretching out from St. Martin's Cathedral. One of them is the Roman-Catholic Cyrilometodská Theological Faculty of the Komenského University, which uses two buildings on Kapitulská Street. Apart from the former Jesuit college the Prepoštský Palace is the centre of the students of theology. A Prepošt-ský House originally occupied the site as early as in 1311. It was used by the Academia Istropolitana in the 15th century. It received the austere ap-pearance of a Renaissance palace during a recon-struction in 1632. Its rich artistic decorations con-trast with the simple façade of the palace. The shade from a small green park in the courtyard conceals a sculpture of a famous native of Brati-slava, St. Elizabeth Hungarian by Alojz Rigele.

## JESUIT COLLEGE (5)

The Jesuit College on Kapitulská Street was built between 1628 and 1635 on a piece of land allo-cated to the Jesuits by the Esztergom Archbishop and Cardinal Peter Pázmaň (Pázmany). The centre for the education of young Jesuits was built by Ja-kub Rava and his son Giovanni, the court archi-tects of the Viennese Jesuits. As the design origi-nated in Rome, Bratislava received a valuable build-ing of the Roman type. The three-story college preserved its original appearance (especially the street-facing side). After the abolition of the Jesu-it Order by a patent from Joseph II in 1782, the building housed a town school, then a office, and in the end was rebuilt for the needs of the Empire-Royal Law Academy, which moved into the city from Trnava in 1858. Among its famous students were, for instance, the Slovakian writer Svetozár Hurban Vajanský (1847 – 1916). Religious educa-tion returned to the building after World War II. The present-day Roman-Catholic Cyrilometodská Theological Faculty prepares the future Catholic priests here.

## DOM U DOBRÉHO PASTIERA (HOUSE AT GOOD SHEPHERD) (1)

Fortunately, the massive clearance of Bratislava's Podhradie quarter, which was carried out before 1973 due to the building of a Nový (New) Bridge ramp across the Danube, avoided one of the most beautiful burgher's houses in Bratislava. The House at Good Sheppard on Židovská Street is a superb example of the so-called Bratislava Rococo style. This smallish architectonic jewel received its name due to the sign on its faćade, which depicts Christ as a good shepherd. The narrow house was built on a tiny trapezium-shaped lot and has only one room on each floor. An interesting exhibition of historical clocks belonging to the City Museum of Bratislava has been in the house since 1975.

## SEGNEROVA MANSION (2)

The burgher's house on the west side of Michalská Street is more than just a valuable Renaissance monument. The house was built for a prominent Bratislava citizen and merchant, Andreas Segner, in 1648. The architect was inspired by the Northern Renaissance style. The faćade of the house is adorned by the coat-of-arms of the family, which is placed above the main portal. The famous scientist and scholar Johann Andreas Segner (1704 – 1777) was born in this house in 1704. After finishing his studies, Johann Andreas returned to his hometown to commence his first scientific experiments. He tested a prototype of a water engine at the Segneovský Mill on the Vydrica Stream. The engine later received his name and is called the Segnerovo Wheel. This invention was a great deed on the field of hydraulics that later led towards the creation of the jet-propelled water engine.

## HUMMELOV HOUSE (3)

The internationally renowned composer Johann Nepomuk Hummel (1778 – 1837) is the most famous native of Bratislava with regards to the music world. He is believed to have been born in a small Renaissance building situated in the courtyard of a residential house on the southeast part of Klobučnícka Street. Hummel, born into a family of musicians, was gifted with his great talent from birth. His father was a member of the Count Grasalkovič's (Grassalkowich) Orchestra and a director of the city theatre. The great W. A. Mozart himself helped the young Johann Nepomuk's development for two years after the family moved to Vienna. The Hummel's Palace now houses a Musical Exposition of the City Museum of Bratislava.

## DOM U ČIERNEHO HAVRANA (HOUSE AT BLACK RAVEN) (4)

To brighten up the small bleak, dark alley that connects Michalská Street and Franciscan Square, the facades of houses were painted white. In addition, a candle-maker called Schneeweiss, lived in the alley in the past. Hence, it received its name Biela (White) Street. The most interesting building is the House at Black Raven, detectable by its valuable Renaissance painting on the street-facing faćade that depicts a scene from the lives of winegrowers. Supposedly, the painter used a sketch by Albrecht Dürer as a model. The symbolical raven above the entry is to remember the Hungarian

King Matthias Corvinus (in Latin corvus means raven). This fine house with a Renaissance courtyard currently houses a stylish restaurant.

### ZELENÝ DOM (GREEN HOUSE) (5)

This house can be easily found in the west corner of the Hlavné (Main) Square in Bratislava. Its faćade is painted green, however its name is derived from the colours used in the interior, painted mainly green and adorned by various floral and figural motifs. The Classicism faćade conceals a Gothic building from the 15th century. Originally the house was a bar serving wine from the local vineyards. A stone relief above the top ledge commemorates this. It depicts a scene from the Old Testament with Joshua and Kalebom carrying a bunch of grapes from Canaan. The Green House also served as a hotel for wealthy guests; sessions of the City Council and of the Hungarian Parliament were held here as well. Even theatre took place here, with plays by Moliére and Shakespeare performed. The house was rebuilt in the Classicism style towards the end of the 18th century.

## OLD TOWN HALL (1)

Bratislava's Old Town Hall on the Hlavné (Main) Square has witnessed a complicated building development during the seven centuries of its existence. Initially, a Romanesque fortified house with a spire from the 13th century occupied the site. It belonged to the Jakubovci burgher family and was bought by the town for the needs of the City Council towards the end of the 14th century. Over the span of the following centuries, the Old Town House was rebuilt a couple of times and new wings and adjacent houses were added. The house is no longer the Town Hall; it now houses the City Museum with expositions of the history of Bratislava and the medieval law system. The museum in the Old Town Hall is the oldest in Slovakia and was founded as early as 1868.

## ACADEMIA ISTROPOLITANA (2)

A university of the Bologna type called Academia Istropolitana was open in Bratislava in 1465. Its establishment was initiated by the Hungarian King Matthias Corvinus and several contemporary scholars were invited to Bratislava. The univer-

sity was closed shortly after the death of king Matthias in 1490, yet despite its short existence it played a great role in spreading the Humanism Movement throughout the then Hungary. The houses on Ventúrska Street still serve education purposes as they house the Theatre Faculty of the University of Musical Arts.

## HUNGARIAN ROYAL CHAMBER PALACE (3)

Bratislava became the temporary coronation city of the country in 1536. Several state institutions and offices moved to the metropolis, among them the Hungarian Royal Chamber. Its role was to manage the royal assets and financial agenda, and to control building activities financed from royal sources. A splendid palace was built for the requirements of the Royal Chamber on Michalská Street in 1756. The Viennese emperor's architect G. B. Martinelli gave the building its majestic Baroque appearance. It became the seat of the Hungarian Parliament in 1780; following heated negotiations in 1848 in the presence of a member of the Parliament, Ľudovít Štúr, a package of so-

cial acts was approved in this place, among others the Act on the Abolition of the Subjection in Hungary. The former seat of the Chamber has been interconnected with the adjacent De Pauliho Palace and both buildings are now a modern multicultural centre of the University Library.

## OLD AND NEW EVANGELIC LYCEUM (4)

The Evangelic School of Bratislava successfully spread education, culture and enlightenment amongst the local Evangelists. It was the centre of the Enlightenment Movement in the 18th century. The ideas represented by the internationally renowned scholar Matej Bel (1684 – 1749), a rector of the school. An Evangelic lyceum was built on the site of the former school in 1783; it is now referred to as the 'Staré' (Old) Lyceum. This building on Konventná Street played an important part during the Slovakian National Revival of the 19th century. A group of national revivalists formed here and was led by the pedagogue of the lyceum, Ľudovír Štúr (1815-1856). The second lyceum building was built nearby in 1855; it is called the 'Nové' (New) Evangelic Lyceum (top picture).

## HISTORICAL BUILDING OF THE SLOVAKIAN NATIONAL THEATRE (1)

The citizens of Bratislava got their first brick theatre in 1776, however as it was not sufficient for the city's needs, it was demolished and the present-day Slovakian National Theatre on Hviezdoslavovo Square was erected on its site. The authors of the project were the renowned builders of theatrical edifices, Ferdinand Fellner and Herman Helmer. Bratislava's new theatre scene was ceremoniously opened on the 22nd September 1886 by the opening of the Bank Opera by Ferenc Erkel Bán. Initially plays were put on only in German and Hungarian, and the building first started to be called the Slovakian National Theatre on 1st March 1920. The most important Slovakian theatre institution began its existence with the performance of the Hubička Opera by Bedřich Smetana. It is now the heart of the opera and ballet scene and also hosts the noble Ball in the Opera event. Since the opening of the new building of the Slovakian National Theatre in 2007, the old theatre on Hviezdoslavovo Square has been referred to as the 'historical'.

## NEW BUILDING OF THE SLOVAKIAN NATIONAL THEATRE (2)

Bratislava and indeed the whole of Slovakia waited for the new building of the Slovakian National Theatre on Pribinova Street for more than twenty years. The lack of financial means for such a demanding project kept postponing the awaited opening of this large-scale modern theatre built near the newly developing Danube embankment. Finally, the ceremonious ribbon was cut on 14th April 2007. The new Slovakian National Theatre boasts seven stories, three main halls, a restaurant with the capacity for 120 people, a club, a cofee shop. This modern building has a hall for the ballet and the opera scenes as well as for the drama scene and also a smaller hall for the theatre studio.

## REDUTA (3)

The most important classical music scene in Slovakia is the Reduta building on Mostová Street. This grandiose Eclecticism building was erected near the Danube embankment in 1915 on the site of a former Baroque granary from the 18th--century. It was designed by Budapest architects Marcel Komor and Dezider Jakab. Reduta is the home of the Slovakian Philharmonic Orchestra. The Bratislava Autumn Music Festival is a great opportunity to see and hear the prominent orchestras and famous interpreters in the Reduta concert hall.

## SLOVAKIAN NATIONAL GALLERY (4)

The Slovakian National Gallery, the most important national institution in the visual arts field, uses several neighbouring buildings on the Danube embankment. Among them is the corner Esterháziho Palace, with its entrance from the Square of Ľudovít Štúr, and the former Vodné Barracks on the Rázusovo Embankment. The originally four-wing arcaded building of the Vodné Barracks lost one of its embankment-facing wings in 1940. It was replaced by a modern addition with a wide window into the inside courtyard. The Slovakian National Gallery collects and exhibits the most important masterpieces by Slovakian artists, such as Medňanský, Benka, Fulla, Alexy, Bazovský and Galanda, and also houses a permanent exposition of Old European Art from the 16th – 18th centuries, Gothic and Baroque Art and 19th century Slovakian Art.

## SLOVAKIAN NATIONAL MUSEUM (5)

The Ancient temple resembling the Slovakian National Museum building is next to the Danube passenger port on the Vajanské Embankment. It was designed by a well-known Slovakian architect, Milan Michal Harminc, and was built as a branch of the Prague Agriculture Museum between 1924 and 1928. The Museum was ceremoniously opened to the public on the 4th May 1930 and its expositions were organised by the Czech Agriculture Museum and the Slovakian Ethnography Museum. A merger of both institutions in 1940 created the Slovakian Museum, the predecessor of the current Slovakian National Museum. The museum houses rich collections of the Natural Science Museum that document Slovakia's natural surroundings. It also houses valuable seasonal exhibitions.

1

2

## PRIMATE'S PALACE (1)

The Primate's Palace on a square of the same name is an architectonic jewel as well as a place that witnessed important historical events. It was built for the highest representative of the Church in the country, Cardinal Baťáni (Batthyányi), in 1781. Built by the Viennese architect Melchior Hefele, the building was the model for the Classicism style to be applied throughout all of Hungary. The palace served the sacral as well as the secular authorities and has witnessed numerous historical events and meetings (Bratislava's Truce after the Battle at Slavkov, the abolition of the serfdom, and the Czechoslovakian Federation Act).

## BRATISLAVA'S TAPESTRIES (2)

A complete set of six monumental tapestries was uncovered underneath the wallpapers during a reconstruction of the Primate's Palace in 1903. This unique artistic collection was made in England in the first half of the 17th century in the royal workshop of Mortlake. It remains to be discove-

red how the tapestries made their way from England to Bratislava. Today the tapestries are one of the main tourist attractions of the Slovakian metropolis. The series dates from the so-called Mannerism era and it is a complete cycle depicting scenes from the tragic Ancient legend about the famous love story of Hero and Leandros.

## MIRBACHOV PALACE (3)

This palace is the best example of the so-called Bratislava Rococo. It was built in the upper section of the Františkánske Square on the site of the fire-destroyed Weitenhof House, where theatre took place as early as at the beginning of the 17th century. Before it came into the possession of the aristocracy, it belonged to a rich brewery owner named Spech. Its present-day name derives from its last private owner, count Emil Mirbach, who left it to the city in his will, providing it would be used as a gallery. His wish has been fulfilled. It exhibits a collection of French reproduction graphic art and replicas of Ruben's Medici Cycle.

## APONIHO PALACE (4)

Near the Old Town Hall stands an elegant Rococo Palace. It was built in 1762 for count Juraj Apponyi of Oponíce, a private counsellor to the Hungarian governor. The building on narrow Radničná Street is a splendid example of how to use a tiny, irregularly shaped lot. The city bought the palace in 1867 with the idea to enlarge the Town Hall. It currently houses a museum with collections of wine-growing and wine-making of the City Museum of Bratislava.

.

## PÁLFIHO PALACE ON VENTÚRSKA STREET (5)

Practically nothing remains of the Garden Palace of the count Pálfi in the Podhradie quarter, however other houses of this important Hungarian aristocrat in Bratislava rate amongst the architectonical jewels of the city. One of them is on the corner of Ventúrska and Green Streets. This Baroque building was built in 1747; special attention should be paid to the richly decorated entry portal lead-

ing from Ventúrska Street. Allegedly, six-year-old Mozart performed a concert in the building. It now houses the Embassy of Austria.

## PÁLFIHO PALACE ON PANSKÁ STREET (6)

One of the oldest monuments in Bratislava is hidden underneath the rather undistinguished Classicism façade of this Palace on the south side of Panská Street. Following the discovery of a Celtic mint it turned out that the palace had witnessed much older history. The Celtic mint producing the then well-known biateky existed here more than two thousand years ago. Detail research of the walls of the palace proved that some of its parts are older than 700 years. Remains of a fortified tower house from the 13th century were uncovered. It was later rebuilt into a Gothic city palace and reconstructed in the Classicism style in the 19th century. It now houses expositions of the Bratislava City Gallery. Various exhibitions are also noteworthy.

## KUTSCHERFELDOV PALACE (1)

This palace is one of the most beautiful Rococo buildings in the city. It was built in 1762 on the site of several medieval lots. Its builders used a rich stucco ornamental style for the façade as well as the interior. The first owner of this palace was Ludwig von Kutscherfeld, the governor of the royal assets in Magyarovári. He sold the house to count Esterházi (Esterházy) in 1800. The Esterházi family hosted the brilliant Russian pianist and composer A .G. Rubinštejn (1829-1894) in the palace in 1847. The then eighteen-year-old artist spent the whole summer in Bratislava and was loved by the citizens mainly thanks to three successful concerts he performed in the City Theatre. He even composed several compositions during his stay in Bratislava, for example the renowned D-mol Concert for the Piano and Orchestra. Kutscherfeldov Palace is now the seat of the French Embassy and the French Institute.

## KEGLEVIČOV PALACE (2)

Contrasting with the nearby typical city Erdődyho Palace, this building on the corner of Panská and Straková Street looks like a country house of a rich yeoman somewhere in the Liptov or Turec regions. It owes its peasant appearance to the low façade with one story, which is compensated by a high red roof similar to those used on old country estates. This Baroque palace is a result of a reconstruction of an older burgher's house of the Keglevič aristocratic family from Croatia. Countess Babetta Keglevičová was a pupil and later a friend of Ludwig van Beethoven. To her the composer devoted the Es-dur Sonata for the Piano and the Composition 7, as well as several other works. The great artist visited Bratislava several times in November 1796 and spent several days here.

## ČÁKIHO PALACE (3)

The city palace built for count Juraj Čáki (Csáky) in 1775 occupies the place where Panská Street opens onto the rectangular Rudnayovho Square. This count of an influential Hungarian family from western Slovakia financed the building of the City Theatre that preceded the present-day Slovakian National Theatre. He had the palace built by a local builder, M. Walch, who successfully proved his skills on the nearby Rococo Palace of count Erdődy on Ventúrska Street. However, the architect used the Classicism style on the palace of count Čáki rather than the previous Rococo and used this experience later when working on both Evangelic Churches on Panská Street.

## ERDŐDYHO PALACE (4)

The city palace in the lower part of Ventúrska Street was built for the country judge Count Juraj Erdődy in 1770 by Matej Walch. The architect used the Rococo style, however already strongly enriched by Classicism elements. The Rococo portal with a balcony is virtually indistinguishable on the broad Classicism façade. Originally, the palace had two stories; the third one was added in the first half of the 20th century. Fortunately, this unsuitable addition was rebuilt between 1997 and 1998 with the emphasis on adhering to the original architectural style. The palace now houses a coffee shop with an exhibition of original paintings by Andy Warhol. Part of the local restaurant is one of the largest „vinotéka (a wine cellar combined with a wine shop) in Slovakia.

## PALACE OF LEOPOLD DE PAULI (5)

The Leopold de Pauli's Palace on Ventúrska Street was built between 1775 and 1776 for the main governor of the emperor's assets on the former royal land. Older Gothic houses originally occupied the site. The building was created by the court architect F. K. Römisch, who probably used building plans by Hillebrandt. The palace is a noble example of the Classicism-influenced architecture, which was prevalent in the city during the last quarter of the 18th century. Its part is a garden with a charming musical pavilion (today part of the University Library). According to some sources, Franz Liszt (1811 – 1886) performed a concert here in 1820; however this is sometimes doubted nowadays.

## GRASALKOVIČOV PALACE (1)

Grasalkovičov Palace on Hodžovo Square, the present-day seat of the President of the Slovak Republic, was built in the gardens outside the fortifications of the then inner city. This elegant Rococo edifice was built for count Anton Grasalkovič (Grassalkowich), the chairman of the Hungarian Royal Court Chamber, the guardian of the royal crown and the head of the Novohradská Council. The garden palace was a luxurious aristocratic residence with a lively social life. A grand and noble ball was held here in 1772 as a tribute to Maria Kristína, the daughter of Maria Theresa, and her husband the governor of the Saxon Tešínsko Region count Albert; famous composer Joseph Hayden conducted the orchestra at the event. The palace served various purposes during the 20th century; among others, it was a seat of the president and was used as the cultural centre of the Pioneers (a scout-like children's organisation during the Communism era).

## ARCHBISHOP'S SUMMER PALACE (2)

The Námestie Slobody Square is one of the most beautiful modern places in Bratislava. Flanked on three sides by modern buildings, its third north side is enclosed by the historical Archbishop's Summer Palace. A Renaissance summer house of the Archbishop F. Forgáč (Forgách) stood here as early as 1614. It had a remarkable garden; its beauty was renowned throughout the whole of Europe. The garden was mainly developed thanks to the Archbishop J. Lipaj hence its name, Lipajova Garden. The present-day garden Baroque palace was built as a summer residency of the archbishop in 1765. The building has undergone several reconstructions and is now the seat of the Government of the Slovak Republic.

## MANSION IN PRIEVOZ (4)

This chateau is idyllically set in the greenery of an English-style park in the Prievoz (part of Ružinov) city quarter of Bratislava. Originally, there was a gamekeeper's house on the site belonging to the Čáki family. The house soon became a summer residence of the aristocratic family. The present-day mansion, built for count E. Čáki (Csáky) and his wife in 1902, boasts an impressive sectional eclectic architectural style. It also contains the Oratory of the Divine Heart of Jesus. The next owner of the chateau, count P. Zolnay, divided part of the park into lots and sold the chateau to the nuns of the Order of the Congregation of the Daughters of St. Francis of Assisi, who opened a hospice inside the chateau. The hospital where nuns still care for patients has remained in part of the building until today.

## BRÄMMEROVA MANSION (5)

A settlement below the castle was once nestled on a narrow space between the Danube and the steep castle hill. It was called Zuckermandel (a garble expression from German meaning 'grab your coat and leg it'; a clear warning for travellers). A large part of Zuckermandel was demolished before the construction of the Nový (New) Bridge and only a few valuable historical monuments have been preserved. One of the most valuable is Brämmerova Chateau on Žižkova Street. This Renaissance building with two massive cylindrical corner towers is a result of a reconstruction of medieval houses, which was initiated by an officer from the castle guard, F. Brämmer, in 1620. The chateau now houses the Museum of Hungarian Culture in Slovakia, which is part of the Slovakian National Museum. The exhibition focuses on history and ethnography.

## CHATEAU IN RUSOVCE (3)

In the southern quarter of Bratislava called Rusovce is a large English-style park with a splendid romantic chateau in its centre. It was built in 1840 on the site of an older mansion from the 16th century. The architects of the chateau chose the romantic English Gothic of the so-called Windsor style, as the wife of the owner of the chateau, count Emanuel Zichy-Ferrari, came from across the British Channel. The chateau had changed hands until 1945 when it was badly damaged by the Red Army soldiers towards the end of World War II. It was also a seat of the folk choir SĽUK, which now uses an adjacent building. The chateau is now awaiting a reconstruction and a new purpose.

1

2

## GRASALKOVIČOVA GARDEN (1)

The public gardens behind the residency of the Slovakian president were established in the 18th century as a Baroque garden of Grasalkovičov Garden Palace. It immediately became one of the most wonderful gardens in the city, remarkable for its floral decorations and a large number of valuable sculptures. It was partially open to the public in the first quarter of the 19th century and it became a large city park in the second half of the 20th century; with a swimming pool, playgrounds, a tennis court and a small zoo. It was used mainly by children as the palace housed the cultural centre of the Pioneers (a scout-like children's organisation during the Communism era). A large reconstruction that ended in 1999 gave the park back some of its original Baroque appearance. One of the sculptures in the park is an equestrian statue of Maria Teresa by J. Fadrusza. The gardens are open to the public.

## MEDICKÁ GARDEN (2)

This city park with a garden, accessible to the public via entrances from Špitálska Street and 29th of August Street, is known amongst Bratislava's citizens as the Medická (Medical) Garden, as there are several buildings nearby linked to medicine. Part of the Medical Faculty of the University of Komenský is housed in Aspremontov Palace on the northern side of the park and the Faculty Hospital is located a bit farther. The lecture rooms are also nearby. The 1769-built Aspremontovov Palace was constructed so that its finer faćade faces the Baroque gardens at the southeast side. Only a part of the area is a landscaped garden; the rest is now a frequented city park. Apart from the modern fountain, there are also sculptures of two famous writers – Sándor Petőfi and Martin Kukučín. The sculpture of Kukučín (a replica) is by a well-known Croatian sculptor, I. Meštrovič.

## ORCHARD OF JANKO KRÁĽ (3)
On the right bank of the Danube lies the Orchard of Janko Kráľ on the embankment between the Starý (Old) and Nový (New) Bridges. This extensive island of greenery was established in the 1870s as one of the oldest public parks in Europe. The first alternations to the riverbanks, which changed the original floodplain forest into an English-style park, were initiated during the reign of Maria Theresa. The park was named after a revolutionary poet of Štúr's generation, Janko Kráľ, whose statue adorns one of the open areas of the park. A small stone summerhouse in the western part of the park is noteworthy. It is a part of the Gothic spire of the Franciscan Church, which was damaged by an earthquake in 1897. Near the river is the Aréna Theatre, the Lebefingen stylish restaurant and the Au Café coffee shop.

## ONDREJSKÝ CEMETERY (4)
Should you like a short trip through the history of old Bratislava, visit the Ondrejský Cemetery. Many of the important citizens of Bratislava are buried in this place, the oldest preserved historical cemetery in Bratislava. The tomb of Karl Jetting (1730-1790), the famous 'Bratislava's Robinson', is noteworthy. Jetting's fate was similar to the one of the castaway called Robinson that was described in Daniel Defoe's famous story. The Ondrejský Cemetery was founded in 1784 and 150 years later, when there were no more burials, it had over 15,000 graves and a large number of tombs. It was to be demolished; however the cemetery has remained intact due to the influence of the public. Although it is a public park nowadays, many graves and tombs remain in place. The entrance to the cemetery is next to a small Classicism chapel that serves Greek-Catholic worshipers.

## HORSKÝ PARK (5)
The largest island of greenery in Bratislava is Horský Park in the northwest part of the present-day Old Town. Bratislava's councillor Henrich Justi (1804-1878) bought these lands with the Študentský Forest in 1869 to establish an English-style park. After a while, the grateful citizens of Bratislava built a monument to Justi. The park houses yet another monument, devoted to the important botanist and mycologist Johann A. Bäumler. Both monuments are by the Bratislava-born sculptor Alojz Rigele. The Horský Park has ordinary tree species, such as oak, beech and elm; however it also boasts numerous exotic trees – baldcypress and tulip tree. The gamekeeper's house at the edge of the park with a pleasant café is a favourite resting place for visitors.

## MAXIMILIÁNOVA FOUNTAIN (1)

The Renaissance fountain on the Hlavné (Main) Square in Bratislava is a favourite place for rendezvous. People started to call it 'Ronald's Fountain' in the 19th century; however the sculpture of a man in armoury does not represent the popular patron and protector of cities, knight Ronald, but rather the Habsburg Emperor Maximilián II. The correct name of the fountain is 'Maximiliánova Fountain,' as this ruler initiated its construction. A dramatic event preceded building of the fountain in 1572. A large fire erupted in the city during Bratislava's first coronation (1563, Maximilián II) and there was nothing with which to extinguish it. Purism modifications were carried out on the fountain in the 19th century. The nude statues were removed and replaced by less disturbing decorations; the original sculptures are now located in the courtyard of a house on Laurinská Street. According to a legend, the fountain turns around 360 degrees at the turn of each new year. However only virgins and chaste people can see this and there are not many of these on the square during the New Year celebrations.

## GANYMEDOVA FOUNTAIN (2)

Ganymedova Fountain has adorned the area outside the Slovakian National Theatre on Hviezdoslavavo Square since 1888. It derives its name from its central sculpture motif by the prominent sculptor and native to Bratislava, Viktor Tilgner. The fountain depicts an ancient legend about the handsome Ganymedes who served the Gods on Mount Olympus. On the top of the fountain is Zeus, changed into a flying eagle carrying a small boy to Olympus. Water gushes from the mouth of the four most typical Danube fish – zander, carp, catfish and pike. Fragments of the southern fortification city walls near the now demolished

Rybárska (Fisherman's) Gate may be admired nearby; they guarded the access way of Bratislava's citizens to the Danube.

### ST. GEORGE'S FOUNTAIN (3)
Nowadays the courtyard of the Primate's Palace is adorned by a Renaissance Fountain of St. George. The centrepiece is an equestrian statue of St. George with a spear in the traditionally depicted scene – the fight with the dragon. This saint is the traditional patron of the city and originally adorned the famous garden of the archbishop Juraj Lipaj at the Archbishop's Summer Palace (see page 30). The fountain was placed in the courtyard of

the Primate's Palace in 1930. There is a replica of the statue of St. George outside the Government Palace near the original site of Lipajova Garden.

### KAČACIA (DUCK) FOUNTAIN (4)
In the middle of a tiny park on Šafárikovo Square is the very popular Kačacia Fountain by Róbert Kühmayer. The park was established in a new Bratislava quarter that sprang up on the left bank at the Starý (Old) Bridge across the Danube after 1891. The motif of boys and ducks on a rock comes from an old Bratislava legend. Some playing boys who were looking after the ducks on the Danube are shown at the moment when an

angry waterman changed them into stones for their frolicking.

### EARTH FOUNTAIN – PEACE PLANET (5)
Hodžovo Square outside Grasalkovičov Palace has undergone radical changes during the past decades. Older edifices gave way to a busy crossroad and modern buildings. The newly created area on the square is adorned by the Earth Fountain – the Peace Planet by Tibor Bártfay. It was built on the site of an older fountain in 1981. It is represented by a round pool with a large steel ball in the centre, which is decorated by relieves of doves representing the symbol of peace.

### DEVÍNSKA KOBYLA (1)

The hill Devínska Kobyla (514 m) is the highest point in Bratislava. This 'greenish island' provides recreation for the citizens of the city's western parts. The sunny south-western and western slopes of this mountainous range are very valuable natural features. The area was declared a protected territory in 1965 (a Nature Reserve at present). The protection concentrates on the rare steppe and forest-steppe vegetation requiring warm and sunny weather. More than a thousand species of vegetation grow here, out of which 25 are protected species. For some of them this is the northern-most border of occurrence. Among the protected fauna are for instance rare orchids, Small Pasque Flower, Yellow Pheasant's Eye, and Stipa Pulcherrima. There is a nature trail going along the range of Devínska Kobyla with splendid views of the countryside.

### SANDBERG (2)

The yellowish rock wall of Sandberg looming above the village of Devínska Nová Ves is a result of the mining for fine sea sand embedded on the bottom of the Tertiary sea approximately 15 million years ago. The sea sediments are extremely rich in various fossils to such an extent that Sandberg has become a term in international palaeontology. The remains of more than three hundred species of various prehistoric organisms have been found here – fossils of various sea animals, sharks' teeth, shells, seal bones and even whales. As this was once a coast, there are also fossils of terrestrial fauna, including mammals from the Tertiary era. Especially remarkable is the finding of the unique Dryopithecus Man-Ape. Sandberg is a protected fossil site and a part of the Devínska Kobyla National Nature Reserve.

### ŽELEZNÁ (IRON) WELL (3)

The forested Malé Karpaty (Little Carpathians) Mountains squeezed between the lowlands are the green lungs of Bratislava. They have been landscaped into a forest park, an excellent recreation area for the city's citizens. The Vydrica Stream

36

eroded the mountains, creating a deep winding valley. It is called the Mlynská Dolina Valley as nine water mills operated here in the past. The oldest were built as early as the 14th century. Most of the historical mills have not survived; some vanished completely and some turned into ruins. However, one has remained intact – the ninth mill. It stands below a popular trip destination called the Železná (Iron) Studňa well. Its name derives from the baths that operated here in the mid-19th century and used iron mineral water from two local springs. Four lakes built for the water mills in the 18th century complete the pleasant atmosphere of the valley. Two lie above the Železná Well and two are located in the lower part of the valley.

### VERNACULAR HOUSES IN ZÁHORSKÁ BYSTRICA (4)

Nooks with a rustic atmosphere with original peasant houses can be found near such a large city like Bratislava even today. One such a place is on the streets of a once independent village, now a part of Bratislava, in the Záhorská Bystrica quarter. A remarkable group of peasant buildings from the 19th century has been preserved in the lower part of Ulica československých tankistov Street. Several brick peasant houses that have undergone only minimal architectonical reconstructions can be found there.

### KAMZÍK (5)

Part of the typical skyline of Bratislava on the northern horizon is the large forested mountain called Kamzík. A TV tower has stood on its top at 439 metres since 1974. It is 194 metres high and houses a revolving restaurant at 68 metres with a splendid view. Two monuments commemorating historical events are located under the peak of Kamzík. The older one commemorates the Turkish threat and dates from 1683. The newer monument nearby is devoted to the victims of the last battle of the Prussian-Austrian War of 1866. East of Kamzík lies the Cvičná Lúka Meadow. In winter, it is a destination of winter sports enthusiasts, while in summer it is a favourite resting place for walkers and tourists.

## NOVÝ (NEW) BRIDGE (1)

The Nový Bridge was opened in 1973 as the second bridge over the Danube. A large part of the Podhradie quarter had to be demolished to make room for the bridge ramp. Despite this, the daring construction was applauded by professionals as a remarkable work of one hundred years. It is now called the Nový Bridge even though there are three newer bridges in Bratislava. The 432-metre long bridge was built to match the height of other landmarks in the surrounding area. The two-shoulder letter A-shaped pylon towers approximately at the same height as St. Martin's Cathedral and Bratislava Castle. There is a viewing restaurant called UFO and also a viewing platform on the roof that resembles a flying saucer spaceship. The pylon construction enabled the spanning of the river without any underwater support as the bridge hangs on massive ropes.

## APOLLO BRIDGE (2)

The name of Bratislava's newest bridge is to remember a former refinery that was bombed during World War II. Its ruins were a hideous sight on the left bank of the river for a long time after the end of the war. The bridge is situated downstream from the Starý (Old) Bridge and upstream from the Prístavný Bridge. Its construction started towards the end of 2002. Due to various aspects, the construction works were remarkable and unique. Part of the bridge construction was assembled on the bank of the river and then turned and fitted into its place above the river by a complicated technical procedure. The ribbon was

ceremoniously cut on the 4th September 2005. The elegant bridge with a fine arch got one of the 2006 OPAL Awards bestowed by the American Society for Technical Engineering upon especially remarkable constructions around the world.

## SLAVÍN (3)

Bratislava was spared larger damages during the march of the front in April 1945, even though human lives were lost. After the war ended, the decision was made to bury the Soviet soldiers in one dignified place. Himmelspitze (Heaven-like) Hill with a field burial side was selected. The building of the monumental Slavín cenotaph was finished in 1960. There are 6,845 Soviet soldiers buried in this pieta place above the town in 6 shared and 278 individual graves. The centrepiece is the Pieta Hall with an almost 40-metre high granite pylon with an 11-metre high sculpture of a victorious soldier on its top. The trees planted in the cemetery come from various parts of the former Soviet Union. Slavín offers a splendid view of the town and its surroundings.

## MONUMENT TO CHATAM SÓFER (4)

An old Jewish graveyard was once just outside the tunnel under the castle on the Danube embankment. It was used for burials from the 18th century. Bratislava's famous Rabbi Chatam Sófer was buried in a tomb here in 1839. The orthodox rabbi came to Bratislava in 1806 as a recognized Talmud scholar. Hundreds of rabbis were educated at his school, and they made his name famous all around Europe. The graveyard was used until 1845 when

it was covered with earth and stones during the construction of the tunnel. Fortunately, the tomb of the rabbi remained intact under an electric tram stop. The place above the graveyard was reconstructed in 2002 and a distinguished monument with an entry into the underground mausoleum was added. It is frequently visited by Jews as well as by tourists from all around the world.

## WATER SPORTS CENTRE IN ČUNOVO (5)

The gigantic Gabčíkova Dam was built on the Danube between Bratislava and Komárno and ever since there have been both opponents and defenders of this huge construction. The upper part of the dam, called Hrušovská Zdrž, reaches onto the territory of Bratislava. A modern water sports centre was constructed near the dyke, built in 1992 to dam up the Danube near Čunovo. It hosts slalom and rafting races even at the international level. Water sportsmen can use two artificial water canals (460-metre and 356-metre long with the altitude difference of 6.6 metres).

## DANUBIANA GALLERY IN ČUNOVO (6)

The Danubiana Gallery was built on a nearby artificial peninsula on the Hrušovská Dam in 2000. It was initiated by a Dutch businessman and art collector, Gerhard Meulensteen. The Gallery exhibits works of modern visual art by Slovakian, Hungarian and Austrian artists. There is an outside section with a collection of sculptures and plastic art and an inside gallery in a modern ship-shaped building.

# WESTERN SLOVAKIA

Western Slovakia is a land of warm lush lowlands with large rivers, fertile soil and also semi- mountainous terrain of the forested hills of Karpaty (the Carpathian Mountain Range). The nature in the region is not as wild as in the eastern part of the country, however it boasts scores of cultural and historical sites and monuments. Apart from Bratislava there are three other large cities in western Slovakia: Trnava, Nitra and Trenčín, and many smaller towns such as ancient Skalica in the Záhorie Region, the bath towns of Piešťany and Trenčianske Teplice in the Považie Region and Komárno, a town of forts situated on the confluence of the Danube and Váh rivers. The most popular tourist destinations in western Slovakia are the Červený Kameň, Smolenice and Bojnice castles. Additionally, the romantic ruins of the castles in Čachtice and Branč and castles in Levický and Topoľčiansky are also highly worth a visit. The Romanesque churches in Diakovce, Bíňa and Štvrtok in Ostrov are steeped in the history of ancient times, while the chateaus and mansions in Dolná Krupá, Holíč, Hlohovec, Moravany, Budmerice and Topoľčianky are elegant testimony of the golden era of the Hungarian aristocracy. Western Slovakia is also a land of floodplain forests, mysterious bogs and moors, water mills, orchards and large fertile fields.

# ZÁHORIE

## PILGRAMAGE SITE IN MARIÁNKA (1)
The village of Mariánka, nestled under the forested Malé Karpaty (Little Carpathians) mountains near Bratislava, is a renowned pilgrimage site. In the 14th century the Order of the Pauline Fathers founded a monastery with a church in the village. The Gothic church with later Baroque modifications features a statue of the Virgin Mary on the altar which dates from the 14th century and is said to have been crafted by a local hermit. The statue with its Romanesque features is a unique masterpiece of Slovak cultural heritage. Pilgrims to Mariánka worship the cult of the Virgin Mary and walk along six small Baroque chapels to a legendary spring and there are Stations of the Cross (the Calvary) on the hillsides of the valley.

## MANSION IN STUPAVA (2)
The most remarkable monument in the small town of Stupava is a large chateau. Originally the chateau was surrounded by a moat and was later rebuilt in the style of Early Baroque by the Pálfi (Pálffy) family in the 17th century. With the turbulent times during the Ottoman invasions and the Estate Uprisings, the chateau was rebuilt as a fortified aristocratic residence. The best view of the chateau is from the English-style park where it is reflected on the surface of a small lake. Stupava hosts the popular Stupavský Širák Folk Festival and the even more famous slávnosti zelá (Cabbage Festival).

## PAJŠTÚN CASTLE (3)
The Pajštún Castle is a favorite trip destination for the inhabitants of Bratislava. Not only is the site steeped in history, it also offers superb views. The ruins of this medieval castle stand atop a cliff above the village of Borinka in the Little Carpathians. The history of the castle dates back to 1273 when it was built as a sentry fort on the Hungarian boarders. The castle was laid to ruins by the Napoleonic army in 1810.

## KORLÁTKA CASTLE (4)
The medieval castle of Korlátko in the Little Carpathians was originally built as a fortification on the western border with Hungary. During this period the castle's founders controlled the so-called Czech Route, an important medieval trade route through the Little Carpathians from the Czech Lands to Trnava (Budín). The castle was built in the 13th century and abandoned in the 18th century and left to fall into ruin. The castle offers a splendid view of the mountain Zárub.

## PLAVECKÝ CASTLE (5)
The hills above Plavecké Podhradie were inhabited as early as the prehistoric times. At the renowned Pohanská archeological site, relics from the Early Stone Age and the Halštalská periods have been unearthed. Also one of the largest Celtic oppida once stood there. The ruins of Plavecký Castle, which dates from the 13th century, are situated on the neighboring hill. The castle was rebuilt into an almost impregnable Renaissance fortress in the 16th century however, it was damaged by the emperor's army in 1707 and derelict.

## VERNACULAR BUILDINGS
## IN PLAVECKÝ PETER (1)

The most complete group of rustic buildings in Záhorie has been preserved in the Plavecký Peter village as a heritage site of rural architecture. The site features a Renaissance church and white peasant houses which are similar to the historical farmhouses in South Bohemia, which represent the architectural style called Peasant Baroque.

## PLAVECKÝ KARST (2)

The hills and valleys of the Little Carpathians above the village of Plavecký Mikuláš are mainly formed of limestone with various karst formations. The Plavecký Karst covers 39 square kilometers and boasts numerous sinkholes, and caves. The rugged rocks called Kršlenica that tower directly above the village offer superb views. There are two interesting caves in the narrow valley above the village. The Tmavá Skala Cave lies on one side of the valley and on the other side is the Deravá Skala where the oldest remains of *Homo Sapiens* ever found in western Slovakia, dating from the Lower Paleolithic Era, were discovered.

## VÁPENNÁ IN THE LITTLE CARPATHIANS (3)

A large hill called Vápenná (752 m) looms over the village of Sološnica. The hill, also known as Roštún, is the third highest in the Little Carpathians after the hills Záruby and Vysoká. A defile of limestone rocks has formed on its forested slopes that drop sharply into the lowlands Záhorská Nížina. The most beautiful rocks, which can be found on the eastern edge of the mountains called Malá (Small) Vápenná, are the home to a rare bird of prey – the jet falcon. Vápenná is forested and was made a National Nature Reserve in 1953.

## VYSOKÁ IN THE LITTLE CARPATHIANS (4)

In some ways the second largest peak in the Little Carpathians resembles Mount Olympus. Seen from some angles it looks like a volcano; however it is not a volcano as it is formed from Mesozoic limestone and dolomite. A popular track to the top of the mountain starts in the village of Kuchyňa. On a fine day the peak (754 m) offers marvelous views with even the Austrian Alps being clearly visible. Vysoká is a Protected Nature Reserve.

### MANSION IN MALACKY (1)

The history of the village of Malacky is associated with the aristocratic family of Pálfi (Pálffy); their family crests featuring a deer forms part of the village's coat-of-arms. According to legend, the deer once saved the life of Count Pálfi. The wealthy Pálfis built a Renaissance chateau in Malacky in 1624 which is remarkable for its exceptionally tall chimneys. The mansion's present-day appearance dates back to a reconstruction in the 19th century, when its splendid English-style-landscaped park with scores of rare trees was created.

### HOLY STAIRS IN MALACKY (2)

There are only three such stairways in the world. The Holy Stairs are a copy of the famous stairway which Jesus had to climb on his journey to the Cross. The original stairway is in Jerusalem, a second is in the Vatican and Malacky boasts the third. They lead up to a side chapel of the fortified Church of the Immaculate Conception of the Virgin Mary from the 17th century. Worshipers climb the stairs on their knees along its left side. Allegedly there are relics of saints underneath each stair, which has made the staircase a very popular pilgrimage site.

### HABÁNSKY MANSION IN VEĽKÉ LEVÁRE (3)

Anabaptists came to western Slovakia after being chased out of Germany and Switzerland in the turbulent times of the religious upheavals during the 16th and 17th centuries. They adopted the lifestyle and habits of the first Christians; they addressed each other as brother and worked on common property. They excelled as craftsmen and were renowned for their brilliant pottery and ceramics. They lived in the so-called 'Habánske Courts'. One of the largest buildings of this type in Europe has been preserved in Veľké Leváre in the Záhorie Region. This unique complex of buildings with a museum is a protected Heritage Monument of Peasant Architecture.

### MORAVSKÝ FLOODPLAIN (4)

The Morava River, which forms the natural border between Slovakia and Austria, was a section in the Iron Curtain and as such was strictly out of bounds for several decades. Thanks to such unusual protection, unique floodplains have been preserved practically untouched. The flat alluvium of the river is a mosaic of flood-plain forests, dead-end river tributaries, marshlands and wetlands, all in very good ecological condition. Two islands of the original floodplain are protected natural reserves called the Horný Les (Upper Forest)

and Dolný Les (Lower Forest) Protected Nature Reserves. An interesting nature trail leads through the countryside of the Moravian alluvium, starting in Devín and ending in Vysoká pri Morave. It can be quite easily managed on foot or by bicycle.

## ŠAŠTÍNSKA BAZILICA (5)

The history of pilgrimages to the village of Šaštín dates back as far as 1564. According to a legend, its origins are associated with a pious lady Angelica who prayed for the lost love and respect of her husband, the Lord of Šaštín Imrich Cobor (Czobor), to the Virgin Lady of Seven Sorrows. Thankful for her fulfilled prayers, the once again loved woman placed a wooden statue of the Virgin Mary into a small newly built chapel. Scores of pilgrims started visiting the statue with miraculous powers to have their prayers and wishes fulfilled. In 1732 Pope Urban VIII issued a decree declaring it a miraculous sculpture as proven by 726 miracles. A Baroque church that houses the sculpture was consecrated on the 15th August 1764; even Maria Theresa was present at the ceremony. In 1964 Pope Paul VI granted the church status of Basilica Minor, the first of its kind in Slovakia.

## BOR (6)

Záhorská nížina is distinct from the other Slovakian lowlands and is filled with the lovely scent of spruce, pine-trees and mushrooms. The forests are very popular with mushroom enthusiasts, mainly from Bratislava, during the mushroom season. The forest in Záhorie called 'Bor' (Pine-Wood) has great importance for this area. Even in the times of Maria Theresa in the 18th century, extensive sand dunes in the region, which formed here during the Ice Age when they were blown here from the Moravian plains, were being artificially forested. If it was not for Bor, sand would be ever-moving and could cover the villages in Záhorie. A large part of Bor is within an extensive army training area. The precious natural lowland is the Záhorie Protected Landscape Area.

## MANSION IN SENICA (1)

Today, Senica is the largest city in the Záhorie Region, larger than Malacky and Skalica. The most significant cultural and historical monument in this lively town is a Late Baroque mansion from 1760. The elegant building bears the signature of the court architect F. A. Hillebrandt. Following a reconstruction in the 1970s, the Záhorská Gallery, devoted to the history and current visual art of the Záhorie Region, was established in the mansion. The chateau is surrounded by an English-style landscaped park. Senica boasts another two mansions – a Classicism building from 1782 and a Late Classicism edifice from the beginning of the 19th century.

## SMRDÁKY (SMELLY) BATHS (2)

The name of the baths in the Chvojnická Pahorkatina hills, Smrdáky (Smelly), comes from their typical odor caused by the local mineral spring with high sulfur content. Skin and rheumatism ailments are successfully cured in this spring, the waters of which have one of the highest sulfur contents to be found in Europe. The baths were established in 1832 by baron Jozef Vietoris. The spa buildings are set in a pleasant green park. Apart from modern buildings, there is a group of Empiricism buildings of high architectonic value. The forested hill Zámčisko with ruins of a prehistoric settlement looms above the baths.

## BRANČ CASTLE (3)

The hill with a castle, the most western slope of the mountain range in Slovakia, is a unique viewing point. It offers a panoramic view of the north and central part of Záhorie. The silhouette of the ruin which stands atop the hill is visible from almost anywhere in the surrounding district. Branč Castle was founded in the 13th century to protect the Hungarian boarders and merchant routes. The lords of the castle owned a large surrounding estate. The castle burnt down in the 17th century, was abandoned at the beginning of the 18th century and over time has fallen into ruin.

## SOBOTIŠTE (4)

In the first half of the 19th century an agile teacher called Samuel Jurkovič was behind the lively economical, cultural and social life of Sobotište. In 1845 he founded the Farming Club. This self-help cooperative was the first of its kind in continental Europe and was founded only three months after the establishment of the world's oldest society of this type in Rochdale in England. The daughter of Jurkovič first flirted with a member of the Štúrovské Movement, Janko Francisci, however she later married a national revivalist, Jozef Miloslav Hurban. Sobotište boasts a mansion, which was rebuilt from an older Renaissance-Baroque building in the 18th century. An Anabaptist Mansion once stood in the village and several of the complex's original peasant buildings have been preserved.

### ROTUNDA IN SKALICA (1)

The most remarkable building in the village of Skalica is the Romanesque Rotunda of St. George. It was built in the 12th century on a small hill with fine views of the dominant rocks and became a part of the fortification system in the 15th century. Its preserved Romanesque disposition is of significant cultural value. The interior houses valuable Gothic murals depicting the classic scene of St. George's fight with the dragon.

### ST. MICHAEL CHURCH IN SKALICA (2)

An unusual triangle-shaped historical square was built in the centre of Skalica in the Middle Ages. Its most prominent landmark is a Gothic parish church consecrated to St. Michael. Written sources mention its existence as early as in 1372, when the king bestowed Skalica with the privileged status of Free Royal Town.

### HOUSE OF CULTURE IN SKALICA (3)

Although it is a relatively modern building situated on a historical square, this edifice deserves special attention. It is the work of the great Slovakian architect D. Jurkovič and was built as the Society House in 1905 in the Art Nouveau style. Its remarkable façade faces the square and is decorated with a colorful mosaic inspired by paintings of the renowned Czech painter Mikoláš Aleš, which depict scenes from vineyards.

### CHATEAU IN HOLÍČ (4)

The Habsburg dynasty, which got hold of the Hungarian royal crown in the 16th century, took over the Holíč estate, including its 16th century Renaissance fortress, in 1736. Between 1749 and 1754 the new masters had the fortress rebuilt into a grandiose summer seat. The Baroque-Classicism chateau once boasted a French garden, pheasant woods, a lake and a group of outbuildings. Unfortunately, most of the chateau with its luxurious interiors furnished in true imperial style

has not been preserved. The husband of Maria Theresa Francis of Lorraine liked visiting the chateau and during that era Holíč was the largest town in the region and boasted a ceramics workshop that produced the famous Holíč Majolica.

## WINDMILL IN HOLÍČ (5)
While the neighboring Czech Republic has several preserved historical windmills, Slovakia only boasts one. It is located near the Moravian boarder in the picturesque town of Holíč in the Záhorie Region. The three-story stone windmill was built in a small wood above the town towards the end of the 19th century and was still in operation after World War I.

## MENHIR IN HOLÍČ (6)
Menhirs, the stone relics of ancient cultures, are mostly found in western Europe, mainly on the British Isles and in Brittany. However, there is one menhir in Slovakia which was found in Holíč during the construction of apartment buildings. The ancient megalithic cult stones were then moved to the courtyard of a former factory in Holíč and symbolically arranged in the shape of a sun dial. French specialists confirmed that the stones are genuine menhirs and possibly date from the time of the megalithic cultures existing approximately between the beginning of the 5th century and the middle of the 2nd century BC.

## ST. MARGARET CHAPEL
## NEAR KOPČANY (7)
A small, secluded chapel devoted to St. Margaret stands in the fields around Kopčany near Holíč. Surprisingly, archeologists have discovered that it is possibly the oldest completely preserved architectonic monument in Slovakia. It was most probably a part of the Great Moravian settlement near Mikulčice, which dates back to the 6th century. The chapel was built between the 8th and 11th centuries and ended up on the other bank of the river following a change in the river's course.

1

2

# PODUNAJSKO
## (Danube River Region)

### SLNEČNÉ LAKES IN SENEC (1)
Water reservoirs in the warmest part of Slovakia are a great benefit for tourism. The regional town of Senec, located about 20 kilometres from Bratislava, makes the most of this advantage. Slnečné jazerá (Sunny Lakes) near Senec are a great tourist destination and their name is very accurate, as the sun shines here up to 2,200 hours per year on average. The lakes were created by sand and gravel mining that started as early as in 1845. The original five lakes connected into a 116-hectare lake are the largest man-dig area in the wide surroundings of the Slovakian metropolis.

### TURKISH HOUSE IN SENEC (2)
The Turkish House in the centre of Senec is a typical example of the Renaissance style. This small chateau, or rather mansion, was built by a Bratislava native and the city head of the county Krištof Baťáni (Bathyányi) between 1556 and 1560. The name of the house commemorates an attack by the Ottomans that happened shortly after it was completed in 1663. It was the seat of Bratislava's county council until 1757. Following a successful reconstruction of the derelict building in 1994, the Turkish House is now a stylish restaurant.

### CHATEAU IN BERNOLÁKOVO (3)
The Bernolákovo's branch of the rich Hungarian family of Esterházi (Eszterházy) managed to get an influential place on the court of the emperor for their support of the Habsburg's interests. Count Jozef Esterházi played an important role in the victory over the Turks that ended in the memorable Szatmárský (Satumarský) Truce of 1711. He received an award that enabled him to build a noble Baroque chateau in Bernolákov between 1714 and 1722. It was once one of the most luxurious aristocratic seats in Hungary. The Esterházi family hosted Maria Theresa, including her numerous company, in their chateau in 1766. The empress expressed her appreciation for the warm hospitality by founding one of the first factories in the area for the production of cloth. The first 18-hole golf course in Slovakia was opened in the historical park adjacent to the chateau in 1995.

### HISTORICAL BRIDGE IN KRÁĽOVÁ NEAR SENEC (4)
An historical bridge spans the slow lowland stream Čierna Voda in Kráľová near Senec. Despite its typical Baroque appearance, the bridge is not that old, as it was built in 1904 as the first park bridge; it replaced an older wooden bridge.

### BEEKEEPING OPEN-AIR MUSEUM IN KRÁĽOVÁ NEAR SENEC (5)
A unique beekeeping open-air museum is located in the Včelárske Paseky locality near the village of Kráľová. Beekeeping has a long tradition here. A cultural and enlightening centre of the Slovakian beekeepers was established here as early as in 1932. Three pavilions sprung up in the area decorated by wood-carving and surrounded by a 10-hectare garden with a research station for the cultivation of honey-bearing plants.

3

4

5

## DUNAJ (THE DANUBE RIVER) (1)

For centuries the Danube has forked out into a tangle of numerous river tributaries and dead-end streams on the drifts it deposited on the island Žitný. These tributaries cut through a huge swampy floodplain forest. However, the natural world of the river marshlands narrowed down into a strip squeezed between the flood gates in the 18th and 19th centuries. A large piece of the area was destroyed by the dam Vodné dielo Gabčíkovo at the end of the 20th century. Larger parts of the preserved Danube floodplains are located on an artificial island that was created between the old river-channel of the Danube and the new manmade canal of the Gabčíkovo. Three villages, Dobrohošť, Vojka nad Dunajom and Bodíky, were also cut off on the island.

## MALÝ DUNAJ (THE LITTLE DANUBE RIVER) (2)

With the area of 1,600 sq km, the Žitný island is the largest European river island. It is bordered by the main river-channel of the Danube on the south while the Little Danube creates its northern boarder. The zigzagging 157-kilometre long lowland river is popular mainly with water-sports enthusiasts. Boating on the stream, which forks out of the Danube downstream of Bratislava and then returns back to the main river near Komárno together with the Váh River, is a very popular sport undertaking.

## ČÍČOVSKÉ DEAD-END RIVER TRIBUTARY (3)

The dead-end river tributary near Číčov on the Žitný Island creates a rather large natural horseshoe-shaped lake. It is also called the lake Lion and was created by a rupture of the Danube flood gate in 1899. It is a small 'island' of the original natural floodplain forests that once stretched on a large territory along the Danube River. An extremely valuable biotope of the water and swamp community protected as a national nature reserve has been preserved in this place. The Číčovské dead-end arm is amongst the most important areas of the Danube Floodplains Protected Landscape Area. Significant archaeological sites are also located in the surroundings of this swampy area.

## VODNÉ DIELO GABČÍKOVO (4)

The waters of the mighty Danube River have been constricted into the Gabčíkovo Dam. The river was dammed up in 1992 near the village of Čunovo, which created the upper part of Gabčíkovo called Hrušovská Zdrž. An extensive artificial lake discharges into a long artificial tributary. The dams of Gabčíkovo are 16 meters above the surrounding lowland terrain. A hydroelectrical plant with eight aggregates uses this level difference; its total output is 720 MW. The plant on Gabčíkovo provides 8 percent of the total electricity consumption of Slovakia. Gabčíkovo is also part of the Danube water traffic way. There are two ship locks at the dyke of the Gabčíkovo. Water flows through an artificial canal below the dam and returns back into the natural river bed near the village of Sap. Gabčíkovo has become a popular tourist destination.

### WATERMILL NEAR JELKA (1)

Water sports enthusiasts like to stop at a watermill situated on the left bank of a large meander of the Little Danube near the village of Jelka. It is a popular camping site that offers pleasant swimming in the river. Hundreds of similar watermills were once on the Danube and its tributaries. The one near Jelka is over one hundred years old. The oldest written record about the existence of the watermill dates from 1894. Initially, it belonged to Jozef Németh and later to his son. It was originally build as a boat mill, however its reconstruction started as early as 1900 and it operated again in August, 1906. The mill worked until April, 1951. The historical mill was successfully reconstructed in 1992 thanks to the Ethnography Museum in Galanta and the Municipal Office in Jelka, and even today it could be once again put into operation.

### WATERMILL NEAR DUNAJSKÝ KLÁTOV (2)

Below the Jahodná village northwest of the Dunajská Streda, a charming tributary separates from river Malý Dunaj (Little Danube) near the village of Dunajský Klátov, after which it receives its name, the Klátovské Tributary. It is just as attractive for water sports enthusiasts as the meander of the main canal of the Little Danube. An old watermill stands near the water in a place which is covered with the white blossoms of water lilies every summer. It was probably built in the 19th century and received its present-day appearance during a reconstruction in 1920. It was in operation until the 1940s. A successful reconstruction was carried out on the historical mill in 1987 and

it is open to the public as an exposition of the Museum of Žitný island based in Dunajská Streda.

### WATERMILL NEAR TOMÁŠIKOVO (3)

The watermill on the bank of the Little Danube near the village of Tomášikovo is set in a splendid natural environment and shadowed by romantic old willow trees. The historic mill with acacia-wood wheels was built in 1895 and used until 1960. And even today, it could grind again thanks to a successful reconstruction in 1982. The watermill is accessible to the public as an exposition of the Ethnographic Museum in Galanta. Visitors can learn about the rich history of the miller craft in Southern Slovakia and admire this technical monument.

### WATERMILL IN KOLÁROVO (4)

The river island near Kolárovo on the forked out Little Danube is connected with the town by a covered wooden pedestrian bridge. It is 86 meters long and is the longest of its kind in Europe. There is a unique wooden boat watermill on the island. In fact it is a river craft consisting of two large boats anchored on the left bank of the right of the two tributaries of the Little Danube. Originally the mill was not in this place. Many of its parts come from a mill which once anchored on the Danube near the village of Radvaň nad Dunajom below Komárno. It was disassembled in 1965 and placed in a depositary of the Museum of the Slovakian Village in Martin. However, it was decided in the dockyards of Komárno to re-build the mill again. The result was a success and the newly reconstructed Radvanský Watermill could be seen on the Danube tributary in Komárno for some time before it was moved to Kolárovo.

## ROMANESQUE CHURCH IN ŠTVRTOK NA OSTROVE (1)

Valuable Romanesque churches on the Žitný island are a great cultural and historical wealth of Slovakia. One of the most valuable can be found in the village of Štvrtok na Ostrove. The massive brick Romanesque building with two spires and typical Romanesque windows dates from the 13th century. The Church, consecrated to St. James, was rebuilt in the Renaissance style in the 16th century and received its final appearance in the 19th century. It boasts a valuable original Gothic bell and preserved fragments of medieval murals in the interior. The Neo-Gothic organ built in 1877 by Országh, a master from Budapest, is also noteworthy.

## ROMANESQUE CHURCH IN HAMULIAKOVO (2)

It is worth turning off the popular cycling track along the left embankment of the dam Hrušovská zdrž to the village of Humuliakovo. Its attraction is the ancient Romanesque Church of St. Cross built in the 13th century as a Romanesque rotunda with a polygonal sanctuary. A simple church nave was added later. Despite later building reconstructions, several valuable Romanesque elements have been preserved, such as the façade, the portal and Romanesque windows in the spire. The church spire leans due to the dampness caused by the underground waters and frequent floods. Remains of Gothic murals from the 14th century can be found inside the church.

## ROMANESQUE CHURCH IN HOLICE (3)

To see the largest Romanesque church on the Žitný island, you must visit the Holice village situated west of Dunajská Streda. The two-spire Romanesque church consecrated to St. Peter and St. Paul was built before 1253. Old clerical documents state that the church was built on the order of the King Stephen I (who was later canonised a saint) together with 11 other churches. This originally Romanesque building was partially rebuilt towards the end of the 14th century in the Gothic style. The loopholes in both church spires confirm the fact that strong stone churches were the shelter of the locals in the turmoil times of the Middle Ages.

## ROMANESQUE BASILICA IN DIAKOVCE (4)

The village of Diakovce is known to the public mainly thanks to its thermal spas. However, this village also boasts a great sight that deserves the attention of tourists: a Romanesque basilica from the 13th century. A Benedictine monastery with a church or a small chapel stood on the site as early as 1090. The present-day church was consecrated in 1228 and throughout its almost 800 years of existence it has witnessed complicated building development. The present-day look is mainly the result of a reconstruction carried out in the 19th century. The oldest part of the basilica is the Romanesque chapel of St. Stephen, attached to the south side of the church.

## ROMANESQUE CHURCH IN BOLDOG (5)

A remarkable historical monument is hidden in the tiny village of Boldog near Senec. The church, dating from the 12th century, was originally built in the Romanesque style and has a preserved Romanesque baptismal font. However, its most remarkable feature is the valuable Roman desk built into the wall of the vestry above the bricked-in Romanesque window. It is a Roman gravestone from the 1st century AD.

### RENAISSANCE CHURCH IN GALANTA (1)

The regional town of Galanta, situated on a large plane of the Danubian Lowland, has its history closely tied with one of the most powerful aristocratic Hungarian families from the 15th till the 20th century, the Esterházi (Eszterházy) family. The Galanta's branch of the Esterházi family built two chateaus in the town. The older one was built in the Renaissance style in the 17th century. It now has a Baroque appearance and is used for various celebrations and exhibitions of the town and also houses a ceremonial hall and a town gallery.

### CHATEAU IN LEHNICE (2)

Driving from Bratislava to Dunajská Streda you will pass a chateau in the village of Lehnice on the right side of the road. The building, which resembles a medieval fortress, was built at the beginning of the 17th century in the then popular Late Renaissance building style. However, the original appearance of the church is long gone as its contemporary owner, count Rudolf Benyvoszky, initiated an extensive reconstruction in the so-called Pseudo-Gothic style that was used on the Italian and Scottish chateaus of this period. The chateau is currently a medical centre and is situated in a beautiful forest park, which refreshes the monotonous plains of the Žitný Island with its greenery.

### MANSION IN DUNAJSKÁ STREDA (3)

The heart of the Žitný island is Dunajská Streda. This pleasant town with a compact centre boasts the so-called Žltý (Yellow) Mansion named after the colour of its faćade. There once was also the Biely (White) Mansion, however it was demolished. It took quite a long time to build the Yellow Mansion. The construction was finished after several decades in 1770. Originally Baroque, it was rebuilt in the Classicism style in the 19th century. It was built for a bishop Mikuláš Kondé and now houses the Museum of Žitný Island, which was moved here from the demolished White Mansion, a romantic building from the end of the 19th century, in 1972.

## MANSION IN TONKOVCE (4)

The jewel of the small village of Tonkovce in the upper part of Žitný island is a Baroque church from the beginning of the 18th century. Its indisputable elegance was enhanced by a reconstruction in the then fashionable Romanticism style carried out in the 19th century. Although this building, set in the splendid greenery of an English-style-landscaped park, has weathered out, its greenish façade is still enchanting. The surrounding park is also remarkable. In the past it was called the 'sentimental' garden. Sound equipment was mounted on the middle spire of the chateau and when the wind was strong it made sounds resembling organ music, which brought out a sentimental mood.

## MANSION IN ŠAĽA (5)

In the centre of the regional town of Šaľa on the left bank of the lower Váh River is a Renaissance mansion from the second half of the 16th century. It was built on the site of an original fort-like building. Written sources mention the existence of a fortified monastery in this place as early as the 13th century. It was later rebuilt into a water castle and was turned into a fortress with corner towers in the turmoil times of the Ottoman wars. The designer, Syroth Kilian of Milano, used the seat of the wealthy family of Thurzo in Bytča as a model. The mansion in Šaľa is valuable mainly for its well-preserved Renaissance appearance with an arcaded courtyard.

## PEASANT HOUSE IN MATÚŠKOVO (6)

Southern Slovakia witnessed great changes in the second half of the 20th century. The traditional village with original peasant buildings was replaced by modern-style villa buildings. One of the few preserved traditional rustic buildings is the house in Matúškovo near Galanta. This peasant house with a courtyard facing windows and peasant annex building dates from 1847 and is now a valuable protected heritage building. The building has been open to the public since 1984 as the Folk Living House and it belongs to the Ethnographical Museum in Galanta. The interior with adobe bricks has white plaster.

## FORTRESSES IN KOMÁRNO (1)

One of the largest fortification monuments in Europe has been preserved in the border town of Komárno. Essentially, it is a complicated system of fortresses that also includes the strongholds in the Hungarian part of the town (Komárom) on the opposite bank of the Danube. The fort in Komárno was built between 1546 and 1557 to protect the town against the Turks. Originally the site was occupied by a 13-century castle. The first Renaissance building with bastions was enlarged between 1663 and 1673 and a Nová (New) Fortress was added to the

Stará (Old) Fortress. However, that was not the end of the building works on the fortification system. An outside protecting ring made up by two lines of bastions and four small outer strongholds was added in connection with the Napoleon wars at the beginning of the 19th century. Thus, the largest fortification system in the then Austria-Hungary was created. The town has recently received the fortification system into ownership and is planning to carry out a gradual reconstruction with the view to opening this monument to the public.

## EUROPE'S COURTYARD IN KOMÁRNO (2)

One of the most appealing tourist attractions in this town with ancient history and scores of cultural and historical monuments is the modern urban project called Europe's Courtyard. It is situated in the very centre of the town near the square Námestie Generála Klapku. The entry gates of the courtyard are named after Hungarian kings. The foundation stone was laid in 1998 and although the project has not yet been completed, the courtyard has a very attractive look. It is a square surrounded by a colourful spectre of replicas of edifices in various building styles. Individual houses

on the courtyard represent architecture typical for various places all around Europe and are the symbol of the shared values and roots of the nations living on our continent.

### MONUMENT TO MÓR JÓKAI (3)

Several great figures were born in Komárno, such as the Hungarian King Ladislaus Posthumus (1440), the world renowned operetta composer Franz Lehár (1870) and the famous writer Mór Jókai (1825). The citizens of Komárno build a stately monument to Mór Jókai, whom they consider one of the greatest Hungarian writers. The monu-

ment, by an artist from Komárno named Julius Bereca, was unveiled in 1937 in a small park outside the entrance to the Museum of Hungarian Culture and the Podunajsko Region.

### OFFICERS' PAVILION IN KOMÁRNO (4)

One of the finest buildings in the centre of Komárno is the former Officers' Pavilion. The Neo-Gothic building was built between 1858 and 1863 in the so-called English Tudor Gothic style. The two-story U-shaped building features four towers, and there is a park in its inner courtyard. Originally it served as an army building with flats for officers

and representative premises for important visitors including the emperor and his court. It now houses important social events.

### ROMAN CAMP IN IŽA (5)

In the Roman times the Danube near Komárno was the natural northern boarder of the Roman Empire and was protected by the Limes Romanus fortification system. Its part was also the Brigetium Army Camp situated opposite the present-day Komárno. Roman leagues built a Roman stronghold called Kelemantia on the opposite (left) bank of the Danube. Its remains were unearthed by archaeologists in the Leányvár locality (Dievčenský Castle) near the village of Iža. It was one of the largest Roman constructions outside the boarders of the empire. Professional lectures are provided to the public during the summer tourist season by employees of the Archaeology Institute (SAV).

### OBSERVATORY IN HURBANOV (6)

An historical observatory is hidden in the greenery in the town of Hurbanovo, famous for its popular Zlatý bažant beer produced in the local brewery. It coordinates the well-organized network of Slovakian amateur astronomy. The observatory was established in 1871 by a well-known Hungarian astronomer named Mikuláš Konkoly Thege (1842–1916). It was among the best equipped astrophysical work stations in the world. The owner left the observatory to the state. A larger cupola was added to the older building. There is a meteorological station near the observatory which boasts the longest observing radar in Slovakia.

### STEAM PUMPING STATION NEAR VIRT (7)

A stylish brick chimney looms between the villages of Virt and Patince east of Komárno. It belongs to a unique technical monument, the steam pumping station from 1897. Apart from the chimney a coal storage room and a building with regulation equipment of the contemporary pump room has been preserved. It originally served the water economy and regulation purposes and was to pump water from the often flooded territories affected by the waters from the Danube and old Žitava rivers.

## FRANCISCAN MONASTERY IN NOVÉ ZÁMKY (1)

The most remarkable cultural and historical monument of the modern town of Nové Zámky on the left bank of the Nitra River is a monastery of the Franciscan Order. It is situated in the north-west corner of the large rectangular Hlavní (Main) square. It was built between 1626 and 1631 and consecrated by the Esztergom cardinal Peter Pázmaň (Pázmány) on 24th May 1631. The architecture of the monastery resembles medieval monasteries with a central Eden Garden. Part of the building is now used by an ethnographical museum and part is once again occupied by the monks of the Franciscan Order.

## BLACK DEATH COLUMN IN NOVÉ ZÁMKY (2)

After the Black Death plague of 1740 in Nové Zámky receded, its grateful citizens build a column in 1749. Thus, the town received a very valuable monument that combines elements of the Baroque and Rococo styles. It is probably the work of Italian artists. The column was moved several times and has adorned the Hlavné (Main) square in the centre of the town since 1993. The conically shaped column is richly decorated with statues. The centrepiece is the statue of the Trinity placed on the top of column. On the front is a statue of Immaculata standing on the Globe and entwined by a snake, and there are also statues of St. Joseph, St. Sebastian, St. Rochus and St. Rosalie.

## MONUMENT TO VENUS OF HRÁDOK IN HRÁDOK IN NITRA (3)

Nitriansky Hrádok (part of the Šurany village) has received the nickname 'Slovakian Troy' thanks to its enormous wealth of archaeological findings. One of the largest archaeological sites in central Europe, which boasts 5 thousand years of history of settlement, is in the Zámoček locality. Archaeologists discovered the so-called tell in this site, a kind of prehistoric dumping site. The most famous discovery of Nitriansky Hrádok is the almost 4,800-year old clay statue of Venus – Magna Mater. Its enlarged copy by sculptor Ján Gubrica has been a part of a remarkable monument

in the centre of the village since 1988. Including its pedestal it measures 2.7 metres, which is ten times larger than the valuable original.

## MANSION IN PALÁRIKOVO (4)

Palárikovo near Nové Zámky is a traditional destination of hunters who use the former local manor, now a luxurious hotel. It was built in the 1740s in the Baroque style for count Károli (Károly). His son count Alojz Károli had the chateau rebuilt according to a design by Mikuláš Ybl in 1866 when it received its present-day Classicism appearance. The chateau is surrounded by a fine 50-hectare English-style-landscaped park with local as well as exotic trees. A small forest is adjacent to its south-eastern border. In the past it was a place of renowned hunting events with great hunting trophies and it is still used for this purpose today. The forest was established by the family of Károli in 1752 as a pheasant wood, which was unique in Europe at the time. Small hunting animals were once bred here seasonally.

## ROMANESQUE BASILICA AND ROTUNDA IN BÍŇA (5)

Bíňa near Štúrovo is one of the many villages to be found in Southern Slovakia, yet it was very different in ancient times. At the times of the Great Moravian Empire it had a settlement on the area of 100 hectares, the importance of which went well beyond the boarder of region. And Bíňa remained a significant place even during the times of the establishment of the Austria-Hungary Empire. The local Romanesque Basilica of Our Lady commemorates the famous past times. The two-spire church was built before 1217 and once belonged to a monastery. It is now a cultural and historical monument of European importance with scores of preserved original Romanesque and Gothic building elements. Another valuable monument is the nearby Romanesque rotunda (about 100 meters away, which is remarkable) with medieval murals from the 12th century. The wall paintings as well as the windows feature the Romanesque style despite the rotunda being rebuilt in the Baroque style in 1755 (72 years after it was damaged).

## BRIDGE OF MÁRIA VALÉRIA IN ŠTÚROVO (6)

Štúrovo attracts tourists mainly with its thermal swimming pool, called Vadaš, and the option to visit Esztergom, which boasts many more monuments. In the past both cities were connected by the pedestrian bridge of Mária Valéria built in 1895. It was destroyed at the end of World War II and only a ferry enabled the crossing of the river. However, the significant bridge of Mária Valéria was reconstructed in 2001 and it is now a pleasant link between the two towns standing on opposite banks of the Danube, as well as a part of the splendid panorama visible from the Slovakian side of the Danube. There is no lie in the saying that the basilica in Esztergom is the most beautiful monument of Štúrovo, for it is at its most charming when watched from across the river (from the Slovakian side).

### PARÍŽ MOORS (1)

The lowland Paríž stream now flows on the bottom of the long ago deserted wide valley of Žitava. Its slow stream created large marshlands on the flat bottom of the valley near Gbelce, which have been a very valuable and protected territory since 1966. The importance of the marshland is highlighted by the fact that it is listed amongst the so-called Ramsar locality, i.e. marshlands of European importance. The vegetation of Saccharum, Tupna and Carex are a popular resting place for scores of birds on their long migrations. The only occurrence of nests of the valuable Moustached Warbler in Slovakia was also discovered here. The Paríž moors can be seen from a bird's eye view from a viewing tower on the eastern edge of the marsh.

### SANDS IN MARCELOVÁ (2)

Strong winds blowing across the cold tundra that spread on our land in the Ice Age blew sands from the alluvium of the Danube and its tributaries and deposited them in the lowlands Podunajská nížina in the form of small sand dunes. Among the largest ones are the sand dunes on the territory of the cadastre of Marcelová east of Komárno. This unique territory has been a protected nature reserve since 1988. Scores of valuable and endangered flora and fauna species are dependent on the sandy soil of sands in Marcelová's.

### MARTOVCE (3)

Most of the sides of the village of Martovce near Hurbanov are surrounded by extensive marshes with romantic willow trees, poplars. They developed on a flat alluvium created by the rivers Nitra and Žitava. Part of the marshes situated south of the village and crowded between the two river beds has been the Alúvium Žitavy Protected Nature Reserve since 1993. The water is ever-present in Martovce. There is a fine lake in the middle of the village created by a dead-end tributary of the Nitra River. Its surface reflects the silhouette of a rustic building from 1871, which houses an exhibition of peasant architecture and living as well as a permanent exposition on fauna and fishing.

## BURDA (4)

The Danube River flows through a chasm below Štúrovo. It is called the Vyšehradská Gate and goes through the volcanic mountains of northern Hungary. The mountain range called Burda jut out steeply to 388 meters on the left side of the lowlands of the Danube (still on the Slovakian territory). It is remarkable for its effusive andesite cliffs. A tourist village called Kováčov with a swimming pool lies in the southern slope of Burda. The rocky slopes of the hills provide an ideal environment for thermopile virgin flora and fauna and are the protected Burdov Nature Reserve. The natural beauties of this interesting area and lovely views of the Danube can be appreciated when walking along the local Nature Trail. Another biotope has developed on the northeast side of Burda. The broadleaved species grow in the colder and more humid environment of the Leliansky Les National Nature Reserve.

## THERMAL SWIMMING POOLS IN PODHÁJSKA (5)

It is said that Slovakia has its 'Dead Sea' in Podhájska, as water from the local geothermal bore has a similar mineral composition to waters of the famous lake. The deep geothermal source was drilled in 1973. Water of 80 degrees gushes out of the bore every second from the depth of 1900 metres. Today it is used in large glasshouses nearby, however it mainly supplies water to the pools of the much visited local thermal baths. The first pavilions were built in 1974 and currently visitors enjoy the well-equipped facilities of a relaxation centre which is open year-round.

## THERMAL SWIMMING POOL VADAŠ IN ŠTÚROVO (6)

Crowds of tourists and holiday-makers swarm Štúrovo mainly because of its thermal swimming pools, called Vadaš. Its history goes back to 1952. The still existing Staré (Old) Pool used thermal water from a bore made in 1949. The

Nové (New) Pool was built on a meadow called Vadaš in 1973 and over the times it has developed into a large well-equipped sport and relax centre. An especially popular enormous swimming pool with a surface of 3,800 sq meters and artificial waves was added in 2002. The advantages of the centre are its outdoor pools, good infrastructure and last but not least the nearby border crossing.

## THERMAL SWIMMING POOL IN PATINCE (7)

The village of Patince near Komárno lies on the left bank of the Danube and is the most southern village in Slovakia. It is popular with tourists mainly because of its thermal swimming pool, situated east of the village. This place combines two important attributes of good summer recreation – warm dry weather and thermal waters. There are three swimming pools, a toboggan and a boating and water-cycling lake in this 30-hectare centre.

# MALOKARPATSKÝ REGION (LITTLE CARPATHIANS REGION)

### CHURCH OF THE HOLY TRINITY
### IN SVÄTÝ JUR (1)
The Church of the Holy Trinity in the centre of Svätý Jur was built in 1654. Originally it belonged to the Evangelists, however was dispossessed only 20 years later to become Catholics place of worship. The jewel of its mostly Baroque interior is a Baroque organ made by the Moravian master Vymola which is the only organ in Slovakia that has been preserved in its original box. A Piarist monastery was added to the church in 1720 and was later enlarged to include a college. The glazed ceramic sundial on the façade of the monastery was created by the monks of the Piarist Order. Brewing of Kláštorný ležiak beer was revived in the monastery in 1995.

### PÁLFIHO MANSION IN SVÄTÝ JUR (2)
On the western side of Prostredná Street, the main road in the village of Svätý Jur, lies an ancient looking building which is the Pálfi mansion. The building bears the name of the prominent Hungarian family for whom it was built as the Renaissance seat of Katarína Pálfi (Pálffy) and Štefan Ilešházi (Illésházy) in 1609. The mansion was possibly built on the site of an older medieval building and belonged to the Pálfis for three hundred and one years until Ján Pálfi gave it to the Francis Joseph Children Hospital in Bratislava in 1907. The reconstructed mansion is now used by the private Academia Istropolitana Nova School.

### NEŠTICH (3)
In the direction of the Little Carpathians, the small town of Svätý Jur narrows down into one street, which runs through the area called Neštich where the Church of St. George from the 13th century is situated. This simple Gothic building houses a valuable altar of St. George made of white sandstone. The altar was completed in 1527 by the craftsman Štefan Pilgram, who combined both Gothic and the Renaissance styles in the design. The St. George Church has no steeple, but a wooden belfry from the 17th century stands next to the church which houses an old bell from around 1400. According to a legend, the bell was buried during the Ottoman incursions and was later dug up by a pig. Neštich is also of historical interest for its preserved mounds which are remains of an ancient fortification.

### ŠÚR (4)
According to historical sources a lake similar to the Nezider Lake existed in the Roman times near modern Bratislava and possibly covered the territory of what is the large, swampy Šúr Forest. The terrain of the area east of Svätý Jur indicates the previous existence of a lake that gradually turned into a swamp. This significant natural area is protected and a National Natural Reserve was established here in 1952. The rare moor and bog alder forest, which changes into natural thermophilic oaks at the edges, is strictly protected. Springs with alkaline sulphur water are located on the west edge of Šúr and were used as local baths in the 17th century.

## MANSION IN PEZINOK (1)

A Medieval castle with a moat was built in the 13th century on the site upon which now stands a mansion. In 1609 the Ilešházi family turned the castle into a fortified Renaissance stronghold with a moat and then in 1844, the Palfi family had the place rebuilt in the Classicism style and created a charming English-style park, which to this day forms an impressive setting for this monument. Thanks to its last owner Ján Pálfi, the mansion was enlarged with six salons and the stately Historical Hall which have been preserved in their original form. The administration of Pezinok bought the mansion in 1931 then sold it to a winemaking cooperative five years later. Today the excellent Pezinok wines are produced here.

## PEZINOK TOWN HALL (2)

Pezinok's Renaissance town hall was built in the first half of the 17th century when the town's inhabitants were striving to gain autonomy. Their efforts were rewarded in 1647 when the town was granted the privileged status of Royal Town. Apart from the judge and council rooms on the first floor, the town hall boasted several shops and a pharmacy on the ground floor and a prison and a torture chamber were located in the basement. The town hall was reconstructed in the Classicism style after a fire in 1832, yet the original Renaissance elements influenced by German architecture have been preserved and the building is now one of the best architectural monuments of this style in Slovakia.

### BIRTHPLACE OF JÁN KUPECKÝ
### IN PEZINOK (3)

The prominent painter Ján Kupecký, renown throughout Europe, was born in Pezinok in 1667 into a family of a weaver of Czech origins in a house on a street bearing his name in the northern part of the town. Kupecký was one of the best portrait painters of his time. Among the famous people he painted were the Russian Tsar Peter the Great, Emperor Joseph I and also the great Slovakian enlightener and scholar Matej Bel. His paintings are on permanent display in numerous significant European galleries. The birthplace of Kupecký is managed by the Malokarpatské Museum in Pezinok.

### MALOKARPATSKÉ MÚZEUM
### (MUSEUM OF THE LITTLE
### CARPATHIANS) IN PEZINOK (4)

The interesting collection of this museum provides a comprehensive picture of winegrowing traditions in the region below the Little Carpathians. The museum is in the Kaviak House which is also another fine example of Renaissance style architecture in the town. There are Renaissance features both on the simple street-facing façade with a cylindrical jetty, and on the arcade in the inner courtyard. The house belonged to a rich wine merchant and according to the date on the portal, the house was built in 1638.

### PARISH CHURCH IN PEZINOK (5)

The oldest sacral monument in Pezinok is the parish church located away from the central Radničné Square on a small street called Farská Ulica. The church was built in the Gothic style at the beginning of the 14th century on the site of an older Romanesque sacral building. The builders of the Late Gothic vault of the church were inspired by St. Vitus Cathedral in Prague. The tall spire was added later and it is a landmark of the town. The interior of the church houses a valuable Renaissance baptismal font from 1523 and an epitaph of the patrons of the church, counts from the villages of Svätý Jur and Pezinok, and the burial chapel of the Ilešházi family.

### SCHAUBMAROV MILL
### NEAR PEZINOK (6)

The ancient Schaubmarov Mill is located on the north edge of the Cajla town quarter of Pezinok. It was built by the Pálfis of Pezinok's mansion in 1767 as the largest of the fifteen mills located in the larger Pezinok area. The mill belonged to a miller's family called Schaubmar with Bavarian origins. The group of mill buildings surrounds a courtyard. The mill is a remarkable technical monument and the only one of its kind that has remained in its original place. The mill was in use until 1951 and is now a branch of the Slovakian National Gallery and houses an interesting collection of naive art including a valuable collection of paintings from the Slovakian enclave in the Kovačica region of Serbia.

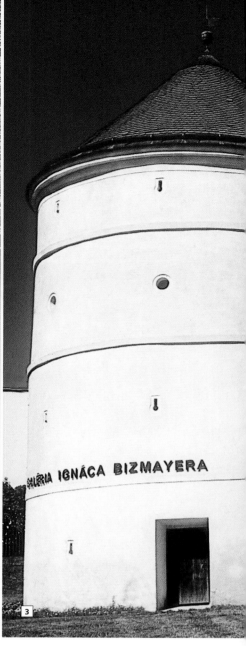

### CHURCH OF ST. JOHN THE BAPTIST IN MODRA (1)

To see the oldest sacral monument in Modra, walk to the old cemetery on the town's southern edge where the famous Slovakian national revivalist Ľudovít Štúr was buried. The cemetery was built in Gothic style in the second half of the 14th century and it has a lot of architecturally valuable Gothic elements. The largest church in Modra consecrated to King St. Stephan was built much later. It is located in the centre of the town and was built in the Neo-Classicism style in 1876.

### HORNÁ GATE IN MODRA (2)

When Emperor Rudolf II granted Modrá status of Free Royal Town in 1607, fortifications could then be built. A ring of fortified walls rose around the town between 1610 and 1646. Originally, there were three entry gates, however only one has survived and been preserved, although it no longer serves its original function. Horná (Upper) Gate is now an inseparable symbol of the town and its tower hosts various prestigious exhibitions.

### GALLERY OF IGNÁC BIZMAYER IN MODRA (3)

The rotunda-like bastion from the 17th century located on the Námestie Slobody Square is only a mere fragment of the original stone fortifications. The Gallery of Ignác Bizmayer (a part of the Ľudovít Štúr Museum in Modra) was opened in the bastion in conjunction with the World Ceramics Congress held in the town in 1994. The premises house remarkable pieces of ceramic art by Ignác Bizmayer, a folk artist from the village of Košolná near Trnava. The artist, who studied at the ceramics school in Modra and later worked as a head teacher at the Slovakian Folk Majolica School in Modra, has worked independently since 1957. His work is strongly influenced by the traditional Habaners ceramics, which were eagerly collected by Heřman Langsfeld from Košolná. This type of ceramic style is adorned with figural decorations with scenes from rural life.

### MONUMENT TO ĽUDOVÍT ŠTÚR IN MODRA (4)

The Monument to Ľudovít Štúr is a landmark in the centre of Modra. It was erected by Fric Motoška in 1939 to commemorate the last years of the life of this Slovakian national revivalist and codifier of the formal Slovakian language associated with the town. Štúr came to Modra in 1851 upon the invitation of his widowed brother Karol, a professor and a rector of the local Evangelic School and took on the role of the preceptor of Karol's children. During a hunt shortly before Christmas 1855 he accidentally shot himself in an unfortunate fall and died of the injury three weeks later on 12th January 1856. Several places in Modra are connected with Štúr. His grave is in the cemetery on the southern edge of the town, there is a Museum of Ľudovít Štúr in the former Town Hall and if you climb the tourist trail up to the Veľká Homoľa hill in the Little Carpathians, you will pass a bench, which is devoted to Štúr and was built at a spot he liked visiting on his rather rare walks.

### PEZINSKÁ BABA (1)

A path that connects Pezinok and Pernek in the Záhorie area cuts through the Little Carpathians range that rises between two valleys. The highest point on this path is the Pezinská Baba mountain saddle at 527 meters. A tourist centre of the same name lies in the saddle in the midst of beech woods. This summer crossroads of tourist trails becomes a favourite skiing centre in the winter as it boasts excellent conditions for downhill as well as cross-country skiing. Pezinská Baba is also a well known spot amongst car sports enthusiasts thanks to the popular annual uphill car races held on the Pezinok's side of the mountain.

### HARMÓNIA (2)

Harmónia near the village of Modra is one of the oldest recreational areas in Slovakia. It was developed when tourism and recreation were almost unknown terms in our country. The history of the centre dates back to 1850 when the small forest at the opening of the Údolie Kamenného Potoka valley in the Little Carpathians was a popular day trip destination with the inhabitants of Modra. Construction of cottages and villas started to flourish at the end of the 19th century with the first villa called Harmónia being built in 1889. Soon more buildings sprang up, built between the wars mainly by rich citizens of Bratislava. Today there are some 600 cottages in Harmónia.

### ZOCHOVA CHALET (3)

Germans settled in a mountain village called Piesok in the heart of the Little Carpathians back in the 14th and 15th centuries. They worked mainly in the forest and searched for ores and minerals. Tourists from Modrá started to visit this place in the 19th century and the town built the Panský House here in 1889 to provide accommodation for tourists during the summer season. The most famous building in Piesok is the popular Zochova Chalet which was built by members of the Slovakian Tourist Club and named after an Evangelic bishop, Samuel Zoch, the first head of Bratislava's Council of the interwar period. Unfortunately, Zoch did not live to see the ceremonious opening

of the chalet in 1933. Several marked tourist trails which crisscross the surrounding forested landscape start at the chalet.

## VEĽKÁ HOMOĽA (4)

It was pretty easy to decide where to build a tourist viewing tower near Modra. The best spot is the prominent hill called Veľká Homoľa located in the middle part of the Little Carpathians and quite easily accessible from Zochova Chalet. The peak is at 709 metres and was the site of an old lookout tower. The view tower was built in 1894 and was one of the oldest in Slovakia. It has fallen into ruin over the years and the new 20-metre wooden viewing tower was erected in 2001. The new construction rises well above the highest treetops offering magnificent views. If you climb the 115 stairs to the viewing platform on a fine day you can see as far as to the peaks of the Austrian Alps.

## TRAJA JAZDCI (THREE RIDERS) (5)

Just a few minutes' walk from the tourist viewing tower on the mountain Veľká Homola in the Little Carpathians is a bizarre rock formation called Traja Jazdci or Kamenná Brána which consists of three rocks standing in one line. The central rock is the highest and looms above the surroundings by approximately 15 metres and thus offers a pleasant view. Most of the rocks in the Little Carpathians are of limestone, however this one is a quartzite formation just as are the rocks Tisové Skaly above the Zochova Chalet. Quartzite is a very hard rock and is ideal for mountaineering.

## ČERVENÝ KAMEŇ (1)

The castle called Červený Kameň (Red Stone) on the eastern edge of the Little Carpathians above the village of Častá is one of the best preserved castles in Slovakia. Unlike many others, it withstood the Ottoman invasions, estates uprising and also the march of the Napoleonic Army. A lookout fortification stood here possibly as early as the 13th century. A rich ore merchant, count Anton Fugger, chose this strategic spot as the site for his massive Renaissance stronghold. Originally, it was more of a secure warehouse for copper and other of the Fuggers' goods than a family seat. However, when the mayor of Bratislava M. Pálfi (Pálffy) gained the castle through marriage in 1588, it was turned into a residence for the rich Hungarian family and remained in their ownership until World War II. It is now a museum open to the public which houses interesting historical collections. There are also tours of the former warehouse premises.

## SMOLENICE CASTLE (2)

The castle above Smolenice looks as if it is taken from a fairy tale. It was built in the New-Romanticism style at the end of the 19th century upon the

site of a medieval castle from the 13th century (which protected the so-called Bohemian Route). The architect was J. Hubert who also designed the Bojnice Chateau for the Pállfis. The Smolenice Castle now belongs to the Slovakian Science Academia, and is used as a congress centre.

## MOLPÍR HILL-FORT (3)

In the past, Molpír Hill above Smolenice provided natural protection for the founders and inhabitants of the prehistoric hill fort. The significant fortified settlement covered more than 12 hectares and was established approximately in the 6th century BC. Both Celts and old Slavs inhabited Molpír. Only traces of the fortifications of these ancient settlements remain. Archaeologists have found a large amount of valuable historical articles on this site; weapons, jewellery and objects of daily life. There is a small museum in the old parish building where findings from the site are on display. A nature trail with splendid views of the Smolenický Castle starts at the parish and leads up to the Molpír site.

## ZÁRUBY (4)

Záruby are the highest peaks in the Little Carpathians, though they are not amongst the highest peaks of the Carpathian Mountains. Nonetheless when viewed from Smolenice they appear to be massive, as they jut out from a valley to heights well over 500 meters. The highest peak (767 m) is formed from dolomite and limestone and protrudes along the top of this huge mountain range in a line of rocks. The rocks Havranie scaly on the eastern side are popular with climbers and there are remains of a castle called Ostrý Kameň in the western part. Beech forest swathes the slopes of Záruby reaching right up to the peak and even though it restricts the view, a trip up here is certainly pleasant.

## WATER RESERVOIR BUKOVÁ (5)

This lake was created on the Hrudka Creek, which flows towards the Záhorie Region in the Little Carpathians. The 50-hectare lake lies in the centre of a plain spreading on the northern side of the Záruby Mountain. The lake is used for recreation, swimming and fishery and there is a caravan site on its north bank.

## OSTRÝ KAMEŇ (6)

From the walls of the Ostrý Kameň Castle the garrisons had a perfect view of the trade path. Historians call it the Bohemian Route as it connected the Czech Lands and Moravia with the towns of Trnava and Budín. The route lay below the castle across the plain in the Little Carpathians Mountains near the Buková village. The castle was built as a lookout post on the border in the 13th century. Later it became the seat of a large domain including a large part of the Záhorie region. It was damaged during the Rákociho (Rákoczi) Uprising at the beginning of the 18th century during which it was abandoned and has been left to ruin. The ruin perched on the rocky bill in the western part of the Záruby Mountain offers splendid views of the Buková Lake, which is the starting point for the shortest trail up to the castle.

# TRNAVA REGION

## ARCHBISHOP'S PALACE (1)
Trnava is called a small Rome as it boasts scores of churches and sacral (Catholic) institutions including the seat of the Archbishop of Trnava. This high office moved here when the archbishop of Esztergom and the Hungarian primate left their city following its occupation by the Ottoman Army. The Archbishop's office moved into an elegant house in 1562. Located on St. Nicholas Square, the Renaissance palace was built under the guidance of Archbishop M. Oláh. His coat-of-arms adorns the main façade of the palace together with the coat-of-arms of Archbishop J. Selepčéni (Szelepcsényi). In 1615 Archbishop F. Forgáč (Forgách) added a new wing to the palace with an archive and a library and his coat-of-arms is on the Baroque portal. Archbishops of Esztergom remained in the building until 1820. The palace is now the seat of the Trnava-Bratislava archdiocese.

## CHURCH OF ST. NICHOLAS IN TRNAVA (2)
Trnava received town privileges as the first city in Slovakia way back in 1238. At that time, the original parish church was a Romanesque style construction built in the in the 11th century and consecrated to St. Nicholas. When Trnava started to rapidly grow, a better place of worship was needed, so a Late Gothic three-nave basilica was built on the site of the original church. It was finished before 1421 and rebuilt into the mainly Baroque Church of St. Nicholas in 1630 under the guidance of Cardinal Peter Pázmaň (Pázmány). Although it is now a parish church for many years it had status as a cathedral basilica with the diocese and Hungarian church synods taking place here between 1543 and 1820. The church is the main place of worship in the town.

## TOWN FORTIFICATION IN TRNAVA (3)
Medieval Trnava is easily identifiable on the current town map as the historical centre is enclosed by an almost coherent ring of the town walls. There are not many towns in Slovakia with such well preserved fortifications. The walls surround a rectangular space of 56 hectares and judging by this area, Trnava was among the largest medieval towns in Europe. The fortified walls were built gradually between the 13th and 16th centuries and were partially demolished in the 19th century.

Fortunately, only a small part of the fortifications were destroyed, therefore one can still admire the brick walls, mainly on the western, northern and southern sides. The total length of the walls is 1.5 kilometres. Of the several original gates to the town only one, the Bernolákova Gate situated on the western side, remains.

## UNIVERSITY CHURCH IN TRNAVA (4)
The first pure Baroque style to appear in all its beauty in Slovakia was the Cathedral of St. John the Baptist in Trnava. The church is amongst the most precious monuments of this style in the country and was built between 1629 and 1637 on the site of a former Gothic monastery of the Dominican Order. A great patron of the building was the Hungarian palatine Mikuláš Esterházi (Eszterházy). According to a legend, this was the last of seven churches built by Esterházi to redeem his sins. The church is called University Church as it was an important centre of university life in the town. Pope John Paul II honoured this place when he gave a sermon to the mass inside this splendid building on 11th September 2003.

## TROJIČNÉ SQUARE IN TRNAVA (5)
Trojičné námestie is the busiest place in the centre of Trnava and is named after a grandiose Baroque column with the sculpture of the Holy Trinity in the middle of a former rink. This remarkable work designed by J. K. Khien was

built in 1698. The Renaissance Mestská Spire is a landmark in the pedestrian-zone square and is located on the northern side. It was built in 1574 by Master Jakub. According to a legend, it was built at the time of the Ottoman invasions to enable citizens to spot the enemy at a distance. The tower is open to the public and offers splendid views. The third noteworthy building on Trojičné is the building of the Ján Palárik Theatre on the west side, which was converted from a restaurant in 1831.

## MONUMENT TO ANTON BERNOLÁK IN TRNAVA (6)
An enlightened Catholic priest Anton Bernolák (1762-1813) and the leader of the first generation of Slovakian national revivalists worked in Trnava as the secretary and chancellor of the archbishop's vicarage between 1791 and 1797. Together with Juraj Fándly, he founded the Slovakian Scholar Association at the Trnava University in 1792. The Association strived to spread culture and enlightenment in Slovakia and, for the first time in history, they also tried to codify the formal Slovakian language based on the western Slovakian dialect. A monument to Anton Bernolák was unveiled in Trnava in 1937 near the western gate. The statue of Bernolák facing the Slovakian nation with an appeal to write in the Slovakian language is the work of sculptor Ján Koniarek.

### ARCHBISHOP'S PALACE, CHURCH AND ST. CLARA MONASTERY IN TRNAVA (1)

In the southeast quadrant of the rectangular historical centre of Trnava stands the former monastery of the Order of St. Clara. The Clarisan nuns settled in this place as early as in 1239 and in addition to the monastery a Gothic church was also built. The church received its mostly Baroque appearance after a fire in 1683. Following the abolition of the Order of St. Clara the monastery was turned into an army hospital. It is now the home of the Museum of Western Slovakia and houses a unique collection of historical bells.

### CHURCH OF ST. HELENA IN TRNAVA (2)

A small but significant sacral monument is located on the bustling pedestrian zone in Trnava. The Gothic Church of St. Helena, also called the Špitálsky was built on the site of a former Romanesque church in the middle of the 14th century and was rebuilt and enlarged in the 15th and 17th century when certain Baroque elements were also added. The three-part Gothic aedicule with sculptures of St Barbara, St. Helena and St. Elizabeth above the portal is an especially valuable piece of art in the church. There are also valuable desk paintings from the 16th century on the main altar which dates from the 19th century.

### CHURCH OF ST. JOSEPH IN TRNAVA (3)

The St. Joseph's Church in Trnava is away from the main streets and the square on a small side street called Paulínska. Its location as well as appearance owe to the fact that the church was originally Protestant. St. Joseph's was built between 1616 and 1646 in the Silesian Renaissance Style. It was given to the Order of Pauline Fathers (The Order of Saint Paul the First Hermit) in 1671 during the Catholic Reformation and consecrated to St. Joseph. The Chapel of the Virgin Mary of Loreto was added to the north side of the church and a monastery building followed later in 1724. It served as a seminary for all of the Pauline monks in Hungary. The former monastery was later turned into an apartment building.

## DOM HUDBY IN TRNAVA (4)

Trnava boasts a rich musical tradition. The prominent Slovakian composer M. S. Trnavský (1881 – 1958) was born and later worked in the town. Trnava also hosts the attractive Dobrofest Music Festival. Dom hudby (House of Music) is located on the Ulica M. Schneidera Trnavského Street. This originally Renaissance house is under the administration of the Museum of Western Slovakia and between 1620 and 1622 it housed the Hungarian royal crown during the Bethlenov's Estate Uprising. The study of Trnavský has been preserved as a memorial to the composer. The Hall of Fame of Goodness is devoted to the Slovakian native John Dopyer who invented the rezophonic 'dobro' guitar. The hall is the only museum in Europe that exhibits these interesting musical instruments.

## OLÁHOV SEMINARY (5)

A significant cultural and historical monument is located near the St. Nicholas Church in Trnava. The first Theological Seminary in Slovakia was established here in 1561 and is named after Archbishop Mikuláš Oláh who was behind the establishment of this institution. Trnava's archdiocese established this institution upon the request of the Trident Council, which demanded that each diocese had its own seminary for the education of future priests. The Renaissance building was damaged by fire in 1566, and following reconstruction served as a hospice for old priests and then as a library of canonry. Currently it is the seat of the Literary Culture Museum, which is a part of the Museum of Western Slovakia.

## SYNAGOGUES IN TRNAVA (6)

The Jewish community formed a lively part of Trnava life as early as in the 14th century. However, the Jews were expelled from the town in 1539 upon an order issued by King Ferdinand I and were not allowed to return until 1781 thanks to the Patent of Toleration of Emperor Joseph II. The Jews built two synagogues in the 19th century. The synagogue built in 1891 is an impressive building with two spires and elements of Oriental style. The original glass dome stands in its centre, and there is a Monument to the Jewish Victims of World War II.

## MANSION IN HLOHOVEC (1)

The grandiose mansion in Hlohovec is best observed from the Šianec viewing point, which also offers views of a large part of Western Slovakia. The Baroque mansion is located below Šianec but above the town of Hlohovec and was built on the site of a 12th century medieval castle, which stood on the site of an ancient settlement from the times of the Great Moravian Empire. The castle, occupied for short periods by both Hussites and Ottomans, became derelict in the 17th century. It had several owners until the Erdődy family had a large mansion built on the ruins of the castle in 1720. The adjacent park with a pond and French terraces contains the oldest theatre building in Slovakia, which was built in the Empirical style in 1802. The bust of Ludwig van Beethoven outside the theatre commemorates this brilliant world-famous artist who performed a concert here upon the invitation of the Erdődys.

## MANSION IN DOLNÁ KRUPÁ (2)

This mansion was built in 1796 by the family of Brunswick in Dolná Krupá and is the work of great contemporary artists. The chief architect was Ján Talherr of the Hungarian Royal Building Chamber. When the architect A. P. Rigel introduced the noble spirit of Classical Roman architecture to Slovakia in 1813, the mansion was rebuilt in this new style and thus received a unified architectural style. A Belgium garden planner Henry Nebien landscaped a marvellous English-style garden with a central pond surrounding the mansion, giving an atmosphere of perfect harmony to the surroundings. Ludwig van Beethoven visited the family of Brunswick in Dolná Krupá several times between 1800 and 1809 and allegedly he composed the *Moonlight Sonata* as a gesture of appreciation to their hospitality, devoting the piece to Terézia Brunswick. The Rococo Beethoven Pavilion located near the mansion currently houses exhibits of the Music Museum. Allegedly, this is the exact place Beethoven stayed in on his visits.

## FRANCISCAN MONASTERY IN HLOHOVEC (3)

The monastery with the Church of All Saints in Hlohovec was built in 1492 by Franciscan monks from Bosnia. In the turbulent times of the 16th and 17th century it was occupied by Evangelists who founded here a Valentín Mackovič book press, one of the first to exist in Slovakia. The monastery was a significant centre of culture and education in the 18th and 19th centuries. The poet Ján Hollý worked in the building of the old vicarage. The monastery's preserved library houses many important documents, among which are two highly valuable medieval documents written in the Cyrillic alphabet in an old Slav language from Dalmatia. The Ethnographical Museum moved to the monastery in 1959. Its most valuable part is the historical refectory with original Renaissance and Baroque stucco decorations and contemporary furniture. The Minor Franciscan Order returned into the building in 1990 and assists the priest of Bratislava-Trnava Archdiocese in Trnava.

## CHATEAU IN BUDMERICE (4)

The three mansions located around Trnava are occupied by the Slovakian artistic community. Visual artists have the mansion in Moravany near Piešťany, musicians meet in the mansion in Dolná Krupá and writers gather in the mansion in Budmerice. The latter mansion, the elegant House of Slovakian Writers, was built in 1899 and is set in the midst of a lovely English-style park in the village of Budmerice. Nearby is the site of historical battle where the Emperor's army crushed the uprising lead by Francis II Rákoci (Rákoczi) in 1705. The mansion in Budmerice is a fine example of the Historicism style boasting precise and well implemented details. Apparently, the count Ján Pálfy was charmed by this style as he had his mansions in Smolenice and Bojnice built in a similar Romanticism style. A legend has it that there was a lady with who he fell in love with behind his keen enthusiasm for the French style mansions.

## ROMANESQUE ROTUNDA IN KRIŽOVANY NAD DUDVÁHOM (5)

Initially the Church of the Elevation of the Holy Cross built in 1938 in the village of Križovany nad Dudváhom southeast of Trnava looks just li-

ke many other village churches in the surrounding area. However, this building deserves special mention. The architect, A. Kapalín, designed it to include the preserved Romanesque rotunda from the 12th century on the left side of the altar. Previously this unique architectural monument formed part of a smaller Baroque church. The date 1172 engraved in the niche of the apse of the Romanesque building, however, it is not considered reliable as it is written in the then unused Arabic numbers. More reliable is the written reference about the existence of the rotunda in a document from 1296. The village sits in an area that is exceptionally rich with archaeological findings, the most important being a settlement from the era of the Great Moravian Empire discovered not far from the nearby village of Majcichov.

## KATARÍNKA MONASTERY
### NEAR NAHÁČ (2)

The ruins of a monastery amid the woods of the Little Carpathians near Naháč have a mysterious atmosphere similar to buildings in the romantic English countryside. The monastery was founded in 1618 on the spot where according to a legend St. Catherine appeared. The saint's name was given to the entire locality called Katarínka. The monastery with the Church of St. Catharine of Alexandria belonged to the Franciscan Order. Following its abolition by a degree issued by Emperor Joseph II it was deserted and the fleeing monks give away its inventory to various monasteries in the area. Deserted buildings and the church gradually fell into ruin. Nevertheless the place was not been forgotten and became a pilgrimage site. Moreover, a group of volunteers has been working on the site since 1994 trying to partially repair the monastery, therefore the history of the monastery is not yet finished.

## LEANING TOWER IN VRBOVÉ (3)

The belfry on the western side of the Námestie Slobody Square is a landmark of the small town of Vrbová located in the eastern foothills of the Little Carpathians and was built near the St. Martin's Church between 1832 and 1835. Following persistent rains, the belfry suddenly leaned to one side on 28th October 1930 due to the damp in its foundations. A survey conducted in 2000 established that the tower is leaning 90 centimetres off its vertical axis. Given that it is 38 meters high, we can easily call it a leaning tower, though obviously it cannot in any way compete with the famous Leaning Tower of Pisa in Italy.

## NATIVE HOUSE OF M. BEŇOVSKÝ
### IN VRBOVÁ (4)

A count called Móric Beňovský (1746 – 1786) from Vrbová was an adventurer and a traveller. On his journeys he went as far as Kamchatka, America and Madagascar, where natives made him their king. One can visit his birthplace in the town of Vrbové west of Piešťany. The aristocratic mansion was built towards the end of the 17th century in the Baroque style and now serves as a library which houses a historic collection and is also a venue for various social events organised by the town.

## ROMANESQUE CHURCH
### IN DECHTICE (5)

Located in the foothills of the Little Carpathians, Dechtice became one of Slovakia's pilgrimage sites in 1994. Allegedly, a local young man saw the Virgin Mary here at the beginning of December and later the same vision was experienced by another six locals. If not the for the pilgrimage site, Dechtice is worth a visit for its historical monument; the smallish Romanesque Church of All Saints dating from the 12th century stands in the village's cemetery. There is nothing exceptional about the façade, yet it hides an ancient Romanesque rotunda. Historians have identified this church as a unique example of metric analogy with the Pantheon in Rome. Romanesque murals in the interior, which date from between the 12th and 14th century and depict scenes from the life of the Christ, are further evidence of the ancient origins of this edifice.

## DOBRÁ VODA (1)

Dobrá Voda is one of the few villages located in the heart of the Little Carpathians. Ruins of the castle of the same name are located on the forested hill above the village. This originally royal castle dating from the 13th century went into the ownership of Ctibor of Ctiborice and later exchanged hands several times. When it was in the ownership of the Erdődys at the end of the 16th century, it began to fall into disrepair and was soon after abandoned after a fire in 1762. The short climb to the castle from the village passes through a cemetery with the grave of a Slovakian poet Ján Hollý (1785 – 1849). He lived in a nearby parish and was visited by Štúr, Hurban and Hodža who asked him to adjust the codification of formal Slovakian.

## KÚPEĽNÝ ISLAND IN PIEŠŤANY (1)

Most of the spas in Piešťany are located on an island surrounded by the Váh River and its tributary. The backwaters of the tributary create excellent conditions for the formation of Piešťany's famous therapeutic mud. Apart from the mud, local warm gypsum-sulphur springs also have curative qualities. There are historical as well as modern spa buildings on the Kúpeľný Island, most of which is covered by a park. The park is prettily landscaped and kept and is complemented by scores of sculptures which were placed here during renowned sculpture workshops. One of the symbols of the spas in Piešťany is the beautiful *Victoria Regia* water plant, which adorns the small lake in the park.

## NAPOLEONSKÉ SPA (2)

When Adam Trojan of Benešov wrote a poem celebrating the healing powers of the spas in Piešťany in 1642, the Napoleon Spa had not yet been constructed on the Kúpeľný Island. This is now the oldest building and was constructed between 1821 and 1862 on the site of an older spa building, which was destroyed by catastrophic flood in 1813. Napoleon's Spa consists of three Classicism buildings constructed above the hot mineral springs that emit a typical bad-egg-like smell. Its name has nothing to do with the French emperor and great conqueror, perhaps apart from the fact that Napoleon adored the Empire style, which is remarkable on these buildings.

## MANSION IN MORAVANY NAD VÁHOM (3)

The village of Moravany nad Váhom lies only three kilometres from Piešťany and is well-know mainly for the discovery of a precious Neolithic sculpture (the so-called Moravian Venuša – Venus), made from mammoth tusk more than 20,000 years ago by an unknown prehistoric artist. You will not be able to see the famous sculpture in this village on the left bank of the Váh as the original is safely stored in the depository of the Slovakian National Bank. However, its perfect copy is exhibited in the Balneologic Museum in Piešťany. Nevertheless, in Moravany one can admire a fine Renaissance mansion with an English-style garden. The Renaissance building from the 16th century is remarkable mainly for its preserved gable attic and is currently the seat of the House of Slovakian Artists and Architects.

## SĹŇAVA (4)

Piešťany is one of the warmest and sunniest towns in Slovakia. The name of the Sĺňava (Sunny) Water Reservoir constructed on the Váh below the town is therefore fitting. Before a dam was built above Šaľa, the river represented the lowest level of the Váh cascade. The artificial 430-hectare lake was created by building of a dam above the Drahovce village in 1956. The reservoir contains over 12 million square meters of water. It was built for the electricity production and as a protection against floods. However, it also has an important leisure purpose. The Protected Study Surface, for the protection of the biotope of numerous water birds, was established here in 1980.

## THERMIA HOUSE IN PIEŠŤANY (5)

The Napoleon Spa is the oldest building in Piešťany while the Thermia House could be called the most beautiful. This elegant building on Kúpeľný Island is a precious example of the Art Nouveau style. It was built together with the balneal and sanatorium called Irma between 1910 and 1912 according to the design of H. Böhm and Á. Hegedűsa. Many prominent contemporary artists created the building's decoration. The first noble guest of the Thermia House was the Bulgarian Tsar Ferdinand and numerous prominent visitors followed; the president Eduard Beneš, the actor Vlasta Burian, the painter Alfonz Mucha as well as the founder of the tennis Davis Cup, Sir Henry Davis.

## KOLONÁDNY BRIDGE IN PIEŠŤANY (6)

The covered pedestrian Kolonádny Bridge, also called Sklenený (Glass) for the large amount of glass used in its construction, was built by prominent Slovakian architect E. Beluš and connects Kúpeľný Island with the town. The bridge has been popular with spa guests since 1933. At the town end of the bridge there is the famous sculpture of the Barlolámač ('the one who thrusts aside his crutches'). This symbol is also a part of the coat-of-arms of the town and is a witty illustration of the great curative powers of the spa. The sculpture is the work of R. Kühmayer. The mid section of the bridge was destroyed by fleeing Germans at the end of World War II. Its reconstruction was completed in 1956 and preserved the original Functionalist appearance of the bridge.

## PRINCE'S SETTLEMENT NEAR DUCOVÉ (7)

During the Great Moravian Empire between the 9th and 10th centuries a prince's settlement once stood on the bare hill Kostolec above Ducové in the western foothills of the mountains Považský Inovec. It was an important defence on the Považská branch of the ancient Jantárová (Amber) Path. Extensive archaeological excavations in this important locality have unearthed a seat of a prince of the period, which was fortified with mounds and palisade walls. A Great Moravian building was erected here on a previous prehistoric settlement. The earth mounds are still clearly visible in the terrain and a replica representing the former palisade walls and stone foundations suggest the ground-plan of a pre-Romanesque rotunda. The charm of the Kostolec above Ducové is enhanced by unique views of the enchanting landscape around the Váh River.

# TRENČÍN REGION

## TRENČÍN CASTLE (1)

The powerful lord Matúš Čák ruled the Trenčín Castle dominion during the 13th and 14th centuries. For his great influence and wealth he was nicknamed the Lord of the River Váh and the Tatras. The history of the castle goes back to the 11th century. Initially a royal castle, it soon became the seat of the contemporary lord mayor. The emperor's army conquered the castle in the 17th century and subsequently occupied it for over a hundred years. It burnt out in 1790. The present-day appearance of the castle is the result of an extensive reconstruction; however the site is experiencing serious static problems. The castle is visible from afar, especially its landmark, a Romanesque tower from the 13th century. The three Gothic houses around the tower were added between the 14th and the 16th centuries. Trenčín Castle houses an exposition of the Trenčín Museum with historical collections.

## STUDŇA LÁSKY AT TRENČÍN CASTLE (2)

The historical well in the courtyard in the lower part of the castle dates from the 16th century. It took the castle guards and local vassals a full forty years of hardship as they dug 80 metres deep in the hard rock until they reached water. The task was finished in 1570 when the castle was owned by the Zápoľský family. However, one of the most famous Slovakian legends has a different explanation for its construction. A young man called Omar allegedly dug the well to redeem his love, a girl called Fatima. Three years it took him before water appeared at the bottom of the well. He took Fatima away, leaving a note for the lord of the castle: 'You have got water now Zápoľský, but heart, heart you haven't got.' Next to the castle well, which is also called Omar's Well or the Love Well, is a Gothic chapel and a terrace with a magnificent view of the town.

## PARISH CHURCH IN TRENČÍN (3)

The parish church in Trenčín is not part of the town centre. It stands in a fortified town called Marienburg on the way from the town to the castle. It is consecrated to the Birth of the Virgin Mary and was built on the site of an older church from the 13th century in 1324. The church burned down during a siege by the army of the emperor Ferdinand of Habsburg in 1528 and was then left derelict for forty years. Its present-day appearance is the result of a reconstruction carried out at the beginning of the 20th century due to a fire in 1886. The church houses the tomb of the Ilešházi (Illésházy) family from 1648 with decorations by a talented pupil of the great Baroque artist G. R. Donner.

## KARNER OF ST. MICHAEL IN TRENČÍN (4)

Besides Trenčiansky Castle, the Karner of St. Michael is the best preserved Gothic monument in Trenčín. This significant historical building was erected in the 15th century next to a parish church in Marienburg as a charnel house, and thus became part of the town fortification system. The karner was used as a chapel in the 16th century and masses were performed here until the parish church, damaged by the emperor's army, was repaired. It now belongs to the Museum of Trenčín; however it is not open to the public. The terrace outside the karner offers a splendid view of the town.

## FARSKÉ STAIRS IN TRENČÍN (5)

You can reach the parish church by walking through the tangle alleys and streets below Trenčín Castle or climb the Farské Stairs. This covered Renaissance staircase was built in 1568 for the members of the town guilds.

## HEADSMAN HOUSE IN TRENČÍN (6)

The house on Matúšova Street in the Hôrka quarter set in the steep slope of the Trenčín Castle Hill stands out due to its medieval appearance. This building from 1580 resembles a bastion and catches immediate attention with its wooden balcony on the first floor. It is called the Headsman House, as according to a legend the city headsman once lived there. It now houses the *Law and Order in Old Trenčín* exposition.

### COUNCIL HOUSE IN TRENČÍN (1)

At the west end of the Mierové Square in the historical centre of Trenčín stands a building that once hosted the former Council House. It was built by the Ilešházi family near the now vanished Horná Gate in the 17th century. Another story was added to the house between 1760 and 1764 when it was also reconstructed in the Late Baroque style. The historical coat-of-arms of Trenčín's county council on the façade above the balcony is supported by Tuscany pillars and is to remind passers-by that this was the location of the council historical meetings. The building now houses the Museum of Trenčín with natural, historical and ethnographic collections of the region.

### DOLNÁ GATE IN TRENČÍN (2)

One of the significant privileges of the free royal town of Trenčín was the right to build city fortifications. Two gates led inside the inner town that once surrounded the present-day Mierové Square. The Horná (Upper) Gate was demolished in 1783; however the Dolná (Lower) Gate has been preserved and is now a valuable historical monument. The 32-metre high gate was built in 1543 and is also called Turecká or Mestská. The six-story tower has a Gothic vaulted gate. Originally, a barbican protected it on the outside. There is a Latin inscription on the façade of the tower: *'In vain shall the guards watch the town unless God protects it'*. The terraces of the tower are accessible to the public.

### PIARIST CHURCH AND MONASTERY IN TRENČÍN (3)

The monastery complex with the Church of St. Francis Xavier of the Piarist Order, located on Mierovo Square in Trenčín, was founded between 1653 and 1662 at the time of the expansion of the Baroque style in the country. It was built by the Jesuits, who were invited to Hungary to support the Catholicism movement. The two-spire church is the work of the Italian Spazzav brothers and is based on the architecture of the Jesuit church in Vienna. The church's Baroque decoration is based on legends about St. Francis Xavier and is the work of Krištof Tausch, a pupil of the great Jesuit artist Andrea dell Pozzo. The illusive paintings in the dome of the church nave are especially impressive and are considered to be one of the best Baroque art pieces in Slovakia.

### TATRA HOTEL IN TRENČÍN (4)

The Tatra Hotel nestled below Trenčín's castle rock was built for Baron Armín Popper, who, along with all his other possessions, soon lost it in a card game. The first guests arrived at the hotel on the 1st January 1901. At that time the fashionable building style was Historicism, yet the hotel also bears some features of the upcoming Art Nouveau style. Apart from replicas of Baroque decoration, the façade is adorned by floral and figural ornaments typical for the Art Nouveau style. Since its beginnings, Tatra has been one of the best hotels in the country. Munich beer, Tokay wine and Swiss cheeses were served here before the war to the intellectual company that met in the foyer, including renowned writers such as Ján Smrek, Martin Rázus and Zuzka Zguriška.

### ROMAN INSCRIPTION IN TRENČÍN (5)

You can admire a valuable inscription of European significance from the window of the terrace of the Tatra Hotel in Trenčín. The message engraved into the castle rock from 179 B.C. is believed to be authentic evidence of the stay of a Roman legion of the Emperor Marcus Aurelius in this spot, located rather far from the northern boar-

1

der of the Empire. The text states that it was ordered by Marcus Valerius, the legate of the 2nd Auxiliary Roman Legion, to commemorate the victory over the German Quadi. It mentions the name Laugaricio, from a Roman camp of the victorious legion. The authenticity of this valuable Roman monument was confirmed thanks to the discovery of a pedestal of the mentioned legate Maximian, which describes his extensive army career in his service to Rome. The text also states the stay of the legion in Laugaricio.

1

2

3

## SKALKA MONASTERY (1)

The ancient Skalka Monastery lies on the right side of a strikingly narrow valley of the Váh River above Trenčín and seems as if it is carved into the rock. It was founded in the 13th century by the Benedictine Order on the site linked with an ancient legend about a monk called Benedict. Supposedly, this monk from the Zobor Monastery near Nitra was a hermit and lived in the rocks above the river. After being killed by a group of thieves, his body was thrown into the Váh. A flying eagle brought attention to the spot where he was later found. Benedict was buried with honour in the castle Church of St. Emmeram of Regensburt in Nitra next to his teacher, friar Svorad (Zvorard). Both monks were canonized in Rome in 1083.

## HAMMAN
## IN TRENČIANSKE TEPLICE (2)

The most impressive building in the Trenčianske Teplice Spa Complex is the Hamman building. It is a part of the Sina Spa House and was built in the Historicism-Moorish Style in 1888. The spa was built as a copy of the summer seat of the Egyptian vice-king Izmail, a model of which was displayed at an international exhibition in Paris. The contemporary owner of the spas, Ifigénia d'Harcourt, noticed the building and persuaded the Egyptian ruler to allow her to have a similar one built in Trenčianske Teplice. The court architect, F. Schmoranz, supervised the construction work. Both the faćade as well as the interior of Hamman exude an impressive oriental atmosphere. The main foyer is particularly remarkable with its arcades and rich decorations in the Moorish-Arabic style.

## MOST SLÁVY (BRIDGE OF FAME)
## IN TRENČIANSKE TEPLICE (3)

Trenčianske Teplice has a lot in common with the Czech spa town of Karlove Vary. Apart from both towns being located in a very similar wooded valley, there is also their connection with the art of film. The Artfilm International Film Festival is held in Trenčianske Teplice annually in June. It originated in 1993 and since then this spa town in the Považie Region has hosted numerous international celebrities from the world of cinematography. Since 1995 the Hercova Misia Prize has been awarded at the festival. The first person to receive this award was the famous Italian actor Franco Nero. Names of the many others awarded are on the signs on the Bridge of Fame outside a hotel of the same name: Jean Paul Belmondo, Sophia Loren, Gina Lollobrigrida, Catherine Denevue and Klaus Maria Brandauer.

## STUD FARM IN MOTEŠICE (4)

The village of Motešice in the area called Trenčianske Záhorie is famous mainly for horse breeding. A stud farm was founded here in 1923 and soon after it was used for army purposes. The farm acquired the great Furioso breed, which is perfect for dressage and jumps. For instance the three-time winner of the famous Czech Velká Pardubická horse race comes from Motešice. The farm includes the largest indoor riding hall in Europe and stables for 250 horses. The management of the farm sits in a Renaissance mansion in the Horné Motešice quarter. It was built as a fortified aristocratic seat with four towers in 1620 and received its Baroque appearance in the 18th century. The Seldner family still

used this luxurious place surrounded by a large park at the beginning of the 20th century.

## OMŠENSKÁ BABA (5)

A massive hill called Omšenská Baba looms above the village of Omšenie above Trenčianske Teplice. It is 668 metres high and is made of limestone and dolomite. Thermophilic vegetation with several protected species grows on its sunny southern slope; the Omšenská Baba Nature Reserve was established here in 1967. Its rocky peak is a favourite tourist destination as it provides a splendid view of the southern part of the hills Strážovské Vrchy. Daniel Krman Jr., a Slovakian enlightened writer and translator well-known for his anti-Catholic polemics, was born in Omšenie.

## KRASÍN (6)

The sharp massive rock Krasín (516 m) that looms above the village of Dolná Súča is completely different from its surrounding less dramatic flysch countryside that is typically dotted with hills. Krasín belongs to the narrow rocky range that basically cuts through the whole of Slovakia. Súča Castle was built on the limestone rocks in the western part of Krasín in the 13th century. Originally one of the king's possessions, it went to Ján Zápoľský who, however, later lost it following his unsuccessful fight for the Hungarian crown, and the castle went to the Podmanický family. The army set the castle on fire in 1550 and over time, the mostly wooden building has almost vanished. Krasín is now visited not for its almost indistinguishable castle ruins, but for the splendid views it offers.

### VEĽKÁ JAVORINA (1)

Slovaks and Moravians share the TV antenna on the Mountain Veľká Javorina (970 m). People from both sides of the border have been meeting atop the highest peak of the White Carpathians since the 19th century to display their shared traditions and culture. A tireless initiator of these meetings was the national revivalist J. M. Hurban. The tradition of mass meetings of Czechs and Slovaks started on 25th July 1933. Today the gatherings on Javorina are amongst the most significant social events of the region. Veľká Javorina is a popular destination for skiers in the winter while in the summer it is sought after by tourists. A tourist chalet called Holubyho was built on the Slovakian side in 1924. It is named after J. Ľ. Holuby, a Slovakian Europe-renowned flora expert, botanist and a great expert on the Podjavorinský area. The chalet serves tourists who climb the peak of Veľká Javorina. There is a fine view of the country beyond the mountain range from the top.

### CHURCH
### IN ZEMIANSKE PODHRADIE (2)

The Evangelic church in Zemianske Podhradie from 1801 is a remarkable architectonic rarity. There is probably only one similar building in

the world, located in Germany. The design of the building was drawn up by baroness Ester Príleská who lived in a mansion in Podhradie. The church was built in the Empire style and has a round ground-plan with a central round hall vaulted by a dome. Twelve covered arcades are attached around the perimeter of the church. A long ladder leads from the gallery to the attics. It was used by Ľudovít Štúr while he was hiding in Zemianske Podhradie from the emperor's army after the unsuccessful uprising in 1848. A zealous nationalist and an Evangelic priest working in Podhradie, Brother Samuel, gave him shelter.

## MANSION
## IN ZEMIANSKE PODHRADIE (3)
The village of Zemianske Podhradie sits in the valley Bošácka dolina famous for the production of excellent slivovitz (distilled fermented plum brandy). The centre of the village is occupied by a mansion from the 17th century. The originally Renaissance building was reconstructed into a family seat by P. Príleský at the beginning of the 18th century. He also landscaped the surroundings into a park, which boasted scores of foreign trees and was unique at the time. The mansion received its present-day Classicism appearance during a reconstruction at the beginning of the 19th century. It later belonged to the Ostrolúcky family (by a marriage) from Ostrá Lúka near Zvolen. Adela Ostrolúcka is well-known to the public, for she was a great tragic love of Ľudovít Štúr.

## VEĽKÝ LOPENÍK (4)
The large forested Mountain Veľký Lopeník (911 m) is perched above the picturesque and undulating landscape of the Bošácka dolina. Slovakia shares this mountain, one of the highest in the mountains called Biele Karpaty (White Carpathians), with the Czech Republic. In the past it was a place with lovely views but it later became overgrown with high forests. However, it is now once again the destination of far-reaching lookout enthusiasts; a 22-metre wooden viewing tower with a stone base was erected here in 2005. Previously there were several similar towers, however they all vanished. The last one perished in the 1970s.

## CHURCH IN HALUZICE (5)
There is a small village on the northern side of the Bošácka dolina called Haluzice. It is set at an interesting altitude and boasts a romantic ruin of an ancient fortified church situated on a fine spot at the edge of the village. It was originally Romanesque (1240), but was then rebuilt in the Gothic and Renaissance styles and deserted in 1810. Fortunately, the ruins were reconstructed so it is now an attractive and impressive sight. The Late Renaissance statue of the Madonna from the 15th century, which adorns the parish church in Beckov, was originally on the façade of the Haluzice church. The famous Czech writer Alois Jirásek was captivated by the romantic ruin for he mentioned it in his Bratstvo Trilogy. However, there is no evidence that members of the Bratríci Movement ever stayed in this place.

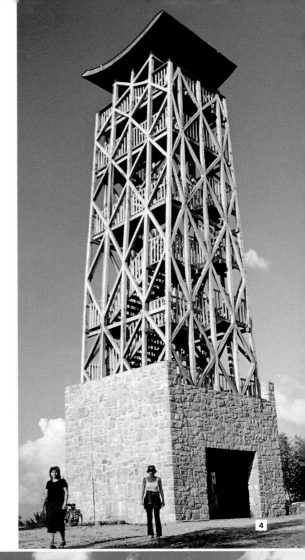

4

5

## BECKOV CASTLE (1)

The Beckov Castle atop a sharp rock above a village of the same name is a very impressive sight from anywhere. A famous legend describes its origins. Allegedly a count Ctibor of Ctiborice built it for his jester Beck in appreciation of his wit. However, according to historians, the castle stood on the rock already before Ctibor lived, which is proved by a document from 1255. The castle was known to be an impenetrable stronghold, which was proved in 1599 when it withstood an unsuccessful Ottoman attack. However, flames managed what the army could not. A fire that broke out in the town in 1709 soon spread onto the castle. This was the end of its fame and only its ruins are to be admired now.

## ČACHTICKÝ CASTLE (2)

The legend about the bloody countess of Čachtice has been a favourite topic for writers as well as film directors. Alžbeta Bátoryová lived in the Čachtice Castle build on a narrow mountain range north of the Little Carpathians. In 1610 she was accused of killing young girls from surrounding villages to bathe in their blood, driven by the desire to obtain their youth and beauty. However, only her servant Fick was charged with the capital crime. The countess, a member of the aristocracy, was only imprisoned in her castle where she died on 21st August 1614.

## DRAŠKOVIČOV MANSION IN ČACHTICE (3)

The mansion in Čachtice was built in 1668 for the Croatian count Mikuláš Draškovič, and it was enlarged before the end of the 17th century. Later it belonged to the Forgáč (Forgách) family. Its last private owner, count Csenkay, was renting the derelict building out and when he died leaving no heir, the mansion went to the state. It now houses a detached exposition of the Museum of Trenčín, with historical and ethnographical collections from Čachtice and its surroundings. Apart from very popular exhibits associated with the countess A. Bátory (Báthory), the written and visual documents about the Literary Association called Tatrín, which was active during the Enlightenment Period in Čachtice, are also noteworthy. An important step in the process of the Slovakian National Revival Movement, which set out and unified its diverse trends, was taken at its memorable meeting.

## TEMATÍN CASTLE (4)

The ruin of the Medieval Tematín Castle lies in a rather remote spot in the heart of the Považský Inovec Mountains. It is accessible by a demanding track with a high level of elevation from the villages at the western foothills of the mountains; however, there is a much more convenient route to the castle form the Bezovec tourist centre. The history of Tematín goes back to the 13th century. The fortification system of the castle was improved in the 16th century, however despite this the fortification did not withstand the fights of the Rákoci (Rákoczi) Uprising at the beginning of the 18th century; the castle was damaged and became uninhabitable.

## MANSION IN BRUNOVCE (1)

The fine Renaissance mansion in Brunovce was built in 1697. The four-wing building with an inner courtyard was rebuilt in the Baroque style in the 18th century when it received its characteristic domes above the corner spires. This reconstruction also removed one of its wings and the double attics with battlements. The mansion belonged to the Berčéni (Bercsény) family of Tematín until 1710. For some time it was also owned by the Medňanský family, who gave us the famous painter Ladislav Medňanský (Mednyanszky). The descendants of the last owner, now live in Austria and Spain. The mansion is in rather good condition, with a lot of original architectonical elements and decorations preserved in the interiors. The paintings on the vault of the former chapel are especially valuable. The mansion is currently not accessible to the public.

## MANSION IN LÚKA (2)

The massive fortified mansion above the village of Lúka was built as a Renaissance fortress and protection against the Turkish threat and estate uprisings during 1674. It later became a comfortable seat of the Šándor family who moved here from the cold and remote Tematín Castle. The energetic lady Katarína got involved in the design of the mansion and changed the original plans of her husband Gašpar. Perhaps that was the reason behind a Hungarian inscription, which appeared on one of the walls and parodied dominant women. The mansion is now used by the Slovakian Ministry of the Interior as a holiday resort called Platan (Sycamore) after the prevalent type of tree in the surrounding park.

## PARISH CHURCH
## IN NOVÉ MESTO NAD VÁHOM (3)

Despite being called Nové (New) this town is no newcomer among Slovakian towns. Its history goes back to the 13th century. It received the town privileges from the king Belo IV as early as 1253. It is called Nové Mesto (New Town) because it was completely rebuilt after being destroyed by the Ottomans. Its most remarkable monument is the fortified Church of the Birth of the Virgin Mary built in the Romanesque style in the early stages of the town's development. It received its Gothic appearance between 1414 and 1423 and was once more rebuilt in the spirit of the Baroque style in 1675 when three Baroque naves replaced the original Gothic nave.

## BEZOVEC (4)

Bezovec (743 m) is the most popular hill in the Považský Inovec Mountains. Although not one of the highest, it is quite easily accessible thanks to a road that leads to cottages in its southern foothills. Most people visit Bezovec during the winter for its ski slopes and lifts. Bezovec is one of the few skiing centres with good snow conditions to be found at the edge of the Carpathian Mountains. Its pleasant landscape of open meadows is also well-liked in the summer when it is a popular tourist destination. The Bezovec Chalet is a brilliant starting point for a tourist trek to Tematín Castle.

## TUMULUS IN OČKOV (5)

The discovery of the burial mound of a chieftain of the Velatice-Baierdorf Culture, which developed in Slovakia between the 13th and 10th century BC, made the Očkov village known in European archaeology. A unique burial site was unearthed here, one of the largest urnfields in Slovakia. The famous discovery was made at the beginning of the 20th century. The tumulus-shaped burial place of an ancient ruler was originally 10 metres high and was 25-metres in diameter. The burial chamber lies 8 metres below the present-day terrain. It is believed that the burial ritual for the chief was accompanied by human sacrifices; however no direct supporting evidence has been found in Očkov. A further 250 graves, urns with ashes, were found near the mound. A unique finding is the alabaster urn, as nothing like it has ever been found in Europe.

## ROCK NEAR IVANOVCE (6)

Trains going from Nové Mesto nad Váhom to Trenčín pass by a rocky hill on the left side with an ostentatious umber colour. The hill near the Ivanovce village shows traces of stone quarrying and it is an important archaeological site called Skala. A well-planed archaeological excavation discovered traces of a prehistoric settlement dating from several thousand years ago. The prehistoric people settled on Skala as early as in the Late Stone Age; however most remarkable is the discovery of a fortified settlement from the Bronze Age. The unearthed remains of a dwelling and strong fortifications from the 16th century BC are among the oldest stone buildings ever discovered in Central Europe.

## ŠTEFÁNIKOVA MOHYLA MONUMENT ON BRADLO (1)

The snow-white structure on the hill called Bradlo (543 m) in the Myjavská Pahorkatina Hills is visible from afar. The plateau on the top of the hill is adorned by a monumental memorial to the general M. R. Štefánik. It is a dignified final resting place of one of the greatest personalities of modern Slovakian history. It was made of white travertine brought from the Spiš region by the significant Slovakian architect D. Jurkovič (1868 – 1947). Two Italian army officers, who also died in the plane crash near Ivanka pri Dunaji in 1919, are buried on Bradlo as well. Most people visit Bradlo during the May commemorative celebrations.

## NATIVE HOUSE OF M. R. ŠTEFÁNIK IN KOŠARISKÁ (2)

It is no coincidence that the general M. R. Štefánik (1880-1919) was buried atop the Bradlo Hill. This beautiful spot was selected because his native village, Košariská, is visible from the memorial. This prominent astrologer, soldier and politician, active in the establishment of Czechoslovakia in 1918, was born on 27th July in 1880 in the family of an Evangelic priest. His native house, the local Evangelic parish from the 19th century, is in the village of Košariská in the south-eastern foothills of Bradlo and now houses an exhibition of the Museum of Slovakian National Councils in Myjava (a part of the Slovakian National Museum network). The exposition gives a comprehensive outlook into the versatile personality of Štefánik.

## POMNÍK HURBANOVSKÝCH BOJOV NEAR BREZOVÁ POD BRADLOM (3)

Slovakians were also involved in the revolutionary events that shook Europe between 1848 and 1849. The Slovakian Voluntary Organisation, which protected their national interests, operated near the town of Myjava in September 1848. The first battle with the enemy, the Hungarian National Guard, broke out on 22nd September near the village of Brezová pod Bradlom, and the organisation of approximately 800 volunteers won its first victory here. The spot of the memorable battle on the way from Brezová to Bukovec is commemorated by the Monument to the fights. The pyramid-like monument is made of stone and there is a marble desk with an inscription. The author is a Slovakian architect, D. Jurkovič.

## MUSEUM OF SLOVAKIAN NATIONAL COUNCILS IN MYJAVA (4)

The most important chapters of the history of the town of Myjava were written in the mid-19th century. Myjava was one of the places which witnessed the formation of the modern ideas of the independent Slovakian nation. The first meeting of the Slovakian National Council, which declared the independence of the Slovakian nation and initiated the anti-feudal Slovakian uprising, was held on 19th September 1848. The Museum of Slovakian National Councils (a part of the Slovakian National Museum network) was opened in Myjava in 1968 on the occasion of the 120 year anniversary of the establishment of the first Slovakian legislative body.

# HORNÁ NITRA

### BOJNICE CHATEAU (1)

A medieval castle was built on the travertine hill in Bojnice as early as the 11th century. The oldest written record of the castle is in the famous document of the Zoborovské Abbey from 1113. The castle with the estate belonged to the king and was bestowed onto the popular members of the aristocracy. The Thurzo family received the castle as a present in 1527 and when this family died out, the building went to the Pálfis in 1643. The last private owner was count Ján F. Pálfi, who devoted great effort and spent large sums of money to have the castle rebuilt into a grandiose Romantic chateau. The main architect was Josef Hubert from Bratislava and the large New-Gothic reconstruction was completed in 1910; however Pálfi did not live to see the result, as he died two years earlier. His will to have the chateau open to the public was fulfilled in 1950. Today, the Bojnice Chateau is swarmed by tourists, who are anxious to see the famous Bojnice Altar, the tomb of count Pálfi, and scores of valuable art pieces, as well as the historical furniture. Part of the tour of the chateau is a karst cave underneath the chateau.

### ZOO IN BOJNICE (2)

The zoological garden in Bojnice is rightfully considered to be the most beautiful in Slovakia, due to its attractive position near the chateau as well as the diversity and amount of kept animals. It was the first zoo in Slovakia and was established in 1955 on a 42-hectare piece of land. There are more than 1,500 animals representing approximately 350 species. The elephant pavilion is the most popular with visitors. The zoo has been greatly successful, mainly in the breeding of large snakes, ostriches, beasts of prey, zebras, antelopes and other rare animals.

### BOJNICKÉ SPA (3)

The spa complex in Bojnice lies in a quiet park area southeast of the town. Its history reaches back to the 16th century, when the first healing procedures started near the local mineral springs upon the initiative of the then ruler of Bojnice Castle, Alexander Thurzo. The oldest written record, which mentions the existence of the spa, dates from 1549. Pavol Pálfi (Pálffy) had the spa enlarged in the 17th century and further modern development was carried out in the 1930s by another owner, the famous Czech businessman Jan Baťa. The mineral waters of the nine local springs successfully cure disorders of the locomotor system and neurological diseases.

### PREPOŠTSKÁ CAVE (4)

The historical square in the centre of Bojnice is on the so-called Farská Travertine Hill. The plateau lies at the east edge of the town behind the church and ends at a steep slope. There is a large entrance into the Prepoštská Cave below an overhanging rock. The cave is a significant Palaeontological site. The Museum of the Prehistoric Era was established outside the entrance into the cave; it boasts a well-presented exhibition about the life of prehistoric mammoth hunters.

## PIARIST MONASTERY IN PRIEVIDZA (1)

The most significant monument of Prievidza, the metropolis of the Horná Nitra region, is the monastery of the Piarist Order located on Ulica Andreja Hlinku Street. It is considered one of the most remarkable Baroque buildings in Central Europe. It was built on the site of an older Gothic stronghold from the 15th century. Building works on the monastery with the church started in 1666 and were carried out according to the design of an Italian architect named Biberlli. A Piarist college, erected on the land of a citizen of Prievidza, was ready for students in 1674. The Piarists started to build the Baroque Church of the Holy Trinity in 1740 according to the design of their own builder, Father H. Hang-

he. The rather modest exterior of this sacral monument hides an unusually rich interior.

## CHURCH IN HANDLOVÁ (2)

The most important monument of the mining town of Handlová at the tip of the Hornonitrianska Kotlina valley is the Roman-Catholic Church of St. Catherine. It was built in the Gothic style between 1330 and 1360 and reconstructed in the Renaissance style at the beginning of the 17th century. It was seriously damaged by a bomb during the movement of the front in 1945; however a successful reconstruction was carried out in 1959. It is now a jewel of Námestie Baníkov Square, sitting in the midst of a charming garden with floral decorations. The city greenery, with scores of artfully arranged blossoms, is the traditional pride of the inhabitants of Handlová.

## CHURCH IN PORUBA (3)

The remarkable Gothic Church of St. Nicholas the Bishop lies in the Poruba village in the eastern foothills of the Strážovské Vrchy Hills. It was built in the first half of the 14th century and later rebuilt several times. Gothic murals from the 14th and 15th centuries are preserved in the interior together with one of the few preserved wooden painted Renaissance pillars in Slovakia.

## CHAPEL IN KOŠ (4)

Life in the village of Koš near Prievidza was largely influenced by mining activity. Part of the village had to be demolished due to the mining of brown coal. The Gothic chapel from 1409, built

originally next to the Church of St. Andrew, was also located on the territory endangered by the mining. A technical solution, unique in Slovakia, was carried out in 2000 to save this valuable monument with preserved medieval murals. The 400-ton building was moved to a safer place. The relocation was executed by equipment borrowed from Germany.

## CHURCH IN NEDOŽERY-BREZANY (5)

The village of Nedožery-Brezany in the Horná Nitra region is a result of the merger of two villages. The Nedožery part is interesting as it is the native village of the renowned humanist scholar and professor of Prague Charles University, Vavrinec Benedikt (1555 – 1615), while the Brezany part boasts the ancient Church of St. Helena and Christ the King. It was built in the Gothic style in 1409. A new church according to the design of B. Štorm was added in 1939. The church is a Protected National Cultural Heritage.

## CHURCH IN DIVIAKY NAD NITRICOU (6)

One of the oldest historical monuments of the Horná Nitra Region is the Romanesque Church of All Saints in the village of Diviaky nad Nitricou. The two-towered Romanesque building dates from the middle of the 13th century, however historians allow for the possibility of even older origins of the church, as the Benedictine monks from the Zobor in the Nitra area are believed to have been active in the territory of the village.

3

4

5

6

### SQUARE IN NITRIANSKE PRAVNO (1)

This once prosperous town was also called Aran-prouwa (Golden Pravno). Although it is now a village, its large quadrant central square surrounded by burghers' houses still recalls its town-like character. Its main landmark is the huge parish Church of the Beheading of St. John the Baptist. The original Gothic building from the 14th century was destroyed by a large fire in 1827 and it was decided after a slow-paced gradual reconstruction that the church would be demolished, apart from the Chapel of St. Michael, and be completely rebuilt. The new church received a Neo-Gothic appearance and was finished in 1907. The town hall in the centre of the square, from the beginning of the 20th century, was built on the site of an older town hall from the 17th century. A Baroque Marian Column stands outside the Town Hall.

### MANSIONS
### IN DIVIACKA NOVÁ VES (2)

The village of Diviacka Nová Ves in the southeast foothills of the Strážkovské Vrchy Hills boasts as many as three mansions. The oldest one dates from the beginning of the 15th century and was built as a Gothic stronghold and rebuilt into a Renaissance mansion in 1568. The second mansion was also originally built in the Renaissance style and rebuilt in the 19th century. The third mansion, called Mačací (Cat) Mansion, has been left derelict since the 18th century.

### MANSION
### IN ZEMIANSKE KOSTOĽANY (3)

The name Zemianske (Yeomen) suggests that this village near Nováky was a bastion of yeomen power in the past. Several family seats of the lower aristocracy have remained here – mansions and manor houses. Only a fragment has been preserved from the oldest Renaissance mansion, also called the Black Mansion, from the beginning of the 17th century – a two-story building with an L-shaped ground-plan and only two of the original four square corner towers. Another Renaissance mansion from the 17th century also has only two towers, this time of a round shape. Apart from this, Zemianske Kostoľany boasts yet another mansion, in the Baroque style, from 1727 and three manors. The mansions once belonged to the Kostoláni (Kosztolány) family.

## TEMEŠSKÁ ROCK (4)

Temešská Rock (910 m) looms high above the Temeš village in the valley of the small Nitrica River. It is the only peak at the northeast of the Malá Magura Mountain in the eastern part of the Strážovské Vrchy Hills. The top of the rocks offers a magnificent panoramic view, and there is a small cave just below the limestone peak. Xerophile and calciphile vegetation grow on the steep slopes of the hill; a 58-hectare Nature Reservation was established here in 1986.

## REMATA RECREATION CENTRE (5)

Near the town of Handlová on the western edge of the Kremnické Vrchy Hills lies the Remata recreation centre. This tourist complex is popular all year round. In the summer it offers brilliant opportunities for sport activities, including fishing in the local lakes. Moreover, traditional folklore festivals of the Horná Nitra region are held here annually at the end of June. Remata is well-equipped for the winter period two. It has three ski slopes and four ski lifts. The slopes were the first in Slovakia to be equipped with artificial lighting. Remata has been the main centre of the Slovakian Paralympics Team since 1989.

## NITRIANSKE RUDNO (6)

The countryside around Nitrianske Rudno in the projection of the Hornonitrianska Valley is flanked by the slopes of the Strážovské Vrchy Hills on three sides. They are reflected on the surface of the water reservoir built above the village on the small Nitrica River. The silhouette of the Malá Magura Mountain on the eastern side received a well-fitting nickname, the 'Sleeping Monk'. This area is famous thanks to the renowned Slovakian botanist and natural healer, František Madva (1786-1852); he has a monument in the nearby village of the same name. Nitrianske Rudno is a popular destination for summer holidays with brilliant swimming and water sports conditions. Tourists can use the campsite and a tourist office. Nitrianske Rudno is a superb gateway for hiking in the nearby Strážovské Vrchy Hills.

### SIVÝ KAMEŇ (1)

The remains of this medieval castle from the 14th century sit atop an andesite rock in the western foothills of the Vtáčnik Mountains. The castle is mentioned in a document from 1352 under the name Kaseleukeu. Originally it belonged to the king and was managed by the castellan of Bojnice Castle until 1388. It was used until the 16th century, however after that it became derelict and went to ruin. The preserved remains give us no idea about its original size or appearance. A large part of the walls was destroyed by the locals who used it as building material. The preserved ruins are the remains of a quadrant tower and a palace. Sivý Kameň is accessible from the village of Podhradie.

### KLÁŠTORSKÁ ROCK (2)

The third larges peak of the volcanic Vtáčnik Mountains is the peak Kláštorská (1279 m). It is a part of the main range and offers splendid views of its neighbour, the highest mountain Vtáčnik. The rocky towers and walls are the remains of a crumbled andesite lava stream. They have the characteristic structure created by tiny horizontal cracks.

### BYSTRIČIANSKA DOLINA (3)

Bystričianska Dolina Valley is considered the most beautiful in the Vtáčnik Mountains. It is named after the nearby village of Bystričany. The beauty of the valley is emphasized by thick beech woods and numerous cliffs. The largest rock formations are on the south side of the valley. The Buchlov Peak (1041 m), located in the side fork of the range, stands out for its beauty and uniqueness. A nature trail that leads from Buchlov to the neighbouring Žarnov cliff cuts through the valley.

### BIELY KAMEŇ (4)

This mountain (1135 m) dominates the northern part of the Vtáčnik Mountains. Its peak was formed by an andesite lava stream which crumbled into bizarre rocky formations; it is a Protected Nature Reserve.

### VEĽKÝ GRIČ AND MALÝ GRIČ (5)

Two conical hills loom on the west horizon of the mining town of Handlová. The right one is called the Malý (Small) Grič (876 m) while its left neighbour is Veľký (Large) Grič (971 m). Both peaks are accessible by marked tourist trails and offer fine views accentuated by andesite rock formations.

### VTÁČNIK (6)

In the Lower Tertiary Era the Vtáčnik Mountains were a complex of active volcanoes. Their highest peak of the same name looms to the height of 1,346 metres. Only the Poľana Peak is higher in the Slovakian volcanic mountain ranges. The slopes of Vtáčnik are overgrown mainly with beech and beech-fir woods. The most valuable vegetation of the virgin forest type is protected in the Vtáčnik National Nature Reservation, which was established in 1950. The top parts have openings at places and the andesite rocks offer magnificent views. A natural trail leads to the peak of Vtáčnik.

# STREDNÉ PONITRIE

### CHURCH OF ST. NICHOLAS
### IN BÁNOVCE N. BEBRAVOU (1)

The oldest and most significant monument in Bánovce nad Bebravou is not the parish church dating from the beginning of the 19th century on the Námestie Ľudovíta Štúra Square in the centre of the town, but the old Church of St. Nicholas on its eastern edge. Rather a large amount of wood was used in its façade. It was built in the first third of the 15th century in the Gothic style and later rebuilt in the Renaissance and Baroque styles.

### MANSION IN HORNÉ OZOROVCE (2)

Originally, Horné Ozorovce was an autonomous village from the 13th century. However, in 1976 it became a part of the town of Bánovce nad Bebravou. Its most noteworthy monument is a 17th century mansion, which used to belong to the local aristocratic family of Ottlík. Only two wings with a letter L-shaped ground-plan remain of the original building.

### NATIVE HOUSE OF ŠTÚR
### AND DUBČEK IN UHROVEC (3)

Remarkably, two significant figures of modern Slovakian history, Ľudovít Štúr (1815-1856) and Alexander Dubček (1921-1992), were born in the same village, and what is even more interesting, in the same house! Their birthplace in Uhrovec near Bánovce nad Bebravou is a National Cultural Monument. It houses an exposition of the Museum of Trenčín devoted to the life and work of the two famous citizens of Uhrovec. And there is yet another unusual coincidence; the manor house belonged to the family of Zay, a member of which was the great political opponent of Štúr, count Karol Zay.

### UHROVEC CASTLE (4)

The Uhrovec Castle is not directly above the village of the same name, but upon a wooded hilltop of the Strážovské Mountains above the village of Uhrovské Podhradie. Built in the second half of the 13th century it was mostly in the possession of the king during the 14th and 15th centuries. King Ferdinand I gave the estate to a Hungarian František Zay of Čerer in 1547 and it then remained in the ownership of this family and was used as their seat until the 18th century. When they moved into a more luxurious mansion in Uhrovec, the castle then served as a prison. After being burned out by radical fanatics in 1848 it became a ruin.

### JANKOV HILL (5)

The Jankov Hill (533 m), which looms in the Strážovské Vrchy Hills east of Uhrovec, is an interesting tourist destination for two reasons. First of all, it is a grandiose monument and secondly, it is the site of popular uphill car races. The monument was unveiled on the deforested viewing place in 1951 and boasts a mound and a mausoleum commemorating the victims of World War II. The Partisan Brigade of Jan Žižka operated on the hill. Seven injured partisans were burned alive by the Nazis in a local bunker in December 1944. Celebrations marking the Slovakian National Uprising are held here annually at the end of August.

## ROKOŠ (6)

The landmark of the Nitrické Vrchy Hills in the south-eastern part of Strážkovské Vrchy is the rocky Rokoš (1010 m). The slopes of the hill, covered by mainly beech forest, are dotted with rock formations. Rare flora that grows on the mineral-rich limestone soil is protected. The 460-hectare Rokoš National Nature Reserve was established here in 1974. There is a splendid view of Rokoš from Uhrovec Castle.

## KARST IN SLATINA (7)

Above the village of Slatina nad Bebravou spreads a karst territory called the Slatinský Karst. Numerous karst formations formed on the surface and beneath on the Mesozoic limestone. There are a few karst sinkholes in the Veľká lúka area, and dry valleys on the southern side of the mountain. The most famous underground area is the 128 metres long cave Dúpna Diera and evidence of a prehistoric settlement were found here. The remarkable sights of the area are two huge karst streams that never freeze over. A nature trail leads through the Slatinský Karst.

## NÁMESTIE M. R. ŠTEFÁNIKA IN TOPOĽČANY (1)

In the centre of Topoľčany lies a large square named after the general M. R. Štefánik. In bygone times it was the most important market place in the entire region. The most interesting building on the square is the Art Nouveau town hall dating from 1911, which replaced an older building that once stood in the centre of the quadrant square, like the large Roman-Catholic Church of the Assumption of the Virgin Mary. The one-nave church with its Prussian vault was built between 1790 and 1802 on the site of a medieval sacral building. The exterior of the church has a Classicism appearance while the interior houses some Baroque elements, for instance the illusive painting in the vault. A Lourdes Cave was added to the eastern side of the church in the second half of the 19th century.

## MANSION IN TOVÁRNIKY (2)

There is a large mansion with an extensive park in the town quarter of Topoľčany called Továrniky. It was built by the Beréni (Berényi) family between 1600 and 1610 so they could move from their castle in Topoľčany into a more luxurious manor house. They brought the entire inventory from the castle with them. Originally, it was built as a Renaissance stronghold with loopholes for cannons and a water moat. However, one of the four wings was demolished in 1752. This opened up the inner courtyard and the redundant moats were also covered. The building was turned into a noble Baroque residence under its new owners, the family of Stummer. They invited the renowned contemporary Viennese architect Hillebrand, who worked mainly for the Emperor, to rebuild the mansion in the second half of the 18th centu-

ry. The mansion witnessed dramatic events in 1945; it was looted and burned down by the locals. The present-day appearance is the result of an ongoing reconstruction that commenced in 1984.

## TOPOĽČIANSKY CASTLE (3)

There would be no point to look for Topoľčiansky Castle in the town of Topoľčany, for it is situated 12 kilometres to the northwest above the village of Podhradie. The romantic ruin is perched on a rocky tip at the eastern edge of the Považský Inovec Mountains. The castle was probably built before the Ottoman invasion. Originally, one of the king's castles, it went to the family of Sečéni (Szécsényi) towards the end of the 14th century. It was also the centre of the Hussite movement in the Nitra area between 1431 and 1434. Several families owned the castle later. The Beréni family

moved from the hostile stone castle into a more comfortable mansion in Továrniky and since that time the castle has been abandoned. Fortunately, some reconstruction work was carried out in the 19th century, which stopped the monument from falling into complete ruin. The central stone tower has been preserved and it is still a landmark of the Stredné Ponitrie area.

### MANSION IN ŠIMONOVANY (4)
This rare and valuable historical monument stands in the middle of the villas in the Šimonovany quarter of Partizánske town. The mansion is nicknamed the Water Castle and is possibly the oldest of its type in Slovakia. As its name suggests, it was built on a loop of the meander of the Nitra River in the 14th century. The oldest written record of the mansion dates from 1426 when it belonged to the family of Šimuni. The present-day appearance of the old Gothic building is the result of reconstruction carried out in 1897. The mansion in the middle of a meadow consists of a two-storey building and a quadrant sentry tower.

### MANSION IN VEĽKÉ UHERCE (5)
The village of Veľké Uherce near Partizánske boasts a mansion that resembles English medieval castles. It was built as a Renaissance manor house by Michal and Margaréta Béšáňi in 1622 and was reconstructed in the Baroque style in the 18th century. However its present-day romantic appearance is the result of reconstruction carried out by the contemporary owners, the family of Thonet, between 1845 and 1860. The style of the Tudor Gothic was used on the exterior as well as in the interiors of the buildings.

The most valuable part of the interior is the Knights Hall with busts of knights on the walls. Original wooden lining is preserved in other stately halls as are decorated parquets, tapestry and a relief portrait of Baron Thonet from 1904.

### MANSION IN BRODZANY (6)
The village of Brozdany near Partizánske is visited mainly by those interested in literature and its history for its remarkable museum located in a 17th century mansion. There are sound reasons for placing an exhibition dedicated to Alexander Puškin here. The mansion was acquired by the Viennese banking family, the Voglovs, in 1844, one of whom married Puškin's sister-in-law A. N. Gončarovova. Thus, a lot of articles belonging to the great poet found its way here and became the corner stone of the current exhibition. The park

around the mansion contains sculptures of famous Russian writers including a sculpture of Lev Tolstoy.

### DUCHONKA (7)
The 17-hectare Duchonka Water Reservoir is one of the most popular summer leisure centres in the Stredné Ponitrie Region and has a camp site with capacity for 300 people, scores of cottages, restaurants and sport centres.

### ČERTOVA PEC (8)
The cave called Čertova Pec is located near the path between Radošina and Piešťany that passes through the Považský Inovec Mountains. It is accessible on foot. You can walk through this tunnel-like 27-metre long cave, which according to archaeological findings, was inhabited by Neanderthal Man in pre-history. It is a protected nature site.

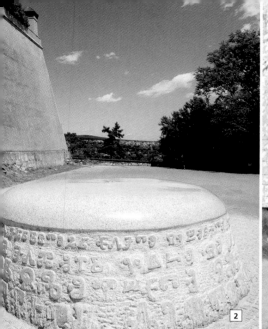

# NITRA REGION

## NITRA CASTLE (1)

Nitra Castle is an inseparable landmark of the town of Nitra. It was already a clerical centre in the times of Prince Pribina and the seat of the Bishop of Nitra. Its key site is the large Cathedral of St. Emmeram (of Regensburt) consisting of three sacral buildings. The older one (11th century) is a Romanesque church consecrated to this saint. The Gothic Horný (Upper) church was built in the 14th century and the younger Baroque Dolný (Lower) church was added in the 17th century. The relics of St. Zorard and St. Benedict are stored in the cathedral. The large Bishop's Palace is next to the church. Since the oldest times, Nitra has been strategically important and thus its fortifications were built gradually from the early Middle Ages to the 17th century.

## PROGLAS MONUMENT(2)

The Proglas Monument has adorned the terrace near the entrance to the Nitra Castle since 2000. The oldest known Old-Slovakian poem called Proglas is carved into a stone block resembling a round table. It is written in the oldest Slavic alphabet, the Glagolitic alphabet (predecessor of the Cyrilic alphabet). Its author is Saint Cyril who together with his brother Methodius came to the territory of the Great Moravian Empire with the mission to spread Christianity in the Slavic language. The poem was preserved in a document from the 14th century; it is stored in the archive of a monastery on the Greek island of Athos.

## SCULPTURE OF THE BROTHERS OF CONSTANTINOPLE (3)

Nitra is the place where the oldest history of the Slovakian language was written. A merger of the Nitra Princedom of Prince Pribina with the Moravian Princedom of Prince Mojmír resulted in the creation of the Great Moravian Empire, which became the basic cornerstone of the Slovakian state. The sculpture of two brothers from Constantinople was built below the walls of the Nitra Castle in 1990 by Ľudmila Cvengrošová.

## KLUCHOV HOUSE IN NITRA (4)

A grandiose stone sculpture of Atlas is to be found on the corner of the house of the Bishop Kluch (the famous supporter of A. Bernolák) in the Horné Mesto quarter of Nitra. It was created by sculptor V. Dunajský in 1820 and it is known as Corgoň, who was a hero of an ancient legend.

## PRIBINOVO SQUARE IN NITRA (5)

The Horné Mesto quarter and is remarkable for being the seat of mostly religious institutions. It is peaceful and is spared the bustling life of the city. Its centre is Pribinonovo Square, with a grandiose sculpture of Nitra's prince Pribina in the middle. The Veľký (Large) Seminary was built between 1768 and 1877. A valuable diocese library, which houses 66,000 books, is in one of the most beautiful buildings of the town. Opposite is the Malý (Small) Seminary, built in 1884 in the elegant Late Classicism style.

## SVÄTOPLUKOVO SQUARE
## IN NITRA (1)
The so-called Dolné Mesto square is the hub of Nitra. It is divided by the busy Štefánikova Avenue, which was converted into a pedestrian zone and ends at the large Svätoplukovo Square. This large space with a nice view of Nitra Castle was founded on the site that was destroyed by a bomb raid during World War II. The landmark of the square is the modern Theatre of Andrej Bagar building, the nestor of the modern Slovakian theatre. The theatre hosts the popular Nitra Theatre Festival. Another outstanding building on the square is the elegant Neo Renaissance edifice of the Town Court from 1882, which is now the seat of the Nitra Museum.

## PIARIST CHURCH AND
## MONASTERY IN NITRA (2)
The grandiose complex of the Piarist church and monastery is perched on a small hilltop above the Dolné Mesto in Nitra. The two-towered church is a significant landmark of the town. The Piarist Order came to Nitra in 1698 with the mission to educate and teach children from poor families. The construction of the monastery Church of St. Ladislaus was delayed because of a fire in 1716, thus the church was not consecrated until 1798. The fire also damaged the monastery, which became the seat of the Piarist grammar school in 1723. Outside the monastery sprawls the Cyrilometodské Square with twelve Baroque sculptures of the apostles by A. Brandl; they are placed around the perimeter of a small park and there is a cross in their centre.

## CALVARY IN NITRA (3)
The best view of Nitra with its castle and the silhouette of the Zobor Peak in the background is from the site of the Nitra's Calvary. The Stations of the Cross were built on the northern slope of a limestone hill in the southern part of the town. A Gothic church stood on the site as early as in the 14th century and it received its present-day appearance in 1723 after it was rebuilt following serious damage caused by the Kuruc wars. The church consecrated to the Mother of God is much visited mainly because of the wooden sculpture of the Virgin Mary of Sorrows. Legends about its miraculous powers attract many visitors to this place. The large building next to the church is the seat of the God's Word Association and also houses the unique Mission Museum.

## AGROKOMPLEX EXHIBITION
## CENTRE AND OPEN-AIR MUSEUM
## IN NITRA (4)
The tradition of Farming and Food Production Fairs started in Nitra in 1952. Today, the premises of the Agrocomplex Exhibition Centre in the Chrenová quarter also host other exhibitions and events, for example the popular Autosalón (Car Exhibition). Visitors can take the interesting field train, which was used on a large farming estate in Želiezovice, to the back part of the exhibition grounds to see the remarkable Open-Air Museum. This outdoor museum is managed by the Slovakian Farming Museum in Nitra and is devoted to traditional ways of Slovakian peasant life and farming. It shows the lifestyle (as most museums of this type); however it also presents the different traditional crafts and farming methods such as beekeeping, bread making and seed flail.

## FARMING UNIVERSITY
## IN NITRA (5)
There are two universities in Nitra. Apart from the humanism and pedagogy orientated University of Philosopher Konštantín, there is also the Slovakian Farming University. It was established as the Higher School of Farming in 1952 and became a university in 1996. Its part is the university campus in the Chrenová town quarter, which is rightfully considered one of the best works of Slovakian modern architecture. The complex boasts six modern pavilions built between 1960 and 1986 on the site of swampy meadows and fields.

## ZOBOR (1)

The ancient Nitra lies at the southern foothills of the massive Zobor Peak (587 m). The huge hill located in the narrowest part of the Tríbeč Mountains is an inseparable landmark of the town. A city quarter of the same name (Zobor) with scores of villas sprawls on the sunny slope of the hill. A cable car went to the peak of Zobor until recently so the peak can only be climbed on foot now. There is a terrace near the closed top station of the cable car with a fantastic view of Nitra and its wide surroundings. The terrace is on a hill called Pyramída (553 m). The Millenary Monument was placed here in 1896, however only a foundation remained from the monument, which was built on the occasion of the celebrations of the establishment of Hungary. The damage was completed in 1921 as the attitude towards the monument was rather controversial.

## FOREST STEPPE ON ZOBOR (2)

The Zobor's Forest Steppe National Nature Reserve was established on the deforested southwestern slope of Zobor above Nitra. The sunny slope on almost 30 hectares has been protected since 1952. The limestone bedrock is brilliant for the vegetation typical for the rock and forest steppe conditions. Valuable oaks grow on the granite. There is a splendid view of the surrounding landscape from the meadow on the northwest slope dropping down towards the village of Dražkovce.

## MONASTERY IN ZOBOR (3)

The St. Hyppolite Monastery set in the slope of the Zobor Peak in Nitra is most probably the oldest monastery in Slovakia. Historians allow that it already existed during the Great Moravian Empire period. Even King Svätopluk was its secret monk, according to a legend. Monks of the Benedict Order played an important role in the colonization of the Slovakian territory in the 11th and 12th centuries. They controlled the settlement in the Carpathians and spread new craft and farming technologies. It is believed that they also founded the famous vineyards on the slopes of Zobor. The monastery on Zobor was abolished in 1467; however it was successfully repaired in 1695. The Camaldolese (part of the Benedictine Order) monks settled below Zobor for some time until the order was abolished by the emperor Joseph II in 1782. A sanatorium for curing of the tuberculosis and respiratory diseases is now on the site of the monastery. Only a few ruins are preserved from the former monastery in the park near the sanatorium. A part of the monastery was incorporated into the building in the southern part of the complex.

## GATE MONUMENT – DOCUMENTS OF ZOBOR (4)

The two oldest original written documents in Slovakia were made in the Benedictine monastery below Zobor. They are known as Zobor's Documents. The older was written in 1111. It lists evidence supporting the monastery in a case over its right to collect a toll and fees. The younger document dates from 1113 and it lists extensive assets and estates of the monastery. It is valuable evidence of the existence of many villages in Western Slovakia and it is the oldest preserved written document in Slovakia. To commemorate the precious written treasures, a monument was erected in the small park at the sanatorium on Zobor. It bears a bronze desk with a sculpture and the inscription 'Gate-Zobor's Documents' by the academic sculptress Zuzana Marciňová-Hetminská.

## CAVE AND SPRING OF ZVORARD (5)

The entrance into the Svoradova (Zvorard) Cave is in the western slope of the Zborov Peak above the former Zobor's Monastery. The stone altar of St. Zvorard has been inside this smallish karst cave for several centuries. According to a legend the saint lived here as a hermit at the beginning of the 11th century and was buried in the St. Emmeram Cathedral at the Nitra Castle together with St. Benedict, another monk from the Zobor's Monastery. Legends about these two saints are an important cultural heritage of Slovakia (see also pages 93 and 115). An iron cross towers above the cave. It was placed here in 1932 and is more than 450 years old. It originally adorned the spire of St. James Church, which once stood on the site of the present-day Svätoplukovho Square. A karst sinkhole called Svoradov Spring is below the Svoradova Cave.

## CHURCH OF ST. MICHAEL THE ARCHANGEL IN DRAŽOVCE (1)

The Church of St. Michael Archangel's simple building impressively completes the silhouette of the bare hill above the village of Dražovce at the western edge of Nitra. The simple architecture, which resembles the original ancient settlement on this site, emits hundreds of years of the history of this place that goes back to the 11th century. The view from the church over the landscape as far as Nitra Castle is magnificent.

## CHURCH IN KLÍŽSKE HRADIŠTE (2)

There is a small church in the cemetery in Klížske Hradište (part of the Veľký Klíž village). At first glance, it looks like a very old building. It is made of stone and features an apse and a round tower – which are signs of Romanesque architecture. However, the history of the church is not very clear. Supposedly, it was built in the 12th century, ceased to fulfill its function in the 19th century, and later became a ruin. A complex reconstruction that started in 1936 resulted in the present-day unified appearance of the ancient monument. Masses started to be held here again in 1994. Legends have it that the church was consecrated to St. Michael, however the truth of this has been doubted and the church is now awaiting the bishop's decision about its new name.

## CHURCH OF ST. STEPHEN THE KING IN KOLÍŇANY (3)

The Tríbeč Mountains are lined with a ring of quartzite rocks and peaks. The ancient Church of St. Stephen the King is perched on one of them above the village of Kolíňany, northeast of Nitra. It was built in the 12th century and, despite later reconstructions, maintained several of its Romanesque elements.

## CHURCH OF ST. GEORGE IN KOSTOĽANY POD TRÍBEČOM (4)

No special attention was paid to the Church of St. George in the village of Kostoľany pod Tríbečom until 1990. However, the discovery of old frescoes triggered off a new, extensive reconstruction, which in turn initiated archaeological research that brought some interesting results. It turned out that the church is amongst the oldest fully preserved buildings in Slovakia. Its oldest part was built at least in the 10th century. This, to a great extent, applies also to the discovered murals in the interior that date from around the turn of the 10th and 11th centuries.

## CHURCH OF THE VIRGIN MARY, THE QUEEN OF ANGELS, IN KLÁTOVA NOVÁ VES (5)

The small, lonely ancient Romanesque-Gothic church sits atop a round hill above the Sádok locality (part of the Klátova Nová Ves village). It was founded in the mid-13th century, allegedly by the pupils of St. Metodius. The original Romanesque building was later reconstructed in the Gothic spirit. The church is protected by a wall which was built on the site of the fort hill that once existed here. Inside the walled area is an old burial site with tombstones originating from the 12th to 14th century. The massive church spire houses a bell from 1785.

## GÝMEŠ CASTLE (1)

According to a legend, Gýmeš Castle was given to a master named Andrej as a reward for helping the King Belo IV during an Ottoman siege. The descendants of Andrej living in the castle soon started to use the name Forgáč (Forgách). Apart from a few short intervals, members of this prominent Hungarian family owned the castle for centuries. The castle survived the tumultuous times of the Kuruc wars despite the fact that its owner, Šimon Forgáč, was an army officer of the army of Francis II Rákoci (Rákoczi). Moreover, it withstood an attack of the Emperor's army. The Forgáčs invested large sums in order to convert the castle into a luxurious aristocratic seat that would be used for hunting events. It was not to be lived in permanently as the family moved to a more comfortable mansion in Jelenec in 1722. The castle began to fall into disrepair in the mid-19th century.

## OPONICE CASTLE (2)

This castle, hidden in the woods of Tríbeč above the village of Oponice, must have been lovely once, for poet Eloise Beutelová called it the jewel of Hungary. However, this is difficult to judge today as the castle has been in ruin since the mid-17th century. It was founded in the 12th century and was documented to be in the possession of Matúš Čák in 1300. It belonged to the family of Aponi (Apponyi) for a long time; however its members moved to a mansion in the village after the castle was hit by lightning in 1645. The damage was completed by the Emperor's army at the beginning of the 18th century as it served, at some point, the rebellious army of Francis II Rákoczi. The most convenient way to reach Oponice Castle is from the village of the same name. Even the name of the village is derived from the name of the Aponi family.

## MANSION IN MOJMÍROVCE (3)

The village of Mojmírovce once was a small yeomen town called Urmín, settled by the inhabitants of southern areas fleeing from the Ottomans in the 17th century. Among the refugees was also the Grasalkovič (Grassalkowich) family, who soon found its way into the aristocratic elite in Hungary. Anton Grasalkovič, the original owner and founder of the Grasalkovič Palace in Bratislava, – the current seat of the president of Slovakia – was baptized here in 1694. Another significant family of Mojmírovce was the Huňady (Hunyady) family. They had a Late Baroque mansion built in the village in 1721 and a splendid garden landscaped around it. The garden was considered one of the finest in the then Hungary. It included a botanical garden and a glasshouse. An historical building of the former stables is located in the garden and is reminiscent of the very first horse race that took place in Mormírovce as early as 1814. After a fire in 1866, the mansion was reconstructed in the Classicism style and was converted into a hotel and a congress centre.

## HUNTING MUSEUM OF THE FAMILY OF APONI (4)

The Aponi family left another – this time smaller – Renaissance mansion in Oponice. Fortunately it is in much better condition than its larger relative. Several architectural styles left their mark on its

elegant present-day appearance. It now houses the Hunting Museum of the Aponis.

## MANSIONS IN BELADICE (5)

One of the two mansions in the village of Beladice situated on the road from Nitra to Zlaté Moravce is a fine example of an aristocratic seat that has become a luxurious hotel. It was built by the vice-head of the Tekov Council Jesenský in the Pustý Chotár locality in 1820. Its later owner, baron Henrik Lindelóf, had the mansion rebuilt in the Neo Classicism style. The size of the mansion was reduced when its side wings were demolished in 1937. The mansion in Beladice is a Cultural Heritage together with the surrounding garden. The second mansion in this village once belonged to the family of Sentiváni (Sentiványi) and also boasts a fine park. Apart from other trees it also has huge linden trees. The oldest tree is possibly 700 years old and is a National Cultural Monument.

## CHURCH OF THE ASSUMPTION OF THE VIRGIN MARY IN VRÁBLE (1)

The town of Vráble has been connected with the Catholic religion since its beginnings. It was the centre of the Esztergom clerics in the 12th century and became the seat of the lower aristocracy in the 15th century. That is why it was visited by the Church dignitaries in the past. The Esztergom Archbishop and Cardinal František K. Vasary performed a confirmation mass in Vráble in 1897. As he was a keen enthusiast of the cult of the Virgin Mary and profoundly enjoyed the singing of the local worshipers during mass he decided to give a new church to the village. It was completed in 1901 and consecrated to the Assumption of the Virgin Mary. Faulty design of the church started to take a toll over time. A part of the walls from the previous church that were incorporated into the new building caused a dangerous leaning of the building, and its foundations had to be supported to stop the movement of the construction. The slim spire remained in the leaning position; its top leans one and a half metres off of its vertical axis.

## STONE BRIDGE IN NOVÁ VES NAD ŽITAVOU (2)

The path westward from the village of Nová Ves nad Žitavou goes over the Drevenica Bridge. Nearby is an old well-preserved stone bridge from the end of the 16th century. It was built at the times when the Ottoman army was devastating the surrounding villages, hence its name, the Turkish Bridge. The stone construction with three arches was built on a trade path from Levice to Nitra. An allegedly miraculous spring lies about 300 metres from the bridge. The pilgrims have come to the site to pray to the Virgin Mary since 1874. A Lourdes Cave was built over the miraculous spring in 1955. The main pilgrimage takes place in August at the anniversary of the Queen Virgin Mary.

## MANSION IN KLASOV (3)

The small village of Klasov lies off the road from Nitra to Vráble. If you visit the village you can admire the Neo Gothic style of the local mansion. It was built by the baron Pavol Weisz on the site of an older manor house. It received its present-day appearance during a large reconstruction at the end of the 19th century in the spirit of the so-called Tudor Gothic. A collection of valuable antiques and oriental art pieces was placed in the mansion in 1945. The interior of the mansion in Klasov has a Neo Gothic ribbed vault and is decorated with Art Nouveau figural and ornamental paintings.

## MANSION IN TAJNÁ (4)

The Classicism mansion in the small village of Tajná, which is a result of a merging of four villages and situated in a large valley of the Širočina Stream northeast of Vráble, is a very impressive building thanks to its architecture. It quite resembles the more famous mansion in Dolná Krupná near Trnava. It was built as a family seat by Ján Taynai in 1840. The mansion is surrounded by a park on an area of 10 hectares and it is now used as an orphanage.

## CHURCH OF ST. JOHN OF NEPOMUK IN LÚČNICA NAD ŽITAVOU (5)

When the two neighbouring villages of Vajka and

Marinová merged in 1960, a suitable name for this new village was searched for. The local administration asked the management of the prestigious folklore choir Lúčnica whether the village could take on its name. Apart from a Baroque mansion with a park, Lúčnica boasts the Baroque-Classicism Church of St. John of Nepomuk. It was built in 1763 and reconstructed in the middle of the 19th century.

### MANSION IN NOVÁ VES N. ŽITAVOU (6)

There are three mansions in the village of Nová Ves nad Žitavou, north of Vráble. The oldest building dates from the beginning of the 18th century. Originally a Baroque edifice, it later changed its appearance as well as purpose, for it was converted into a granary and later also used for hatching chickens. Count Jozef Berchtold had another mansion built near the river at the beginning of the 19th century. Another count, Ján Klobušický, and his family had the third mansion built in 1872. Its architect, A. Weber, decided on the Neo Classicism style and placed the mansion in a lovely English-style garden with local and exotic trees.

## TOPOĽČIANSKY MANSION (1)

The most powerful society of the country once visited Topoľčianky. The Habsburg family first owned the local mansion, and later it became the summer seat of the first Czechoslovakia president Tomáš G. Masaryk in 1923. The last head of state who spent a pleasant time of relaxation here was Antonín Zápotocký. The mansion in Topoľčianky is a jewel from an architectural point of view. The Viennese architect Alojz Pich designed the aristocratic seat of the then lords of the Keglevič family. A grandiose Classicism wing was built in 1818 on the site of a demolished wing of the original Renaissance fortress. The inner arcaded courtyard and three remaining wings retained the original Renaissance appearance. A museum with original furnishings and a library collected by the archduke Joseph August Habsburg was placed into the Classicism wing. A large park is also part of the mansion.

## NATIONAL STUD FARM
## IN TOPOĽČIANKY (2)

Topoľčianky can easily be called the Slovakian hippo-metropolis as it is the seat of the national stud farm, which counts among the most significant European breeding centres of the noble 'warmblood' breed. It was founded in 1921 and bred the Arabian, Lipizzan, Hucul Pony and sport breeds. The farm has approximately 5,000 horses and also keeps cattle and grows grapes. A part of the farm is a racing field and a colourful Hipologické Horse Museum with an exposition on the co-habitation of horse and man that has lasted for centuries.

## MANSION
## IN ZLATÉ MORAVCE (3)

The town of Zlaté Moravce experienced its biggest fame in the 18th century when it had the special status of the seat of the Tekov County Council. The town became its seat in 1735 and the council meetings were held here. The mansion came into the ownership of an army supplier, baron Jural Palaška, in 1711; he retained it until 1799. The prominent family of Migazzio, who supported the boom of the town, lived in a local mansion from the 17th century. Originally a Renaissance building, it received its Baroque-Classicism appearance during a reconstruction in 1789 initiated by the Viennese Cardinal Krištov Migazzi. The north wing of the mansion houses a branch of the Ponitrianske (the Nitra River District) Museum. It was established as one of the many museums opened on the occasion of the 1,000 anniversary of the existence of Hungary in 1896. Originally, it was only a private collection of articles of scholars and aristocracy and was not open to the public. The collections were moved to Nitra in 1924. The new Tekovské Museum was opened later, in 1955. Its centrepiece was a collection from Bojnice. There is a statue of Janko Kráľ made of Bulgarian white marble in the courtyard. This great poet of the Štúr period lived in Zlaté Moravce from 1862 until his death in 1876. He worked here as a lawyer and was involved in public life although only until 1867, when following the Austria-Hungary Compromise he was completely set back.

## EUROPEAN BISON FARM
## IN TOPOĽČIANKY (4)

Although the European Bison Farm is connected with Topoľčianky, this is not exactly correct. It should be said that the Farm lies near the village of Lovce, which is less than 10 kilometres from Topoľčianky. It was established in 1950 when there were only 150 European Bison, also called Wisent, the largest mammal in Europe, left in the world. Out of the total of 140 hectares of the area, the breeding station takes up only 27 hectares. It has three centres and a capacity for 12 bison. During its approximately 50 years of existence the farm has bred 120 European Bison in total. The animals were sent to various zoological gardens, parks and private zoos. According to the international regulations the names of European Bison born in Slovakia begin with the syllable Si.

## ARBORETUM IN MLYŇANY (1)

Count Štefan Ambrózy-Migazzi founded a botanical garden with a park near the village of Tesárske Mlyňany in 1982. Its aim was to experimentally grow various exotic trees. The task was successful and the village now boasts the largest and most visited arboretum in the land. The meticulously looked after park landscaped around a romantic 1894-built mansion includes 2,300 species of local and foreign trees and takes up an area of 67 hectares. It is divided into geographical sections; the East-Asian, North-American and Korean sections. Lakes, sculptures and exotic pavilions that evoke the landscape of China and Japan complement the park tastefully.

## MONUMENT
## NEAR VEĽKÉ VOZOKANY (2)

A bronze lion on a stone pedestal in the middle of the fields near the town of Veľké Vozokany near Zlaté Moravce overlooks the countryside in Southwestern Slovakia. This monument commemorates the battle between the Ottoman and Hungarian armies on 26th and 27th August 1652. Hungarian soldiers were greatly outnumbered, yet managed to beat the enemy. The Esterházi (Eszterházy) family had a 5-metre high stone obelisk erected on the battlefield in 1734 to commemorate four members of their family who fought bravely and lost their lives in the battle. The original obelisk was replaced by the present-day bronze lion on a travertine pedestal. It holds the Ottoman flag in its front paw.

## CASTLE IN SKÝCOV (3)

A romantic building resembling a medieval castle stands in the centre of the mountain village of Skýcov in the Tríbeč Mountains. It was built many centuries ago as a Gothic castle; however it had a completely different appearance then. A Renaissance mansion was built on its site in 1663. It was fortified to protect the inhabitants against possible attacks of the Ottomans. Count Arthur Odescalchi bought the derelict building in 1813 and restored it in the spirit of the then fashionable Romanticism style. The mansion gradually turned into a replica of a Romanesque castle featuring a spire, a moat and a drawbridge. The castle in Skýcov was damaged by Germans at the end of World War II during an army operation against the local partisans. It was partially reconstructed after the war.

## HRUŠOV CASTLE (4)

The romantic ruin of Hrušov Castle is hidden in the midst of the forests of the Tríbeč Mountains. It was built on a quartzite rock called Skalka (488 m) in the mid-13th century. The castle changed owners; it belonged to Matúč Čák, to the Levický family and to the king. Its castellans were infamous for plundering the surrounding villages and their hostility towards the monastery in Svätý Beňadik. The castle later became the seat of the Hrušov aristocracy and changed hands several times. It was given to the lords of Topoľčianky in the 16th century. The castle did not withstand (as many others did) the Kuruc wars. It was set on fire and demolished by the Emperor's army as revenge for the support its owners gave to the army of Francis II Rákoci (Rákoczi). It turned to a ru-

in standing on the original ground-plan with preserved towers, bastions and scores of other architectonic elements.

### ŽIVÁNSKA TOWER IN JEDĽOVÉ KOSTOĽANY (5)

A lonely stone tower stands in the forested landscape on the way from the village of Malá Lehota in the northeast of the Tríbeč Mountains. It is called the Živánska Tower and it also features in various legends as the Bandit Tower. The rather derelict building looms on the top of a rock above the valley of the small Žitava River. Its architectonic style is similar to Hrušov Castle so it is believed that it was probably built as early as in the 13th century as a sentry tower to protect carriages bringing gold from Kreminca to Nová Bana. It was possibly occupied by members of the Sikulové Tribe from the nearby village of Jedľové Kostoľany. The first written record of the Živánska Tower is not very old; it is mentioned in a travelogue called Turňa dating from 1781. The tower once had four floors and was 4 metres high.

# LEVICKÝ REGION

### LEVICE CASTLE (1)

The history of Levice Castle goes back to the period when a large part of Slovakia was ruled by the powerful Matúš Čák. The castle was an important base for the protection of the country against the Turks in the 16th century. Its defenders successfully held the castle during the Turkish attack in 1544 and even managed to chase the enemy out of the town. The castle was enlarged in 1560, a Renaissance mansion was added to it, and its fortification was also reinforced in the 16th century. Despite this the Turks conquered the castle in 1663, but only because its ruler Gašpar Bartakovič (Bartakovics) gave in without a fight. They did not hold the castle long, as the emperor's army recaptured it only a year later. This army destroyed the medieval part of the castle in 1708 for it was a base of the Kuruc soldiers of Francis II Rákoci (Rákoczi). The mansion has been preserved until today; it served as an aristocratic seat for a long time and now houses the ethnographical collection of the Tekovské Museum.

### ROCK SETTLEMENT
### IN BRHLOVCE (2)

The small village of Brhlovce near Levice looks as if it was moved to Slovakia from a Turkish Anatolie. There is a group of unique stone dwellings in a lane called Šurda. Apart from traditional houses the locals made their dwellings as well as work places by carving them into the soft turf. This original way of building, or rather digging, houses was used from the times of the Turkish wars, and even Matej Bel mentioned it. The complex of stone buildings in Brhlovce is now a Folk Architecture Monument Reserve. One of these dwellings houses an exhibition of the Tekovské Museum in Levice, which was awarded the prestigious Europe Nostra award in 1994, as the first in Slovakia.

### CALVINIST CHURCH
### IN KALINČIAKOVO (3)

An ancient Romanesque church is preserved in the village Kalinčiakovo, which is now part of Levice. It belongs to the Calvinism religion and was built as early as the 12th century. It was damaged by a fire in 1833; however a reconstruction fortunately restored its more or less original Romanesque appearance (with only small amendments). Valuable medieval paintings were discovered during the reconstruction. Originally, the church was protected by a wall, however only fractions have been preserved, including a small mound. According to a legend, the church was connected with the Levice Castle by a secret corridor.

### MANSION IN KALINČIAKOVO (4)

The Romanesque church in Kalinčiakovo cannot be overlooked as it is situated right next to the main road. If you are interested in seeing the local mansion, then turn west. The mansion was built in the Baroque style in the 18th century, but now has a Classicism appearance received during a reconstruction in 1820, carried out by its contemporary owners, the Majténi (Majthényi) family. It now resembles a Roman temple.

### CHURCH IN STARÝ TEKOV (5)

The ancient village of Starý Tekov sprawls on the right bank of the Hron River and boasts a famous history. It was a regional town and the seat of Tekovská county. The village was amongst the first that received the autonomous privileges as early as in the 13th century (1240). The head of Tekov's county lived in the now vanished medieval regional castle. The medieval Gothic monastery also have not survived the time and the only preserved monument from the period of fame and prosperity of Starý Tekov is the large Church of the Assumption of the Virgin Mary from the 13th century.

### OUTLOOK TOWER ON VÁPNIK (6)

You can make a pleasant trip when swimming and relaxing at the popular Margina and Ilona, swimming pools, near Levice. An outlook tower stands nearby on a hill called Vápnik (274 m). This monument from World War II is an important landmark of the landscape, and it was erected on the peak of one of the largest travertine mounds in Slovakia. Travertine was actively quarried here in the past and its reserves were almost exhausted. Several valuable fossils were discovered in the local quarry and the locality is a Protected Natural Monument.

## CHURCH OF ST. NICHOLAS
## IN PUKANEC (1)

Pukanec was once a prosperous town with the privileges of a Free Royal Town, and a member of the exclusive association of rich medieval mining towns. In many cases, the present-day small towns and villages hide superb town walls. Pukanec boasts a particularly large and splendid Gothic church from the 11th century. It was consecrated to St. Nicholas and was originally part of the town fortification which is documented by the sentry tower in the east side of the church, which once was a watchtower. The present-day tower of the church was built at the west side of the church after the town walls were demolished. The interior houses several preserved Gothic elements, the most valuable being four Neo Gothic wooden altars. Pukanec initiated a pleasant tradition that later spread to other villages in the surrounding area. The altar is adorned with special decorations made from autumnal farming products.

## WATER MILL NEAR BOHUNICE (2)

The road from Levice to Banská Štiavnica passes an historical water mill behind Bohunice. This valuable technical monument was built at the end of the 19th century and is one of the many mills that once operated in Hont and Tekov. The mill of Pavol Turčan on the Sikenica Stream was successfully reconstructed and opened to the public; it is part of the Tekovské Museum exposition in Levice.

## CHURCH IN PEČENICE (3)

The village of Pečenice sits in a splendid spot on the sunny southern slopes of the Štiavnické Hills and is surrounded by vineyards dotted with traditional houses, the so-called hajloki. The fortified Roman Catholic church dominates the village. It was built in the Romanesque style in the 13th century and improved by Gothic elements in the 14th century. Despite later building reconstructions the

church has kept its ancient appearance. There is a fine mansion near the church.

## WATER RESERVOIR IN BÁTOVCE (4)

The Lipovina Lake, which sits in the north-eastern tip of the Podunajská Nížina Lawlands, enjoys a warm, dry climate. It is a popular tourist destination during hot summers. The 25-hectare lake was built on the Jabloňovka Stream in 1968.

## STONE BRIDGE IN BÁTOVCE (5)

There is an historical stone bridge over the Sikenica River, which flows through the village of Bátovce. The Baroque bridge was built in 1780 and is adorned by a sculpture of the traditional patron of bridges, St. John of Nepomuk.

## HUSSITE CHURCH IN JABLOŇOVCE (6)

A remarkable sacral monument with fortification walls can be admired in the village of Jabloňovce, at the southern edge of the Štiavnické Vrchy Hills. It is referred to as the Hussite Church. The original Gothic church from 1459 later became the sanctuary of this reformed religion. The Tolerant Belfry from 1782 stands near the church, as well as the so-called Tolerant Linden Tree, which was planted in the same year. The beautiful Jabloňovský Roháč National Nature Reservation protects the original oak, european hornbeam and maple trees.

## HORŠIANSKA DOLINA VALLEY (7)

The Sikenica River leaves the Štiavnické Vrchy Hills and flows through the hills in the eastern part of the Podunajská nížina Lowlands. It cuts into the turf layers, which originated from the local volcanoes in the Early Tertiary era, near the village of Horša, northeast of Levice. Thus the river created a sharp and almost canyon-like valley that has been a Nature Reserve since 1976.

## MANSION IN ŽELIEZOVCE (2)

The town of Želiezovce in the lower Pohronie region can boast a past visit of a famous guest. The composer Franz Schubert was the private music teacher of daughters of Count J. K. Eszterházi (Eszterházy), during the summer months between 1818 and 1824. The count owned the Želiezovce estate and lived with his family in the local mansion. The originally Baroque building from 1720 was later rebuilt in the Classicism style. The partially reconstructed four-winged building is set in a large park with a pond. There is another Classicism edifice in the park, the so-called Soví zámoček, where Schubert stayed during his visits. There is a special room managed by the Tekovské Museum in Levice which is devoted to the Austrian artist's stay, as well as a monument to the musician in the park.

## DUDINCE SPA (3)

The Dudince Spa has an excellent locality in certainly one of the warmest areas in the whole of Slovakia. The area at the eastern part of Podunajská nížina lowlands has a very pleasant climate. The town boasts 700 years of history, not including the ancient times of the builders of the so-called Roman stone pools almost 2000 years ago. Several Roman elements have been discovered here, such as ceramics and coins. The warm mineralized water is used for curing of the locomotive system, nervous system and heart diseases. The water content is similar to the waters from the French Vichy Spa. There is a number of modern, well-equipped sanatoriums.

## TRAVERTINE IN SANTOVKA (1)

The curative powers of the mineral spring waters in Santovka have been known for more than 500 years. They are mentioned in a document from 1578. Today, they are amongst popular mineral waters and are successfully used for skin diseases, diabetes and inappetence. The popular Santovka mineral water was first sold as early as 1858 and nine years later it was honoured at an international fair in Hamburg. It later received a further 27 awards. The mineral springs in Santovka are connected with the local travertine formations in various stages of development. Apart from the old travertine moulds, in the Wellness Thermal Pool you can watch as the water of the spring makes strange foam, which over time will turn into strong travertine rock.

## COUNTY COUNCIL IN ŠAHY (4)

It was decided after the fire of the county council in the Hungarian town of Kemence in 1806 to move the seat of the council to nearby Šahy. This increased the importance of this small town immediately. It was decided to build an apt building for the council in 1822, however the prolonged construction works lasted until 1859. Šahy remained the district town also after the establishment of Czechoslovakia until 1923, when the council was moved to the town of Krupina. The edifice of the former county council now serves as the town hall. There is a memorable desk with the bust of the poet of the Štúr movement, Janko Kráľ, on its façade. He was arrested in this spot in 1848 and was imprisoned in the district prison together with Ján Rotarides before they were moved to Budín. His Šahy poem is a bitter testament of this experience.

## TRAVERTINE IN DUDINCE (5)

The mineral springs that provide water for the Spa in Dudince are on an important tectonic zone at the south of the Tertiary volcanic area. They are part of numerous travertine formations, which are at different developmental stages. The sedimentary rock is created by the influence of warm water seeking to reach the surface. Many of the travertine moulds are only dead rocks now; however there is a place near the swimming pools in the Štiavnice River bed where travertine forms right in front of your eyes. It has been a protected area since 1964. The most famous travertine formation is a group of travertine hills called the Roman Baths or Močidlá. There are 32 basins resembling baths that were perhaps used by the Roman legionaries. The travertine hill with a semicircular crater is called Tatársky prameň. The largest formation is the 6-metre travertine formation called Kúpeľný prameň.

# CENTRAL SLOVAKIA – NORTH

Splendid nature has wedded scores of historical monuments, which document the creative lives of the past generations of inhabitants of Horné a Stredné Považie regions, in the north of central Slovakia. The axis of the entire area is the River Váh. It has two sources; one rises in Vysoké Tatry (the High Tatras) Mountains and the second in the Nízke Tatry (the Low Tatras) Mountains. The Váh is the longest Slovakian river, flowing through several historical regions. Its upper current goes through the Liptov area, surrounded by a ring of high mountains. Below Ružomberok it touches the cold Orava, the hostile yet beautiful region that sprawls along the river of the same name. After leaving a defile in Veľká Fatra (the Greater Fatra) Mountains the Váh flows through the Turiec area, called the Slovakian Garden for its picturesque and pleasant environment. Another mountain range stands in the way of the river below Vrútky, where it goes through a chasm in the Malá Fatra (the Lesser Fatra) Mountains to reach the city of Žilina. Here the Kysuca River, which collects waters from the once poor but beautiful Kysuce area, pours into the Váh. Finally, the river turns left and slowly sulks across the wide flat land of the Podunajská Nížina Lowland.

# STREDNÉ POVAŽIE (CENTRAL VÁH RIVER REGION)

### VRŠATEC CASTLE (1)
The ruins of Vršatec Castle are hidden amongst the rocks of one of the peaks in the area and thick greenery. It sits at 805 metres and is counted among the most highly situated castles in Slovakia. It was built in the 13th century on a great naturally protected spot and often changed owners. It turned into a ruin following a gunpowder blast in the 18th century. There are in fact two castles on the limestone rock. The upper castle is situated directly in the rocks on the crest and offers splendid views. The younger, lower castle sits in the steep northwest slope of the rock. A tunnel once connected the two castles.

### VRŠATSKÉ ROCKS (2)
The bizarre belt of rocks at the east side of the White Carpathians is an eye pleasing variety to the monotonous landscape of sandstone formations (flysch). The peaks of the Vršatec Rocks boast the most rugged and fascinating shapes. From below the castle they look like massive stone walls with castellation, from the Chmeľová viewing peak (925 m), the third highest in this range, the rocks resemble a sharp knife sticking out of a loaf of bread. Apart from the rock of the Vršatec Castle, the rest of the rocks are not accessible to tourists; you can, however, admire them from a path that skirts the rocks.

### ČERVENOKAMENSKÉ ROCK (3)
A sharp, needle-like rock looms above the village of Červený Kameň in the White Carpathians. The limestone Červenokamenské Rock (723 m) is an important landmark of the landscape. Only climbers can reach its peak so tourists must admire this bizarre rock formation, a Protected Nature Reserve, from the surroundings. The slope of the hill situated on the eastern side of the valley can be managed to the same height as the peak of the Červenokamenské Rock, and there is a wonderful view of the scenery with the Vršatské Rocks in the background.

### LEDNICE CASTLE (4)
The builders of Lednice Castle ingeniously used the natural environment of the splendid landscape around a village of the same name in the White Carpathians. It was a royal border castle that protected the route to Moravia. The building seems as if it grew into the limestone rock of the peak where it sits. The castle, which resembles an eagle's nest, was built in the 13th century. It was occupied by robber barons during the 15th and 16th centuries who terrorized the wide surroundings. Brothers of the Podmanický family and Imrich Telekessy of Lednice Castle were beheaded for their crimes. The castle is now a derelict ruin. There is a settlement around the castle with a tunnel carved into the rock which leads to the castle.

## FRANCISCAN MONASTERY
## IN PRUSKÉ (1)

Juraj Jakusič (Jakussits) became the lord of Vršatec Castle in 1640 and later became the bishop of Veszprém and Jager. Being a Catholic and a priest, his main concern was to bring his mainly Protestant vassals back to the Catholic religion. He invited the Franciscan Order to pursue this task, who built a monastery in the village of Pruské on his estate in 1642 and later added the Church of St. George. Hugolín Gavlovič (1712 – 1787) was one of the monks of the monastery. He was the author of a well-known book on morality and chastity. The monastery is now used as a social services house.

## MANSION IN PRUSKÉ (2)

There is a Renaissance mansion from the 16th century in the village of Pruské, which was settled by colonists from Prussia and Silesia in the 13th century. The four-winged building in the middle of an English-style park was rebuilt in the Baroque and Classicism styles in 1787. However the Renaissance core of the building survived; there are two corner protection towers and an arcaded courtyard. The disposition of the mansion in Pruské resembles to a certain extent the mansion in Bytča. Perhaps both aristocratic seats were built by the same builder from the workshop of master Kilian of Milan.

## FORTRESS IN ILAVA (3)

The fortress in this village was originally a medieval castle built at the turn of the 11th and 12th centuries to protect the trade path along the Váh River. It was occupied by the knights of the Order of the Temple during the reign of the Arpád dynasty and then went to a Croatian count who improved the building greatly. The so-called Lower Castle was rebuilt into a noble aristocratic seat. The monks of the Order of Trinity settled in the Lower Castle at the beginning of the 18th century building a Baroque monastery and a church. Its two towers are a landmark of the fortress. The minster became a parish church after the monks left Ilava in 1783. The church became part of a prison during a rebuilding of the fortress in 1856.

## ROMANESQUE CHURCH
## IN POMINOVCE (4)

There was once a village named Pominovce near Ilava in the Middle Váh River District. It suffered floods from the nearby Váh, so its inhabitants left it and founded a new village named Sedmerovec in a safer place. Pominovce vanished from the map; however it left behind a valuable Romanesque Church of St. John the Baptist. This small sacral monument located in the middle of the fields far away from people and their houses was founded in the 12th century, or perhaps even earlier, above the village of Dražovce near Nitra. The ancient stone church houses several original Romanesque elements such as the simple church spire, the apse and windows in the south wall of the nave.

## MANSION IN LEDNICKÉ ROVNE (5)

The Slovakian Glass-Blowers Museum is rightfully placed in the village of Lednické Rovne. This village in the Stredné považie area has a long and rich tradition of glass production. Glass is still produced here. The museum was placed here in 1988 into a reconstructed mansion from the 16th century. The building was enlarged during a reconstruction in the 18th century and it received a new façade in the 19th century. For some time, it was used as a school. In the past the mansion was the seat of the aristocratic Schreiberci family, who owned the local glass works. Modern glass production that was developing after World War II built on the tradition of this company. Expositions of the museum present the entire history of glass production.

### STRÁŽOV (1)

The Strážovské Vrchy Hills received their name from their highest peak, Strážov (1,213 m). The landmark of the massive mountain range that spreads between two areas, Stredné Považie and Horná Nitra, looms above the colourful mountain village of Zliechov. It has five peaks and all are higher then 1,000 metres. There is a group of rocks at the upper part of Strážovské Vrchy. The highest one offers splendid views far beyond the borders of the mountain range. The original mainly oak forests on the slopes of Strážov are a National Nature Reserve.

### VÁPEČ (2)

This mountain (955 m n. m.) above the village of Horná Poruba, is not among the highest peaks in Strážovské Vrchy, however it usually rates first in surveys regarding the most beautiful hill. It is an almost perfect cone topped with a limestone-dolomite rock. The view from Vápeč is unique and you can see as far as to the foothills.

### KOŠECA CASTLE (3)

Not much is left from Košeca Castle in the Strážovské Vrchy Hills. This medieval aristocratic seat from the 13th century was taken by the army of the palatine Imrich Esterházi (Eszterházy) on the 16th November 1670. The soldiers of the Habsburg dynasty blew up the castle in rebellion against the local lord Imrich Petróci, who was an active member of the Vešeléni (Wesselényi) Uprising. He even planned to kidnap the emperor Leopold I, who was to be captured during a hunt and imprisoned in the Košeca Castle. The plan did not work out, though. The uprising was repressed and Petróci escaped to Transylvania (Sedmohradsko).

### ZLIECHOV (4)

The village of Zliechov has a splendid location. It is nested in a valley in the heart of the Strážovské Vrchy Hills and surrounded by forested hills. Among them is also the highest peak of the mountains, Strážov. The village is very old; the oldest written document mentions its existence as early as in 1272. People inhabited the mountains rather early as the old trade path between the Považie and Ponitrie areas cut through the mountains. Zliechov is an attractive tourist destination thanks to its preserved folk architecture and excellent skiing conditions.

### NIMNICA SPA (1)

The ink has not yet dried on the birth certificate of the Nimnica Spa as it is only slightly over fifty years old. During the building of the Priehrada Mládeže Dam in 1953, some water appeared in the foundation walls. It was strange as the water was salty and sparkling. Drilling revealed a source of valuable mineral water and it later resulted in the building of the Nimnica Spa. The youngest spa town in Slovakia is in a beautiful setting at the bank of the Nosice water reservoir and specialises in curing perspiration and digestion illnesses.

### NOSICE WATER RESERVOIR (2)

There are still many old-timers who remember the post-war euphoria and participated in the construction of the Priehrada Mládeže Dam (Dam of the Youth). Dozens of young people were active in the building of the first great work of the Socialism era in Slovakia between 1949 and 1957. Priehrada Mládeže is now called Nosice and it is one of the levels of the Váh Cascade hydro-energy system. The artificial lake filled up a narrow valley of the river with a pronounced meander. The dam is 500 metres long and 35 metres high and holds 36 million square metres of water. Its main purpose was the production of electricity. The plant has three Kaplan Turbines that produce approximately 160 million kWh of electricity.

### MANSION IN ORLOVÉ (3)

The town of Považská Bystrica acquired a valuable historical monument when the village of Orlová was joined with it – a mansion from the 17th century. It was built in the Renaissance style by Žikmund Balaša (Ballasa) in 1612; however it burnt down only four years later and was rebuilt and enlarged in 1733. A fine Baroque fountain was placed in the arcaded courtyard. The man-

sion was occupied by interesting personages, such as the count Hohonlohe and the Czech violin virtuoso Jan Kubelík. Several historical details are preserved in this rather large four-winged building with a nice park, for instance the interior of the Chapel of St. John of Nepomuk. The collections of an Ethnographical Museum were placed in the mansion in 1984. The park behind the mansion has remarkable rare trees.

### POVAŽSKÝ CASTLE (4)
The forested hill with a ruin above the right bank of the Váh River on the way from Považská Bystrica to Žilina cannot be overlooked. It is also called Bystrický (as the town of this name is nearby) and was probably founded in the 13th century as a royal sentry castle that controlled the trade route along the Váh. King Matthias Corvinus gave it to the powerful Podmanický family in 1458, but it returned to the crown after the death of brothers Ján and Rafael who were infamous as robbers. Its last owners, the Balašovci family, moved out of the castle after a fire in 1630 into a Renaissance mansion in Považské Podhradie. The castle was demolished in 1698 on the order of the Emperor Leopold, for it was a refuge of the members of the Tököli (Thököly) Uprising. The castle has never been repaired as the owners of the estate preferred to stay in their Rococo mansion in Považské Podhradie from 1775.

### MANSION IN JASENICE (5)
The village of Jasenice in the lower part of the Papradianska Dolina Valley boasts a finely reconstructed mansion. It was built for the family of Sunyoghovci in 1618 and later modernized several times. The mansion received a simple but impressive appearance during the last reconstruction. A natural exposition of the Ethnographic Museum in Považská Bystrica was opened in the mansion in 2006; previously it was located in a mansion in Orlové. The botanic and geological exhibition from Stredné Považie area completes the zoological collections.

1

2

## MANSION IN BYTČA (1)

When the wealthy baron František Thurzo became the owner of the extensive estate in Bytča in 1563 the small stronghold did not correspond with his majestic attitude. As business with copper brought him sufficient funds he could build a grandiose Renaissance mansion on its site between 1571 and 1574. To carry out the building works he took on an Italian builder, Kilian from Milan. His portrait is on a fresco on the ground floor of the mansion. After the mansion was damaged by members of the Hajdúš Uprising between 1605 and 1612, another Italian artist, A. Pocebello, was invited to repair the mansion in Bytča. The Esterházis obtained the mansion after the last of the Thurzo family died at the beginning of the 17th century. Their perception of the building was rather different as they turned the luxurious aristocratic seat into out-buildings. The memorable court proceedings with the bloody countess Alžbeta Bátoriová (Báthoryiová) took place in the mansion. And it is worth mentioning that the famous rebel and national hero Juraj Jánošík served here as a soldier, and perhaps the history of his outlaw life was started right in Bytča after he met prisoner Tomáš Uhorčík here at the beginning of the 18th century.

## WEDDING PALACE IN BYTČA (2)

When the Italian builder A. Pocabella came to Bytča at the beginning of the 17th century to manage the repairs to the local mansion, the nobleman of the local large estate Juraj Thurzo gave him another task. Having seven daughters, he had a Renaissance wedding palace built next to the mansion. The weddings of the noble brides as well as other social events took place here. There is a large wedding hall inside this elegant historical building, which was once the biggest of its type in Slovakia. The palace currently belongs to the Museum of Považie Area in Žilina.

## HRIČOV CASTLE (3)

The ruin of Hričov Castle is perched on a high rock in the Súľovské Mountains. It is a nice trek to the ruin. The castle was built in the 13th century and it remained the seat of the Hričov lords until the 16th century. Its owners were members of the influential Hungarian high ranks. One of them was the influential nobleman František Thurzo, who brought his seat from the castle to the mansion in Bytča. The last building works on Hričov Castle were carried out in 1622. Later on the aristocracy did not care much for the badly accessible castle and it deteriorated and turned to ruin. There is a nice view of the surroundings from its half-demolished walls.

## HRIČOVSKÁ IHLA (4)

A strange rock can be seen from the windows of the train near the village of Hričovské Podhradie on the eastern side. Although almost lost in the bushes, Hričovská Ihla (Needle) still looms above and adorns the landscape at the west edge of the Súľovské Mountains. This sharp rock formation is an eroded remain of a crumbled limestone rock, which in the long vanished past was a part of a coral reef of the tropical sea that lay in this area in the Late Tertiary era. The damaging erosion has caused the rock to lean. There is a narrow rock window. It is a Protected Nature Monument.

3

4

### LARGE AND SMALL MANÍN (3)

The enchanting landscape of the Váh River area around the Považská Bystrica has two large 'guards' as it is symbolically protected by a pair of huge rock peaks. When looking from the Váh, the Large Manín (891 m) looms on the right side and the slightly smaller Small Manín (813 m) on the left. The two big mountains hug the Manínska Canyon created by the Manínsky Stream flowing from the mountains. Both mountains are made of limestone with its typical geomorphologic shape and differ from the majority of the rocks that also belong to the Súľovské Mountains range and that are made of conglomerate.

### MANÍNSKA CANYON (4)

This canyon is the largest of the three canyons in the valley of the Manínsky Stream in the Súľovské Mountains. It is the lowest of the three and is squeezed between the huge rocks – the Large and Small Manín. There is a narrow paved road thought the constricted rocky canyon that enables access to the mountain villages. However, it takes some skills for a driver to safely manage the narrow path flanked by steep rock walls. The bizarre limestone rocks rise to 400 metres on both sides of the Manínsky Stream. Water eroded the bottom of the stream, creating large potholes. The narrow canyon receives sunshine only rarely and the snow sometimes stays there until May. The valuable natural surroundings of the canyon are a Protected National Nature Reserve.

### BOSMANY (1)

The Kostolec and Manínska Canyon line up nicely when observed from the massive rock above the village of Kostolec. The large limestone rock formation is one of the three rocks called Bosmany. Limestone is typically full of small karst cavities that were eroded by rain water. Various vegetation grow on the limestone bedrock. It is protected together with the interesting and various geomorphologic formations.

### KOSTOLECKÁ CANYON (2)

Before the Manínsky Stream escapes out of the Súľovské Mountains and flows across the Podunajská Nížina Lowland into the Váh, it must go through three canyons. The highest one lies between the villages of Vrchteplá and Kostolec. Below Kostolec the valley narrows for the second time into the Kostolec Canyon, which is about 300 metres long and is a Protected Nature Reserve. The stream eroded the huge limestone wall with a big rock overhang, the largest in Slovakia, on the northern side. Just above the canyon stands a school building which houses the Room of Peter Jilemnický.

### SÚĽOVSKÉ ROCKS (1)

The Súľovské Rocks are called the Slovakian Dolomites for their fairy tale-like appearance and bizarreness. They are the largest group of rock formation in Slovakia, apart from the Tatras area. In our conditions they are a unique natural phenomenon. This is not to say that Slovakia lacks rocks and rock formations, however only the Súľov Rocks are made of conglomerate leaving out the rocks in the neighbouring Strážovské Vrchy Hills and Žilinská Kotlina Valley. They are a central area of the Súľovské Mountains range. One or two rings of the rock crests with an oval ground-plan encircle the Súľovská Kotlinka Valley, which lies in the heart of the mountains and is made of the softer slate. The narrow rocky Súľovská Canyon connects the valley with the village of Považské Podolie.

### SÚĽOV CASTLE (2)

The remains of the medieval Súľov Castle are hardly visible in the conglomerate Súľovské Rocks. The castle was called Roháč, just as one of the local hills, in the past. It was founded in the 15th century and became the reason for squabbles between two aristocratic families (Podmanický and Sirmiensis) in the next century, which ended in the castle being burnt out. In any case, it was reconstructed and further used until the end of the 16th century, when the family moved into a mansion and only a sentry remained at the castle. It was abandoned in 1780 and started to fall apart. The climb to Súľov Castle is a demanding yet pleasant tourist trip. The reward for the difficult trek is the impressive view of the fairytale world of the Súľovské Rocks.

### BRADA (3)

It is no easy task to scramble up the Brada Hill (816 m) in the Súľovské Rocks. You can reach the area just below the peak quite easily by following a tourist path; however there is a rock tower to be managed in the end, which is difficult and is an undertaking even for a mountaineer. However, there are plenty of accessible spots around Brada with wonderful views of the scenic and bizarre Súľovské Rocks.

### HLBOCKÝ WATERFALL (4)

The outer range of the conglomerate Súľovské Mountains above the village of Hlboká nad Váhom is divided by a valley. The Hlbocký Stream manages the stone obstacle in a cascade of two waterfalls. The total height of the waterfall is 14 metres. The falling water eroded several spiral potholes into the rock – bowl-like holes.

### GOTHIC GATE (5)

The phenomenon of nature created various amazing rock formations in the Súľovské Rocks. With a little bit of imagination you can see animals, people and fairy tale characters. Apart from rock towers, bastions and needles, the rocks also boast rock gates and windows. The highest gate is in the northern slope of the Súľovský Canyon. It is 13 metres high and called the Gotická brána.

1

## ŽILINA REGION

### PARISH CHURCH IN ŽILINA (1)

The pair of towers of the Parish Church is an inseparable part of the silhouette of the historical centre of the town of Žilina. They are a landmark of the southern side of Námestie Andreja Hlinku Square and loom above even the roofs of the burgher houses on Mariánske Square. This church, which was consecrated to the Holy Trinity, was built at the beginning of the 15th century at the site of an older town castle. The original Gothic building was later rebuilt in the Renaissance style. Valuable altars and paintings by the prominent Slovakian painter Jozef G. Klemens are inside the church. The church spire is 51 metres high; there is another tower only 6 metres away, a belfry called Burianova built in the 16th century in an Italian style.

### MARIÁNSKE SQUARE IN ŽILINA (2)

This square is a unique urban place in Slovakia. The area in the middle of the historical core of the town is encircled by arcaded burgher houses, which is unprecedented in any other Slovakian town. Even some of the houses on the side streets have arcades. Historical squares in Czech

and Moravian towns bear a similar appearance. The fashion of arcaded houses came to Žilina in the 16th and 17th century when the town was inhabited by the Evangelists who sought building inspiration in Protestant Europe, mainly in Germany. The only sacral monument, the Jesuit Church of St. Paul with a monastery, was built on Marian Square with the uplifting of the Catholic spirit in Žilina in the 18th century.

### WOODEN CHURCH IN TRNOVÉ (3)

Apart from in the eastern part of the country, wooden churches are a rare sight in Slovakia. Moreover, the one in Trnové at the eastern edge of Žilina is of the Roman Catholic religion as opposed to the churches in the east. According to written sources it existed as early as 1582, however some Gothic elements suggest that the origin of the church goes even further back. It consists of a wooden one-nave building with a shingle roof

and an attached wooden spire. The main altar is Baroque and dates from the 18th century. The bells are older; they were cast in the 17th century. The Renaissance painted ceiling in the presbytery also dates from the 17th century.

### BUDATÍN CHATEAU (4)

The work of tinkers is typically considered the oldest Slovakian craft. Tinkers sat out on journeys throughout Europe and even reached America. A unique exposition of the Museum of Považie located in the Budatín Chateau is devoted to this craft and the art of production of everyday articles from this material. A stone castle was built in the then independent village of Budatín (now a suburb at the northern edge of Žilina) in the 13th century to protect the trade path to Silesia. Its lords managed a large estate reaching as far as Kysuce. The Budatín Chateau is now one of the best preserved monuments of its type in Slovakia.

## CHURCH OF ST. MARTIN IN TEPLIČKA NAD VÁHOM (1)

The Church of St. Martin in Teplička nad Váhom near Žilina is visited by local worshipers as well as by tourists. Its main attraction is a coffin with a glass top with the remarkably preserved body of the famous humanitarian Žofie Bosňáková. The wife of F. Vešeléni (Wesselényi), the palatine of the Strečno Castle, was much loved amongst the vassals for her piety and charity. After she died in 1644 her mummified body was placed into the crypt of the castle where it was discovered 45 years later without any visible sings of decay. The same can be said about the body 400 years later.

## DOMAŠINSKÝ MEANDER (2)

The wall of the Lesser Fatra Mountains stands in the way of the Váh River between Vrútky and Strečno. However, the longest Slovakian river managed to get over this obstacle by creating a narrow chasm through the mountains. The valley on the bottom of the chasm created the deep Domašinský Meander. The local rail track does not follow the large bend of the river but rather uses a shortcut through a tunnel; but the frequented Hradská Road skims the left bank of the river. However, a quick drive will not provide sufficient time and tranquillity to admire the beauty of the Meander. Fortunately, this cannot be said about the rafting on the river, which is a great tourist summer attraction and is linked with the old tradition of the scouring of wood down the river. Rafting is a safe entertainment nowadays as the dangerous places near the infamous Margita and Besná rocks, which scourged rafters in the past, are no longer there.

## STARÝ CASTLE (3)

This castle is perched atop a rocky point above the right bank of the Váh River. Previously it was called Varín, but lost its name when the younger Strečno Castle was built. Starý Castle was built in the 13th century and was mainly owned by the bandit barons called the Pongrács (Pongrácz) who used it as a safe shelter as well as a base for looting. They unjustly collected the spoil from the rafters that floated wood down the Váh from the Carpathian forests. The lords of the castle moved to the nicer, more comfortable mansions at a lower altitude in the 17th century. The castle was abandoned at the beginning of the 18th century and has gradually turned into a ruin. A tourist trail that meanders nearby is a part of the popular crest trek of the Kriváň part of the Lesser Fatra Mountains. The castle walls and particularly the rock above the castle offer a splendid view of the Domašinský Meander in the chasm of the Váh River.

## MONUMENT TO FRENCH PARTISANS NEAR STREČNO (4)

The defile of the Váh River through the Lesser Fatra Mountains has been a strategically important point since the oldest times. Whoever controlled it ruled the entire area. Heavy fights over the defile erupted in September 1944 during the Slovakian National Uprising between the Slovakian partisans and German Nazi. Many voluntary antifascist fighters from abroad were amongst the partisans. There was a large group from France.

Despite being outnumbered by the Germans, the partisans bravely defended their positions for a long time and many died as heroes. To commemorate the victims of this army operation a Monument to French Partisans was erected on the Zvonica Hill above the village of Strečno between 1952 and 1956. This impressive artistic work made from white travertine from the Spiš region is placed in the lovely surroundings with a view of the nearby Strečno Castle.

## STREČNO CASTLE (5)

The place where the Váh leaves the defile through the Lesser Fatra Mountains is guarded by two castles that were once enemies. The bigger is perched on a steep rock above the left bank of the river and is called Strečno Castle. The medieval castle was built at the turn of the 13th and 14th centuries and was in the king's possession until the mid-15th century. It later became the seat of the powerful noblemen that owned the extensive surrounding estate. The fate of the castle was sealed by the participation of its owners in the estate uprisings. Its last owner was František Vešeléni (Wesselény), a leader of the anti-Hapsburg uprising. As revenge the emperor's soldiers destroyed the castle in 1674 to such an extent that it was inhabitable and became a ruin. However, the ruin was later preserved and following a successful reconstruction the castle is now one of the most popular tourist destinations in the region.

## TERCHOVÁ (1)

Even the steel sculpture of the legendary Jano-šík erected above the village of Terchová can tell us nothing about the legendary hidden treasure of this famous hero and outlaw of Slovakia's past. The author of this grandiose 7-metre high symbol of Terchová is the academic sculptor Ján Kulich. You can learn more about Jáno-šík at an exhibition of the Museum of Považie in the building of the former school. The exhibition is devoted to Terchová and its famous native. And to make it even more interesting you can visit the meadow in Terchová, where the legendary folk hero was born on the 25th January 1688.

## VEĽKÝ KRIVÁŇ (2)

The defile of the Váh River divides the Lesser Fatra Mountains to the southern Lúčanská Fatra part and northern Krivánska Fatra section. The higher and more rugged Krivánska Fatra section was designated a National Park and received its name from the highest peak of the range, Veľký (Large) Kriváň (1,709 m). The conspicuous cone hill lies a bit away from the main crest of the mountains, and a short turn leads to it from the main trail. On a fine day the view from Veľký Kriváň is far-reaching. Malý (Small) Kriváň (1,671 m) is also nearby.

## VEĽKÝ ROZSUTEC (3)

Although it is not the highest peak (it is the fifth highest) in the Lesser Fatra Mountains, Veľký (Large) Rozsutec (1,610 m) is generally perceived as the most beautiful and most popular mountain. It ranked first in a number of surveys about the most beautiful mountains in Slovakia. Its rugged silhouette sharply contrasts with the neighbouring soft-lined Stoh Peak with a completely different geological formation. There are rocky but much lower mountains on the other side of Veľký Rozsutec, the Poludňové Rocks and Malý (Small) Rozsutec. The physically demanding climb to the peak of Veľký Rozsutec is a splendid touristic undertaking. And there is no need to feel sorry even if you don't find the treasure, allegedly hidden here by Jánošík, as the view of the landscape is breathtaking.

## JÁNOŠÍKOVE DIERY (4)

The very attractive trek through the Jánošíkove Diery rock formation can be a part of the climb to Veľký Rozsutec. The huge mountain range is divided and rugged by a group of narrow rock defiles and gaps with numerous waterfalls in the east. Similar to the more famous defiles in the Slovakian Paradise, Janošíkove Diery can also be managed only thanks to ladders, chains and other technical equipment. The Dolné (Lower) Diery are in the lowest part, and above them

continue the Horné (Upper) Diery. There is a Nature Trail through the Jánošíkove Diery, which includes a fine view of the rugged landscape of defiles and rocks.

## TIESŇAVY (5)

The rocky, narrow Tiesňavy Canyon leads into the Vrátna Dolina Valley from Terchová. The symbolic guard of this natural gate is the Skalný Mních Rock. The portal of Tiesňavy is made by two embracing rocks called Sokolia and Boboty. There is a chapel on the rock above the Vrátaňka River and a sign that shows the level of water at the time of the great flood in June 1848. A deluge of mud and stones fell off of Veľký Rozsutec and killed 14 people.

## ŠTEFANOVÁ (6)

The interesting village of Štefanová sits in the middle of a valley in the northwest part of the Kriváň part of the Lesser Fatra Mountains. It is now part of the village of Terchová and boasts one of the most splendid and most photographed natural scenes in Slovakia. Veľký Rozsutec and Stoh mountains create a breathtaking setting for this colourful village with preserved vernacular wooden architecture. However, no longer do the inhabitants carry on with the traditional farming as they work mainly in the tourism industry.

## KUNERAD MANSION (1)

A romantic building set in a pleasant natural environment is to be found in the forested valley on the western side of the Lúčanská part of the Lesser Fatra Mountains. It was built for a count named Bellestrém as a hunting mansion in 1915. Its builders copied the then fashionable French style of building. The Bellestrémci family visited their hunting mansion twice a year even after the establishment of Czechoslovakia, and to make it a pleasant stay it was luxuriously equipped. It even had its own electricity plant. However, for the second time the war changed the fate of the mansion. It was burnt down by German fascists in September 1944 for being a refuge of partisans. Following a reconstruction it was turned into the sanatorium of a spa with the same name. The Kunerad Mansion is a starting point for treks to Martinské Hole Mountain.

## LIETAVA CASTLE (2)

The castle on the rock south of Žilina is called Lietava, allegedly after the Slavic goodness Lietva. The castle was built after the Ottoman attack in the second half of the 13th century. The oldest history of the castle is connected with the Bebek family, who ruled a large estate in the Rajčianska Dolina Valley. It went into the possession of the powerful Thurzovci at the beginning of the 17th century; the Hungarian palatine Juraj Thurzo was even born at the castle. Many Slovakian castles had an unlucky fate as their owners joined the anti-Habsburg uprisings. In the case of Lietava, another problem was a squabble over its rightful heirs. For this reason there was no real castellan on the castle and it became derelict in the 18th century. The core of the Lietava Castle is Gothic and the last reconstructions were carried out in the Renaissance style, which gave the castle its romantic charm, mainly thanks to the attractive arched attic. It is currently undergoing a large reconstruction.

### ROCK NEEDLE IN POLUVSIE (4)

Next to the main road from Rajecké Teplice to Žilina near the village of Poluvsie is an interesting natural formation. A 15-metre rock needle protrudes from the ground. It is the result of an erosive separation off of a rock wall at the south of the Skalky Mountain. It is a Protected Natural Monument.

### SLOVAKIAN NATIVITY SCENE IN RAJECKÁ LESNÁ (5)

The pilgrimage village of Rajecká Lesná in the Rajecká Dolina Valley is much visited because of the miraculous sculpture of the Virgin Marry the Charitable as well as for the famous Slovakian Nativity Scene. It is the largest work of its type in Slovakia and was carved from wood by a local folk artist, Jozef Pekar. The Slovakian Nativity Scene in Rajecká Lesná is a large picture book of Slovakian geography and history. It boasts important woodcarved national symbols and monuments and includes basically all regions from Bratislava to Eastern Slovakia. It features castles, churches, town halls, burger houses, and folk buildings, as well as the national Kriváň Peak. There are approximately 300 figures and about half of them are movable. Master Pekara worked on the nativity Scene until 2002.

### ČIČMANY (6)

The tradition of painting decorations on the facades of wooden houses in the mountain village of Čičmany is at least 200 years old. The painting, done with whitewash, was not done merely for aesthetics reasons; it also had conservative and

protective purposes. The house in Čičmany inspired the prominent Slovakian architect D. Jurkovič, who used this idea in his project about peasant life and farming for an ethnographical exhibition held in Prague in 1895. He later helped to reconstruct the houses, which burnt down in 1921. The collection of the wooden painted houses in Čičmany was declared a Folk Architecture Monument Reserve in 1977. There is an ethnography exposition in the one-story Radenov House belonging to the Museum of Považie in Žilina. Another exposition was opened in the Gregorov House in 1986, which documents life in Čičmany at the beginning of the 20th century.

### NÁMESTIE SNP (SLOVAKIAN NATIONAL UPRISING) SQUARE IN RAJEC (7)

Rajec was a more important town in the past than it is today. It was an even larger centre of the region than Žilina. The better times of this picturesque town in the Rajecká Dolina Valley are remembered by the large central Námestie SNP Square with a roughly quadrant ground-plan. The location of the streets that lead out of the square in the corners is the typical sign of the Gothic urban development. Although the historical buildings were replaced by modern edifices, a few original burgher houses have been preserved. One of them, on the southern side of the square, is the Renaissance house from the 17th century with a stone balcony and arcades. It houses the Town Museum with collections documenting the life in the region. There is a Renaissance town hall from the 16th century in the middle of the square.

### RAJECKÉ TEPLICE (3)

This spa town is nestled below the splendid Skalka Rock and clad in the greenery of the park. It was founded near warm mineral springs. The curative powers were already known by people living in the 14th century. The palatine Juraj Thurzo liked visiting the springs from his nearby Lietava Castle in the 16th century and tried to cure his sciatica here. The spa settlement developed here in the 17th century and the first water analysis of the local mineral springs was made in 1795. After it was visited by the archduke Karol Ľudovít, the spa became popular with noble clientele. The spa is now among the most important in Slovakia and specializes in diseases of the locomotive and nervous systems, as well as the back, chronic muscle pain and post-traumatic problems.

# KYSUCE

### OIL SPRING IN KORŇA (1)

When the great oil fever broke out at the beginning of the 20th century due to the invention of the automobile, for a while the inhabitants of the Kysuce region thought that they would enjoy riches on a par with the Texas oil magnates. The reason for their unfulfilled dreams, was an oil well discovered in the area around the hilly village of Korňa which is the only source of oil of its type in central Europe. However, the well proved not viable for commercial exploitation, so at least the locals filled their buckets and used the crude oil at home.

### KYSUCKÁ GULA IN MEGONKY (2)

Amongst the uniform flysch of basic sedimentary rock prevalent in almost the whole of the Kysuce region lies a narrow hill range with the mysterious stone balls. They lie in an area of about 15 kilometres and half a kilometre wide that stretches through the Turzovské Hills north of the villages of Čadec and Turzovka. The origin of the mysterious sandstone balls is not clear. Their almost perfect geometrical shape led to speculation about them being created by some ancient civilization or even by extraterrestrials. The balls can be found in several places. The best way to see them is to visit an abandoned stone quarry near the border village of Megonky. The so far, the largest ball discovered is called Mary and is 3 metres in diameter. People have collected a lot of these balls as garden decorations and one has been turned into a monument which stands in the village of Klokočov.

### ŽIVČÁKOVÁ NEAR TURZOVKA (3)

Allegedly, the Virgin Mary appeared on the Živčáková Hill above the village of Turzovka for the first time on 1st June 1958. Similar visions were reported six more times by 14th August of the same year. News spread fast and the first pilgrimage to the site commenced on the 8th September. The village is now called the Lourdes of Slovakia and the Živčáková Hill above Turzovka is now one of the most important pilgrimage sites in Slovakia. Cardinal Ján Chryzostom Korec gave permission for the village to build the pilgrimage Chapel of the Virgin Mary the Queen of Tranquillity in 1992. The chapel was consecrated one year later and is currently the destination of thousands of pilgrims from the whole of Slovakia and abroad.

### VEĽKÝ JAVORNÍK (4)

The recreational village of Kasárne located directly on the border was previously only accessible from the neighbouring Czech Republic until a new road was built from the village of Makovo. Kasárne is a popular skiing centre in the winter, while in the summer it is the most convenient starting point for treks to the Veľký (Large) Javorník Mountain (1,071 m). The largest peak of the flysch Javorníky Mountains is near the border with the Czech Republic and is a popular tourist destination mainly for its splendid views of the Slovakian and Moravian sides of the mountains range. On a fine day, you can see the Lesser Fatra while the peaks of the Moravian-Silesian Beskids Mountains loom in the opposite direction. The peak is within the Veľký Javorník National Nature Reserve, which was established in 1967 to protect the beech and spruce of rain forest character.

## MANSION IN RADOĽA (1)

The inhabitants of the Kysuce District were vassals of the lords from the neighbouring regions, mainly from the Budatín and Bytča areas. With no local aristocracy, this district has almost no castles or mansions. One of the few exceptions is the Renaissance mansion in the village of Radoľa near the Kysucké Nové Mesto town. However, even this mansion had no local owner. It was built in the 16th century possibly on the site of a medieval sentry tower and went to the possessions of the family of Čáki (Csáky) as part of the Budatín estate in 1798. The complex of the mansion once included outbuildings, a brewery, a mill and a lumber-mill. The expositions of the Kysuce Museum in Čadec were open to the public in the mansion in 1983; they focus on the oldest history and burgher living in the Kysuce region in the 19th century.

## MANSION IN OŠČADNICA (2)

The village of Oščadnica also boasts a mansion. However this is the last of the mansions in the Kysuce region. The mansion in Oščadnica is much newer than the one in Radola. The former dates from the first half of the 19th century, which is evident from its romantic appearance resembling Alpine hunting chateaus. The mansion is now an exhibition hall of the Kysuce Gallery in Čadec containing a collection of toys created by Slovakian artists. The mansion is surrounded by a natural park with a pond. If you visit the mansion at the end of May you can also experience the popular Oščadnická Heligónka International Music Festival.

## VEĽKÁ RAČA (3)

The largest peak of the Kysucké Beskydy (Beskids) Mountains called Veľká (Large) Rača (1 236 m) lies on the border between Slovakia and Poland and is the highest peak in the entire Kysuce area. Apart from the peak, which is covered by bilberries, the slopes of the hill are lined with flysch rocks that are mostly overgrowned with dense forest. Beech and fir trees and also interesting pseudo-karst cavities lie within the Veľká Rača National Nature Reserve which covers 313 hectares. One of the best tourist centres in Slovakia is on the west side of the mountain. The popular Snowparadise skiing centre is divided into three hubs which bear names of the nearest villages; Dedovka, Marguška and Laliky. Skiing enthusiasts can enjoy 14 kilometres of downhill ski pistes and three cross-country trails. The Snowparadise turns into Sunparadise in the summer with scores of tourist attractions.

## MUSEUM KYSUCKEJ DEDINY IN VYCHYLOVKA (4)

There are not many preserved original folk buildings in the Kysuce area as they were replaced with scores of unsightly, unstylish modern edifices after World War II that were built by the local inhabitants with money earned in the mines of Ostrava. However, some examples have been preserved and moved to one place. Museum Kysuckej Dediny was established in the beautiful surroundings of the Chmúrna Dolina Valley in Vychylkov (part of the village of Nová Bystrica) in 1981. This interesting open-air museum is a unique opportunity to learn about the life in old villages of the area. It boasts 34 living, sacral, technical and farming edifices from various places in Kysuce. For example, there is the original pub that once again serves its original purpose.

## LOGGING BACK SWATH RAILWAY IN VYCHYLOVKA (5)

The appeal of the Museum of Kysuce Village in Vychylovka is enhanced by a unique logging back swath railway which passes through the open-air museum. The restored historical railway is a unique technical monument, the only of its type in Europe. The only other type, of this railway still working are in the Peruvian Andes and the Rockies in the USA. It was built by the Italian war prisoners in 1915 and was originally 61 kilometres long and connected the village of Oščadnica in the Kysuce area with the village of Lokča in the Orava region. A steam train climbed an elevation of 217.69 metres along the steepest 2.5 kilometre stretch of the railway on the border between the two districts. Three switchbags enabled the train to make the climb. The railway line was extended to a length of 110 kilometres in the 1920s. Reconstruction of the most culturally significant stretch of the line was started in 1974 which enabled sporadic operation of the railway between Kubatkovce and Chmúrna stations. The railway was extended in 1995 with the stretch that now leads through the open-air museum up to the first switchbag. The historical train, which originally transported logs to lumber-mills, now serves tourists.

**1**

## MATICA SLOVENSKÁ
## IN MARTIN (1)

The town of Martin is rightfully called 'the most Slovakian town' as it witnessed several landmark events in the history of the Slovakian nation and is now the seat of several national institutions. One of them is the Matica Slovenská, an institution founded in 1863 with the aim of reviving the national spirit and spreading enlightenment amongst Slovaks. The first building of Matica Slovenská dating from 1864 is in the centre of the town and is now used by the Slovakian National Literary Museum and has a permanent exhibition about the oldest Slovakian literature. The present-day headquarters of the Matica Slovenská institution are in a building dating from 1925 situated to the east of the town centre.

## NATIONAL CEMETERY IN MARTIN (2)

Every nation has a Pantheon or similar place of rest for great national personages. The Slovakian National Cemetery is in the town of Martin and is a National Cultural Monument. It was founded in the second half of the 19th century when Martin was the hub of the forming modern Slovakian nation and is situated at the southeast edge of the centre of the town. The first person to be buried at this, for Slovakians sacred place, was the vice-chairman of the Matica Slovenská Institution Karol Kuzmány in 1866. There are approximately 300 hundred important people from across the spectre of Slovakian culture, science, politics and social

**2**

sphere buried here. Among them are the tombs of Janko Kráľ, Svetozár Hurban Vajanský, Jozef Gregor Tajovský, Jozef Cíger Hronský, Janko Jesenský, Martin Kukučín, Martin Benka, Ľudovít Fulla and Andrej Kmeť.

## SLOVAKIAN NATIONAL MUSEUM IN MARTIN (3)

The most important museum in Slovakia, the National Slovakian Museum, was established in the town of Martin upon the initiative of the Slovakian Museum Association, which managed to open its first permanent exposition in Martin in 1908. It was housed in the purpose built edifice financed from a national donation fund. Currently, the Slovakian National Museum curates 40 percent of all museum collections in Slovakia with almost 4 million art pieces. Martin is now the seat of the Slovakian National Museum, the Ethnographical Museum, the Andrej Kmeť Museum, the House of Martin Benka and the Jahodnícke Háje Open-Air Museum.

## TURČIANSKA GALLERY IN MARTIN (4)

The centre of the town of Martin has been converted into a pleasant pedestrian zone. The historical former county council building from 1740 stands at its southern end. This originally Baroque building was rebuilt in the Classicism style for the requirements of the Turiec County Council, which moved to Martin from Sklabiňa Castle. The table in the meeting hall of this institution was always laid with a red cloth. The red colour symbolised the blood of two yeomen of Turiec killed at the Ónod Gathering in May 1707. The vice-head of the council, Krištof Okoličáni, and the council notary, Melchior Rakovský, got into a fight with Francis II Rákoci (Rákoczi) and were maliciously killed by supporters of the last anti-Hapsburg uprising. The former County Council now houses the Turčianska Gallery.

## MUSEUM SLOVENSKEJ DEDINY – JAHODNÍCKE HÁJE (5)

The open-air museums in Slovakia usually have a specific regional character as they represent life in a particular region. However, Museum Slovenskej Dediny in Jahodnícke Háje at the southern edge of the town of Martin has a truly national character, for this open-air museum covers the regions of the entire country. The first art arrived in the museum in 1982 and today there are approximately one hundred exhibits, yet the project is still far from complete. There is place for dozens more folk buildings and monuments. The edifices are separated according to the region of their origin. Apart from the Turiec area, the Orava, Liptov, Kysuce and other regions and areas are represented here.

## MARTINSKÉ HOLE (6)

Looking down upon the town of Martin from Martinské Hole is like a view from an aeroplane thanks to the elevation of more than a thousand metres. The climb is demanding task, but the view can be enjoyed without excursion ascent by taking the cable car which goes from the Podstrá-ne quarter and rises to the Martinské Hole Chalet (1245 m). From there it is only a short walk up to Veľká Lúka (1457 m), the highest peak of the Lúčany section of the Lesser Fatra Mountains. The peak offers a splendid panoramic view. Martinské Hole is an excellent skiing centre that is often open until May thanks to the high elevation.

## ŠÚTOVSKÝ WATERFALL (1)

It is pretty easy to climb up to Šútovo Waterfall in the Šútovská Dolina Valley on the southern side of the Kriváň section of the Lesser Fatra Mountains, thus it is a frequented tourist destination. The beautiful mist of water that falls from a rock step 38 metres above is about an hour's walk from the village of Šútovo. It is the largest waterfall in the Lesser Fatra Mountains and one of the largest in Slovakia.

## ŠÚTOVSKÉ LAKE (2)

Near the point where the Váh River leaves the Kraľovany Gorge there is an abandoned stone quarry. The bottom of this large gorge in the hill above Šútovo village is flooded by the waters of Šútovské Lake. This lake with turquoise blue water is situated in beautiful surroundings with the silhouettes of peaks of the Kriváň section of the Lesser Fatra Mountains in the background. The banks of the lake are swarmed with swimmers during the summer and its clear waters attract scuba divers who like to train in this lake.

## SKLABIŇA CASTLE (3)

Sklabiňa Caslte at the north of Turiec withstood the difficult times of the Middle Ages as well as the turmoil of the estates uprising. However, it did not survive World War II. when it was occupied by partisans and German fascists burnt it down in September 1944. The castle was built above the village of Sklabinský Podzámok in the 13th century. Originally it was royal property and the administrative centre of a large estate. It was also the seat of Turiec County from 1320 until the middle of the 18th century. The royal visits of Ľudovít I and Sigismund of Luxemburg were a testament of its former importance. It was well fortified and difficult to conquer. According to a legend, the outlaw and Slovakian hero Juraj Jánošík managed to get to the castle, but by cunning not force. Supposedly this happened in 1712. Although that there is no evidence of this feat, people loved the story.

## CHURCH OF SIMON AND JUDE
## IN PRÍBOVCE (4)

The village of Príbovce in the heart of the Turčianska Kotlina Hollow is an important transportation hub. The advantageous location of this area was recognised even in the Bronze Age. Here, archaeologists have discovered a valuable burial site of the Lužická Culture. The medieval history of the village goes back to the 13th century. Gatherings of the county council were held in Príbovce, the centre of the county, in the 17th century. The most noteworthy monument in the village is the Roman-Catholic Church of St. Simon and St. Jude built in the Gothic style in the 14th century. The shingle roof of the main nave and the small spire is remarkable. The village also boasts one of the most beautiful Evangelical churches in Turiec.

## CHURCH IN SVÄTÁ MARA
## IN SOCOVCE (5)

The entire Turiec area can be viewed from Stráž Hill near the village of Sosovce. And it is easy to understand why this lovely landscape is called the Turčianska Záhradka (Turiec Garden). According to archaeological findings, the strategically located hill in the centre of the Turčianska Kotlina Hollow

was settled back in the Bronze Age. The medieval village called Svätá Mara replaced the Great Moravian era settlement on the hill and the inhabitants built the ancient church hidden in the shadow of high trees on the northern slope of the hill. This impressive Early Gothic sacral monument dates from the 13th century and it has maintained some of its oldest architectonic elements such as the Gothic windows and a fragment of a mural from the 15th century on the south façade. The vaulted crypt houses the tombs of members of the aristocratic family of Rakovský.

## CHURCH OF ST COSMAS AND
## DAMIAN NEAR ABRAMOVÁ (6)

The lonely church situated in the open space near the village of Abramová is a jewel of the landscape southwest of Turiec. The church is consecrated to St. Cosmas and St Damian and was built in the Gothic style in 1375. The interior is mainly Baroque and houses an historical organ. The spire was not added until the 20th century.

meetings here during the estate uprisings in the 17th century. A secret gathering of supporters of the palatine František Vešeléni (Wesselényi) who were planning the uprising took place here in 1666. The present-day spa complex consists mainly of modern buildings, an exception being the historical Modrý Kúpeľ building from 1885. This Neo-Classicism dome-shaped building creates a sharp contrast with the straight-edged forms of the buildings dating from the second half of the 20th century. The famous Slovakian painter M. Galanda (1895 – 1938) was born in the town and there is a gallery in his childhood home. Another attraction of this spa town is its aqua park.

## KĽAK (3)

The German settlers of the 14th century gave the Kľak Mountain (1,352 m) in the southwest tip of the Lesser Fatra Mountains a suitable name; they called it *Nasenstein*, i.e. the Stone Nose after its crooked sharp rocky top. Comparing this hill with the Kriváň Mountain is also apt as Kriváň is similarly jagged. The particular shape of Kľak is due to its geological formation. The top part is created by layers of the Mesozoic dolomite. The less steep side of the rock was formed in the direction of the layers while its steep slope was created at their front. The trail to Kľak from the Vrícko direction passes by the 30-metre-high Kľacký Waterfall and the peak offers magnificent views. Slightly below the peak are remains of a derelict chalet. The memorial plaque on a nearby rock commemorates the airdrop of Soviet soldiers just before Christmas 1944 who came to support the Slovakian National Uprising.

## ZNIEV CASTLE (4)

In terms of altitude, at 988 m Zniev Castle is among the highest castles in Slovakia. Historical sources record the existence of a fortification called the Castrum Turucz (the Turiec Fort) at this site back in the 11th century. It was rebuilt in stone in the mid 13th century; from which time a quadrant tower has been preserved. The castle was the seat of Turiec county council until the 14th century when it was moved to Sklabiňa Castle. Afterwards the importance of Zniev Castle waned. It belonged to the Premonstratensians from Kláštor pod Znievom who used it to store the archives of the Turiec convent. Like the county council, the archives were also moved to Sklabiňa Castle in the 17th century. The castle was damaged by the Kuruc soldiers who looted and burnt the castle twice. The demanding trek up to the castle is rewarded by the wonderful view of the almost entire Turiec region.

## VYŠEHRAD (5)

The name Vyšehrad (Higher Castle, 829 m) indicates that there was once a castle on the rocky peak in the Žiar Mountains. There was an old Slav settlement at this strategic point between the 8th and 11th centuries. According to the old legend of the White Lady of Vyšehrad, the castle was ruled by a man called Velen who promised the hand of marriage of his beautiful daughter Belana to the man who could dig a well at the castle. A young man called Milot from the nearby settlement on Zniev started with the task while another suitor called Sebeľub preferred to spend his time court-

## SLOVAKIAN GRAMMAR SCHOOL IN KLÁŠTOR POD ZNIEVOM (1)

The Kláštor pod Znievom is historically a very important seat of Turiec for two reasons. A monastery was founded here in the early Middle Ages by the Benedictine monks from Zobor attempting to colonise the Turiec, Orava and Liptov counties. Secondly, the town found its way into history books because it had one of the first three Slovakian grammar schools. The school here was founded in 1869 and like the other two original grammar schools in Revúca and Martin, it was financed by funds from a patriotic charity. The spiritual father

and the director of the grammar school in Kláštor pod Znievom was Martin Čulen. Although it was closed down in 1874, the school played a very important role in promoting national consciousness throughout northern Slovakia. The historical building of the school still stands on the village's main street.

## TURČIANSKE TEPLICE SPA (2)

The first spa buildings in Turčianske Teplice were built way back in 1532 when the land was owned by the mining town of Kremnica. The Hungarian aristocracy rebelling against the Habsburgs held

ing the lovely girl. Milot's effort was successful and he ran to show the first goblet of water to the princes only to find her in the arms of his rival. He angrily cursed the lovers who then fell into the mountain. From that time White Lady, the unhappy Belana, haunts Vyšehrad begging in vain for forgiveness.

## MANSIONS IN DIVIAKY (6)

The village of Diviaky (Wild Boar) was incorporated into the town of Turčianske Teplice of which it is now a part. According to a legend, a certain Blažej of Blatnice fought with a huge wild boar and as a reward for killing the beast he was given a large estate. The village that Blažej founded was named Diviaky in celebration of the event. Indeed, the legend is older than the two beautiful mansions in the village. The older dates from the 17th century and is remarkable for its splendid Renaissance style. It now houses the Slovakian National Library. The younger mansion from the second half of the 18th century is a fine example of Rococo and partially Classicism styles.

## TURIEC RIVER (7)

The river Turiec flows through the entire Turiec region. It rises below Flochová in the Kremnické Vrchy Hills and flows into the Váh at Vrútky after a journey of 66 kilometres. There are long stretches on the river's course on her way where its natural unregulated state has been preserved. Other Slovakian rivers also looked like this in the past. Official data about the length of the river is probably not very accurate as the river coils and zigzags into numerous meanders. The most beautiful part of the river is between the villages of Moškovec and Raková. You can find magical places in the shade of the willow trees on the banks.

### MANSION IN MOŠOVCE (1)

The small town of Mošovce at the southeast of the Turčianska Kotlina Hollow was once a prosperous place with famous craft production. This town with a number of monuments boasts a fine Baroque-Rococo mansion from the second half of the 18th century. The mansion is in a large English-style park with a mausoleum from 1911. The building with the Art Nouveau and New-Gothic elements now houses the Museum of Mošov Craftsmen. The statue in the small garden outside the mansion commemorates Ján Kollár (1793-1852), who was born in Mošovce. An exposition dedicated to this artist, the Museum of Ján Kollár, is located in a former granary near the site of his birthplace.

### MUSEUM OF K. PLICKA IN BLATNICA (2)

The village of Blatnica in the Turiec region witnessed the birth of Slovakian cinematography. The first Slovakian movie called Jánošík was made here by American filmmakers of Slovak origin Daniel and Jaroslav Siakeľs who chose their native village as the set for its beautiful surroundings. Many inhabitants got a role in the film and the premiere of this silent Slovakian movie was shown on 3rd January 1923. There is an interesting exposition of the Slovakian National Museum in the village's Baroque-Classicism mansion from the mid-18th century. The mansion houses a collection presenting the life and work of the prominent photographer, filmmaker and ethno-

grapher Karol Plicko (1894 – 1987). The exposition was opened in 1988.

### BLATNICA CASTLE (3)

Blatnica Castle is situated in a very interesting location. From one side of the castle walls there is a nice view of the entire Turčianska Kotlina Valley, while on the other side, there is a splendid view of the Gaderská Dolina Valley which takes a sharp 90-degree turn just below the castle. The castle was built in the mid-13th century to protect the trade route that connected Turiec and Nitra counties and was a possession of the king. However when trade shifted to a new route further west, the castle lost its significance and the king passed it to the

nobility. The powerful family of Révaj (Révay) took ownership of the castle in the 16th century and built a settlement below its walls. The troubled times of the estate uprising did not spare the castle and it was damaged during the second half of the 17th and at the beginning of the 18th centuries. The derelict building was repaired in 1744, nevertheless the castle was abandoned after 1790. The ruin is accessible to the public tough it is rather dangerous due to its ruinous state.

### TLSTÁ AND OSTRÁ (4)

The Tlstá (Fat) and Ostrá (Sharp) mountains differ greatly from each other. They both have similar geological formation; both hills were created on a romain of the Mesozoic sheet and both are formed of dolomite and limestone. The biggest difference between the two is pretty clear from their names. When viewed from the valley below, the left hill, the Fat (1,373 m), is a wide massif with typical rock galleries at the top. The slightly lower Sharp (1,247 m) boasts a slim silhouette ending in a short tip of a rock. The popular Chodník Janka Bojmíra trail leads to the top of the Tlstá Mountain. The trail is named after the great promoter and admirer of the nature in the Turiec area and keen organiser of tourism in the region.

### GADERSKÁ AND BLATNICKÁ DOLINA (5)

The Gaderská and Blatnická valleys in the Greater Fatra Mountains are an inseparable couple of this area. Both meet just before the beginning of the Turčianska Kotlina Hollow near the popular recreation cottage area of Gader near Blatnica. There is a nice, easy climb through Gaderská Dolina which coils around the Tlstá Hill from the north, to the main crest of the mountain range in the Kráľova Well. The central part called Dedošova Dolina Valley is the most interesting part of the 18-kilometre long gorge. It is full of rock formations, small waterfalls, huge pots and lush greenery and is considered to have some of the most splendid natural scenery in Slovakia. The Vlkanová Dolina Valley is similarly charming. Tourists usually climb to the viewing hill called Drienok.

### BORIŠOV (6)

Tourists frequently turn off the popular Greater Fatra Ridgeway to relax or spend a night at the favourite Chata pod Borišovom Chalet. If you walk to this mountain chalet located in a splendid spot in a meadow of the slope you will not be able to resist climbing up Borišov Peak (1,510 m), which boasts lovely mountain scenery. The climb up to this landmark peak in the centre of the mountain range is rewarded by stunning views.

### KRÁĽOVA STUDŇA (7)

The crossroads of tourist trails in the southern part of the Greater Fatra Mountains at Kráľova Studňa is an important point, as tourist trails from five directions meet here. This charming place was named after a local spring (well) that was once used by sheep and cattle grazing on bare plains typical for the highest part of the Greater Fatra. An eye-catching rock looms above the crossroads. It is called Kráľova Rock (1,377 m). There is a mountain hotel, on the bare south-facing slope, which is a great gateway to the popular Ridgeway trek through the Greater Fatra Mountains.

## ORAVA

### BABIA HORA (1)

This giant mountain is called the queen of the Orava Region and the mother of its inhabitants. It lies at the Polish border and is the highest peak (1,729 m) in the Slovakian mountains of the flysch rock origin. It has a smaller neighbour at the western side – Malá (Small) Babia Hora (1,615 m). Most tourists climb the mountain from the Polish side; the traditional Slovakian trek from the Slaná Voda Gamekeeper's lodge is a Nature Trail. The climb is demanding, however it is rewarded by a fantastic panoramic view on a fine day.

### HVIEZDOSLAVOVA LODGE (2)

The story of the famous epic poem Wife of the Gamekeeper by the poet Hviezdoslav is set in a gamekeeper's lodge in the village of Rovne at the southern foothills of Babia Hora, hence the name of the lodge. An alley between the house and the Slaná Voda Chalet also bears the name of the famous Oravian bard. There is an exhibiti-on about the life and work of the famous Slova-kian writer Milan Urban, who lived, for some time, in the house next to the lodge. Near by is a Nature Trail, which is the most popular trek to the Babia Hora.

### SLANÁ VODA (3)

The locals knew the salty water from the springs near the village of Oravská Polhora by the Medie-val Ages and used it instead of salt. That is why

they called the place with the springs Slaná Voda (Salted Water – for this mineralized water has a very salty taste). The water from the spring once poured into a stream making the stream salty as well, just as the lower situated Polhoranka River. The name of one of the local villages, Slanica, is also connected with salt. Warm baths were established near the springs in 1865. They received the name of the nearby village of Polhorany and quickly became popular. Towards the end of the 19th century, hundreds of people were staying in the spa. The spa was even compared to the world-renowned salt spa near Florence, Italy. However, the fame of the spa faded at the end of World War I. The derelict buildings were not restored and only a tourist chalet called Slaná Voda reminds us of the former spa.

## PEAT BOGS NEAR MÚTNE (4)

Orava is a landscape of rough beauty and typically has a cold climate. Moreover, it is also rather wet and thus has excellent conditions for peat bogs. No other place in the whole of Slovakia can boast as much peat as Orava. At first glance, the peat bogs resemble those in the Siberian taiga. Specific vegetation grows on the flat swamps where water stands, including alder trees and several rare flora species. The Dolina Zlatného Potoka Valley near Mútne provides an excellent opportunity to see the bogs. The tourist trail passes two peat bogs; the higher one is called Spálený Grúnik and the other, located very near the village, Mútňanská Píla.

## VODNÁ NÁDRŽ ORAVA (5)

This lake is called the Orava Sea as it is one of the largest water reservoirs in Slovakia. The first project about a dam that would deal with the traditional problem of frequent floods on the Orava River was done as early as in 1830. Its wooden model was exhibited in the Orava Castle until recently. However, the daring idea had to wait more than 100 years before it was realized. The construction works of the dam started in 1941 and were finally completed twelve years later. The water flooded an area of over 33 square kilometres, displacing 3,200 people from their homes in the fully or partially flooded villages. The area of the town of Námestovo was decreased as it ended on the bank of the huge artificial lake.

## SLANICA ISLAND (6)

The construction of the Orava Lake rang, as they say, the death bell for some villages. It ended, among other things, the existence of the Slanica village, the native place of the famous national revivalist Anton Bernolák in 1762. Only a Baroque church was left, for it was on the top of a hill where the water could not reach. The piece of dry land with the church is now called Slanica Island. It was quite fittingly nicknamed the 'Island of Art' as the church no longer serves its original purpose but houses exhibitions of the Oravská Gallery in Dolný Kubín. There is a nice exhibition of valuable stone folk sculptures outside the church.

## CHURCH OF ST. ANNA
## IN ORAVSKÁ LESNÁ (7)

There is an interesting church in the remote village of Oravská Lesná in the picturesque landscape on the border of the Orava and Kysuce regions. It is remarkable not for its age but for its attractive Art Nouveau appearance. The church for the Roman Catholic worshipers started to be build in 1910 on the initiative of the vicar Štefan Moheľ and was finished four years later. A lot of wooden elements were used on the very attractive façade. The length of this one-nave building is 37 metres, exactly the same as the height of the church spire. The rather large interior can accommodate 2,200 worshipers, 500 of them seated. The altars come from an old church and some of them were brought from as far as Tyrol. The wooden carved chandeliers in the interior from the workshop of the local woodcarver Rudolf Svinčák are noteworthy

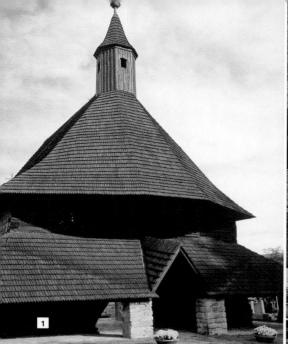

## WOODEN CHURCH IN TVRDOŠÍN (1)

The wooden church in the village of Tvrdošín nestled impressively in the greenery of a cemetery is a unique sacral monument in Slovakia. It rates among the oldest churches in Slovakia and was probably build in the second half of the 15th century. It belonged to the Evangelists in the mid-17th century, however was later returned to the Roman Catholic worshipers whom it serves even today. The large shingle roof and a small hexagonal spire is a landmark of the building. Its interior is mainly Baroque. There once was a Gothic wooden altar; it was replaced with a Baroque altar after 1768. Only one wing with a painting of St. Peter and St. John the Baptist is preserved from the Gothic altar. Its central part was moved to a museum in Budapest.

## VERNACULAR BUILDINGS IN PODBIEL (2)

A group of wooden peasant buildings lies directly at the main road in the village of Podbiel in the Orava Region. It was designated a Folk Architecture Monument Reserve in 1977. It is situated in the locality of Bobrová Roľa and consists of 74 wooden cottages from the 19th and 20th centuries. It is one of the largest groups of rustic buildings in central Europe. Several buildings are used as recreational cottages.

## ORAVICE TOURIST CENTRE (3)

The significant Oravice tourist centre in the close vicinity of the Polish border is on the site of the former Oravická Bystrá village, which was founded in the 16th century. Although located in the northern foothills of the Roháče Mountains, Oravice is a popular gateway for attractive mountain treks, a ski centre and a well-liked thermal spa. A geothermal spring discovered before World War II made Oravice attractive, offering year-round swimming in thermal pools. Most visitors come from Poland.

## FRANTIŠKOVA SMELTERY NEAR PODBIEL (4)

The remains of the historical smelting works are by the road from Podbiel to Roháče. The smeltery was constructed in 1836 as an industrial pioneer work in the Orava Region. However, the success of this project was threatened by the lower quality of the iron ore transported from surrounding deposits. The produced iron was fragile and therefore was not very popular. This caused the closing down of the iron works in 1863 and the factory ceased to exist. Today a torso of the hammer mill can be seen near Podbiel as well as the inlet and outlet canal, chamber, factory hall and a blast furnace. A reconstruction of Františkova smeltery started in 1972. Thanks to the great effort of volunteers,' there are exhibitions of historical iron ore melting during the popular Iron Days at the end of August.

## JURÁŇOVA DOLINA (5)

The Juráňov Creek, which collects water from the northern slopes of the Roháče Mountains, eroded a valley called Juráňova Dolina, finding a way through the lower part of the range of resistant limestone and dolomite rock via an extremely narrow chasm. The creek carved bizarre rock formations into the tough rock. The giant potholes created by gurgling water are especially of interest. A path for wood transport once led through the attractive part of this area, called Tiesňavy. Only wooden poles that supported an original wooden gutter remained. A tourist trail goes along the western side of Tiesnavy which is part of a Nature Trail.

## MUSEUM ORAVSKEJ DEDINY NEAR ZUBEREC (6)

Thanks to its attractive location at the foothills of the Roháče Mountains this interesting open-air museum is one of the most beautiful sights in Slovakia. It was opened in the Brestová locality near Zuberec in 1975. Peasant buildings from the entire Orava area were organised to resemble a typical 19th-century village from this region. A mill and a scrubbing-board were placed on a mountain creek. The wooden church from the 15th century was brought from the village of Zábrežie.

## PLAČLIVÉ AND OSTRÝ ROHÁČ (1)

There are a couple of sharp neighbouring mountains in the rocky main ridge of the Západné Tatry (Western Tatras) on the border of the Orava and Liptov regions. The more western is the Plačlivé Peak (2,126 m) while its eastern neighbour is called Ostrý Roháč (2,087 m). The pair of peaks creates a typical silhouette resembling a devil's horns, which gave the name to the western part of the mountain range, Roháče (Horns). A trek along the crest climbing both peaks is a worthy alpinism tour. The more demanding parts must be managed via chains and iron footrests.

## BANÍKOV (2)

The massive Baníkov (2,178 m) is not the highest peak of the Western Tatras. It rates the fourth amongst the giants of these mountains. However, it holds two first positions: it is the highest peak in the main ridge as well as in the entire Orava Region territory. The name of the peak (Mining) suggests that iron ore was mined in the area in the past. Baníkov can be accessed by trails from three sides and offers a fine panoramic view. The most popular and easiest trail goes from the western Baníkovské Sedlo mountain saddle. The trail from the opposite direction (from Smutné Sedlo at the east) is much more challenging, with difficult chain-secured sections.

## ROHÁČSKE VODOPÁDY (3)

The water of a mountain creek falls over the rocky cascades of Roháčske waterfalls above the end of the Spálená Dolina Valley just before the main Roháčska Dolina Valley. The largest waterfall in the area is 18 metres high and is an attractive stop on the way along the Nature Trail towards the Roháčske Plesá Tarns.

## SIVÝ VRCH (4)

This mountain (1,805 m) is a grand end to the Ridgeway of the Western Tatras Mountains. The most western peak of the range is different than its western neighbours. It is made of limestone and dolomite while most of the rocks in Roháče are granite and schist. Thanks to its rocky top and regular cone-like silhouette Sivý Vrch is considered one of the most beautiful mountains in Slovakia. The rocks on the top create a fascinating 'rock town' with bizarre shapes. It is a National Nature Reserve.

## ROHÁČSKE PLESÁ (5)

The area of Roháče was once covered by icebergs. The largest one filled up the extensive valley called Roháčska Dolina. It was 12 kilometres long and 200 metres deep and after it melted, small lakes remained in the holes it created. They are called plesá (tarns). Four tarns on the rocky edge now adorn the splendid landscape of Roháče. The largest (2,22 ha) and lowest (1,562 m) tarn is plesá Prvé Roháčske Pleso. The highest tarn (1,719) is called the Štvrté Roháčske Pleso. A Nature Trail leads to the tarns.

### ORAVSKÝ CASTLE (1)

Since the oldest times, the lords of Orava controlled their extensive estate from Oravský Castle. The site on which the medieval builders chose to build the castle is amazing. The position and building of the castle is dramatic mainly when looking from the north. Originally there was a small wooden construction that was replaced by a stone castle after an Ottoman attack. The castle became the seat of the Orava County Council and its rulers. The wealthy Thurzo family, who received the castle in 1556, were responsible for its largest reconstructions. The castle burnt down in 1800 and was left to become derelict, however a large reconstruction after World War II restored its appearance from 1611. Today Oravský Castle is an attractive exposition of the Oravské Museum and is the most visited monument in the whole of the Orava Region.

### ORAVA RIVER (2)

The historic Orava Region is united by a river of the same name. Its right tributary, the 112-kilometre long Váh River, collects waters from a territory partially located in Poland. The Orava River has two sources, Biela Orava and Čierna Orava which once had the confluence on the site which is now on the bottom of the Oravská Priehrada Dam. In its central part the Orava flows through picturesque landscape decorated by numerous limestone rocks. Tourists can raft on the river and admire its beauty in the summer season. A narrow chasm on the Orava just above the Váh tributary, which can also be managed by a raft, is an impressive tourists attraction.

### MANSION IN HORNÁ LEHOTA (3)

One of the raft ports on the Orava River is near a Renaissance mansion in the village of Horná Lehota. The nicely reconstructed historical monument with corner towers is associated with the old aristocratic family of Abafi (Abaffy) and was built in the first half of the 16th century. It is considered the most northern historical monument influenced by the Italian Renaissance in the world.

### ORAVSKÁ GALLERY IN DOLNÝ KUBÍN (4)

The town of Dolný Kubín is the metropolis of the Orava Region. Its history reaches back to the 14th century and although it did not have the Free Royal Town status and was under the rule of the lords of Oravský Castle, it prospered greatly thanks to several privileges. The development of the town was strongly supported by a decision in 1683 when it became the seat of the Orava County Council, which received a stately building towards the end of the 17th century. The remarkable building on the central square, now called Hviezdoslavovo Námestie, was enlarged and reconstructed in the Baroque style in 1758. A sandstone coat-of-arms of the county from the 18th century on the main façade is reminiscent of its original purpose. Today, it is the seat of the Oravská Gallery which curates over 7,000 art pieces documenting art development in Orava from the 15th century up to the present. There is also an interesting exposition of the local painter M. Medvecká.

### ČAPLOVIČOVA LIBRARY
### IN DOLNÝ KUBÍN (5)

The Čaplovičova Library lies in the southern section of the Hviezdoslavovo Námestie Square, which is impressively complemented by the silhouette of the mountain Veľký Choč. It was built in 1911 to store the historical scientific library founded in 1839, thanks to the all-life-effort of V. Čaplovič. The collection, given to the Orava County Council by Čaplovič, has around 45,000 titles in total, including books, newspapers, magazines, maps, pieces of music as well as precious manuscripts, graphics and engravings. Collections of articles related to astronomy, medicine, numismatics, mineralogy and palaeontology from Čaplovič's travels around Europe are also part of the library. The building also houses the Oravské Museum of P. O. Hviezdoslav, which manages the library. There is a statue of this national bard in a small park outside the building.

### WOODEN BRIDGE
### IN DOLNÝ KUBÍN (6)

The historic part of the town sprawls on the left bank of the Orava. When the city spread to the right bank of the river in the second half of the 20th century, a new pedestrian bridge was needed. The wooden colonnade bridge over the Orava is part of the pedestrian zone which connects the centre of the town with the Bysterec housing estate.

## VYŠNÝ KUBÍN (1)

This town below the majestic peak of Veľký Choč is known mainly as the native place of the greatest Slovakian poet P. O. Hviezdoslav (1849-1921). This cult poet, who mainly celebrated the beauty of Orava was born into an impoverished yeomen family. A monument commemorates his birth house, which burnt down. The tomb of the poet is at the cemetery in Dolný Kubín. Vyšný Kubín is a town of rich yeomen tradition and boasts several preserved manor houses. The older 17th century Renaissance mansion is next to the main road. The second mansion from the 18th century, of the Kubíni (Kubínyi) family, is inside the village. There are several others as well.

## OSTRÁ AND TUPÁ (2)

A couple of rocky peaks loom above Vyšný Kubín opposite the Veľký Choč Mountain. The peak on the right side finished off by a sharp peak is called Ostrá Skala (813 m), while to the left is the lower and wider Tupá Skala Peak. Both limestone rocks are protected. Ostrá features interesting small caves, and a mound that once protected an ancient settlement of the Púchovská Culture was discovered on its top. Another settlement, of the people of the Lužická Culture from the Lower Bronze Age, was discovered on Tupá Skala.

## WOODEN CHURCH IN LEŠTINY (3)

Only two buildings are preserved from several wooden Evangelic churches in the Orava area. One of them is in the village of Leštiny at the northern foothills of the peak Veľký Choč. The Evangelists in Orava had strong support from the Thurzo family of Oravský Castle in the 16th century. The Zmeškalec family built the wooden church in Leštiny towards the end of the 16th century. Its historical value is remarkable for it has been preserved without any significant changes to its architecture. The simple shrine was built in a steep slope and bears the typical signs of the articular churches – it has no spire or bells; a belfry was added a hundred years later as an independent wooden building. The simple exterior sharply contrasts with a richly decorated interior remarkable for the colourfulness and variety of decorations.

## MEMORIAL HOUSE TO MARTIN KUKUČÍN IN JASENOVÁ (4)

Orava has bred scores of important personalities, mainly in the area of Slovakian literature. Apart from the poets Hviezdoslav and Bernolák, the writer Kukučín (1860 – 1928) was also born in the region. In contrast with the native house of Hviezdoslav, Kukučín's native house has been preserved. It is in the village of Jasanová, away from the main road from Dolný Kubín to Ružomberok. The Memorial House to Martin Kukučín was opened in this wooden farm from the 19th century. It offers a great opportunity to learn about the life and work of this prominent personage of the Realism style in Slovakian literature.

## WOODEN CHURCH IN ISTEBNÉ (5)

This wooden Evangelic church from the 18th century is at the top end of the village of Istebné. The impressive building from dark wood is harmoni-

cally complemented by a group of old linden trees. The construction of the church was approved in 1686; however it was not finished until 1731. The builders of the church adhered to the so-called articulas (deliberations of the Sopron Congress, which allowed for followers to erect and maintain churches within the Emperor's dominions). The simple building without a tower stands in a sloppy terrain. A wooden construction with the cross ground-plan stands on a stone basis with several crypts; a shingle roof covers the church.

### VEĽKÝ CHOČ (6)
This grandiose mountain (1,611 m) is shared between the Orava and Liptov regions. Inhabitants of both areas consider this peak in the Chočské Vrchy Hills to be their symbol and it has always played the role of their reliable guard and protector. Observed from anywhere, Choč's silhouette with the rocky peak is an outstanding sight. It was formed from Mesozoic dolomite and limestone. The entire geological unit (Chočský príkrov) was named after the peak. The top of the mountain offers a fantastic view; a great deal of Slovakia is visible on a fine day.

### PODŠÍP (7)
This rocky mountain (1,169 m) adorns the picturesque landscape on the border of Orava and Liptov. Its silhouette is beautifully reflected on the surface of the Váh River above the village of Kraľovany, the only village of Orava which is the gate to the region at the Váh. The slopes of the hill with white coloured rocks look as if they have been sprinkled with sugar and descend onto a smallish meadow plateau on the west side. Rocks called Šípske create impressive scenery for the mountainous village of Podšíp, with a unique group of wooden vernacular houses. Part of these original buildings was preserved only thanks to the effort of volunteers. The landscape at Podšíp opens towards the west.

# LIPTOV

### CHURCH OF ST. ANDREW
### IN RUŽOMBEROK (1)

The grandiose Roman-Catholic Church of St. Andrew is a landmark of the Námestie Andreja Hlinku Square which was built on the spot where Germans founded a settlement called Rosenberg in the Middle Ages. The Late Gothic church was built in 1585 on the site of an older sacral edifice from the 14th century. Part of the older church was probably incorporated into the walls of the new bulding. The interior of the church houses a Late Gothic baptismal font from the 16th century. Glass window-panes by Ľ. Fulla are also noteworthy. The church's Neo Gothic spire houses the oldest bell in Liptov. It is called Andreas and was produced by the workshop of the bell-founder A. Sladič from Banská Bystrica in 1585.

### RUŽOMBERSKÉ STAIRS (2)

Six grandiose staircases lead from the Námestie Andreja Hlinku Square in Ružomberok to the lower part of the town. The staircases have 579 steps in total and are called: Školské schody, Tmavé schody, Ružové schody (to Mostová Street), Stairs in Severná Ulička and Kláštorné schody. The Školské stairs with 155 steps are the longest.

### MAUSOLEUM TO A. HLINKA
### IN RUŽOMBEROK (3)

The Mausoleum is beneath the south nave of the Church of St. Andrew; however it is now only a symbolic pieta site. It represents a distinguished memorial to the priest and politician Andrej Hlinka (1864-1938), who was a remarkable personage in modern Slovakian history. His life is closely connected with Ružomberok, where he lived and worked until 1905. After he died at the local parish in 1938, he was buried in a Jesuit crypt and was later (in 1941) moved into the mausoleum designed by J. Švidroň. Before the arrival of the Red Army, however, his relics were moved once again, hidden in a secret place, and have not yet been returned to the mausoleum; the hiding place is known only amongst the privileged circles.

### VLKOLÍNEC (4)

The impressive group of wooden peasant buildings south of Ružomberok looks like an open-air museum, set in the carefully selected gorgeous natural setting of the northern section of the Greater Fatra Mountains. Nonetheless, Vlkolínec is not a museum, but rather a normal village with permanent inhabitants. It consists of a group of 45 wooden vernacular buildings located in a remarkable natural environment. One main and one side street that lead through the village are flanked with wooden buildings. There is also a wooden belfry (1770) on a small square and the 1875-built Malý Church on the edge of the village. One of the wooden cottages houses a detached exposition of the Liptovské Museum in Ružomberok. Vlkolínec was added to the UNESCO World Culture Heritage List in 1993 and it is also a Folk Architecture Monument Reserve.

4

## ĽUBOCHŇA (1)

Ľubochňa is hidden in the greenery of a park at the opening into the long Ľubochnianská Dolina Valley in the chasm of the Váh River between the towns of Ružomberok and Kraľovany. Originally, it was a settlement on the estate of the Likava Castle and a centre of the raft transport of wood along the Váh. A hydrotherapy centre was built here at the end of the 19th century. It became the first spa centre specialising in heart diseases. Count A.Bethlen supported the development of the spa to a great extent. He was also behind the building of Tatranská Lomnice, which is apparent from the parallel between the architectural styles of these two localities. A nice example is the log-built Kolárov House, which has found its way into the history books as it was the site of the meeting held on 16th January 1921 by the Marxism Social Democratic party, which supported the Communist Manifesto.

## JÁNOŠÍKOVA TAVERN IN VALASKÁ DUBOVÁ (2)

According to a legend about Juraj Jánošík, a legendary outlaw who robbed the rich and gave to the poor, he was caught only thanks to treachery. Supposedly it happened in a tavern in Valaská Dubová below the majestic Choč Mountain. Jánošík even managed to get free of the Pandur soldiers but was recaptured after slipping on some spilled peas, thrown in his way by a treacherous old lady. The tavern no longer exists, however a new one was built on its site in the 19th century. It now offers accommodation and runs a restaurant called Jánošíkova Krčma. Tourists visit Valaská Dubová mainly because of this nice memorial to the folk legend.

## ROJKOVSKÁ TRAVERTINE (3)

A visit to the nearby village of Rojkov in a valley of the Váh River near Ľubochňa offers impressive natural scenery. The surface of a round pond (10 metres in perimeter) located on a meadow above the village beautifully reflects the nearby Šíp Hill with its peak dotted by white limestone rocks. The pond with mineralized plaster water was created by the toppling of the Rojkovská travertine mound protected as a Natural Monument. Another interesting natural monument, the Rojkovské Moor, is nearby. It is a Protected Nature Reserve.

## LIKAVA CASTLE (4)

This castle 'attached' to the steep southern slope of the Veľký Choč Mountain was once one of the powerful centres of Liptov. It was built as a sentry castle on the trade path leading through the Orava Region to Poland in the 14th century. Originally a royal asset, it later became the seat of the Head of the Liptov County Council at the end of the 14th century. The castle was considered a luxurious palace in the 16th century for it had several paned windows with glass from the glass works in Ľubochňa. It served as a seat of the Tököli (Tököly) family in the 17th century, however it was later conquered by the Emperor's army for the participation of its then owner in the Vešeléni (Wesselényi) Uprising in 1670. For some time the castle was used as a county prison. Poet S. Chalupka in his poem Likavský Väzeň (prisoner) placed Juraj Jánošík in this prison. However, this is only fictional, as the castle was ruined six years before Jánošík was beheaded. The fate of Likava Castle was sealed by Francis II Rákoci (Rákoczi), who ordered its demolition.

## JÁNOŠÍKOVA PÄSŤ AND LISKOVSKÁ JASKYŇA (5)

A sharp rock is nestled below the steep slope of the forested hill called Mních near Ružomberok. As it resembles a human hand, it is called Jánošíkova Päsť (Fist). However, this natural monument enveloped in legends has rather prosaic origins. It was created by erosion that separated it from a limestone massif, which houses a cave Liskovská jaskyňa. It lies in a smallish hill and its corridors measure more than 4 kilometres. It became very famous in 1874 due to a great discovery of the remains of a prehistoric man, most probably the Neanderthal Man.

## CHURCH OF ST. MARTIN IN MARTINČEK (6)

One of the oldest churches in Liptov is in the village of Martinček near Ružomberok. It is visible from the road from Ružomberok to Liptovský Mikuláš in a crack between two hills. The history of this Early Gothic church consecrated to St. Martin goes back to the 13th century. According to an old legend, it was built by the Knight Templars from a monastery that once stood on the nearby Mních Hill. The hero of the legend is a knight, Johan Gottfried de Herbestein, who helped merchants attacked by highwaymen. He died in an uneven fight and was buried in the nearest stone church, which allegedly was the small church in Martinček. The presence of this mysterious Knight Order in Liptov has not been confirmed though. The church on a hill above Martinček is decorated with splendid medieval murals.

## CHURCH OF ALL SAINTS
### NEAR LUDROVÁ (1)

The ancient Church of All Saints stands in the middle of the fields on the way from Ludrová to Ružomberok. The significance of this valuable historical and cultural monument dating from the 13th century reaches beyond the Liptov Region. The building protected by fortification walls has preserved Romanesque and Gothic architectonical elements. The most important is the interior. The walls were painted by an unknown artist around 1420. The murals depict a remarkable Christological Cycle, which is the most extensive work of this type in Slovakia. It consists of 34 scenes form the life of Jesus Christ. The Bible motifs and the consecration cross are also noteworthy. There is a fragment of fresco on the eastern wall which depicts St. Christopher, and is believed to have miraculous powers; the first worshipper who sees it will become immortal. The lines on the entry portals are also legendary. They were made by the swords of nobles and one of them is supposed to have been carved by the Polish King Ján Sobieský, who stopped here on his way from the victorious battle above the Ottomans near Vienna.

## LUDROVSKÁ DOLINA (2)

The natural features in this valley in the western part of Nízke Tatry (Low Tatras) were named in symbiosis with the character of the place. There is a karst 19-metre deep gorge called Snežná Jama (Snow Hole) for it was used as a natural fridge in which to store delicious local sheep cheese. The water of a creek zigzagging between rocks in the lay-by small valley below Salatín roared and gave this narrow rocky chasm its name of Hučiaky (Roaring). The creek which flows on the bottom of Hučiaky is very cold as it comes from the karst underground and is shaded by the rocks of the deep chasm. It has received the well-fitting name Mraznica (Freezer). These natural wonders in Ludrovská Dolina attract many tourists.

## SALATÍN (3)

This proud mountain (1,630 m) looms above the mountainous landscape at the northeast of the Low Tatras. This conspicuous cone-shape peak was formed by limestone with numerous karst formations. There are bizarre rock formations, narrow chasms and abysses. The underground world of caves is also rich. A forest, almost untouched by man, lies in the poorly accessible terrain on the slopes of Salatín. Mainly oak, fir and maple trees

grow here. A National Nature Reserve on 1,193 hectares protects the valuable nature of the mountain. The top of the mountain offers splendid panoramic views and is a popular tourist destination.

## KORYTNICA SPA (4)

This spa town lies in the splendid scenery of the most western part of the Nízké Tatry National Park. It was founded near mineral springs discovered in the 16th century. The water is bottled and sold as a popular table mineral water called Korytnická. It cures digestive illnesses and liver problems. The village was once called Medokýš. Gold was mined in its surroundings towards the end of the 18th century. And a narrow-gouge railway, called Korýtka by the locals, began operation here in 1908. Trains pulled by a steam engine operated on the 24-kilometre long track from Ružomberok, however the railway no longer exists. Moreover, Korytnica is also a tourist centre with an excellent location below the ridge of the Prašivá Mountain in the western part of the Low Tatras.

## LIPTOVSKÁ LÚŽNA (5)

This interesting village is situated in the middle of a small picturesque hollow below the ridge of the Mountain Prašivá in the most western part of the

Low Tatras. It was founded in 1669 by Štefan Tököli (Tököly) on his Likava estate, and he also invited highlanders from the Orava Region to inhabit it. A visit to this 6-kilometre long mountain valley is a great opportunity to see the peculiar vernacular architecture with authentic and still living folklore; some inhabitants still wear the traditional costumes. The renowned photographer, filmmaker and folklorist Karol Plicko was charmed by the attractive landscape and colourful folk traditions of Liptovská Lúžna.

## BRANKOVSKÝ VODOPÁD (6)

If you would like to see the highest waterfall in the Low Tatras, you must climb to the Veľký Brankov massif in the most western part of this mountain range. The waters of Brankovský Vodopád fall over the limestone and limestone schist rock tables on the western side of the massif. The awe-inspiring waterfall is 55 metres high and rates amongst the highest in Slovakia. It has a rather stabile flow (approximately 3 litres per second). It has been protected since 1980 and it is now a National Nature Monument. At the same time, it is among the five most remarkable Slovakian waterfalls in the category of the most important natural heritage of the country.

## RAKYTOV (1)

Rakytov (1,567 m) is the most dominant peak, the fourth highest in the Liptov branch of the Greater Fatra. Its cone top towers above its surroundings. It is considered the best viewing point in the Greater Fatra for its location in the centre of the range. There is a cross and a viewing rose on the top of the mountain. It can be difficult to climb it in the winter, as its steep slopes are under threat of an avalanche. The most convenient trail to the Rakytov peak is from the Smrekovica Hotel.

## ČIERNY KAMEŇ (2)

This is certainly one of the most photographed mountains (1,479 m) in the Greater Fatra. Although not the highest (it holds the tenth position), it is certainly one of the most beautiful peaks. The popular Greater Fatra Ridgeway does not go over its peak, as the nature of its rocky peak has rare flora and fauna and is strictly protected in a National Reserve. However, that does not matter as Čierny Kameň is splendid mainly from the tourist trail that skirts its western foothills. The dolomite and limestone peak is imposing and extremely photogenic. The denuded sections are of interest from a geological point of view.

## OSTREDOK (3)

The massive Greater Fatra mountain range culminates at its highest peak, called Ostredok (1,592 m). It is in the southern part with only one high main ridge. It is rather inconspicuous as surrounded by only slightly lower mountains with wide round shapes. Ostredok belongs to the section called Hôľna Fatra. High above the high border of the forest is a rough and beautiful landscape of alpine meadows called 'holy'. The slopes of Ostredok and neighbouring Křížna Mountain are overgrown with grassy vegetation with scores of rare species of small plants that managed to acclimatize in these harsh conditions. A popular alpine Ridgeway goes over Ostredok. Dangerous avalanches are a threat on its side slopes in the winter.

## JÁNOŠÍKOVA KOLKÁREŇ (4)

A forested section is to be found in the Liptov branch of the main ridge of the Greater Fatra. It is called Jánošíkova Kolkáreň and is protected as a National Nature Reserve. It is a rather specific section within the mountain range as it is the only protected territory situated on the part of the National Park formed by crystal. The original mountain forest with spruce and rowan trees is preserved in this area. Many spruces are over 100 years old. The ground is covered by carpets of fern, cranberries and bilberries.

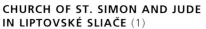

## CHURCH OF ST. SIMON AND JUDE IN LIPTOVSKÉ SLIAČE (1)

Three villages, Nižný, Stredný and Vyšný Sliač, merged to create Liptovské Sliače. The inhabitants of the three villages agreed to build one church on the Kostolná Hora Hill in the 13th century. Allegedly, after the first day of building works the site was mysteriously moved overnight to another place in Stredný Sliač. Thus, God wished the church to be built elsewhere and the present-day Roman Catholic Church of St. Simon and St. Jude was built on a hill that symbolizes Zion and heavenly Jerusalem in 1329. Precious frescoes from the 14th century by an unknown Italian artist are preserved in this old Gothic church. The author depicted the Virgin Mary the Guardian being crowned by two angels on the eastern side of the triumphal arch. The famous Sliačska Madonna is on the Slovakian thousand crown note.

## SLIAČSKE TRAVERTINE MOUNDS (2)

Remarkable natural formations, protected by the Sliačske Travertíny Natural Reserve, are in a small valley near the village of Vyšný Sliač, which was carved into the picturesque hills of the Liptovská Kotlina Hollow. A travertine for-

mation resembling a small volcano with a crater is on the travertine mould called Čertovica. There are similar shapes in the surroundings, one of them with a small pond that is popular with swimmers in the summer. At the foothill of the knoll is a spring with drinking water (65 litres per second). The spring water is mineralized. Part of the Nature Reserve is a moffete spring – a place with an intense gas emission. This is unique in Slovakia. Small birds sometimes die due to the emitted carbon oxide. Even shepherds avoided this place in the past as it is dangerous for cattle and sheep as well.

## CHURCH IN LIPTOVSKÝ MICHAL (3)
Only a short way from the turn of the highway near Bešeňová is the small village of Liptovský Michal, which boasts the ancient Church of St. Michael from the 13th century. It is amongst the oldest sacral buildings in the Liptov Region. It was documented as a completed building as early as 1237. Its façade includes a large amount of wood and its roof is covered by shingle. A nice belfry, originally a fortification gate, was built next to the church in the 17th century. This church was once a building with unique architecture which, apart from the stone section, included also a wooden church nave; unfortunately it has not been preserved. A painting of Christ was placed in the stone entry area. Sometime after World War II, this allegedly miraculous painting supposedly shed tears over a woman seeking help for her hungry children. It is now placed in the parish.

## WOODEN CHURCH NEAR SVÄTÝ KRÍŽ (4)
A village called Paludza was flooded by the water of the Liptovská Mara Dam at the beginning of the 1970s. However, its wooden church was

too valuable to be destroyed, so it was dismounted and rebuilt on a meadow between the villages of Svätý Kríž and Lazisko. This wooden 1693-built Articular church is amongst the largest wooden buildings in central Europe. This large Protestant church was admirably built by a wood carving master named Lang within 8 months.

## CHURCH OF ST MATTHEW THE APOSTLE IN PARTIZÁNSKA ĽUPČA (5)
This town was once amongst the most important places in Liptov prospering mainly due to banking. Originally it was called Nemecká (German) Ľupča for it was inhabited mainly by Germans from the 14th century until the end of World War II. Its current name is reminiscent of the activities at the end of World War II (Patrizánska - Partisan). The town is famous for the production of wooden storage vessels used to keep and transport the popular local 'bryndza' sheep cheese. The past fame of the town is commemorated by preserved burgher houses and the large Church of St. Matthew the Apostle with a fortification wall and loopholes. It boasts one of the highest church spires in northern Slovakia; its nave can accommodate up to 6,000 worshippers.

1

## LÚČANSKÝ VODOPÁD (1)

The impressive cascade of this waterfall located in the park of the Lúčky spa town looks like a miniature of one of the famous waterfalls at the Plitvice Lakes in Croatia. Water gushes over a travertine step on the Teplianka Stream from the height of 12 metres. Lúčanský Vodopád and Lúčanské Travertine Knolls are protected National Nature Monuments. Travertine is created on warm springs on the tectonic band on the boundary of the Chočské Vrchy Hills and the Liptovská Kotlina Hollow.

## LÚČKY SPA (2)

People have been coming to this spa town, nestled in the south-eastern foothills of the Choč Mountain, since 1761. The first spa building was built by the local lord Adam Turanský. At first, the spa specialised mainly in gynaecological problems, however it now also cures mobility illnesses. The basic of the successful cures is the plaster-bole carbonic mineral water from the local spring with a temperature of 32 degrees.

## MANSION IN BEŠEŇOVÁ (3)

Apart from a thermal pool and attractive travertine formations, this village also boasts a nice Renaissance mansion from the first half of the 17th century. The mansion was built by the Dvorník family and its interior was rebuilt in the Baroque style in the 18th century. Part of the mansion is a chapel consecrated to the Trinity from 1890. The elegant edifice with quadrant corner towers and a shingle roof is situated in a pleasant English-style park. The mansion is a private property; however it houses the Hunting Collections of the Liptovské Museum.

## THERMAL POOLS IN BEŠEŇOVÁ (4)

Mineral springs connected with the local travertine rise in this village. It was believed that rich sources of geothermal waters are underground due to the favourable hydro-geological conditions of the Liptovská Kotlina Hollow. This idea turned out to be accurate and water of 60.5 degrees gushes from the 1,987-deep bore. The rich source of thermal water gave rise to the popular thermal pools open year-round. The modern Thermalpark houses 7 outdoor pools with the temperature between 27 and 40 degrees. The place is especially attractive in winter as it offers unrepeatable views of snow-covered Tatras peaks. The outdoor swimming pools are interconnected with the indoor pools.

## TRAVERTINE KNOLLS IN BEŠEŇOVÁ (5)

If we compare Lúčanský Vodopád with Croatia's Plitvické Lakes, the travertine knolls in Bešeňová resemble the American Yellowstone Park, indeed only as its miniature relative. Springs with mineralized water are located in a hill above the railway near the village of Bešeňová. Layers of travertine have formed from the springs. Here you can see why they say that travertine is a stone born of water. The congealed travertine creates a group of small terraces, which resemble the large ones in the above-mentioned American national park. The traver-

2

tine cascade is a very attractive element of the local landscape mainly thanks to its colourfulness. The local stone is not white as it is in Dreveník in the Spiš Region. It has a range of colours due to various, mainly iron elements. There is a pallet of shades from yellow and brown to bronze and red. The travertine terraces are an important paleontological and archaeological site and are therefore a Protected Monument.

## LIPTOVSKÝ CASTLE (6)

This castle is amongst the highest located castles in central Europe. It was built before 1262 to protect the trade path from Liptov to Orava through the Sestrčská Dolina Valley. The Liptov County earned independence around 1340 and the castle became the seat of its ruler. The Hussites got the castle in the 15th century and were later changed by the highwayman knight Rikolfi, who was plundering villages in Liptov and Orava. It is documented to have been deserted in 1453. King Matthias Corvinus ordered that the castle be demolished in 1474 as its owner P. Komorovský supported his adversary, the Polish King Ladislaus II Jagilleon. Only a small ruin has been preserved from this medieval castle. Archaeological excavations are underway and the area is being partially restored.

3

5

4

6

## LIPTOVSKÁ MARA (1)

The building of the Liptovská Mara Dam between 1970 and 1975 brought great changes to life in Liptov. Eight villages were flooded by the dam with an area of 21.6 square kilometres. One of them gave its name to the dam. Only a spire from the Gothic church from the 13th century is preserved from the vanished village of Liptovská Mara. A small exhibition about the flooded villages was opened in the spire. The dam destroyed several villages and a large area of fertile fields, meadows and orchards; however on the other hand it turned the area into an attractive tourist destination. The reservoir was built to prevent floods on the Váh River and to produce electricity and it supported the development of recreational activities, concentrated on the northern bank of the lake around the village of Liptovský Trnovec. The southern bank of the dam is not used for recreational purposes as it is skirted by a railway and a highway. The only building here is the popular Dechtáre Roadhouse, which offers the excellent Slovakian speciality 'bryndzové halušky' (potato gnocchi with sheep cheese).

194

## ARCHAEOLOGICAL OPEN-AIR MUSEUM HAVRÁNOK (2)

A visit to the partially forested hill above the western bank of Liptovská Mara is an interesting opportunity to go back in time by two thousand years. A remarkable archaeological open-air museum called Havránok is situated in the slope. After the discovery of the remains of a Celtic settlement from the 1st century BC, its replica was built here. The central unit of this settlement is a courtyard with a pottery workshop furnished with an historical double-chamber kiln. A log cabin with outbuildings stands in the middle of the courtyard. A cult area was constructed in the upper part of the settlement with an historical replica of the palisades. It commemorates the place where Celtic druids carried out various pagan rituals with sacrifices to their gods. Old Germanic people settled in this place after the Celts; however Havránok was deserted at the times of the Roman period with life returning only in the 12th century, when a wooden estate, which vanished in the 15th century, was built here.

## PROSIECKA DOLINA (3)

The mountain range of the Chočské Vrchy is so narrow that some creeks flow across it. They rise at the slopes of the round hills of Oravská Vrchovina and flow through Chočské Vrchy via narrow rocky chasms. The most bizarre is the Prosiecka Valley. Just the entry into this wild valley from the village of Prosiek is imposing; it is created by a narrow rock cleft between two steep rocks with a fitting name Vráta (Doors). The valley forks into two in its wider central part. A 15-metre high waterfall called Červené

Piesky is in one of the branches. The second rocky chasm is called Sokol and can be managed only using steel leathers. The pass through Prosiecka Dolina is a part of a Nature Trail. The valley is a National Nature Reserve.

## KVAČIANSKA DOLINA (4)

This valley is located to the east of Prosiecka Dolina and metaphorically could be called its sister. It is a National Nature Reserve and it is almost unbelievable that a road to Hútě and two other remote villages on the other side of Chočské Vrchy once led through this wild rocky chasm. The tourist trail, a part of a Nature Trail, skirts the eastern slope of the valley, reaching the height of 70 metres above the bottom of the valley in some sections. The small village of Oblazy is in the top part of the chasm. It boasts two wooden water mills that used the waters of three creeks. The upper mill is called Brunčiakvský and the lower one Gejdošovský. These technical monuments were preserved mainly thanks to the work of volunteers who devoted hundreds of hours maintaining these monuments. The historical so-called gátrová water-impelled saw located in the lower mill was produced by the Viennese company Gustav Topham. It was state-of-the-art technology in its time.

## CHURCH OF ST. LADISLAUS IN LIPTOVSKÉ MATIAŠOVCE (5)

Liptovské Matiašovce used to be a quite village on a dead end road off the Hradská Road. However, the village is now a busy centre due to the new road between the Liptov and Orava regions. A nice Renaissance-Baroque church from the beginning of the 16th century stands left of the

road just outside the village. The attractive appearance of this sacral monument is complemented, to a certain extent, by its outer stone fortification with loopholes and round corner bastions. The church was built by the Nitra Bishop L. Matiašovský on the site of an older church consecrated to St. Helena. Valuable furnishing from the 17th century has been preserved inside the church; the 17th-century Baroque altar of St. Ladislaus and the crypt of the yeomen family of Matiašovský. Liptovské Matiašovce is the gateway into the Suchá Dolina Valley located in the most western part of the West Tatras; it has the popular cave called Dúpna Diera.

## OUTLOOK TOWER IN VEĽKÉ BOROVÉ (6)

Three mountain villages called Huty, Veľké Borové and Malé Borové are on the border of Liptov and Orava regions. They belong to the Liptov Region, however are on the other side of the narrow Chočské Vrchy Mountains. A narrow rugged path through Kvačianska Dolina once connected these villages with the world; today there is a better modern road. All three of the villages have a splendid location and a large amount of preserved folk buildings. Even though it does not seem to be that way the tourist outlook tower is a rather new tourist attraction of this wonderful nook of Slovakia. It was built on the ridge of the Oravská Vrchovina Hills above the village of Veľké Borové and in an interesting architectural style; the tower received the appearance of an old church spire and looks as if it has stood here for centuries. The terrace of the tower offers beautiful views of the Orava Region and Roháče Mountains.

## CHURCH OF ST. NICHOLAS
## IN LIPTOVSKÝ MIKULÁŠ (1)

This town is the hub of Liptov. In the past it was a traditional centre of tanner production, while today it is one of the main tourist centres in Slovakia thanks to its excellent location. The large Námestie Osloboditeľov Square is in the centre of the town, with the landmark of the Church of St. Nicholas. This Early Gothic monument dating from the 13th century is the largest in Liptov. It served as the parish church for Liptovský Mikuláš as well as several other surrounding villages. Together with a nearby manor of the local yeomen called Pongrácov, it was enclosed by fortification walls in the 15th century, becoming a now vanished town castle. For periods of time the church was owned by the Catholics and Protestants during the 16th and 17th centuries. The Czech exile Juraj Tranovský held sermons here in the turmoil times. This famous author of the Cithara Sanctorum hymnal was buried in the underground crypt of the church. There are three incomplete Gothic altars inside the church. The main altar was brought here from the church in Liptovský Trnovec that was flooded by the waters of Liptovská Mara Dam.

## CHURCH OF THE SACRIFICE OF OUR
## LORD IN SMREČANY (2)

The most valuable historical monument of the village of Smerčany is the ancient Church of the Sacrifice of Our Lord, which is listed as a National Cultural Heritage Monument. Its oldest part with the vault of crossed Romanesque ribs dates from 1349. A larger part of the church is

Gothic and is the result of building reconstructions in the 16th century. The church is valuable mainly thanks to the preserved medieval murals in the interior and a beautiful wooden ceiling decorated with ornaments. The Baroque altar and the Late Gothic bell by Master Andrej from 1509 are also noteworthy.

## MUSEUM OF JANKO KRÁĽ
## IN LIPTOVSKÝ MIKULÁŠ (3)

Janko Kráľ is the most famous from the scores of important personages born in this town. This prominent poet of the Štúr movement was born here in 1822 into a family of a butcher and an innkeeper. An ethnographical museum located in the former manor of the family of Illésházi (Illésházy) was named after this poet to commemorate his life and fame. The Museum of Janko Kráľ on the Námestie Osloboditeľov Square was built in 1955. Its aim was to collect and present historical, ethnographical and artistic materials about the Liptov Region. Another exposition, *Chapters from the history of the town of Liptovský Mikuláš,* was opened in 1993. The Late Renaissance manor was acquired in 1712 for the requirements of the Liptov County Council. It is possible that the famous court proceedings with the outlaw J. Jánošík was held here. Jánošík was sentenced to death by hanging on 17th March 1713 and the sentence was carried out on the Šibeničky Hill beyond the town nine months later on 18th December of the same year. The difficult moments preceding Jánošík's death are presented in the exposition in the underground of the museum

called Mikulášska Torture Room. Presently there are significant interests to confront the legend about this hero with the historical truth.

## FRANCISCAN MONASTERY AND CHURCH IN OKOLIČNÉ (4)

The monastery of the Franciscan Order reflected on the surface of the Váh River is the largest sacral monument in Liptov. This originally Gothic architectonic jewel was built towards the end of the 15th century and was later rebuilt in the Renaissance style. The grandiose Church of St. Peter o Alcantara is part of the complex and was completed in 1492. The Late Gothic church is a parish church and serves worshipers from the villages around Liptovský Mikuláš. Interestingly, a bus takes the worshipers to masses. The traditions of the Franciscan Order are once again held in the monastery next to the church.

## MANSION IN OKOLIČNÉ (5)

Okoličné was once an independent village, however it is now a town quarter in the eastern part of Liptovský Mikuláš. It was in the possession of an old yeomen family named Okoličáni (Okolicsány) from Liptov. Their seat was a Renaissance mansion built in the first half of the 17th century on the site of an older building. The two-story building on the rectangular ground-plan with corner bows is in fact a Renaissance monument with later Baroque amendments. It is set in a green park. Okoličné boasts another, younger Baroque-Classicism mansion from the second half of the 18th century.

## MUSEUM OF LIPTOVSKÁ DEDINA
## IN PRIBYLINA (1)

A problem with preservation of the most valuable cultural and historical monuments from the villages that were to be flooded arose before the construction of Liptovská Mara. A solution was to move the most valuable folk buildings to a meadow above the village of Pribylina next to the road from Liptovský Hrádok to Podbanské. The Museum of Liptovská Village was open here in 1991. This remarkable open-air museum with the splendid scenery of the Western Tatras is among the most visited tourist attraction of the Liptov Region. The Gothic-Renaissance mansion and the Early Gothic church from the village of Liptovská Mara are mostly of interest. The open-air museum hosts many attractive events during the summer, such as the Nedeľa Rodákov held in June, and presents folklore shows and crafts.

## BYSTRÁ (2)

The Western Tatras were once rather fittingly called Liptovské Hole. This high mountain range reaching over 2,000 metre contrasts with the rocky High Tatras as it is covered by large 'holes' (Alpine meadows located above the level of dwarf pine). Numerous herds of cattle and sheep once browsed the meadows; today they are a favourite destination of alpinism enthusiasts. The highest peak of the Western Tatras is Bystrá (2,248 m) located in the eastern part of the mountains. It is not in the main ridge but in a short southern fork. The traditional trail to Bystrá starts in Podbanské and goes through the Bystrá Dolina. This valley was formed by an iceberg, which melted and left two smallish tarns called Bystré Plesá, and a tiny lake called Anitino Očko. A lovely panoramic view is the reward for the challenging climb.

### ŽIARSKA DOLINA (3)

This is the most popular valley in the southern section of the Western Tatras situated above the village of Žiar between two forks of the mountain ridge, Jalovská Kopa and Baranka. The huge Baranec Mountain towers above the bottom of the valley at a height of more than 1,000 metres. The 7-kilometre long Žiarska Dolina was formed by an iceberg, which formed ice cauldrons and a rock step with the Šarafiový Waterfall. This is the only valley with a tourist chalet. Žiarská Chalet was built in 1950 at the elevation of 1,325 metres on the site of an older chalet. A pieta site was created near the chalet in 1995 to commemorate all victims of accidents in the Western Tatras. It is similar to the Symbolický Cintorín Cemetery near the Popradské Pleso Tarn in the High Tatras. At the end of Žiarská Dolina is the Smutné Sedlo mountain saddle at 1,965 metres. A trail connecting the Liptov and Orava region goes through this saddle.

### JAMNÍCKA DOLINA AND RAČKOVA DOLINA (4)

Two splendid valleys are situated in the central part of the Liptov section of the Western Tatras. Jamnícka Dolina is on the left when looking from the Liptovská Kotlina Hollow, while Račkova Dolina is to the right. For a long section they are interconnected and only forks out after approximately 2 kilometres from the entry to the hollow. A sharp rocky crest of the Otrhanci Peaks is between the valleys and it culminates by the Jakubina Mountain (2,194 m), the second highest peak in the Western Tatras. Both valleys, Jamnícka and Račkova, were formed by icebergs which melted and created tarns in both valleys. The largest is called Nižné Jamnícke Pleso and even though it is the third largest in the range it has less than 2 hectares. Vyšné Račkovo Pleso in Račkova Dolina is even smaller. Both valleys can be accessed from the Museum of Liptovská Dedina near Pribylina.

### BARANEC (5)

The Western Tatras were created by similar asymmetric tectonic upheaval as the neighbouring High Tatras. The southern part of both these Carpathian Mountains is higher than the northern therefore the highest peaks are located in the southern forks. Apart from the peaks Bystrá and Jakubina, Baranec (2,184 m), the third largest peak in Western Tatras is also in this location. The silhouette of this peak is a typical landmark of the mountain scenery in northern Liptov. It is a popular destination for alpine tourism and offers magnificent views reaching over more or less the entire Liptov area. The most convenient trail up to Baranec starts at the Žiarska Chata chalet.

## DEMÄNOVSKÁ DOLINA (1)

This 16-kilometre long valley on the northern side of the Low Tatras has two different faces. Its upper part lies in the northern slopes of the Chopok Mountain and was formed by ancient icebergs, while the lower part was created mainly by water eroding limestone massif and creating a splendid underground world of caves. The upper part of the valley opens widely like a large natural amphitheatre that houses two iceberg valleys. The conspicuous Ostredok Hill is wedged between the fork of two valleys, Repiská Dolina and Široká Dolina. The upper part of Demänovská Dolina is a heaven for skiing enthusiasts while its lower part is a strictly protected territory. At the point where the valley enters the limestone sections it narrows down considerably and a creek, called Demänovka, disappears underground at places. Its large bed full of round boulders is dry for most of the year as the creek goes underground through the complicated system of Demänovské Caves. Both sides of the narrow lower part of the valley are flanked by numerous splendid, bizarre limestone rocks. A narrow valley called Vyvieranie joins the main valley from the right side.

5

### DEMÄNOVSKÁ ĽADOVÁ JASKYŇA (3)

This ice cave is located in the lower section of Demänovská Dolina and is a part of the local cave system. It is remarkable for its permanent ice cover and it is the second largest cave of its type in Slovakia after the Dobšinská Ľadová Ice Cave. So far two kilometres of corridors have been discovered and explored in Demänovská Jaskyňa. This was known to the people in the Middle Ages and it is mentioned in a document of the Esztergom Capitola dating from 1299, which talks about an unspecified cave opening in Demänovská Dolina. A description by J. P. Haim from 1672 describes this cave in more detail. The bones of a cave bear were discovered in the cave; at first they were thought to belong to a dragon. The cave was opened to the public as early as in the mid-19th century. The present-day tour is almost 650 metres long.

### VRBICKÉ PLESO (4)

This tarn is the evidence of past times when icebergs covered some northern valleys of the Low Tatras. This tarn in Demänovská Dolina was created by a front iceberg moraine during the last glaciation. The Low Tatras have fewer tarns than the High Tatras, which is why Vrbické Pleso and its surrounding is protected in a National Nature Monument. The splendid mountain lake lies in a forested landscape near the Mikulášská Chata Chalet at 1,113 metres and, with an area of 0.73 hectares, it is the largest in the Lower Tatras. It is eight metres deep, however it is slowly disappearing.

### DEMÄNOVSKÁ JASKYŇA SLOBODY (2)

The eastern side of the lower part of Demänovská Dolina hides the largest cave system in Slovakia. It boasts the impressive Demänovský Karst with a labyrinth of caves and corridors totalling 30 kilometres. And the exploring of the caves has by no means been finished. The most beautiful section of the cave system is called Demänovská Jaskyňa Slobody; it is open to the public. Its immensely colourful and rich stalagmite and stalactite decoration places it rightfully amongst the most beautiful caves in Europe. The length of the thus far discovered cave corridors is eight kilometres. The underground corridors and halls are located on several storeys with the underground Demänovka River flowing on the bottom of the lowest story. The discoverers of the cave, A. Kráľ and his assistants, entered the cave in 1921 though one of the places where the river flows underground. Today, visitors can select from two tours of the cave. The traditional tour is 1,150 metres long, while the exclusive tour is twice as long.

### CHOPOK (5)

According to its height (2,024), this mountain is only the third highest in the Low Tatras, however it is certainly the most visited, as thousands of skiers swarm it in the winter. Skiing lifts make Chopok easily accessible in the winter, however it is slightly more demanding to visit the peak in the summer. The cableways on the northern and southern side only take tourist to the middle of the slope. However, to walk the several serpentines from the top station Luková to the peak is an easy tourist undertaking. More challenging is to climb to the top from Kosodrevina at the southern side of the mountain, which requires approximately double the time. It was much easier in the past as even in the summer the cableways from both sides of the mountain took tourists right up to Kamenná Chata Chalet just below the peak. The Low Tatras Ridgeway goes over Chopok.

## ĎUMBIER (1)

The 80-kilometre long main ridge of the Low Tatras has only four peaks higher than 2,000 metres. The highest of them is Ďumbier (2,043 m). At first glance you can see its two very different faces. The steep slopes of this huge mountain descend into deep hollows mostly shaded by dark shadows at the north with snow staying in these parts until late summer. The northern hollows of Ďumbier are a peaceful home to the chamois species. The southern hills are very different. They are much gentler with almost no rocks but with a huge carpet of screes and dwarf pines. Unless the day is cloudy they are bathed in sunshine. Originally, the Low Tatras Ridgeway led along the entire massif, however tourists can now access only the western ridge as the trail is closed on the eastern side.

## GRANARIES IN LIPTOVSKÝ JÁN (2)

Several interesting folk buildings are preserved in the village of Liptovský Ján. Three historical granaries are a fine example of folk architecture. They are located on Svätojánska Street and were originally used to store grain and other farming products. They now provide accommodation.

## THERMAL SPRING
## IN LIPTOVSKÝ JÁN (3)

The mineral springs in Liptovský Ján were already known in the Middle Ages. A local inhabitant, M. Sentiváni, wrote a scientific work about the springs in the 17th century. He later became a rector and a professor at Trnavská University. The springs started to be used in 1919 when Svätojánske Spa was opened in the village on the initiative of count J. Gemerský-Sentiváni, who invested into the larger bore and had his mansion converted into a spa pavilion. Moreover, he had built the baths and the outdoor and indoor swimming pools. The spa specialised in the curing of skin diseases, rheumatism and heart-vascular problems and was officially closed down in 1938. Its tradition is kept alive in the thermal swimming pool near the Máj Hotel, which uses waters from the Rudolf (1979) thermal spring. The original lake is now a tourist attraction.

## JÁNSKA DOLINA (4)

This valley is the eldorado of speleologists with the underground full of suprises and the possibility of the discovery of new caves. Mainly the Jaskyňa Zlomísk Cave is remarkable. With the length of its explored underground corridors (10 kilometres) it is the fourth largest cave system in Slovakia. The absolute victory is held by a valley in the Krakovská Hola massif. Speleologists explored the Starý Hrad Cave here, which is the deepest in Slovakia. There is an elevation difference of 495 metres between its highest and lowest corridors. The Ľadová Priepasť Abbys is also noteworthy. It is 125 metres long and an ice cone (15 metres high) stands on its bottom throughout the year.

## YEOMEN MANSIONS AND MANORS
## IN LIPTOVSKÝ JÁN (5)

The village of Liptovský Ján boasts a rich history created throughout the centuries by the local famous yeomen. It was owned by the prominent Sentiváni (Szentiványi – Svätojánsky) family for centuries until the abolition of serfdom. They built a wooden castle in the slope of the hill above the village in the Medieval Ages, and it was the only castle in Liptov that was not owned by the king. Although the times of yeomen are a long gone history in Liptovský Ján, the present-day village boasts more than twenty mansions and manors built by them. In no other place in Slovakia have so many manor houses of the lower aristocracy been preserved. Manors and mansions are rich in style, ranging from the Renaissance to the Classicism; however, many need to be repaired. One of the mansions was rebuilt into a Culture Centre and it houses the small Svätojánske Museum.

## OHNIŠTE (6)

The Ohnište (1 538 m n. m.) Hill is a wonderful work of nature with scores of remarkable natural formations. It stuns the tourist with imposing rock galleries and a karst plain with a large amount of karst formations. It boasts škrapy and sinkholes as well as a 182-metre deep abyss called Havran. A 20-metre high rock window was created near the peak of the mountain. It is the highest natural rock opening in Slovakia. The massif of Ohnište is a National Nature Reserve. A Soviet army plane flying to support the Slovakian National Uprising crashed into its northern neighbour of Onhište, called Slemä, on 13th October 1944. All its crew (19 people) was killed in the accident.

## LIPTOVSKÝ HRÁDOK CASTLE (1)

A sentry tower that guarded the merchant path along the Váh River gradually developed into a royal castle at the beginning of the 14th century. It was captured by the Hussites in 1433 and owned by several yeomen later. The Gothic castle was enlarged when a Renaissance palace was added to it at the beginning of the 17th century. Liptovský Hrádek was an important strategic point of the Emperor's army during the Estate Uprising and scores of fortifications, mounds and bastions were built around it. It burnt out in 1803 and only the Renaissance palace was restored. Following a successful reconstruction it was transformed into a luxurious hotel.

## WEIGHTING ROOM AND CLAPPER IN MAŠA (2)

Ores were mined in the past around Liptovský Hrádok Castle at the upper part of the Liptov Region. Inhabitants of several villages were involved in mining. The iron ore was smelted in the first blast furnace founded in 1792 near the Váh River between the villages of Kráľova Lehota and Liptovský Hrádok. The historical furnace has not

been preserved; only a weighing building and a clapper remain in the village of Maša. Both are valuable historical monuments.

## ČERTOVICA (3)

One of the few places where the massive mountain barrier of the Low Tatras is slightly weaker is a mountain saddle called Čertovica Sedlo. The main crest lowers to 1,238 metres here, and the only road across the mountain range connecting the areas of Horné Povážie and Horehronie leads here. An important tourist centre has developed in the saddle thanks to this significant connection.

## LIPTOVSKÁ TEPLIČKA (4)

This peculiar village was founded during the Walachian colonisation in the 17th century. It is set in a splendid natural environment of the eastern part of the Low Tatras and is well-known for preserved folk buildings as well as for still maintained authentic folklore traditions. Remarkable are mainly dozens of small grassy hills – cellars at the back of the houses – for the storage of potatoes.

## BOCIANSKA DOLINA (5)

The road from the Čertovica Saddle towards the Liptov side descends into a picturesque valley called Bocianska Dolina, which separates the Ďumbier and Kráľova Hoľa parts of the Low Tatras. Both villages have a rich mining history and are used mainly for recreational purposes.

## VÝCHODNÁ (6)

This colourful village in the upper Liptov is well known in the world mainly due to the high quality of folklore. An international folklore festival has been held here since 1953. It is the greatest event of this type in Slovakia and is rightfully considered one of the best traditional folk culture happenings in the world. The history of the festival in Východná goes back to 1953. The festival is now a member of CIOFF (International Organisation of Folklore Festivals). Until 2005 the folklore groups were presented in a natural amphitheatre at the edge of the village, however the village now boats a fine festival hall.

## VAŽECKÁ JASKYŇA (7)

The entry into this cave is located on the south-

ern edge of the village of Važec at the upper Liptov area. Although it is not one of the longest caves in Slovakia (only 503 metres long), it is very popular among the experts as well as lay public for its remarkable stalagmite and stalactite decorations. It was created in a limestone massif at the edge of the Kozie Chrbty Hills and thanks to the discovery of the remains of a cave bear, it counts amongst the most renowned paleontological sites in Europe.

## VODNÉ DIELO ČIERNY VÁH (8)

A hydro-power plant was built in the upper Liptov area between 1974 and 1981. This technical work, which is environmentally friendly, consists of two water reservoirs. The lower lake was built on the Čierny Váh River above Svarín and the other was built on the karst plain of Kozie Chrbty. The artificial lake is dammed, at places, 75 metres high, and mould is situated 430 metres above the lower reservoir. The dam is an interesting technical construction, moreover the upper reservoir offers unrepeatable views of the breathtaking panorama of the Tatras Mountains.

# CENTRAL SLOVAKIA – SOUTH

At the south of central Slovakia the harsher Carpathian countryside mixes with the influence of the warm and dry Panonia lowlands. Horehronie (Upper River Váh Region) lies at the north of this area. It boasts peculiar and colourful folklore traditions and the attractive Čiernohronská Forest Railway. The east is lined with impressive extinct Tertiary volcanoes with a long tradition of ore mining. The wealth from the mines supported the thriving development of the Golden town of Kremnica, Silver Banská Štiavnica and Copper Banská Bystrica. However, there are other towns and villages with scores of cultural and historical monuments. The east part of south-central Slovakia is covered by the extensive Slovenské Rudohorie Mountains, overgrown with endless forests. People in this part were also active miners; however they also developed long-established glass production. The natural wonders are best preserved in the territory of the Muránska Planina Plain, which was designated a National Park. The most southern regions of central Slovakia along the Hungarian boarder offer a pleasant landscape of hollows and low mountain ranges with a mosaic of colourful meadows, orchards, vineyards, forests and picturesque towns and villages. The largest towns of the region are Lučenec and Rimavská Sobota, while the smallest Slovakian town, Modrý Kameň, is also to be found in this locality. The most popular tourist area in the south is the Cerová Vrchovina Protected Landscape with charming volcano hills; the volcanic activity in this area extricated in the relatively recent geological past.

# HOREHRONIE

### HOREHRONIE MESTSKÝ CASTLE
### IN BANSKÁ BYSTRICA (1)

The group of historical buildings on the Námestie Štefana Moyzesa Square in Banská Bystrica formed one complex in the past – the town castle. The castle was to serve as a refuge to the wealthy inhabitants of the town. Its oldest parts date from the 13th century and the castle best fulfilled its function during the mining uprising between 1525 and 1526. The walls were strengthened during the 16th and 17th centuries due to the Ottoman threat. When the protective purpose of the castle ceased to be important later on, most of the fortification walls were demolished. Only a few isolated architectonically interesting buildings, listed below, have been preserved until the present day.

### CHURCH OF ST. CROSS
### IN BANSKÁ BYSTRICA (2)

The smallest of the two churches of the Mestský Castle is consecrated to the St. Cross. This one-nave building dates from the 15th century and was converted from an old Gothic chapel, which was mentioned in historical documents as Slovakian. The reconstruction of the church was financed by the Slovakian inhabitants of the town who wanted to have masses served in the Slovakian language; hence the name Slovakian Church. It belonged to the Evangelists in the 17th century and was given to the Jesuits in the 18th century. The Jesuits carried out the rebuilding in the spirit of the Baroque style. A fire in 1782 destroyed a large part of the interior furnishing; only the Altar of St. Alois, the baptismal font and benches have been preserved.

### MATEJOV DOM
### IN BANSKÁ BYSTRICA (3)

At first glance the five-story house in the back part of Mestský Castle seems to be very old, as it has maintained its medieval appearance. It is called the Matejov House after the coat-of-arms of the King Matej on its southern façade. It was built in 1479 for a king's representative, who controlled the mining activities and collected tax for the ruler. The building of this house enlarged the northern side of the castle next to the preserved stone Banícka Bastion and a fragment of the fortification walls.

### STARÁ TOWN HALL
### IN BANSKÁ BYSTRICA (4)

As the Námestie SNP Square in the town has a new town hall, the historical edifice at the eastern side of Mestský Castle is called Stará (Old) Town Hall. It is also called Pretórium. It was built in the Gothic style by a rich burgher and the Head of the County Council Vít Mühlstein, after a fire in the town in 1500, as the seat of the town council. It was rebuilt in the Renaissance style between 1564 and 1565, when an arcaded balcony was added to its facade. Today, the town hall houses the Stredoslovenská Gallery with one of the largest collection of graphic art in Slovakia.

## NÁMESTIE SNP
### IN BANSKÁ BYSTRICA (1)

Together with other privileges Banská Bystrica also required the right to mine gold, silver and other ores as early as 1255, thus securing its long term prosperity. Mainly copper was successfully exported to numerous foreign lands in Europe; this gave Banská Bystrica its nickname, the Copper Town. Its inhabitants enjoyed showing off their wealth and built luxurious palaces on the main square. This large unevenly shaped place is called Námestie SNP and boasts extremely valuable historical buildings, most of them dating from the Middle Ages. Splendid Renaissance burgher palaces with rich artistic decorations were built by merging old, narrow Gothic houses. This resulted in the very attractive appearance of the present-day square, which invites town inhabitants as well as visitors for pleasant walks along the pedestrian zone.

## CLOCK TOWER
### IN BANSKÁ BYSTRICA (2)

The narrow spire of the Clock Tower is a landmark of the upper part of Námestie SNP Square. It was built in 1552 above the town prison. Its cellars contained torture rooms and cells, and the tower also housed a weighing room with town measurements and weights and was therefore called Vážnicová (Weighting) Spire. Its current name is associated with the two clocks on its square-facing façade. The spire was rebuilt several times. The last reconstruction caused a leaning of the spire by approximately 40 centimetres; it is visible at first glance.

## BENICKÉHO HOUSE
### IN BANSKÁ BYSTRICA (3)

This house at the northern side of the Námestie SNP is the most eye-catching amongst the remarkable buildings of the square. Similarly to other houses on the square, it was built by the interconnection of two older Gothic houses after 1660. This splendid Renaissance edifice bears the characteristic signs of the work of the Italian architect Jakub de Pauli. By including the corner arcade balcony into the façade of the house this artist completed the impressive yet practical unification of the inner part of the building with the outside area of the large square. Graffiti and murals dating from between the 16th and 18th centuries, discovered during the last reconstruction, enhance the beauty of the Benického House. The Renaissance portal with the coat-of-arms of the Sentiváni (Szentiványi) family is also noteworthy. It depicts a couple of well-dressed miners with typical hammers.

However, the house was not named after them, but rather after Tomáš Benický of Mičiná, who owned it in the second half of the 17th century.

## EVANGELIC CHURCH IN BANSKÁ BYSTRICA (4)

Compared with the busy Námestie SNP, Lazovná Street in the northern part of the centre of Banská Bystrica is much more peaceful. This applies mainly to a pleasant small park outside the Evangelic Church. It was built for the Evangelic religion of the Augsburg Profession between 1803 and 1807 outside the city walls near Lazovná Gate. The elegant Classicism building replaced the original wooden Articular church similar to the church in Kežmarok. There is a painting of Christ on the central altar by Daege. It was given to the local church in 1842 by the Prussian King Friedrich Wilhem IV. There are the tombs of several personages of Slovakian culture – Ján Botto, Martin Rázus, Terézia Vansová, Viliam Figuš Bystrý and Alexander Matuška – at the Evangelic cemetery behind the church. There are buildings of the Evangelic parish and former Evangelic school at the eastern side of the park outside the church. It was the seat of the Literary and Musical Museum until 2003, when it was moved into the attic of the historical building of Štátná vedecká knižnica (National Science Library) on the street of the same name.

## TOWN FORTIFICATIONS IN BANSKÁ BYSTRICA (5)

In the 16th century Banská Bystrica was one of the best fortified towns in Slovakia. The reason was the prevalent threat of the Ottomans, who occupied a large part of Hungary after the battle at Moháč in 1526. Building of the fortification continued until the 17th century. None of the original five city gates has survived. They were demolished towards the end of the 19th century and the beginning of the 20th century. However, the demolition was not very consistent, so fragments of the walls and four bastions can still be recognised in buildings in the historical centre. Two belonged to the fortification of Mestský Castle and two were part of the southern side of the fortification. The Mäsiarska Bastion at the Pamätník SNP Monument is a very nice example of medieval fortification. The nearby Čižmárska Bastion has also been preserved.

## MONUMENT TO SNP AND MUSEUM OF SNP IN BANSKÁ BYSTRICA (6)

The modern history of Banská Bystrica is closely connected with the Slovakian National Uprising (SNP). This huge army operation against the government of the Slovak Republic in Bratislava and German fascism started here on 29th August 1944. Slovakia got into the victorious antifascist block of nations thanks to this uprising, which was one of the most powerful in Europe during World War II. The rebellious town received a dignified monument in 1969. At the same time it serves as the Museum of Slovakian National Uprising. It collects and presents various documents of the antifascist fight in Slovakia. The monument is in the midst of a park, which was converted into a remarkable open-air museum of the army weaponry used by the partisans.

## TAJOV (1)

This village west of Banská Bystrica is the native place of two famous personages. The Slovakian writer and dramatist J. G. Tajovský was born in a wooden cottage in the centre of the village on 18th October 1874. He spent a beautiful childhood in Tajov and kept returning all his life, and even though he died in Bratislava, they buried him at the Tajov cemetery together with his wife Hana, who was also a writer. The exposition of the Literary and Music Museum in Banská Bystrica was opened in the native house of Tajovský. It is devoted to his life and work as well as the history and ethnography of the village. The priest and scientist J. Murgaš was born in the building of the former school in the community of Jabriková on 17th February 1864. He was a priest, however his heart was in painting; he also became famous in the area of electrical engineering due to the discoveries in the field of the wireless telegraphy. However, you would search for the tomb of Murgaš at the local cemetery in vain, as he was buried far away in Pennsylvania in the USA. A room devoted to his life and work was opened in his native house.

## ŠPANIA DOLINA (2)

Banská Bystrica received its nickname, Copper Town, mainly thanks to this village. Copper ore was once mined in this locality in a side valley of the Starohorské Vrchy Hills. It later became the source of wealth of the rich burghers of the town. Špania Dolina can be certainly counted amongst the most beautiful villages in Slovakia. A unique group of old log-built houses stands in its centre. They were built during the 17th and 18th centuries and were designated a Folk Architecture Monument Reserve. Some houses in the village are even older and boast preserved Renaissance paintings. The most valuable historical monument of Špania Dolina is the Church of the Transformation of Our Lord from the 13th century with a roofed staircase with 162 wooden steps. The historical building of clapper is reminiscent of the mining past of the village, yet the most visible witness is the great hill of tail called Hálňa which is heaped on the steep slopes, offering splendid views. Laceworkers sit outside their houses during the summer to present their great art. Apart from the lace, Špania Dolina boasts an old tradition of copper and enamel crockery production.

## MONUMENT TO SNP IN KREMNIČKA (3)

A significant pieta site hides in the shadows of the forest at the southern edge of Banská Bystrica. It commemorates tragic events of the modern history of the Slovakian nation. The Monument to SNP (Slovakian National Uprising) was unveiled here in 1949. It commemorates the victims of the cruel fascist regime during World War II. This great work from pink ryolit was erected on the site of the largest mass grave from the period of World War II in Slovakia. In total 747 people including soldiers, partisans, and civilians were murdered at this place between 5th November 1944 and 5th March 1945. Amongst the victims of the fascist headsmen were also 58 children. Another monument was

built in Kremnička in 1995. Its creator, an Israeli architect named Arieh Fatran, gave it the shape of the Menorah. This traditional Hebrew symbol commemorates the 400 Jewish victims who were amongst those murdered.

### KRÁLIKY (4)

This interesting village lies at the eastern foothills of Kremnické Vrchy Hills. Situated in a splendid natural environment, it boasts several valuable preserved folk architecture buildings. The easily accessible Králiky are a popular tourist destination of the inhabitants of Banská Bystrica and serve mainly a recreational purpose. The slopes above the village have excellent skiing conditions. Králiky are also popular for cross-country skiing; the long-distance races called Biela Stopa SNP take place in this locality. There is the tourist Chata nad Králikmi Chalet above the village, which is a great starting point for treks to Kremnické Vrchy.

### HARMANECKÁ JASKYŇA (5)

Woodcutters once hid in the entry to this cave (once called Izbica), when the weather was bad.

The cave system was first accessed in 1932, when a speleologist M. Bacúrik dug his way into the Objaviteľský Hall of the Harmanická Cave. Paradoxically, he received no reward for the discovery. Quite to the contrary, he was fined for an unauthorised entry onto the lands of the forests belonging to the town of Banská Bystrica. The cave was not made accessible until 1950. So far, speleologists have explored 2,763 metres of its underground system in the limestone massif at the edge of Greater Fatra. The tour of the cave is 1,020 metres long. The rather challenging climb to the entry into the cave, situated 260 metres above the bottom of Harmanecká Dolina Valley, is rewarded by the remarkable beauty of the stalagmite and stalactite decoration in the corridors and halls of the cave. Soft sinter is typically found in this cave, and it has a large colony of wintering bats.

### ZVOLEN (6)

This massive hill looming north of Donovaly has the same name as the famous town of Zvolen in central Slovakia. It is the highest mountain (1,402 m) in the Zvolen Mountains in the south-

eastern section of the Greater Fatra. Its grassy top with a panoramic view is easily accessible by a cable car, which goes from Donovaly to the lower sub-peak Nová Hoľa. The eastern side of Zvolen is an excellent skiing slope for adept skiers.

### DONOVALY (7)

Climbing the mountain saddle of Donovaly (850 m) is one of the few ways to relatively easily climb the huge mountain barrier between the Horné Považie and Horehronie regions. The first coalmen settled here in the 17th century. One of their settlements developed into the present-day village of Donovaly; it was named after its founder, a coalman named Donoval. This once poor mountain village is now a popular tourist centre with scores of chalets and other tourist facilities. Several old log cabins, with the typical glassed veranda, and a Classicism church from 1825, have been preserved. The popular skiing centre, Park Snow, is located in Donovaly. It gets very busy during the traditional dog-team races, which gave the locality its nickname – 'Donovalská Alaska'.

## BADÍNSKY PRALES (1)

Walking through this forest along the local Nature Trail is a remarkable experience. Actually, the term walking is not accurate as it is a challenging trek with numerous obstacles, which were created by the forest and almost untouched by man. Badínsky Prales is one of the oldest protected territories in Slovakia; it was designated as early as 1913. It is an extremely valuable area with preserved original fir and beech trees, as well as several other leafy tree species. There are also rare elm trees; Britain's Prince Charles visited the forest to see them in 2000.

## CHURCH OF ST. MARTIN BISHOP IN ČERÍN (2)

The Church of St. Martin Bishop on a hilltop above the village of Čerín is one of the most significant sacral monuments of the region. It was built in the Gothic style in the 14th century. Valuable medieval murals from the 14th and 15th centuries and a painted wooden ceiling dating from the 16th century are preserved in the interior. A stone wall with loopholes was erected around the church during the Ottoman threat in the 16th century. Inside the fortified area is a triangle-shaped fine wooden belfry.

## WOODEN CHURCH IN HRONSEK (3)

In the past more wooden churches for worshipers of the reformed religions existed in Pohronie, however only one has been preserved until today. This unique church is located in the village of Hronsek south of Banská Bystrica. This beautiful edifice was remarkably built within one year and eight days. The church was consecrated on 31st October 1726. Its interior has a very economical solution, the ground-plan has the shape of the Greek cross and the church is 26 metres long and 11 metres wide. Yet, up to 1,100 seats were placed inside. This building is unique in Slovakia from an architectonic point of view. Its builders ignored the traditional log-cabin style (from the Protestant Germany) and used a pillar-frame construction with a bearing wooden frame and desk filling. The detached belfry is also noteworthy. It dates from the same time as the church. The poet Andrej Sladkovič married a local girl, Júlia Sekovičová, in the church on the 15th September 1847.

## MANSIONS IN HRONSEK (4)

The aristocracy from the village of Hronsek near Banská Bystrica gained an important social position as its members held high offices in the Zvolen County Council and even at the emperor's court in Vienna. They built two mansions in Hronsek on the right bank of the Hron River. The older building dates from the 15th century and was rebuilt from an original water castle in the Renaissance style in 1576. It was well fortified due to the Ottoman threat; it received four protection towers and a moat. Allegedly, coins were minted in the mansion during the Rákoci (Rákoczi) Uprising. It is worth mentioning that one of the owners of the mansion, Žigmund Géci (Céczy), had a daughter named Juliana, who is famous as the Levočská White Lady thanks to a novel by Mór Jókai. The younger mansion in Hronsek (1775) is baroque.

## MIČINSKÉ TRAVERTINE KNOLLS (5)

This is an important natural science locality and a National Nature Monument. The occurrence of travertine in Slovakia is rather common; however most of them are solid rocks that calcified into nicely shaped decorative stones. Travertines near Dolná Mičiná are attractive knolls and their formation has not yet been finished. Travertine is created right in front of your eyes in this spot – directly from water. You can see a flat, low knoll with a crater on the top filled with bubbling salty-iron water. It brims over the edges and runs down the gentle slopes of the knoll on a wet meadow along the Lukavica stream. It loses its mineral elements on the flat surface creating sediments of mud and bog fresh water limestone. This is the first stage of travertine creation.

## ĽUPČIANSKY CASTLE (1)

Many Slovakian castles did not survived the Estate Uprising, and others became derelict as their owners moved into more comfortable mansions. One of the few that are fully preserved stands above the village of Slovenská Ľupča in the Horehronie Region. Its history goes back to the 13th century, when it was a part of the dowry of Hungarian queens and was visited by the kings for hunting in surrounding forests. It was acquired by the family of Séči (Széchy) in 1620 and later came to the Hungarian palatine J. Vešeléni (Wsselényi) through a marriage to Mária Séčiová. The risk that the castle would end up a ruin like many others increased by this event as its lord joined the anti-Hapsburg uprising. Surprisingly, the Emperor's army spared the castle. Its functionality was increased thanks to the New Gothic reconstruction at the end of the 19th century. It is now a private property and is not accessible to the public.

## MONUMENT TO SNP IN NEMECKÁ (2)

This village in Horehronie witnessed the tragic events of January 1945 when German troops murdered about 900 people, including members of the Hlinka Guard and even civilians. Participants of the anti-Fascist movement in Slovakia together with innocent civilians were shot dead in a former limekiln. Apart from Slovakians, Russians, French, Romanians and Americans died here as well. The site was transformed into the Monument to SNP (Slovakian National Uprising) and it was designated a National Monument. A fragment of a kiln and a Memorable Room with a permanent exhibition are also part of this pieta place.

## CHURCH IN PONIKY (3)

It happened on 6th January 1678. 'The Turkish attacked Poniky' and hauled off 239 local boys and girls. The village has never recovered from this tragedy, which was described in the famous poem Turčín Poničan by Sam Chalupka. It ceased to be a town with privileges that had prospered from mining. The Church of St. Francis of Seraphim is reminiscent of the past times of the town. It was built in 1310 and has maintained its medieval appearance despite later rebuilding. It houses valuable murals from the 14th century and a Gothic altar of the Virgin Mary from 1512. The Neo Gothic baptismal font with the date inscription (1512) was probably produced in the workshop of Master Pavol of Levoča. The British Crown Prince Charles honoured the church with a visit in 2000.

## BRUSNO SPA (4)

This spa town sits in a calm environment in the forested valley along the Brusnianka Creek that cut into the northern edge of the Veporské Vrchy Hills. Brusno lies in the opening of the valley into the Horehronské Podolie and its architecture has almost merged with the village of Svätý Ondrej across the Hron River. Inhabitants of Brusno are famous for their craft of lacing; they successfully traded lace in far foreign lands. The oldest written

record of the local alkaline-sulphur springs is in the parish chronicle of the village of Medzibrod and dates from 1818. The first spa pavilion was built in 1837. The spa specialises in digestion and heart-vascular diseases and mobility problems. Most patients came here for gall-bladder and liver therapy. Apart from the older buildings, for instance the Paula spa pavilion, there are also modern edifices. The most remarkable is the Poľana spa pavilion.

## ĽUBIETOVÁ (5)

When the King Ľudovít I bestowed the privileges of the free royal town upon Ľubietová, it became one of the seven privileged wealthy mining towns in central Slovakia. Gold, silver and other ores were mined here in the past, even nickel and cobalt. The Empress Maria Theresa visited the town in the 18th century. Today, Ľubietová is not a town but only a larger village in the Hutná Valley at the northern hills of the Poľana massif. Several historical monuments are reminiscent of better times, when it was a prosperous town.

Apart from burgher houses and two churches there is an interesting house built in the Historicism style on the foundations of a medieval building from the 14th century. Ľubietová is known in the mineralogy circles. Recently, an unknown mineral was discovered in the Podlipa locality with old tunnels, shafts and piles of tail. It is called libetenit after the locality where it was found.

## KALIŠTE MONUMENT (6)

The second phase of the Slovakian National Uprising started towards the end of October 1944, as the rebels were outnumbered by the better equipped fascist army. They withdrew into the mountains and started a partisan war against the occupants. Their best hinterland became the villages of Baláže and Kalište in the Starohorské Vrchy Hills. Their inhabitants paid a cruel price for helping the partisans though. The Nazis sent a troop to the locality in March 1945, burning down Kalište and murdering some of its inhabitants. Baláž met the same destiny two days later. After the li-

beration survivors returned to Baláž, however Kalište has never been restored. A monument to the victims of fascism was erected in the ruined village and was designated a National Cultural Monument in 1961. An exposition of the Museum of SNP in Banská Bystrica was opened in two reconstructed houses.

## HRB AND VEPOR (7)

A striking mountain range forks to the north from the massif of the Tertiary Poľana volcano. There is a rocky double-peak, whose shape resembles a high table sagging in the middle. The southern part of the 'table' is the higher Vepor Mountain (1,277 m), also called Ľubietovský Vepor according to the nearby village at the western foothills of the mountains. The northern Hrb (1,255 m) Peak is an important geographic point. According to calculations it is the geological centre of Slovakia. Hrb offers splendid views and there is the tourist Chata pod Hrbom Chalet at its northern foothill.

## TÁLE (1)

Tále is a wide strip of meadows along the foothills in the spot where the Bystrá Dolina Valley leaves the Low Tatras. A tourist centre of the same name was founded here in the second half of the 20th century. The first tourist facility, the large Partizán Hotel, was built in 1961. There is a natural swimming lake in a meadow outside the hotel. Tále is a popular tourist centre in the summer. A relatively new facility is Gray Bear, the first 18-hole golf course in Slovakia. Tále also offers excellent skiing conditions in the winter; the six lifts can take up to 3,000 skiers onto the slopes in an hour.

## MÝTO POD ĎUMBIEROM (2)

This interesting village lies on an important road from the Horehronie to the Liptov Region via the Čertovica Saddle. It was founded in the 15th century and iron ore, gold and silver were mined in the surroundings from the 17th century. Apart from precious ores the locals also earned a living by sheep breeding and the production of cloth and canvass while using the local fuller mill. The present-day Mýto pod Ďumbierom is an important tourist centre. In the summer it is visited by tourists attracted by the nearby Nízke Tatry National Park while in the winter there are good skiing slopes (4.5 km) with artificial snow available right in the village.

## BYSTRIANSKA JASKYŇA (3)

The entry into this cave is at the southern edge of the village of Bystrá. The part of the cave called Stará Jaskyňa has been known since the oldest times. J. Kovalčík and E. Laubert entered the then unknown part of the cave in 1923. Tourists had the first opportunity to visit the Bystrianská Jaskyňa in 1939, however still without electric lighting. The present-day tour is 490 metres long and has been open to the public since 1968. It is a river type cave with an underground karst system created in an island of limestone at the northern edge of Horehronské Podolie. The Bystrianka Creek flows through the cave and it resurfaces in a well in Valaská; it propelled a stone mill in the past. Bystrianska Jaskyňa is specific for it offers speleotheraphy.

### BYSTRÁ DOLINA (4)

This is one of the most beautiful valleys on the southern side of the Low Tatras. It starts at Tálov and leads right into the heart of the mountain range. Its lower part lies at the southern slopes of Chopok and Ďumbier and it cuts deeper and lower between the fork of the Baba and Veľký Gápľ mountains. The Bystrianka Creek flows on the bottom of the valley. The path that climbs the valley ends at the Srdiečko Peak (1,216 m). A cable car from Srdiečko goes right to the 300 metres higher situated Kosodrevina Chalet. The Alpine tourisms enthusiasts use this way to get to the main ridge of the Low Tatras, while in the winter the slopes below Chopok are swarmed by skiers. Below Srdiečko is the Trangoška Hotel, called after the valley which starts at it and goes to the Chata M. R. Štefánika Chalet below Ďumbier.

### VAJSKOVSKÁ DOLINA (5)

Although less visited, this valley on the southern side of the Low Tatras is very pretty. Its lower part is below Poľana and Kotlisky in the main ridge of the mountains and the valley continues for 10 kilometres before it ends at the Horehronské Podolie west of Krpáčov. An iceberg covered Vajskovská Dolina in the Ace Age. The Vajskovský Creek flows on the bottom of the valley and several waterfalls gush over its rock steps. The largest cascade is called Horný Vajskovský Waterfall and it is almost 50 metres high. The Dolný Vajskovský Waterfall is 16 metres high. Species of chamois enjoy the conditions of the upper part of the valley. Several monuments in the valley commemorate its partisan-connected past. Another monument is in the side Kulichová Dolina Valley at the site where an avalanche fell of the Žiarská Hoľa, killing 16 forest workers in 1956.

### CHATA GENERÁLA M. R. ŠTEFÁNIKA (6)

This chalet is an important point for the tourists who trek the long Low Tatras Ridgeway. It provides excellent facilities. It sits at 1,740 metres and its foundation stone was laid in 1924. It was built to replace a hostel which was once at the peak of Ďumbier.

## SQUARE IN BREZNO (1)

There was enough space in the free royal town of Brezno to build a large central square, which would accommodate burgher houses and other pretty buildings. The almost quadrant square is named after the general M. R. Štefánik. The former Classicism town hall from 1770 stands in its centre; it now houses the Horehronské Museum. Next to the town hall is the Baroque Church of the Assumption of the Virgin Mary, which is slightly younger and houses a precious organ by Master J. Pažický of Rájec. The landmark of the southern part of the square is the 31-metre high Classicism Mestská Tower from 1830. Around the square are several Renaissance and Baroque burgher houses from the 17th and 18th centuries. The Ďumbier Hotel at the eastern side of the square is a fine example of Art Nouveau architecture. The Piarist monastery with a chapel from the end of the 17th century near the hotel is one of the oldest monuments of the town.

## HEĽPA (2)

Although a popular folk song describes Heľpa as a pretty town, the truth is that it is beautiful; however it is not a town but rather a colourful village with scores of preserved vernacular architecture and, most of all, thriving folklore traditions. Heľpa is a never ending source of various forms of folk art and culture. This was appraised even by one of the best experts on the Slovakian countryside living and folklore, K. Plicka, who said that the folk costumes, people and traditions in this village have been preserved at their purest. He made a lot of photo and camera documentation from traditional games of the youth of Heľpa, which were later used in the brilliant movie Zem Spieva. You can experience the sparkle and authenticity of the local folklore if you visit the Horehronské Days of Singing and Dancing Festival, which is held annually in Heľpa at the beginning of summer.

## TELGÁRTSKA SLUČKA (3)

The construction of the railway between Červená skala and Margecany between 1931 and 1936 was an important task in the Slovakian transport network. The designers of this challenging work selected several interesting technical solutions. For example they dealt with the problem of a steep terrain above the village of Telgárty, while incorporating the railway into the countryside as well as possible. Trains enter the loop tunnel, a unique construction in Slovakia, behind the village. The 1,239-metre spiral loop with a semi-diameter arch of 400 metres reaches the required level of the terrain while the distance between the end and the beginning of the tunnel is only 83 metres. The bank of the railway in the tunnel is 12.5 % and it leads onto the Chramošský Viaduct, a brick bridge with nine arches. It is 113.6 metres long and 18 metres high and spans the Gregorová Dolina Valley.

## KRÁĽOVA HOĽA (4)

Only Kriváň can compete with Kráľova Hoľa in popularity with regards to the national symbol that these two peaks represent and in their re-

presentation in folk songs and legends. Kráľova Hoľa at 1,946 metres fascinates by its mightiness. It is located in the most eastern part of the Low Tatras ridge between the Horehronie, Liptov and Spiš Regions. It deserves its nickname of the 'Roof of Slovakia' as four important Slovakian rivers, Hron, Čierny Váh, Hornád and Hnilec, rise on its huge slopes. At the peak are rugged rocks. On a fine day the top offers phenomenal panoramic views reaching from the Hungarian border to Poland. There is also an important trigulation point. A TV transmitter was built slightly below the peak in 1960 and it has become the typical sign of the mountain visible from afar.

### ROLLING MILL IN VALKOVŇA (5)
The village of Valkovňa was created in 1954 by the merging of several small communities in the valley of the Hron River between Pohorelá and Šumiacie. Their inhabitants had rather different lifestyles than the farmers and shepherds in the surrounding villages. Iron works developed here in the past, employing people with craft and workman skills. Several hammer-mills and rolling mills were built in the Horehronie Region as a part of the Coburgovské Ironworks in the 18th and the 19th centuries to process local iron ore. One of the first in Slovakia, a workmen colony developed in the village of Nová Maša in the second half of the 18th century. The remains of the original sheet mill from 1832 are in the village of Valkovňa, which operated until 1926.

### MEANDERS OF HRON (6)
After ten kilometres of its long journey from its source to the Danube, the Hron River meanders in the section below Telgárt until the village of Červená Skala. Coiling lazily, the river creates numerous meanders. The meadows around the zigzagging river are permanently wet, providing thus excellent conditions for humid species of vegetation with many rare species. A peat bog is forming on the surface of the meadow with standing water. It is the Meandre Hrona Nature Reserve.

1

## ČIERNOHRONSKÁ FOREST RAILWAY (1)

Hundreds of kilometres of narrow-gauge railways once existed in Slovakia; they transported wood from the Carpathian forests. The first 11 kilometres of the forest railway in the northern part of Veporské Vrchy Hills was opened in 1908. It gradually extended to an unbelievable 132 kilometres. One of the railways went through the Dolina Kamenistého Potoka Valley to the village of Sihla, another one ended at the Dobročský Prales forest. Demolition of the Čiernohronská railway was seriously considered in the 1980s, but fortunately there were enough enthusiasts who have managed to restore this valuable, and now very popular, technical monument. Thanks to their work Horehronie acquired one of its greatest tourist attractions. The historical Čiernohronská forest railway now operates in two sections. The longer one connects the stations Chvatimy pri Hronci with Čierny Balog, the second goes from Čierny Balog to the open-air forestry museum in Vydrov.

## VODROVO FOREST OPEN-AIR MUSEUM (2)

The pleasant journey by the Čiernohronská railway can be even more interesting. Another unusual and very resourceful local tourist attraction, the open-air forestry museum, was opened in the Vydrovská Dolina Valley in the summer of 2003. The entry is at the last stop of the upper section of the railway. A large amount of exhibits associated with forests and woodcutting are in this museum. There is a 2,900-metre long nature trail with 47 interesting stops. While walking in the natural environment visitors can learn about traditional and modern wood mining, methods of wood skidding and transportation by a chute or a cableway. A short section of the railway demonstrates the technique of the loading and transporting of logs on carriages pulled by a steam engine. Exhibited is also forest transportation equipment, for example forest tractors and even a helicopter. An important section of the museum is devoted to the protection of the forest its wildlife.

## SIHLIANSKA PLAIN (3)

This plain at the west of the Veporské Vrchy Hills is in a way a large roof with the springs of several important Slovakian rivers: Slatina, Ipeľ, Rimavica and Čierny Hron. The sparse, rugged surface of the plain is deforested to a great extent. There were once fields, however being rather infertile due to the harsh climate, they were replaced by meadows and clearances to a greater extent. Thick forests are only to be found on the steep slopes that surround the plain and on the Poľana Peak that towers above the plain at the west. People found their way to this landscape of high elevation; there are four villages and several communities.

## DOBROČSKÝ PRALES (4)

The Carpathians forests were listed among the UNESCO World Nature Heritage Monuments

2

in 2007. Among them is the Dobročský Prales Forest at the north of the Veporské Vrchy Hills. It was the first National Nature Reserve that protected the rare trees preserved in the status close to the climax vegetation community. There are rare firs; many are the oldest and largest in Slovakia. Until 1964 there was a legendary fir called 'mother of the forest', whose age was estimated at 500 years. And a fir with the record height of 58 metres grew in the forest until 1984.

## TRI VODY SMELTERY NEAR OSRBLIE (5)

A rare technical monument is to be found in the forested valley near the Osrblie village, which is a popular Slovakian centre of biathlon. In the locality called Tri Vody on the confluence of three creeks, a blast furnace, the first in Hungary, was built in 1795. It was a part of the Dreiwasser-Gewerkschaft iron works owned and run by members of the Ľubovietová Mining Association. The blast furnace used charcoal and produced iron from the local iron ore, which was then further produced in the iron works, hammer mill and rolling mill in the nearby Osrblie. Iron pipes, tiles, and pottery as well as cannonballs were produced here. The place in Tri Vody burnt down in 1882 and was taken apart later; however a fragment of the furnace has been preserved. Its 8-metre high armature was conserved and it is one of the remarkable technical monuments reminiscent of the era of the fast development of iron production in this area.

## LOM NAD RIMAVICOU (6)

One of the four villages in the Sihlianska Planina Plain sits at 1,015 metres; it is one of the highest villages in Slovakia (except the villages in the High Tatras). Lom nad Rimavicou was settled during the later phase of the Vallachian colonisation, possibly not before the 18th century. It was later settled by the mountaineers from northern Slovakia who were invited to remove a large slash caused by a tornado. This colourful village sat in a picturesque landscape near the rise of the Rimavie River is remarkable for the high number of preserved wooden folk architecture. There are impressive groups of traditional wooden cottages.

## SIHLIANSKE HUCULE (7)

The cool and moist Sihlianska Plain has excellent conditions for the Hucul Pony breed. A herd of these small but tough horses browses the meadows near the Sihla village; it is the second largest herd in Slovakia, only the stud farm in Topľčianky have more Huculs. The breed is considered to be a descendent of old Eurasian wild horses called Tarpan and Kkertak. Their name is derived from a region in the Ruthenia, settled by mountaineers called Hutsuls. It is not known when people tamed the horses and started using them for hard work. Originally, Hucul was a typical horse of farmers and shepherds in the mountains and foothills of the entire Carpathians, from Slovakia to Romania. Huculs are now successfully used in agro tourism.

# PODPOĽANIE

### PUSTÝ CASTLE (1)

This castle looms at the south above the town of Zvolen and, sprawling on 8 hectares, it is (with regards to the built-up area) the largest castle in Slovakia, even larger than Spišský Castle. Nevertheless, the huge size of the castle is not apparent as only fragments have been preserved from the walls and even these remains are mostly covered by forest greenery. Pustý Castle was built as a royal castle in the 12th century and it later became the seat of the Zvolen County Council. In the past there were two fortifications on the two hilltops, connected by a ridge, on the forested hill above the town. The building development of the castle was completed in the first half of the 14th century, when the powerful Dončc was the Head of Zvolen Council. The period of the great significance of the Zvolen County and Pustý Castle died out after the death of Donč and this role was taken on by the Zvolenský Chateau. Pustý Castle suffered great damage during the fights between the army of Ján Huňady and the soldiers of Ján Jiskra in the 15th century and it fell into ruin after a fire in 1451.

### ZVOLENSKÝ CHATEAU (2)

The powerful head of the Zvolen Council ruled a large territory which also included the Liptov, Turiec and Orava regions. He did not live in the town but in the castle above it. The fortified Gothic chateau in the town was built between 1370 and 1382 as a luxurious residence for the Hungarian King Ľudovít I, who visited the town when hunting in the surrounding forests. An extensive Renaissance reconstruction in the 16th century gave the Zvolen Chateau more or less its present-day appearance. It still played an important part in the protection system of anti-Ottoman fortresses that guarded the access to the rich mining towns in central Pohronie. The

interiors were greatly altered during a Baroque reconstruction in the second half of the 18<sup>th</sup> century. It gave the chateau its most splendid room – the royal hall with a lacunar ceiling which depicts 78 portraits of the Roman emperors and kings from the Habsburg family. The chateau now houses the Slovakian National Gallery with a valuable collection of Gothic and modern art.

## NÁMESTIE SNP IN ZVOLEN (3)

This large rectangular square is in the centre of Zvolen. It is the largest in Slovakia and one of the largest in central Europe. It has a rectangular shape in the direction of the meridian. At its south side is the Zvolenský Chateau, while the northern side is enclosed by the Baroque Finkova Mansion. In the centre of the square is the parish Church of St. Elizabeth from the end of the 13<sup>th</sup> century, the oldest historical monument in the town. The second landmark of the square is the much younger Evangelic church (1923) that protrudes into the square at the north. The former town house at the same side of the square now houses the Wood and Timber Museum. The most beautiful historical burgher houses are at the east side of the square, including the Theatre of J. G. Tajovský. Námestie SNP is a pedestrian zone and also boasts a small park, a fountain and a monument to SNP in the shape of a large typical Walachian axe by J. Kulich.

## TECHNICAL UNIVERSITY IN ZVOLEN (4)

Zvolen is rightfully considered the key town of the forest and timber industry in Slovakia. It has several production, research and educational institutions and companies that operate throughout the whole of Slovakia. At the east edge of the town is the large Bučina timber company and resort and academic research centres roofed by the National Forest Centre. The key educational institution is the Technical University, with its faculties focusing on forestry, woodcutting and ecological and environmental sciences. This university continues with the tradition that was started by the Mining and Forestry Academia founded in 1762 as the first one of its time in Europe. The first future forest engineers joined the University of Forestry and Woodcutting, the predecessor of the current university, in 1952. The present-day Alma Mater of Zvolen uses a modern edifice built near the bus station.

## ARMOUR TRAIN HURBAN IN ZVOLEN (5)

Zvolen was one of the key sites of the Slovakian National Uprising in the autumn of 1944. Three armour-plated trains, called Štefánik, Hurban and Masaryk, were used in the fight by the rebels. They were built in the Zvolen railway workshops as the rebels had insufficient heavy army equipment. There is a replica of the Hurban armour-plated train in the park between the Zvolen Chateau and the train station.

## ARBORETUM BOROVÁ HORA (6)

As the centre of forestry and woodcutting, Zvolen boasts an arboretum that specialises in the research and breeding of trees of Slovakia. The arboretum belongs to the Technical University in Zvolen, however some of its parts are accessible to the public. It was built on 50 hectares in the slope of the Borová Mountain at the northern edge of the town in 1965. It focuses on growing local trees and fulfills science and research purposes. It boasts over 400 species of trees and their 700 forms; in total there are over 30,000 trees. The largest collection of roses in Slovakia in the rosary is also noteworthy. It counts more than 600 types of roses in over 4,000 bushes. It has types of roses from the Czech Republic as well as Slovakia; however there are also species from other countries. Visitors can see the attractive collection of 500 of cactus species mainly from Mexico and South America. The Borová Arboretum has been protected since 1981.

## CHURCH OF ST. MATTHEW
## IN ZOLNÁ (1)

A very important sacral monument is in the small village of Zolná near Zvolen in the valley of the Zolná Stream. The rare fortified Early Gothic Church of St. Matthew from the 13th century was first documented in written sources in 1311. The interior boasts valuable medieval murals; the fresco of St. George fighting the dragon is very interesting. The saint is not depicted in the traditional way; instead of a single he has a double cross on his shield. The church, just like a nearby mansion, was built from the volcano tuf that is plentiful around the village. The stone comes from the Štampľochy quarry; the famous unearthed Zolniansky lahar is nearby. This congealed mud was moved millions of years ago during the wild volcanic eruptions of the nearby Poľana stratovolcano.

## SLIAČ SPA (2)

There are not many places where mineral water springs have a pleasant temperature as well as a high content of carbonic oxide, yet they have such a unique spring in the Sliač Spa, near the town of Sliač. Its water has an ideal temperature and there is no need to heat or cool it. It is successfully used for curing heart-vascular and gynaecological diseases. Its curative powers have been know since the ancient times and a written source about the spring exists from as early as 1244. The first spa procedures started in Sliač in 1657 and it is one of the most popular spas in Slovakian. The complex of the spa pavilions set in the lovely greenery of a park is considered a fine work of modern architecture.

### KOVÁČOVÁ SPA (3)

This spa is a twin of the more famous Sliač Spa about 5 kilometres away. It sits on the right side of the valley of the Hron River at the foothills of Kremnické Vrchy Hills. The spas do not compete as they specialise in the treatment of different diseases. Kováčová cures patients with diseases of movement and some neurological diseases. The local mineral springs have a temperature of almost 50 degrees and come from a depth of 502 metres. They are successfully used in the curing of rheumatism, joint infections and the Bechterev Illness. Kováčová is an old village with a history reaching as far back as to the 13th century, however the spa is much younger, having been opened in 1929. Kováčová is also widely visited by the public, for it has a nice thermal swimming pool.

### DOBRÁ NIVA CASTLE (4)

There is no need to look for this castle near the village of the same name in the Pliešovská Kotlina Hollow, as it looms on a hill above neighbouring Podzámočok, a village situated further north. Dobrá Niva was founded in the 13th century to protect a trade path from Krupina to Zvolen and it was in the possession of queens in the 15th century. It played an important role during the Ottoman wars as an advanced protection of the Zvolen Chateau. The castellan of the estate moved into a new building in the settlement below the castle at the beginning of the 17th century and only a sentry remained at the castle. It came into the possession of the Esterházi (Eszterházy) family in 1614. It was deserted and left to dereliction at the end of the 18th century. Dobrá Niva Castle is an example of how the other Slovakian castles could have looked. Only a part has been preserved from the original building, however it is well preserved and maintained together with its surroundings.

### MANSION IN OSTRÁ LÚKA (5)

Despite the promise of the members of the Štúrovo Movement never to marry for the love of the Slovakian nation, it is no secret that its leader Ľudovít Štúr fell in love with a Slovakian girl, Adela Ostrolúcka (1824 – 1853), from a prominent aristocratic family. They met in the village of Zemianske Podhradie, where Adela's parents had a mansion. Štúr's brother Samko worked here as the local Evangelic curate. Štúr taught the young lady Polish and Slovakian and her father M. Ostrolúcky helped him to get the mandate of the member of the parliament on behalf of the free royal town of Zvolen, as his second family mansion was in Ostrá Lúka near Zvolen. Adéla got typhoid and died in 1853 and was buried in the family tomb near the Renaissance mansion from 1636.

## VÍGĽAŠ CASTLE (1)

When observed from the road, Vígľaš Castle is very inconspicuous; however visitors are very surprised upon entering this large medieval monument. The castle, dating from the 14th century, was recorded as a royal hunting manor as early as 1393. The original three-winged Gothic building with a chapel was rebuilt into a Renaissance fortress during the Ottoman threat in the 16th century. Its strength was tested by the Ottoman attacks, however it was never conquered. It became the possession of the Esterházi (Eszterházy) family in the 18th century, who converted it into a comfortable aristocratic seat. The last reconstructions towards the end of the 19th century were carried out in the spirit of the upcoming romantic Historicism. Vígľaš survived centuries to have its fate sealed at the end of World War II. It burnt down and became a ruin in 1945. A gradual reconstruction of the castle is currently underway.

## FOREST RAILWAY IN VÍGĽAŠ (2)

A monument made of a steam engine with few carriages stands in the village of Vígľaš below the castle of the same name. It is reminiscent of the past times, when trains operated along the forest railway in Vígľaš. The construction of the narrow-gauge started in 1904 and its entire 25 kilometres through Očová to Kyslinky in the Poľana area was completed in 1907. It transported forest workers and wood from the surrounding thick woods of the Poľana mountain. However, it was closed down in 1975 for being uneconomical. It is a pity that calculations omitted the possibility of using the railway for tourism, which would have brought a high profit.

## MONUMENT TO MATEJ BEL
## IN OČOVÁ (3)

For 300 years inhabitants of this village have been proud of its enlightened native and scholar Matej Bel (1684-1749). He was born in this village, famous for interesting and still practiced folklore, and became a great authority active in the fields of history and theoretical theology. He was considered to be the 'great jewel of Hungary'. He was born into a family of a butcher and a farmer; however rose to aristocratic status for his merits in the field of science and pedagogy. His book called *Notitia Hungariaenovae Historico-Geographica* about the history and geography of the then Hungary brought him an international fame. The university in Banská Bystrica was named after him. A monument to Bel was unveiled at the occasion of the 300 year anniversary of his birth outside a basic school in Očová on 22nd July 1984. Bel's jubilee was even listed in the UNESCO anniversary calendar. A monument was erected on the site, where his native house once stood. The central motif of the monument is a statue of Matej Bel by an academic sculptor, J. Kulich.

## DETVA (4)

This small town at the southern foothills of the extinguished Poľana volcano is not famous for historical monuments. Its inhabitants decided to practice folklore and present it in a very attractive and unrepeatable form. Mainly the male traditional costumes are easily identifiable for their typical shirt, which does not cover the belly. A real in-

habitant of Detva has to have a *fujara*, a large folk shepherd's flute of unique design originating from Slovakia. The best players on this instrument are supposedly born in the Detva area. The beauty and charm of the local costumes, dances and songs are best watched at the traditional Folklórne Slávnosti pod Poľanou Festival, which is held annually at the beginning of June in the amphitheatre near the village.

## PODPOLIANSKE LAZY (5)

A charming landscape, which has attracted numerous painters and photographers, lies at the southern foothills of the Poľana massif. This unique scenery, created by a mosaic of fields, meadows, and orchards, is dotted by scarce small farmsteads and complemented by the huge silhouette of the extinguished Poľana volcano. The typical signs of this landscape are dispersed individual farmsteads. Fortunately, the socialist collectivisation, which destroyed the borders of fields eradicating thus the traditional structure of the landscape, did not affect this area. So thankfully numerous narrow strips of small fields, which are reminiscent of Chinese rice fields, have been preserved.

## POĽANA (1)

The best preserved Tertiary volcano in Slovakia lies in the centre of the country. The massive stratovolcano extinguished millions of years ago, however it has maintained several typical signs of a volcano. There is a huge fissure in the centre of the massif which was created by the erosion of the volcanic caldera. Remains of the outside layer of the volcano with regularly alternating valleys and crests sprawl towards the edge of the massif. The prominent boundary between the caldera and the outside layer of the volcano is created by a sharp ridge in the shape of an incomplete ring. In its centre lies the highest peak of the mountain range called Poľana (1,458 m) some maps state it as Zadná Poľana. At the same time it is the highest volcano peak in Slovakia.

## PRÍSLOPY (2)

The mountains that flank the central caldera of the Tertiary Poľana volcano are mostly higher than 1,000 metres. A deep depression lies only in the southern arch of the ridge. The ridge decreases steeply from Drábovka Peak into the Príslopy (956 m) Saddle and rises again on the opposite side into the Želobudzská Skalka Rock. The slope below the rocky peak offers the best views of the Poľana caldera. The surroundings of the Príslopy Saddle dotted with bilberries are amongst the most photogenic places in Slovakia.

## VODOPÁD BYSTRÉ (3)

Tourists climbing up the Bystrá Dolina Valley meet a natural obstacle in its upper part. The waters of the splendid 23-metre-high Vodopád Bystré Waterfall gush over a rocky step made of hard andesite. There is another, smaller waterfall as well. This natural obstacle can be managed via an iron ladder. The rocky step was formed on the bench of harder andesite that is more resistant to the destructive erosions than the surrounding softer pyroclastic rock. A depression of a large block of rock on the tectonic brake also helped to form the rocky step. Vodopád Bystré is amongst the highest waterfalls in the volcanic parts of the Western Carpathians and it is a Protected Natural Monument.

## KALAMÁRKA (4)

Rocky steps in valleys and mainly in mountain crests are typical for the Poľana area. They resulted from the activity of these former stratovolcano mountains with periodic eruptions and lava flow. This created the typical layers, which include the tougher cooled lava and softer products of the volcanic eruptions. The erosion of the volcano consequently formed the hard benches of the former lava as terrain steps, often rock walls and towers. A nice example is the Kalamárka rock. The conspicuous rocky defile of andesite is 20 metres high and towers above the valley of Detviansky Creek in the most southern part of Poľana. The typical sign of rocks in the Kalamárka site are horizontal cracks that divide the rock into numerous horizontal layers and benches.

## MELICHOVA ROCK (5)

The landmark of the landscape of the southern part of Poľana is the Melichova Rock. This conspicuous lonely sharp andesite formation towers above the surrounding terrain at the southern edge of the mountain range above the Skliarovo Lazy locality. This 30-metre high rock needle was created by the weathering and selective erosion of cooled andesite lava. It is a Protected Natural Monument. A tourist trail circles the Melichova Rock; it is used as the fastest trek to the Poľana Hotel. The trail passes a derelict house below the rock. The rock was named after the last member of the family who lived there until 2003.

## BÁTOVSKÝ BOULDER (6)

The caldera in the centre of Poľana, with the Kyslinky settlement and a chalet, once was an enclosed depression. That is no longer true as the upper part of the Hučava Creek moved inside due to bad erosion. The stream flowed into the caldera and now collects waters from the mountain. A huge block of volcanic rock separated from the northern slope of the Hučava Chasm a long time ago and fell onto the flat meadow of the stream. The boulder is 14 metres high and 8 metres wide.

## JÁNOŠÍKOVA SKALA (7)

The massive rock wall visible at the northern slope of Hrochotská Dolina Valley is called Janošíkova Skala. A large opening is visible in the 200 metre long and 30 metre high rocky defile. It could have been formed in a similar way to the Bátovský Boulder. The opening was later enlarged by erosion. It is called Abčiná and is referred to as a cave, although it is not a real cave, as it was not created in limestone. According to a legend, the legendary treasure of the Slovakian hero Jánošik was hidden here.

# CENTRAL POHRONIE

## MESTSKÝ CASTLE IN KREMNICA (1)

According to an old legend, this town was established thanks to a grouse. When the lords of Šášov caught this bird during a hunt they found gold specks in its throat, and this surprising discovery led them to the gold ledge. However, the historical facts have a rather different version about the origins of this Golden Town. A mining settlement called *Cremnychbana* was founded in the heart of the mountains in the 13th century. A parish church with a charnel house and an aristocratic house on the top of the hill were merged into a fortified town castle. A ring of double fortification walls encloses the northern and southern entry gate with the Zámocké Stairs, the Clock Tower and the Banícka Bastion. The central building of the castle is the grandiose Gothic Church of St. Catherine from the 15th century. The Charnel of St. Andrew from the 13th century and the former town hall from the end of the 14th century are also noteworthy. Mestský Castle is open to the public. The Museum of Coins and Medals of Kremnica, located in the castle, presents six interesting expositions about the history, archeology and art of the region.

## CHARNEL OF ST. ANDREW (2)

The oldest building of Mestský Castle in Kremnica is the Romanesque-Gothic Charnel of St. Andrew. The oldest written document about the charnel dates from 1506; however it is much older, dating from the 13th century. This sacral building with a round ground-plan has two stories. The first floor houses an ossuary with Romanesque six-part vault while a Gothic chapel with preserved medieval murals is on the top floor. According to a legend, a murder happened in the charnel in the 15th century and sensitive people can allegedly feel a gentle shaking in the building.

## TOWN FORTIFICATION IN KREMNICA (3)

The wealthy Kremnica, profiting from gold mining and minting, definitely needed a quality fortification system. It was built between 1405 and 1426. A double stone wall with bastions encircled the town and it connected to Mestský Castle at the north. Three gates originally led inside the town, however only one is preserved – the Dolná Gate in the southern part of the walls with a barbican that was added in 1530. It houses an interesting exposition devoted to the history of skiing in Slovakia. Another preserved element of the fortification is the round Čierna Tower in the southwest corner, built at the highest section of the walls. The Červená Bastion at the southeast corner is also well-preserved.

## CHURCH OF ST. CATHERINE IN KREMNICA (4)

The large Church of St. Catherine is a landmark of the impressive silhouette of Mestský Castle in Kremnica. This Late Gothic two-nave church dates from the middle of the 15th century, when it was rebuilt from an older Romanesque church. The date of 1488 appears on the splendid Gothic net vault of the church. The sections of the vault are decorated by medieval paintings of saints, and there are stone epitaphs on the walls of the church. The Neo Gothic interior of the church from 1885 boasts several valuable art pieces, such as the Late Gothic sculpture of Madonna on the side altar and a Renaissance marble baptismal font. A jewel of the church is an organ of great quality. Visitors can enjoy its beautiful sound at the Kremnický Hradný Organ Festival that is held annually in August.

## ŠTEFÁNIKOVO NÁMESTIE IN KREMNICA (1)

The wealthy mining town built a suitably ostentatious central square that later received its name after M. R. Štefánik. In the centre of the square stands a grandiose Baroque Black Death Column with a fountain, set in a green park. An originally Gothic burgher house from the 15th century is on the east side of the square. It was rebuilt into the town hall after 1738, for the original seat of the city council was destroyed by a fire. The Roman-Catholic parish as well as several burgher houses on the square also have Gothic foundations, even though they have newer Renaissance, Baroque and Classicism facades. The spire of the Franciscan church towers above the square at the east. The church is adjacent to a monastery, which was built between 1653 and 1777. The historical mint located in the northwest corner is significant.

## MINT IN KREMNICA (2)

Among the town privileges, which Kremnica received from the King Karol Róbert in 1328, was also the right to mint. Initially, local gold was used and coins of the Florence style called Florény were minted; however the mint produced *Kremnické Dukáty* coins in 14th century which were considered the strongest currency in cen-

tral Europe for the high quality and permanent sterling. The historical building of the mint is the largest in the world and at the same time is one of the oldest permanently working mints; state currency, memorable coins and medals are minted here today. The Museum of Coins and Medals located in a burgher house on the square provides information about the minting and medals production in Kremnica.

### BLACK DEATH COLUMN
### OF THE TRINITY IN KREMNICA (3)

The grandiose Trinity Column on the Štefánikovo Square in Kremnica is one of the most beautiful monuments in Slovakia. There is not another Black Death Column with such rich and splendid decoration. In the past another stone pillar stood on the site (1711); however it was moved into the village of Horná Ves in 1761. The present-day column was built eleven years later and was devoted to the victims of a Black Death plague in 1710. The column is 20 metres high. The sculpture decoration consisting of 14 monumental Baroque sculptures and numerous smaller statues and angels is the work of Dionýz Stanetti and Martin Vögerle; it was finished after the death of these artists by their journeyman T. Mayer.

## CENTRE OF EUROPE IN KREMNICKÉ BANE (1)

The ancient Church of St. John from the 13th century sits in a beautiful spot in the middle of meadows near the town of Kremnické Banie There are several explanations for why it is located in an open landscape. According to a legend, the construction works started in a different location, however all that was built during a day was discovered destroyed in the morning. This mysterious event told them to build in a different place so they went to search for a more suitable spot and found a burning thorny bush. There was a crying child inside the bush and the new location for the church was therefore obvious. It was built in such way that the altar stands on the very spot where the bush was burning. Another legend speaks of an angel who selected the location for the church. Well, there is possibly a less mysterious explanation, as the church served worshippers from several villages so a place suitable to all was selected. A stone next to the wall around the church shows the exact geographical centre of Europe.

## ČERTOVA SKALA (2)

The southern edge of the Kremnické Vrchy Hills descends steeply into a valley of the Hron River. A diagonal Nature Trail up the slope climbs to the National Nature Reserve. Just before the peak, there is a remarkable isolated formation amongst the andesite rocks. Its shape resembles a mushroom and it is called Čertova Skala. The massif in the southern section of the mountains is formed by colourful rocks. The soft tuff is more prone to erosion that the harder andesite lava rock. In the case of formations like Čertova Skala, a large andesite rock prevents erosion of the softer tuffs underneath. However, it is only a matter of time before the 'leg' of the mushroom will become slim to such extend that its 'head' falls down the slope, and the formation will be gone.

## SKALKA (3)

The highest peak of the Kremnické Vrchy Hills Flochová (1,317 m) lies in a relatively remote place and is therefore not very popular. Many more people walk the dense network of tourist trails near the Skalka Tourist Centre, which received its name from the dominant Skalka Mountain (1,232 m) with a TV transmitter on its Suchá Hora Peak. Its high location guarantees good snow conditions in the winter and it is famous amongst snow sports enthusiasts. The skiing season usually last until late spring. There are five lifts and slopes with an artificial snow system and electrical lighting for night skiing. The terrain offers excellent conditions for cross-country skiing and ski-tourism. One of the three stadiums of the Bielá Stopa SNP races is at Skalka. The tradition of the mass cross-country ski marathon, which starts at Skalka or nearby Krahúľe and ends at Králiky, was started in 1974.

## JASTRABSKÁ SKALA (4)

Although not the highest peak in Kremnické Vrchy, Jastrabská Skala Rock (683 m) is a landmark of the landscape. The asymmetrical rock at the top section of Ostrý Vrch, formed by Tertiary ryolits and ryolit pyroclast, gives the peak its typical silhouette. Jastrabská Skala is named after the village Jastrabá at its eastern foothill. A tourist marked trail to the top of this viewing peak starts on the other side of the mountain at the village of Bartošova Lehôtka. The nature beech forest on the volcanic substrate is a Natural Monument; its area exceeds 8 hectares.

## ŠÁŠOV CASTLE (1)

According to a legend, Šášov was built by the lord of Zvolenský Castle for his court jester who saved his life during a hunt. The position of the castle atop a rock at the edge of the Štiavnické Vrchy Hills suggests that it was chosen purposely as it was to control an important side section of the path to Kremnice along the Váh River. According to historians, the history of Šášov goes back to the 13th century. The castellans and later the owners of the castle, the Dócio family, were known as bitter enemies of the monks from the Hronský Beňadikt and regularly ransacked their possession. Tököliho (Thököly) soldiers destroyed the castle in 1677. The castle is now a rather large ruin.

## REVIŠTE CASTLE (2)

This castle looms atop a forested hill at the edge of the Vtáčnik Mountains. Its silhouette reflects on the surface of the Hron River. It was built in the 13th century as part of a project of the Tekov Council to create a protection of the valley along the Hron, which provided access to the wealthy mining towns. The castle went into the possession of the powerful Dócio family in 1490, who were not very friendly with other aristocratic families. Their squabbles with neighbours and also the realistic threat of the Ottomans resulted in the rebuilding of the Gothic castle into a Renaissance fortress. The tragic death of Žigmund Dóci, who was killed by an Ottoman headsman in 1647, was the end of this family, and the Revište Castle went into the possession of the Court Chamber in Vienna. It was conquered and looted by the soldiers of the rebellious Imrich Tököli and has been a ruin ever since. It offers a nice view and is frequent-ly visited in the summer; there is a camp for rafters and boating enthusiasts below the castle on the bank of the Hron.

## STAROHUTSKÝ VODOPÁD (3)

This waterfall is above the village of Stará Huť near Nová Baňa, which boasts one of the oldest Hungarian glassworks. A small creek, the left tributary to the Starohutský Creek, gushes over the 5-metre high step of andesite rock. The current becomes stronger during the spring, when it collects melted snow. This impressive creation is a Protected Natural Monument and is one of the stops along the Nature Trail through the Vtáčnik Mountains.

## MUSEUM OF POHRONIE IN NOVÁ BAŇA (4)

The name of the town of Nová Baňa (New Mine) reveals the occupation of its former inhabitants. Although called Nová (New) this town has a long history reaching back to at least the 14th century. It was built by miners from Pukance as a new mining settlement near the discovered golden ledges. Nová Baňa received the privileges of a free royal town already in 1345. Several valuable historical monuments are reminiscent of the past wealth of the town. The most important is the town hall built for the royal representatives on the square in 1353. It now houses the Museum of Pohronie.

## PUTIKOV VŔŠOK (5)

Central and eastern Slovakia was shaken by volcanic eruptions several million years ago. The epilogue of these natural dramas was the activities of the last Slovakian volcano, located in the valley of the Hron River near Nová Baňa. It was estimated that these events took place more than 100,000 years ago. The youngest Slovakian volcano is an unremarkable hill called Putikov Vŕšok. The hole near the crater and numerous schorches, lapilli and pumice shows that it was a very hot area in the recent geological past. Several lava streams flowed down the volcano into the valley of the Hron. The longest spilled onto the meadow of the river; this helped to determine the time of eruptions. Basalt is mined at the end of the lava streams and is used for the production of insulation material in the nearby factory in Nová Baňa. Splendid meadows growing on the lava streams dotted with several solitary trees complement the lovely scenery.

## MONASTERY
## IN HRONSKÝ BEŇADIK (6)

The Hungarian King Gejza II decided to build a Benedictine Monastery in 1075 above the Slovakian Brána Gate, in the spot where the Hron River leaves the territory of the Carpathians. Benedictines built the three-nave basilica with two towers on the foundations of a Romanesque church between 1346 and 1375. It was consecrated to St. Egídio. A large conversion of the monastery into the anti-Ottoman fortress started in 1565 after the Benedictines left. The monastery was damaged by a fire in 1881 and was reconstructed in the Gothic style afterward. It became a detention camp in 1950 for monks imprisoned by the Communists. The Pallotine Order has been looking after the monastery since 1999. The complex of the monastery in Hronský Beňadik is a National Cultural Monument with scores of valuable clerical and artistic monuments. The basilica houses a precious relic, the God's Blood, which was given to the King Matthias Corvinus by the pope. It is a piece of the renowned Veil of Veronica with dots of the blood of Christ.

# ŠTIAVNICKÝ REGION

## TROJIČNÝ COLUMN
## IN BANSKÁ ŠTIAVNICA (1)

The historic town of Banská Štiavnica, listed in the UNESCO World Cultural Heritage List, sprawls in a rather steep descending valley. The rough, narrow terrain does not provide enough space for a large central square so the town only has small picturesque squares. The most beautiful is the Trojičné Square, named after the Trojičný (Trinity) Column in its centre. The Baroque column of the Holy Trinity was built between 1759 and 1767 to commemorate the dreadful Black Death plague that decimated the population of the town in 1710. The author of the sculpture is Dionýz Stanetti, one of the best sculptors of the times. He made a similar grandiose column in Kremnica. The sculptures of seven saints represent the patrons of miners and protectors of the inhabitants against the plague. The stonework is by K. Holzknecht, who was considered one of the best masons in central Europe at the time.

## STARÝ CHATEAU
## IN BANSKÁ ŠTIAVNICA (2)

The arrival of German settlers in the 12th and 13th centuries in the town was a strong impulse. The colonists came into the Slovakian village of Štiavnica below the Paradajs Hill. The village was growing rapidly and received the town privileges in 1238. These privileges became the example for establishing documents of other mining towns in the surroundings. The medieval town of Banská Štiavnica was rapidly forming around the fortified parish Church of the Virgin Mary, originally a Romanesque basilica from the beginning of the 13th century. The preserved Charnel of St. Michael also dates from this period. A fortified town castle developed around the church in the 14th century; it is now called the Starý (Old) Chateau. The fortification walls encircle a bastion and an entry gate with a tower. The basilica was rebuilt into a Gothic hall church at the beginning of the 16th century; however the castle was rebuilt into a sentry fortress during the Ottoman wars. The castle church was sacrificed in order to strengthen the fortress in the mid-16th century. A palace with corner towers was built over it; tumbling of the vault of the nave created a courtyard. The later Baroque modifications of the Starý Chateau were not significant, affecting mainly the originally Gothic entry tower. It now houses collections of the Slovakian Mining Museum.

## HALLENBACHOV HOUSE
## IN BANSKÁ ŠTIAVNICA (3)

This house is the largest building on the Trojičné Square in the town. It was rebuilt from an old Gothic house in the Renaissance style in the 16th century and received its mainly Baroque present-day appearance in the 18th century. Hallenbachov House originally housed the Mining Court and later went into the possession of the Mining and Forestry Academia. It now houses a mineralogical exposition of the Slovakian Mining Museum. Visitors can see over 400 minerals from several regions. An interesting part of the tour of the museum is the Michal Tunnel; entry into the underground mining corridor has been preserved in the back part of the building. Visitors can access 76 metres of the tunnel.

## NOVÝ CHATEAU
## IN BANSKÁ ŠTIAVNICA (4)

The Nový (New) Chateau was built on a hill south of the historical centre of Banská Štiavnica and it is a landmark of the town together with the Calvary. This Renaissance sentry fortress, built between 1564 and 1571, was a significant strategic point of the anti-Ottoman defence. The town fortification walls once connected to the fortress on both sides, however they no longer exist. Nový Chateau is shaped like a massive quadrant tower strengthened by four identical round corner bastions. A pyramid-like roof topped by a small onion-shaped tower covers the entire building and loopholes were made in the perimeter walls. The chateau also served as a public clock in the past – every quarter hour was announced by blowing a trumpet. The Nový Chateau was built as an anti-Ottoman fortress and therefore it now houses an exposition of the Slovakian Mining Museum about the anti-Ottoman fights in Slovakia.

## STARÉ MESTO
## IN BANSKÁ ŠTIAVNICA (5)

Inhabitants of this town like lizards, for according to an old legend, this small animal was behind the birth of the town. A local shepherd once saw two lizards with shiny skins covered by golden dust. Thanks to this, the boy discovered a rich gold mine. The news travelled fast and gold-diggers and miners soon arrived in Štiavnické Vrchy and established a town in the area. Gold was behind its foundation, yet the town wealth came from silver, hence its nickname Silver Banská Štiavnica. The original mining settlement called Bana was not on the site of the present-day historical centre, but on the Glanzenberg Hill. So even though this part is now called Staré Mesto (Old Town) it has no houses, streets or squares and boasts only a natural environment with rocks and vegetation.

## CHURCH OF ST. CATHERINE
## IN BANSKÁ ŠTIAVNICA (6)

It only has a small spire, however the Church of St. Catherine on the crossroads of the main streets of the town is a conspicuous landmark. The Late Gothic one-nave church was built towards the end of the 15th century and consecrated in 1500. At first, it served miners, as aristocracy and rich burghers went to masses into the parish church in the Starý Chateau. The Church of St. Catherine became the parish church of the town in 1555. It belonged to the Evangelists between 1580 and 1672 and as the mass was held in Slovakian since 1658 it was also called the Slovakian Church. The main nave with the gothic net vault is flanked by lower chapels; the 1775-built Chapel of St. John of Nepomuk was built in a different, Baroque style. There are crypts with tombs of bailiffs and important citizens underneath the church.

## CHURCH OF THE ASSUMPTION OF THE VIRGIN MARY IN BANSKÁ ŠTIAVNICA (1)

This is the parish church of the town and its Empiricism faćade hides one of the town's oldest monuments. It is also called the German Church. It was built as a Romanesque Basilica of St. Nicholas in the 13th century; however this building has not been preserved. After the Dominicans left the town in 1535, their monastery with the church went to the Jesuits and later to the Piarists. The monastery was demolished in the second half of the 18th century. The church underwent several reconstructions, receiving its present-day appearance after 1806. The last reconstruction was carried out due to a fire. The interior of the church is mainly Baroque and Classicism; the medieval architecture is either hidden or unpreserved.

## KAMMERHOF IN BANSKÁ ŠTIAVNICA (2)

The largest public building in the town connected with mining is called Kammerhof. This large three-story building on Kammerhofská Street was created in 1550 by the merging of several Gothic houses from the 13th century. The medieval origin of the building is visible on its uneven ground-plan, prolonged in the direction of the gently descending main road. Kammerhof (Court Chamber) was an important office that controlled mining in the town and its surroundings and managed the mines and mints. Its head was the chief chamber count. This function later went to the director of the Mining Academy, therefore the school administration moved into the building. A stone desk with a line under one of the arches of the Renaissance loggia in the courtyard shows the local, so-called Štiavnický, meridian. Kammerhof houses expositions of the Slovakian Mining Museum about the mining history of Slovakia.

### PIARGSKA GATE
### IN BANSKÁ ŠTIAVNICA (3)

The necessity to protect the town was very relevant at the times of the Ottoman wars during the 16th and 17th centuries. Therefore a fortification system with bastions and gates that included the Nový Chateau fortress was built. The fortification was designed by an Italian engineer, Ferrabosco (involved also in the reconstruction of Bratislava Castle). The hilly terrain of the town had to be considered. The fortification was not enormous and only the Piargska Gate, one of the original five gates into the town, has been preserved. It was named after a mining town, Piarg (presently called Štiavnické Bane), as the road from the gate led to it. It was built in 1554, only several years later than the nearby Nový Chateau.

### CLAPPER IN BANSKÁ ŠTIAVNICA (4)

This Renaissance building in the shape of a quadrant tower with a shingle roof ending in a spire and a couple of mining hammers dates from 1681. It had a special function. The sound produced by hitting on a wooden desk was emitted through the opening at the top of the roof. This was the way to call miners to work; it was also used during various celebrations, meetings, gatherings, funerals and fires. The ground floor of the clapper was used as a prison in the 18th century.

### KALVÁRIA IN BANSKÁ ŠTIAVNICA (5)

The regular conical peak above the town is called Kalvária. This denuded conspicuous hilltop, originally called Scharfenberg (Sharp Hill) was once a basalt volcano, active in the lower Tertiary era. Apart from being a remarkable natural formation it has great cultural and historical meaning. A unique complex of the Stations of the Cross was erected on its slopes between 1744 and 1751 upon the initiative of a Jesuit, F. Perger. The 23 buildings in total were prettily incorporated into the natural environment, thus expressing the accord between nature and human skills. The lowest building is a church with an oval ground-plan and a couple of towers.

There are three chapels at the beginning of the Calvary. The bottom staircase is a replica of the Roman Holy Stairs. The path along the slope connects 14 chapels of the Stations of the Cross leading to the top with a splendid two-towered church. The symbolical God's Grave is behind the church.

### MINING OPEN-AIR MUSEUM
### IN BANSKÁ ŠTIAVNICA (6)

The best and most coherent idea about mining in this area is provided by the natural Mining Museum. This unique mining open-air museum is part of the Slovakian Mining Museum and is located 2 kilometres southeast of the centre of Banská Štiavnica. The museum was established in 1974 by the restoration of an historical Ondrej Shaft and a Bartolomej Adit. Original mining machinery and equipment is on the surface. Visitors to the museum can visit the mine and walk the 1,300 metres of the tour. Its deepest section is 45 metres below the surface. Visitors to the museum can admire traditional and more modern equipment of the mine, although mining in this place ended a long time ago.

### MINING AND FORESTRY ACADEMY
### IN BANSKÁ ŠTIAVNICA (7)

In the past this wealthy town was a centre of culture and education of European significance. Its enlightened inhabitants, such as S. Mikovíny and Josef, Matej and Maximilián Hellovec chose the path of scientific and technological progress. They successfully applied new technologies in mines and discovered numerous revolutionary ideas and inventions. The mining education institutions were concentrated in Banská Štiavnica, which was the preferred centre of the precious ore mining in the 18th century. The oldest Hungarian mining school was established in the town in 1735 and it later became the Mining Academy, the first university of this type in Europe. It merged with the Forestry Academy (1808) in 1846.

### SITNO (1)

Only a few mountain ranges can boast such a dominant hill as Štiavnické Vrchy. Sitno (1,009 m) looms high above its surroundings and its typical silhouette is recognizable even from a great distance. Sitno is a magical hill veiled in legends. One of the most popular ones talks about knights sleeping inside the hill ready to protect the nation in the direst straits. The peak of Sitno looks like a large stone table; it was formed by a fragment of cooled lava channel that spilled from a strato-volcano in the Tertiary era. The top flat area is flanked by steep andesite rock on three sides. Some sections of the rock are crumbling, thus creating bizarre rock towers. Apart from the TV transmitter and a tourist chalet there is also a restored historical outlook tower from 1888 on the top. It was erected on the site of an older outlook tower from 1727, destroyed by a lightning in 1852.

### ŠTIAVNICKÉ TAJCHY – RICHŇAVA (2)

Artificial lakes built for local mines are a great wealth of Štiavnické Vrchy. The German name tajch (lake) is used for them. The oldest written records about tajchy in the Štiavnica area date from the beginning of the 16th century. However, most of them were built in the 18th century. M. K. Hell with his son and the cartographer S. Mikovíni, a lecturer at the mining school in Štiavnické Bane, were involved in the project of the lake creation. Originally there were about

60 mining lakes; today only a third of them is preserved. The builders of the lakes had to deal with the insufficient water reserves in the heart of the mountains and created an ingenious system unsurpassed in Europe. It was designed to catch as much rain water as possible from the mountains slopes, which was then brought to the lakes by a complicated system of ditches. The total length of waterways was 73 km; the sluiceways were 53 km long. Water held in the reservoirs was used in mines and smelteries to propel the mining technology.

### POČÚVADLIANSKE JAZERO (3)

This lake spreads on the west side of the Sitno Mountain. With an area of 12 hectares it is the largest tajch lake in Štiavnické Vrchy. It is also the deepest (11 metres) and the coldest. It was named after a village situated 5 km away to the south. Počúvadlianske Lake was created between 1775 and 1779 according to a design by J. K. Hell. Six dams were needed to retain the water in the lake; the highest one is almost 30 metres high and is the oldest in Slovakia. Use of the lake for mining is now a thing of the past, and it is a popular tourist centre with excellent swimming and water sports conditions. It is also the traditional starting point for the climb to nearby Sitno.

### OTTERGRUNDSKÝ TAJCH (4)

The Chodník Milana Kapustu Nature Trail starts at the Červená Studňa Saddle. It follows a comfortable contour way that traverses to the east-

ern slope of the Paradajz Hill. The path provides an almost constant view on the roofs of Banská Štiavnica from a surprising height. The most beautiful bird's eye view of the historical town is from the dam that holds the waters of the Ottergrundský Lake, a smallish water reservoir at 939 metres, which is the highest tajch in Štiavnické Vrchy. It was created in 1759 to provide water for mines in Banská Štiavnica. Vodárenská Reservoir below the Červená Studňa Saddle is much older, having been built as early as in 1500 as a source of drinking water for Banská Štiavnica.

### ŠTIAVNICKÉ BANE (5)

This locality in the centre of Štiavnické Vrchy is not a compact settlement. It is a group of former mining settlements west of Banská Štiavnica, which were administratively merged in 1948. This area was a centre of intensive mining activities from the Middle Ages until the beginning of the 20th century. Local mines were, at certain times, the most modern mines in the world, which is proved by the fact that in 1627, gunpowder was used in Horná Biberová mine for the fist time in the world. The main pioneer of the modern technologies in Štiavnické Banie was the mining constructer M. K. Hell (1653-1743) who managed to construct the beam mining pump for pumping water out of flooded mines. This pump was the most efficient in Europe at its time. Štiavnické Bane is a Monument Reserve (1995). There are fragments of anti-Ottoman fortification with a pre-

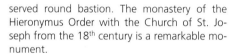

served round bastion. The monastery of the Hieronymus Order with the Church of St. Joseph from the 18th century is a remarkable monument.

### SITNO CASTLE (6)

Sitno is wrapped in legends and guarded by steep rock walls. A castle was built on its fourth (eastern) side. Its history started in the 13th century when the builders continued with the ancient tradition of erecting castles on strategic hills. The oldest history of the castle atop Sitno is veiled in mystery. Historical documents mention it in 1548 with regards to troops sent by the Hungarian ruler to punish the looting lord of the castle M. Balaš (Balassa). The castle was a target of the Ottoman attacks during the 16th and 17th centuries. According to a legend, it was not conquered by the Ottomans thanks to an ingenious scheme. Inhabitants of the castle baked a cake from the last of their flour and rolled it down the hill. Thinking the castle had abundant reserves of food the Ottomans gave up and went away. However, Kuruc soldiers managed what the Turkish could not. The castle was conquered during the Francis II Rákoci (Rákoczi) Uprising and left to become a ruin.

1

2

3

## CHURCH IN BANSKÁ BELÁ (1)

Banská Belá was a free royal and mining town until 1788 when it merged with its stronger neighbour. The Late Romanesque Church of St. John Apostle form the 13th century is a remarkable monument of the town. The key reconstruction of the church was carried out in 1590. The church nave was completely changed; the oldest semi-circle building was replaced by the present-day larger nave. The massive tower of the church remained in its original state. The Renaissance reconstruction was carried out while the church belonged to the Evangelists. Another, smaller church was built following religious disputes and it is currently a Marian pilgrimage site.

## SABÓOVA SKALA (2)

The entry to Štiavnické Vrchy from Hliník nad Hronom has a silent stone guardian. The valley with the path from Sklené Teplíce is protected by the Sabóova Rock. This huge 50-metre high ryolit rock was formed by the erosion of the lava channel from the Tertiary volcano. Geologists have been interested in this locality for a long time for the occurrence of the perlit zone around the perimeter of the rock. It was named after J. Szabó (1822-1894), who was one of the first to conduct thorough geological research into the Banská Štiavnica area. This place was designated a Nature Reserve in 1907, and it was the first protected geological locality in Slovakia.

## VYHNIANSKE STONE SEA (3)

The name of this village derives from its past when iron ore was mined and smelted in the local smelteries (vyhniach). The village boasts the oldest still operating Slovakian brewery (Steiger) founded in 1645, however its natural surroundings are also remarkable. There is a Stone Sea locality on the slope of the valley below the Kamenná Peak. This interesting natural formation owes its name to its large size. It is the largest boulder site of the volcanic part of the Slovakian Carpathians and represents a nice example of the break-up of a ryolit lava channel; this large area is covered by stone boulders of various sizes and forms. Lava spilled from a Tertiary volcano many millions of years ago. Vyhnie still attracts swimming and bathing enthusiasts even though the sea is not real. The village has a thermal pool and there is also the Štiavnické Lake, known also as Rozgrund Tajch, at the upper part of the Vyhnianská Valley.

## SKLENÉ TEPLICE SPA (4)

The history of Sklené Teplice reaches back as far as 1340. Apart from glass production, its inhabitants were also active miners. The existence of the local thermal spa was first documented in 1550. Over the times it was owned by several aristocratic families and when the last owners, the Lipaj (Lippay) family, died out without heirs towards the end of the 17th century, the spa went to the state which gave it to the Mining Institution in Banská Štiavnica for management. Local warm mineral springs with a temperature up to 53 degrees were used for therapy. Moreover, the water was used in smelting furnaces for the production of silver. Apart from water, mud and steam were used in therapies; this tradition is still used in the unique cave bath called Parenica. The spa specialises mainly in curing movement and neurological problems. Water from the springs is cooled down and then used in the local thermal pools.

## BANSKÁ HODRUŠA (5)

This village was created by the merging of two old mining settlements in the valley of the Hodrušský Creek in Štiavnické Vrchy. It sprawls almost along the entire valley and is one of the longest villages in Slovakia. Dolné Hámre with a well-known Sandrik company, which has been producing silver and metal articles – mainly cutlery – since its foundation in 1892, are in the lower part of the valley. Banská Hodruša is of more interest to tourists. It lies below the Kerling Peak and boasts several remarkable monuments. The oldest one is the ancient Gothic Church of St. Nicholas from 1387. There is an entry into the historical Galander Shaft (1479) right next to the church. Another mining history monument of the village is the Renaissance clapper from the 17th century. The Tunnel of the Emperor Francis is also noteworthy, remarkable for its length of over 12 kilometres.

## EVANGELIC CHURCH IN BAĎAN (6)

This village is situated in the southern part of Štiavnické Vrchy and is affected by the warm influence of the Panonian lowlands from the south. Thus, it was inhabited much earlier than the cold mountainous areas at the north. Archaeological findings from the Lower Stone Age support this theory. Baďan, established in the 13th century, once belonged to yeomen families in the southern parts of the Hontianská County. It suffered from frequent attacks by the Ottomans in the 16th century. The village boasts an old Evangelic church, originally thought to have been built in the Renaissance style in 1685. However the building is probably much older, according to several architectonic signs typical for Romanesque rotundas. New research confirmed this and the church started to be referred to as the so-called 'Baďanská Rotunda', which dates possibly from the 12th century.

## ARBORETUM KYSIHÝBEĽ (1)

The renowned Mining and Forestry Academy in Banská Štiavnica is behind several interesting forest projects and experiments realized in the surroundings of the town. One of them is the Kysihýbeľ Arboretum established in 1900. On an area of 7.73 hectares on the territory called the Jubilejný Forest of Queen Elizabeth, J. Tuszon designed an experimental arboretum with various local and foreign trees growing in the mild conditions of the northern hemisphere. Originally, the arboretum had 282 species of trees. Another hundred were added to the 166 species that have been preserved. Northern America has the highest representation of trees. Among the most valuable are Cork-Tree, Paper Birch, Chamaecyparis, Douglas spruce and sequoia. The arboretum still serves as a valuable nature laboratory that tests the acclimatization ability of observed trees in the conditions of Štiavnické Vrchy. Various exotic trees are also in the vicinity of the arboretum. Many of them are from the planting carried out in the Feistmantelová Garden, established in 1836. There is a nature trail with 16 information panels across the research forest area called Malé (Small) Arboretum.

## CHATEAU IN SVÄTÝ ANTON (2)

This village boasts one of the most beautiful chateaus in Slovakia. It is well-known mainly amongst hunters as it houses collections associated with hunting. Slovakian as well as foreign nimrods meet here annually in September during the popular Days of St. Hubert. The local grandiose Baroque-Classicism mansion was built on the site of a vanished castle in 1744. Its builder used the symbol of a calendar, designing 4 entrances, 7 arcades, 12 chimneys, 52 rooms and 365 windows. Its first owner was the head of the county council and the general of the Emperor's army, Andrej Koháry. Later it went into the possession of the noble aristocratic family of the Coburgov with German origins. The members of this family ended up on thrones

of several lands in Europe; the same applies to the last owner, Ferdinand Coburgov, who became the Bulgarian Tsar in 1908. The chateau is accessible to the public and has charming furniture, precious art pieces and a large amount of hunting trophies.

## CHURCH OF ST. EGID IN ILIJA (3)

The fact that the ancient church in Ilija near Banská Štiavnica was consecrated to a hermit – St. Egid – is symbolical as the village is in a relatively remote, yet beautiful, spot at the eastern foothills of the Sitno Mountain in Štiavnické Vrchy. The church ranks amongst the most remarkable sacral monuments in Slovakia. Originally it was thought to date from 1254; however a thorough research into the church came up with several remarkable facts. The remains of an older building and ceramic fragments from the Lower Bronze Age were discovered below the floor of the church. This moves the origin of the church much further into the past. Supposedly, it was built by Benedictine monks from a nearby abbacy in Hronský Beňadik, founded in 1075. Another finding also deserves attention. A skeleton of an approximately 6-year old child was found near the decorated Romanesque portal, which is one of the most beautiful and valuable details of the church. Locals connect it with the legend about the ringer-boy who rang the bell to raise alarm when the Ottomans were coming.

## KRUPINSKÉ BRALCE (4)

South of the village of Žibritov in the Štangarigel locality is the interesting Krupinské Bralce Natural Monument. The protected territory from 1975 boasts unique rocky formations formed from the crumbled andesite lava channel of a Tertiary volcano. The typical feature of the rock is the conspicuous quinquelateral separability. This type is not unique in Slovakia, as there are splendid formations in the Cerova Vrchovina Hills; however it is extraordinary for the size

of the stone columns that are higher than one metre on average. The vertical rocks make up a stone-like replica of a town with skyscrapers. Green moss that covers the rock blocks below the andesite columns enhances the charm of this place. The soft moss is the home to many rare Gastropoda Species.

## CASTLE IN ŽIBRITOV (5)

This village with preserved folk architecture lies in the eastern part of Štiavnické Vrchy. An unfrequented road goes through the village connecting the villages of Svätý Anton and Krupina. The oldest record about the village dates from 1266. It suffered looting by the Hussites in the 15th century; the Ottomans then destroyed it; finally, another disaster fell upon the village in 1807 when it burnt down. Its inhabitants once earned their bread by charcoal production and farming. As the cluster of grapes on the coat-of-arms of the village suggests, it was once a large centre of wine production. You can still find old vineyards here with the largest ones located on the slopes at 520 metres. The village holds a primacy with the highest located vineyards in Slovakia. The picturesque landscape of Žibritov attracts filmmakers. Scenes of the first co-production Slovakian-Hungarian movie, *Dáždnik Svätého Petra*, were shot in the village and its surroundings in the 1950s. An old bastion used as a belfry stands in the centre of the village. It is a fragment of the vanished small castle from the 16th century and served as a sentry tower at the times of the Ottoman wars.

# POIPLIE

### MONASTERY IN BZOVÍK (1)

The count Lampert from the old family of Hunto-Poznan established a Cistercian Monastery in Bzovík near Krupina around 1130. Soon afterward, monks from Moravia arrived to turn the abbey into the Premonstratensian Priorate, which rapidly became one of the largest feudal estates of the area. The monastery was conquered by members of the Bratríci Movement in the 15th century. It was also conquered by invaders from the nearby Krupina. The originally Romanesque building was rebuilt in the Gothic style during these times of upheaval. Žigmund Balaša (Balassa) got hold of the Priorate in 1530, displaced the monks and converted the building into an anti-Ottoman stronghold, building its distinctive round corner bastions and a water moat. It was occupied and burnt out by the soldiers of Tököli (Thököly) in 1678 and later went into the possession of the Jesuits. Although once more in the hands of the church, its original function was not restored. World War II caused serious damage to the building.

### CHURCH IN KRUPINA (2)

Krupina received the privileges of the free royal town before Bratislava; and together with Trnava they were the first privileged towns in Slovakia in 1238. These rights were based on the Magdeburg Law, and later altered to the Krupina Law (14th century), which was the basis of the law order of other medieval towns in this area, such as Žilina, Martin and Prievidza. The good location of the town on the Magna Via trade path facilitated its development. The central Námestie Sv. Trojice Square has maintained its medieval ground-plan; it has mostly modern buildings so visitors have to walk further on to see historical monuments. At the east side is the Church of the Birth of the Virgin Mary from the 13th century. It is basically a Romanesque basilica that was rebuilt a couple of times. Its massive construction and fortifications from around the 15th century give the church its ancient appearance. A jewel of the church is the Late Gothic Altar of the Virgin Mary the Queen of Apostles with valuable sculpture decorations from the 16th century.

### KRUPINSKÁ VARTOVKA (3)

Krupina was a significant strategic point during the Ottoman wars protecting the path to the wealthy mining towns. Thus it got the best fortification. The walls around the town were built by its inhabitants as well as people from surrounding villages; fragments are preserved. There is a system of underground corridors underneath Krupina which has not yet been much explored. Perhaps they were part of the anti-Ottoman protection system; on the other hand they could easily be merely wine cellars. The Vartovka Tower played an important part in the anti-Ottoman defence. It was built in 1541 above the town in the spot called Tanistravár (also Straživar). Its location was excellent as the far southward view enabled spotting the enemy from afar. The sentry were probably very alert as Krupina was never conquered. The 15-metre high stone tower with a wooden balcony was reconstructed and is now used as an outlook tower.

### ČABRAĎ CASTLE (4)

The builders of this castle chose a very good location. They placed it on a hill flanked by the deep valley of the Litava River, thus enhancing its natural protection. It was built in the 13th century, and a document from 1276 states that Derž and Demeter from the Hunto-Poznano family fought over the castle. There were often squabbles over its possession, and the castle often changed owners, at times by force. The loathed count M. Balaša (Balassa) occupied the castle shortly in 1547; however it was then returned to the original owner. Like other castles in the regions this one too was converted into an anti-Ottoman fortress in the 16th century. It successfully withstood two Ottoman attacks (in 1585 and 1602) saving this the mining towns in central Slovakia. In 1622 it went into the possession of the Koháry family, who owned it until it was destroyed by Ondrej Koháry, who preferred a more comfortable mansion in Svätý Anton and burnt Čabraď in 1812.

### STARÁ HORA NEAR SEBECHLEBY (5)

The vineyards have been part of the surroundings of the Sebechleby village at the southern foothills of Štiavnické Vrchy for at least three centuries. The good weather conditions allow the growing and producing of good quality wine. Apart from large vineyards, this picturesque landscape is dotted by smallish vine producing farms. The most famous is the Stará Hora Folk Architecture Monument Reserve. It was founded during the upheaval times of the 16th century. In the fear of the Ottomans its inhabitants carved temporary underground hiding places in the soft tuff, which were used for wine storage in the 17th century. Small houses that provided accommodation mainly during the busiest seasons were built above them. A settlement developed from the temporary houses; the Chapel of St. Urban was built here in 1732.

## MODRÝ KAMEŇ (1)

Modrý Kameň was once a significant town and the centre of the western Novohrad area. Today it is the smallest town in Slovakia with less than 1,500 inhabitants. Although the neighbouring Veľký Krtíš is greater with regards to importance, it cannot compete in regards to historical monuments. As the time stopped in Modrý Kameň, the town has maintained its ancient spirit. The medieval Modrý Kameň Castle from the 12th century was owned by the aristocratic Balaša (Balassa) family. It got into the hands of the Ottomans in 1575 and later became derelict. A Baroque church was built near the ruin in 1730. The preserved mansion houses the Museum of Dolls and Toys, part of which is devoted to regional history and ethnography.

## HRUŠOV (2)

This village is famous mainly for its traditional annual folklore festival held in August called Hontianska Paráda. Old crafts, village and regional culture, farming traditions and costumes are presented in the courtyards of festively decorated vernacular houses.

## PLACHTINSKÁ DOLINA (3)

This valley between the Krupinská Planina Plain and Ipeľská Kotlina Hollow has very favourable warm and dry weather conditions, which are excellent for orchards, vineyards and sweet chestnuts, the local speciality. There are three villages in the valley, Horné, Stredné a Dolné Plachtince. Horné Plachtince boasts preserved folk architecture and produces beautiful, richly embroidered costumes. There is a nature trail above the village that goes to the Pohanský Hill archaeological site. Stredné Plachtince has also kept folk traditions; moreover it is the native place of the famous Slovakian actors, Jul. Pántik, C. Filčík and M. Kňažko. Dolné Plachtince is famous for its good wine and popular traditional festivals called Fašiangy.

## MANSION IN DOLNÁ STREHOVÁ (4)

This village in Ipeľská Kotlina is famous mainly for its thermal pool, however it also boasts an interesting Rococo-Classicism mansion, which is closely connected with the significant Hungarian writer and dramatist I. Madách (1823 – 1864). The famous writer was born and buried in the village of Dolná Strahová. His tomb is near the mansion and is adorned by a sculpture of Adam, the character from his most famous book, 'The Tragedy of Man'. There is a Memorable Room with a permanent exposition about the life and work of this famous man in the mansion.

## EVANGELIC CHURCH IN PRÍBELCE (5)

The village of Príbelce became famous as the centre of the serfdom uprising in the Hontianska County during the revolutionary year 1848. The local teacher J. Rotarides was the leader of the uprising together with his friend, the poet of the Štúr Movement, J. Kráľ. The army suppressed the uprising and both men were arrested and taken to prison in Šáhy. The dramatic events of the uprising are celebrated during the Oslavy Janka Kráľa Celebration. One of the most beautiful churches in the south of central Slovakia lies at the northern edge of the village. Its architecture is impressive but the most charming is its breathtaking position in the open landscape away from the villages.

## EVANGELIC CHURCH IN PÔTOR (6)

The village situated on the road between Veľký Krtíš and Lučenec was once called Peter. According to written documents, a church, consecrated to St. Peter the Apostle, stood in this place as early as in 1297. However, the relation of the present-day church and this ancient building is unknown. It was built towards the end of the 15th century and the Evangelists got it at the end of the 16th century. The massive one-nave building with a polygonal presbytery underwent several later reconstructions; however its Gothic appearance was not significantly altered. A fortification wall was built around the church in 1599 and a detached wooden belfry was build within the area. The nave and presbytery boast a nice wooden ornament-decorated ceiling. The carved wooden Baroque altar with the painting of Jesus Resurrected from 1681 is very valuable.

## CHURCH OF ST. ELISABETH IN MUĽA (1)

The smallish border village of Muľa on the right bank of the Ipeľ River boasts the unusually large Art Nouveau Church of St. Elisabeth. It was built between 1910 and 1918 according to the design of a Hungarian architect named I. Medgyaszay. The façade has a ferroconcrete construction; this was its first usage in the building of a church in central Europe. The church has an octagonal ground-plan with an alcove for the choir and organ. It is roofed by a dome and there are nine sculptures of cherubims along the roof by a sculptor named Sidón. There is a connecting section between the nave and the tower with a pyramid-like roof. The painting of St. Elisabeth, the daughter of King Andrew II born in 1207 at Bratislava Castle and the traditional patron of Hungary, is above the main altar. A crypt with the remains of a lord R. Körfy lies underneath the altar.

## SYNAGOGUE IN LUČENEC (2)

Lučenec is the largest town in the south of central Slovakia. It is mentioned in history books thanks to the memorable battle in which Jan Jiskra defeated Ján Huňady on 7th September 1451. The famous Czech writer A. Jirásek named one book of the Bratrstvo Trilogy Bitka pri Lučenci. The town has no older historical monuments thanks to this battle and other army events and mass tragedies. However, it boasts interesting modern architecture from the last two centuries. A nice example is the grandiose synagogue, built in the Art Nouveau style in 1925 on the site of an older synagogue. It was designed by L. Baumhorn, who built 22 synagogues on the territory of the formal monarchy as well as many beyond its borders. Similar synagogues like the one in Lučenec are to be found in Amsterdam, Brussels and Tel Aviv. The synagogue is the largest in Slovakia; it is 35.5 metres high. Under the dome in the centre of the building supported by four columns was originally an altar

from Karaský marble. The synagogue is derelict and currently awaits reconstruction.

## MANSION IN HALIČ (3)

This mansion is the result of a reconstruction of a medieval Gothic castle into the Renaissance stronghold. The Forgáč (Forgách) family owned it from the mid-16th century until 1848. One legend talks about the young wife of count Forgáč being kidnapped by the robber baron Balaš. He dragged her to his Divín Castle where he cruelly murdered his own wife. However, the unhappy Forgáč saved his wife via an underground tunnel that once allegedly connected the mansion with the castle.

## TURECKÝ BRIDGE IN POLTÁR (4)

The town of Poltár at the north of the Lučenská Kotlina Hollow is known as the centre of traditional glass and pottery production. The Ipeľ River flows along its west side and is spanned by the historical Turecký Bridge that leads to Lučenec from the Zelená quarter. The attractive stone three-arched bridge was built between 1554 and 1593 when this area was controlled by the Ottoman army. Original stones were used for the reconstruction of the bridge to maintain its authenticity.

## CHURCH OF ST. GEORGE IN STARÁ HALIČ (5)

One of the most significant sacral monuments in the Novohrad area is in the village of Stará Halič, southwest of Lučenec. This small community boasts the large Gothic Church of St. George. The windows in the nave of the Romanesque building suggest its ancient origin. It was possibly built in the 13th century; however its architecture is mainly Gothic due to reconstructions during the 14th and 15th centuries. Later rebuilding did not change the building considerably. The nave and presbytery house valuable medieval murals. The Renaissance belfry from the 17th century is also splendid.

## CEMETERY IN VEĽKÁ NAD IPĽOM (6)

It is worthwhile to make a short stop in this village and see the local cemetery with the grave of the priest G. Borbás (1850 – 1909). It has an unusual gravestone. This huge block of rock comes from the nearby Hungarian Village of Ipolytrnóc on the other side of the Ipeľ River. A large amount of similar stones were found around the village. They are valuable fossils from the trunks of prehistoric trees which once grew in the tropical Tertiary forest. These findings made the village one of the most famous paleontological sites in the world; it holds the world prime in the number of discovered fossils of the Tertiary flora and fauna.

### DIVÍN CASTLE (1)

The name of this castle looming above the village of the same name is connected with the world *deva* and *dievča* (girl). According to a legend the security of the castle had to be ensured by the immuring of a virgin in its walls. The history of the castle reaches into the ancient past, when such dreadful traditions were possible. It was built in the 12th century on the site of an extinct old Slavic settlement. It was a sentry castle of the trade path from Novohrad towards the mining towns of central Slo-

vakia. The Hungarian Council ordered a transformation of the Gothic castle into an anti-Ottoman fortress in 1559, however this did not prevent it from being conquered by the Ottomans in 1575. They occupied it for almost 20 years. Divín was later owned by several aristocratic families, the most renowned being the unpopular Balaša family. The castle lord count I. Balaša (Balassa) pillaged the surroundings and terrorized its inhabitants. The castle paid for his bad deeds as it was burnt out by the Emperor's army.

### MANSION IN DIVÍN (2)

The fortified Renaissance mansion is right in the centre of the village at the eastern foothills of the Castle Hill. The lower part of the medieval Divín was built here in the 15th century; the Renaissance mansion was built on its site in 1670 by the unpopular count I. Balaša, for his castle was occupied by the Emperor's soldiers that were to stop his cruel pillaging. The mansion is now a splendid example of a medieval stronghold. The two-winged building with the L-shaped ground-plan is strengthened by four

bastions. Original wooden balconies and fragments of graffito decoration are preserved in the interior and the shingle roof enhances the charm of the mansion.

## CHURCH OF ALL SAINTS
## IN DIVÍN (3)

The troublesome past of this village required a fortification of the castle as well as the mansion and the church. The history of the church goes back to the 13<sup>th</sup> century. It was probably destroyed by the Ottomans, so a new one had to be constructed. However, this one had no lucky fate either as it was destroyed by the Hussites, who hated Catholic churches. And for the third time it was demolished by the Ottomans in 1554. The ruler of the county, J. Balaša, reconstructed the church. He confessed the Lutheran reformed religion so he gave the restored church to an Evangelic priest. It was also surrounded by a fortification wall. It is a unique sacral building with bastion fortification in Slovakia. The rebels around Francis II Rákoci used the church as their base in 1708 for their attacks on the Emperor's army. The new lords of the Divín estate became the Ziči (Zichy) family, who returned the church to the Catholics.

## RUŽINÁ WATER RESERVOIR (4)

This lake of 170 hectares was constructed in 1970 on a small stream near the Ružiná village. This area of central Slovakia is affected by the warm influence of the Panonian lowlands coming from the south via the wide Dolina Krivánskeho Potoka Valley. This makes the shallow lake with splendid beaches one of the warmest in Slovakia. It offers excellent swimming, water sport and fishing conditions and is therefore swarmed by tourists. The recreational activities are restricted only in two areas that are Protected Territories, Ružinská Jelšina and Ružinský Breh, which have valuable marshes with a large population of water birds.

## EVANGELIC CHURCH IN DOBROČ (5)

An ancient church is hidden in the shade of greenery at the cemetery on a hill between the villages of Mýtna and Dobroč at the western edge of the Slovenské Rudohorie Mountains. It was built in the Early Gothic style in the 13<sup>th</sup> century and was affected by later reconstructions during the 17<sup>th</sup> and 19<sup>th</sup> centuries, yet it lost nothing of its charm. A fortification wall with loopholes around the church was built in the 15<sup>th</sup> century and it became a part of the fortification system of Novohrad after the memorable Battle at Lučenec in 1453. The fortified church was used by the Bratríci of Jiskra, who strengthened the wall and dug a moat around it. Evangelists have managed the church since the end of the 16<sup>th</sup> century. A wooden belfry with a shingle roof was built at its south side in the 18<sup>th</sup> century. The most valuable art piece in the interior is the Renaissance painting of the Last Supper at the altar.

## MANSION IN PODREČANY (6)

The village of Podrečany, northwest of Lučenec, was established on the Divín estate as part of the colonization efforts of the castle lords of Tomaj family in the 13<sup>th</sup> century. The lord of the village at the beginning of the 18<sup>th</sup> century was the captain of the Rákoci Army, Andrej Török. He opened a pipe factory in the manor from the 16<sup>th</sup> century used by Francis II Rákoci. The pipes from Podrečany were good products, sold throughout the entire monarchy. The estate was taken over by the Kuchynko family in 1878, who had an Art Nouveau mansion built in the village in 1893. Its builders were inspired by the French style and erected a one-story building with a U-shaped ground-plan and front façade into a garden. Stucco ornaments with French Baroque decorative elements adorn the facades and there is an English-style park next to the mansion.

## FIĽAKOVSKÝ CASTLE (1)

This is an interesting place for naturalists as well as historians. The hill is a remnant of a very young volcano of the Maar type (known mainly from the German Eifel Mountains, these are the remains of highly explosive volcanoes). Only two peaks are left from this maar, which is amongst the youngest volcanic formations in Slovakia – the Castle Hill and the Červený Hill. Both were part of the tuff ring around the crater. Historians are interested in the castle mainly because of its significance during the Ottoman wars. This medieval castle was involved in heavy fighting from the 13th century. The Ottomans managed to conquer it only thanks to

treason in 1554, and they then made it the seat of their administration unit. The liberation of the castle by the Emperor's army in 1593 was famous throughout the whole of Christian Europe. The Kuruc soldiers blew the castle up in 1682. The partially reconstructed large ruin in the middle of the town is now accessible to the public.

## ŠOMOŠKA CASTLE (2)

The sharp silhouette of this castle near Šiatorská Bukovinka is a jewel of the landscape at the south of the Cerová Vrchovina Hills. It was built from basalt in the 14th century. As Budín fell into hands of the Ottomans in 1541 and the castles in the Novohrad area got into the first fighting line, Šomoška was rebuilt into a Renaissance stronghold. Its sentry withstood the attacks for a very long time and the castle was a small island of freedom in the middle of the enemy's territory. It fell 22 years after the conquest of the Fiľakovský Castle, because of a vicious attack by the Ottomans revenging the death of their leader Hasan, according to a legend. It was liberated in 1593 and narrowly avoided demolition in 1709; as its owner Š. Forgáč (Forgách) participated in the Francis II Rákoci Uprising. In any case, the castle was left derelict. Following a partial reconstruction it is now open to the public.

## KAMENNÝ VODOPÁD BELOW ŠOMOŠKA (3)

Tourists walking up the nature trail from the Dolina Bukovinského Potoka Valley can see

a splendid view of a natural formation called Kamenný Vodopád (Stone Waterfall) just below the Šomoška Castle. The remains of basalt columns are in the wall of an old quarry for building material for the castle. The highest columns measure 9 metres. The formation of basalt into quinquelateral and hexagonal columns is rather common, however these columns are specific as they are extremely regular and unusually slim (15 cm in perimeter). They are also arched and resemble falling water that turned into stone. The Šomoška Hill is a leftover of a volcano active roughly 4 million years ago. It has been studied by naturalists and mainly geologists since the 18th century.

## STONE SEA BELOW ŠOMOŠKA (4)

The northern slope of the rocky hill with Šomoška Castle is covered by a large stone sea. It is 100 metres long and approximately 40 metres wide. It was formed by the crumbling basalt rock that formed the top of the hill. Its preserved part can be seen at the Kamenný Waterfall, halfway between the stone sea and the entry to the castle. The best conditions for the creation of the stone sea were during the Ice Age when ice and freezing weather destroyed the basalt rock, braking it into numerous rocks in the form of hexagonal columns. Rocks of a regular honeycomb-like shape fit into each other perfectly.

## MAČACIA QUARRY (5)

The basalt paving stones that once covered the roads in almost all towns in Slovakia are also called mačacie hlavy (cat's heads). Perhaps it is just a coincidence; still the largest basalt quarry is called Mačacia. It is near the village of Šiatorská Bukovinka, and a nature trail from the village leads to it. It was created at the western edge of the largest lava formation in Cerová Vrchovina. Lava spilt from the Medveš Volcano towards the end of the Tertiary Era. The formation has an area of 14 km2 and crates the top part of the table hill with flat peak. Mačacia is a part of the quarry network that is no longer used.

## SOVÍ HRAD (6)

A striking rock looms above the roofs of the village of Šurice near Fiľakov. It is called Soví Hrad (Owl Castle) and represents the remains of a volcano active towards the end of the Tertiary Era. The sharp cone-shaped rock formation from basalt volcanic material cooled down in a channel of a crater of a now extinguished volcano. The peak of Soví Hrad towers almost 100 metres above the surrounding terrain. On one side of the peak is a steep slope, while a steep rock wall is on the other. A medieval castle stood atop the hill in the past. Its history is unknown, but it was possibly built in the 13<sup>th</sup> century.

# WESTERN GEMER A MALOHONT

### HAJNÁČKA CASTLE (1)

A perfectly symmetrical hill looms in the centre of Hajnáčka village in the Cerová Vrchovina Hills. Its conical shape is topped by bizarre rock towers with the almost indistinguishable remains of a medieval castle from the 13th century. The castle was once strong and well able to withhold Ottomans attacks, according to evidence by a noble, Š. Forgáč, from the second half of the 16th century. The battle over the castle had an interesting prelude. One of the Ottoman leaders challenged a noble, J. Bebeka, to a duel, which took place below the walls of Hajnáčka and ended in a huge fight with many wounded. However, despite the good defence of the castle, the Ottomans conquered it in 1556 and held it until 1593. It survived this occupation, but not the last estate uprising, and it burnt out in 1703. Its devastation was so serious that we can only speculate about its original appearance. However, even if not because of the castle, it is still worthwhile to climb up the hill to see the remarkable volcanic rocks. The rock formation at the top is an eroded filling of the volcano vent of a now extinguished basalt volcano from the end of the Tertiary Era.

### POHANSKÝ CASTLE (2)

Cerová Vrchovina Hills with basalt volcanoes is a unique territory in Slovakia. A similar landscape can be found in the French Central Massif, which is why is the area around Fiľakovo and Hajnáčka called Slovakian Auvergne. Volcanoes extinguished towards the end of the Tertiary Era and at the beginning of Quaternary Era, and a great change in the landscape followed. It was basically turned upside down with valleys becoming mountain ranges and vice versa. This applies also to Pohanský Castle (578 m), which is atop a perfect table hill that looms west of Hajnáčka. Its peak is a flat plateau, which provided a safe asylum to pagan people in the prehistoric times, as it was protected by almost uninterrupted walls of basalt rocks. The crumbled edge of the plateau created bizarre rock towers at the southeast. Some fell and formed piles of rock with numerous cavities; they are called pseudokarst caves. The Stĺpová Cave with its 182 long corridors is the longest of its type in Slovakia.

### TILIČ (3)

The smallish Tilič Hill (475 m) gently looms above the surroundings at the eastern slope of the Pohanský Hrad massif. It is a protrusion of a basalt ledge above the surface and as it is harder than the surrounding sandstone, it creates a hilltop. There is a small rock with a fantastic view of the most beautiful part of Cerová Vrchovina. The panoramic view of the volcano peaks that flank the round crater-like Hajnáčska Kotlina Hollow is splendid. A cone hill with a rocky tip looms in the centre of the hollow, and remains of the medieval Hajnáček Castle are on its top.

### RAGÁČ (4)

Ragáč (537 m) is the highest hill at the eastern side of the mountains around the Hajnáčska Kotlina Valley in the centre of Cerová Vrchovina. It is of one of the youngest local volcanoes and was still active in the Pleistocene Era, so time has not erased its volcanic features. Below the peak rock, with splendid views, is a peculiar well-shaped hole, which is thought to be hornitos (an expert name for this particular volcanic form created by a large amount of volcanic gas penetrating lava). A similar phenomenon is at the Etna Volcano in Italy; a large amount of pumice stone in the near surroundings supports this theory. Volcanic rock is light and porous as it has been penetrated by a lot of gas.

### STEBLOVÁ SKALA (5)

The picturesque landscape of Cerová Vrchovina is divided by the long Gortva Valley, flanked by a long flat mountain range with the cone hill Steblová Skala (486 m) in the east. This striking hill was formed on the spot of the skeletonised volcanic vent reinforced by cooled basalt ledges and offers magnificent views. A steep rocky slope descends southwards. There is an interesting rock formation resembling a huge organ with pipes made of large hexagonal basalt columns. They were probably created in the same way as the famous Kamenný Vodopád below Šomoška Castle, however these are higher (over 15 m) and significantly deeper (up to 30 cm).

## KURINEC LAKE RESERVOIR (1)

The popular recreational centre Kurinec – Zelená voda lies south of the town of Rimavská Sobota. It is attractive mainly for its position at the bank of the Kurinec Lake, constructed on the Ľukva River. The dam (22 ha) is popular for swimming, water sports and fishing. The attractiveness of this place is enhanced by nice oak forests that flank the lake on both sides and are suitable for easy walks and mushroom picking. The oak forest is protected by a Nature Reserve on the right bank of the lake. The trees are over 300 years old; it is the original lowland forest.

## COUNTY COUNCIL
## IN RIMAVSKÁ SOBOTA (2)

This town is the centre of the smallish Malohont historical region situated on the upper stream of the Rimava River. It was an independent administration centre called Rimavský Komitát in the 13th century but towards the end of the century it lost its position and was added to Hontianská County, which was not its geographical neighbour. The name Malohont dates from the beginning of the 15th century. It received the district status with relatively great self administration rights including the right to select a vice-head of the country. The local aristocracy tried to put Malohont under Novohrad County, however it merged with Gemer Country at the other side, thus creating Gemer-Malohont County (1786) with the administrative centre in Ri-

mavská Sobota, which existed with two breaks until 1922. The grandiose building of the county council from 1909 adorns the Námestie M. Tompu Square in the eastern part of the centre of Rimavská Sobota.

### HLAVNÉ NÁMESTIE IN RIMAVSKÁ SOBOTA (3)

The medieval Rimavská Sobota with the Sobôtka fortress did not endure wars and natural catastrophes and therefore now has a network of streets and a regular-shaped square. The central quadrant Hlavné Square is a pedestrian zone and could be envied by other towns. Foundations of an older medieval sacral building incorporated into the paving were once visible on the square; however an unattractive modern glass building was built above them. The original Gothic church belonged to the Calvinist religion and was demolished by an order of Maria Theresa in 1771, as the local Calvinists, afraid of losing the church, attacked a Catholic procession two years before. The new Catholic church, built in the centre of the square in 1790, was consecrated to St. John the Baptist. Calvinists have another church (1784) situated in the south corner of the square. A high tower was added to the Baroque-Classicism building and it is one of the landmarks of the town. The Knižnica Mateja Hrebendu building on the southwest side built in 1801 has the prettiest faćade in the town; it was the seat of Gemersko-Malohont County.

### POKORADZSKÉ LAKES (4)

A peculiar landscape sprawls north of Rimavská Sobota. It is on the border of the Revúcka Vrchovina Hills and Rimavská Kotlina Hollow. This border is created by a steep slope deformed by large landslides. The Pokoradzská table, created by volcanic tuffs, is broken and slides at the edges. In the lower parts of the landslides is a peculiar undulated relief with tiny hills and valleys. The valleys are filled with the very small and interesting Pokoradzské Lakes, located right off the road from Rimavská Sobota to Horné Záhoriany. The lakes have almost dried out as earth and peat are slowly filling up the valleys and are turning into protected marshes with rare humid species of vegetation.

### TEPLÝ VRCH (5)

The main advantages of the Teplý Vrch (Warm Hill) recreational centre are spelled out in its name. It has the warmest lake in Slovakia. Moreover, this area is typical for pleasant weather and warm dry summer. The Teplý Vrch Reservoir near the village of the same name was created on the Blh River. The village below its dam was established in the 14th century as the settlement below the nearby Blh Castle. It was pillaged by the Ottomans and rebels of the estate uprising in the 17th century. Its inhabitants once produced weaving equipment and beeswax products and ran carrying-trade.

## REFORMED CHURCH
## IN RIMAVSKÁ SEČ (1)

The village of Rimavská Seč at the south of the Rimavská Kotlina Hollow was established towards the end of the 12th century. It owned some town privileges in the Middle Ages; it received the right of sword in 1347 and fair and market rights in the 15th century. Originally, it belonged to the lords of Blh Castle and was part of the Muránsky estate in the 17th century. The village is part of the tourist Gothic Path, as it has a valuable Gothic church of the reformed religion. Its history reaches back to 1332. A Renaissance tower was added to the north side of the church in 1560. Despite the Classicism reconstruction in 1791 the church maintained its medieval one-nave disposition. At the end of the presbytery are a Gothic cross rib vault and Gothic lancet windows. The complex of the church is enclosed by a ring of fortification walls.

## MANSION IN VEĽKÝ BLH (2)

The valley of the Blh River was ruled by the lords of Blh Castle in the Middle Ages. Its ruin is now in the centre of Čierna Deer Park with mouflon and wild boars. The castle was destroyed during estate uprisings of the 17th century and its inhabitants moved to a mansion in Veľká Blh. The Koháry family had the original Renaissance building demolished and built a new Baroque mansion with a park and a pond on its site in 1720. It was reconstructed in the Classicism style in 1815 and has since maintained its appearance.

## CHURCH OF ST. ABDON
## AND SENNEN
## IN GEMERSKÝ JABLONEC (3)

The Baštianska Kotlina Hollow lies in the bizarre volcanic landscape of Cerová Vrchovina. It is divided by the interesting meandering valley of the Gortva River. There is a splendid view of the picturesque hills in the hollow from a hilltop above the village of Gemerský Jablonec. Atop the hill is the ancient Romanesque Church of St. Abdon and Senen with a cemetery from the 13th century. Its medieval appearance was restored in the 18th century. There is a valuable Late Renaissance painted ceiling in the interior from 1703 and a wooded choir from 1815.

## CHURCH OF ST. JOHN THE BAPTIST
## IN RIMAVSKÉ JANOVCE (4)

A Benedictine abbey once stood in the village of Rimavské Janovce, south of Rimavská Sobota, in the 12th century. A village developed around 1221 (documented as Janus). It belonged to yeomen families for a long time, who built four manors in the area. The ancient Church of St. John the Baptist is a significant monument of the village; its history goes back to the 12th century. It is a simple Romanesque basilica (without side naves). Its present-day appearance is the result of a reconstruction after a fire in 1857. The ancient appearance of the church is enhanced by the unplastered façade. Stones in the walls and the very atypical spire with a bell in its western façade are reminiscent of the Italian or Dalmatian building styles. Murals from 1876 comply with the medieval iconography in the interior.

## REFORMED CHURCH IN ŽÍP (5)

The Gothic Path, which connects valuable Gothic monuments of the Gemer and Spiš regions, goes also into the small village of Žíp in the lower part of the valley of the Blh River. The village, which is out-of-the-way from the main road, is an attractive tourist destination due to the Early Gothic Church of the reformed religion from the 14th century. It was built on the site of an older Romanesque sacral edifice. Its original medieval architecture and preserved murals in the interior from the end of the 14th and the beginning of the 15th century are quite valuable. The themes and appearance of the murals is rather different than usual artistic work in ancient churches in the Gemer area; the illusionary painted altar is most unique. There is a wooden belfry near the church which has maintained its appearance from the reconstruction in 1789.

## ČÍŽ SPA (6)

A farmer from the village of Číž found a mineral spring with especially salty water in the 1860s. He sent a sample to Rimavská Sobota laboratories and it was determined that this rare iodic-bromidic water was curing. Further analysis from experts in Budapest and Vienna confirmed that it ranks amongst the most mineralized waters of its type in the world. The spa in Číž opened in 1889 and specialised in the curing of skin, neurological, movement and blood circulation problems. Patients with illnesses of joints, muscles and back are successfully treated here. The buildings of the spa are architectonically unified; they are modelled after Swiss spa architecture. The pavilions, replicas of Alpine log-cabins, are set in a meticulously maintained park.

## EVANGELIC CHURCH IN RIMAVSKÁ BAŇA (1)

A rare Late-Romanesque church from the last third of the 13th century stands atop a small hill above the village of Rimavská Baňa in the valley of the Rimava River between Rimavská Sobota and Hnúšťa. It belonged to a mining village established on the estate of the Esztergom Archbishop. It was rebuilt in the Gothic style in the 14th and 15th centuries and later adorned with Renaissance graffiti. Moreover, it was also surrounded by a Renaissance defence wall during the Jiskra's Uprising. The upper floors of the tower have a Baroque style. Valuable murals, discovered underneath the layer of lime in 1893, are preserved in the interior.

## DRIENČANSKÝ KARST (2)

The surroundings of the village of Drienčany in the valley of the Blh River are rich with karst formations. The almost 3-kilometre nature trail with nine stops provides information about these natural wonders. There are 160 sinkholes, 32 caves and cavities and several karst springs and wells. Two stops of the nature trail introduce its two larges caves; the 50-metre long Veľká Drienčanská Jaskyňa, inhabited by the people of the Kyjatická Culture 25-30,000 years ago, has a population of bats. The Malá Drienčanská jaskyňa is longer (79 m) and was also inhabited in prehistoric times; traces of cave bears and other animals of the last Ice Age were discovered here.

## EVANGELIC CHURCH IN KRASKOVO (3)

The Gothic Path, which takes tourists to the historical monuments of the Spiš and Gemer regions, goes to the off-beaten villages on the Pokoradzská volcanic plate at the south of the Slovenské Rudohorie Mountains. A significant stop on this popular tourist trail is in the village of Kraskovo, with an ancient Early Gothic church from the end of the 13th century. This splendid village church has kept its medieval appearance despite several reconstructions, mainly thanks to the preserved murals from the 13th and the 14th centuries. They were created by

the technique of frescoes being engraved into wet paint. The murals, originally covered by plaster, were uncovered and restored in 1906. Some of the decorations are from the workshop of the Master of the Ochtinské Presbytery; others are the work of the Master of Kraskovské Paintings, who was considered the greatest artist of Gemer in the 14<sup>th</sup> century. Amongst the depicted topics is the remarkable legend about King Ladislaus and his fight with Kumani.

## MONUMENT TO PEOPLE OF THE KYJATICKÁ CULTURE (4)

Near the former mining village of Kyjatice, with the valuable Evangelic church from the 13<sup>th</sup> century, is the Monument to the People of the Kyjatická Culture. It was built next to the road to the Kadlub community to commemorate that this small village gave its name to the ancient culture of the Bronze Age. The Kyjatická Culture was developing on the territory of central Slovakia and northern Hungary more than 3,000 years ago. Its members were farmers, yet they could make bronze and iron. They lived in caves and huge, highly located settlements. Archaeological findings around Kyjatice provided valuable study examples from an urn-field with 192 graves. The Monument consists of three pyramid-like mounds, a funeral pile and two urn caves.

## EVANGELIC CHURCH IN KYJATICE (5)

The medieval Evangelic church from the mid-14<sup>th</sup> century is an important cultural and historical monument of Kyjatice on the Pokoradzská volcanic plate. Even though this is mainly a Gothic building, it has some elements of other architectonic styles, such as the Romanesque semi-circle window in the south wall of the nave and the attached renaissance tower with a wooden top part and shingle roof. The most valuable is the medieval mural decoration in the interior from the 14<sup>th</sup> and 15<sup>th</sup> centuries. The huge expressive painting on the north side of the nave from the 15<sup>th</sup> century depicting the Last Judgement is especially remarkable. The Renaissance altar from 1678 and the richly

carved Baroque baptismal font from the 18<sup>th</sup> century are also noteworthy.

## EVANGELIC CHURCH IN RIMAVSKÉ BREZOVO (6)

The soaring church spire of the Evangelic Church in Rimavské Brezovo is visible from afar and is a landmark of the village situated in the valley of the Rimava River between Rimavská Sobota and Hnúšťa. The church with the tower is a valuable Gothic monument and a part of the Gothic Path, which takes tourists to see important medieval monuments of the Spiš and Gemer regions. Originally, this was a Romanesque-Gothic church from the last third of the 13<sup>th</sup> century, however an extensive reconstruction in 1893 changed its architecture significantly; the entire orientation of the church was changed, the presbytery becoming a chapel with a Gothic cross vault. This is the most valuable part of the church thanks to preserved medieval murals. The consistent painting from the 14<sup>th</sup> century was discovered underneath the plastering and is believed to be the work of the Master of the Ochtinské Presbytery.

## EVANGELIC CHURCH IN DRIENČANY (7)

The Evangelic church in the village of Drienčany is a valuable monument; however this village is a term in the Slovakian literary history. The most popular Slovakian fairy-tale writer, P. Dobšinský (1828-1885), was a local Evangelic priest for 24 years (1828-1885). He was also buried in the village; his tomb is right next to the church. The site around the church went through a complicated building development. Initially, a Late-Romanesque church was built here in the 13<sup>th</sup> century. It was demolished in 1553 and replaced by a wooden chapel, which burnt down in 1720. The local Evangelists therefore sat about building another wooden church, which was first used in 1724. And the present-day Evangelic towerless church was built in 1793. Its rectangular building has a wooden lacunar ceiling, a segmented presbytery and a Classicism column altar from the 19<sup>th</sup> century. Near the church is a detached brick belfry with a wooden arcade and a shingle roof.

## HRADOVÁ (3)

The huge forested massif of Hradová (887 m) looms high above the town of Tisovec. This popular tourist destination provides splendid views of the town and its surroundings. There is a sharp rocky ridge at the top part, and to climb it is a very challenging task. Once there were two castles on Hradová, however both vanished a long time ago; only tiny fragments are preserved. The oldest castle was built in the 13th century as an aristocratic seat in the spot called Okrúhla Skala. The younger edifice from the 15th century stood just below the main peak and fulfilled the role of a sentry fortress. Both castles had an advantageous position on the hardly accessible peak, which provided an excellent natural defence. The site was also known to prehistoric settlers, who left archaeological traces here. Supposedly, the Old Slavs also settled on this easily defensible hill. Yet despite its great position, the castles did not withstand the attacks of the Bratríci Movement and later the Ottomans, and both were left to become ruins after the estate uprisings.

## EVANGELIC CHURCH IN KLENOVEC (4)

The high spire of the Evangelic church is the landmark of the interesting village of Klenovec in Slovenské Rudohorie. Its ancient appearance is enhanced by the belfry with a wooden balcony and a fortification wall around it. Yet this church is rather new (1906), as the original Tolerance church was destroyed in a fire in 1888. The architects of the church fully respected its original appearance and used preserved building materials. The former Tolerance church from the 18th century also had a predecessor, a church from 1610. According to historical documents, the outlaw J. Jánošík was caught in Klenovec in 1713. The captain came to visit his friend T. Uhorčík, who ended his outlaw career and acquired a new identity as M. Mravec; both were arrested and were sent to prison.

## KLENOVSKÝ VEPOR (5)

Although this mountain is not the highest (1,338 m), it is the most popular in the western part of Slovenské rudohorie. A whole mountain range, Veportské Vrchy, was named after it. The typical shape of its peak is easily recognisable; it is a skeletonised lava channel of an extinct Tertiary volcano. Its peak was denuded to such an extent that it is impossible to say where it stood. Several trails go up forested Klenovský Vepor. The most convenient path starts in Čremoš in the upper part of the Veporský Stream Valley above Klenovec. The viewing place is slightly below the top of the mountain.

## NÁMESTIE DR. VLADIMÍRA CLEMENTISA IN TISOVEC (1)

The village of Tisovec has a splendid location at the southwest edge of the Muránska Planina Plain. Its name is derived from the local yew trees and this original mining settlement developed in the 13th century. It had grown into a town by the end of the 15th century and received town privileges and rights to have markets in 1595. The local industry started to develop in Tisovec towards the end of the 18th century and at the beginning of the 19th century. A blast furnace was built in 1793; it was the largest producer of iron in Hungary around the mid-19th century. In the centre of the village is the smallish but charming Námestie Dr. Vladimíra Clementisa Square, leading into Jozefyho Street at the west; it was named after the Slovakian leftist, intellectual, politician and publicist (1902-1952). His native house with a memorable sign is on the west side of Jozefyho Street, which bears the name of yet another famous native, the Evangelic priest and teacher P. Jozefy (1775-1848). The Classicism town hall from 1798 and the adjacent Classicism Evangelic church from 1832 are landmarks of the centre of Tisovec.

## COG-RAILWAY POHRONSKÁ POLHORA – TISOVEC (2)

Brezno and Tisovec are connected by the railway built in 1895 for the requirements of the ironworks in Tisovec that need to be connected with the Hronec ironworks in the Horehronie Region. The railway had to manage the mountainous terrain of the Veporské Vrchy Hills with a rather high elevation. Original cog-adhesion engines once operated on the railway; they were produced in Floridsdorf especially for this railway. First the tendrové engines, one of the best cog-engines in the world, operated on the railway. The more technically demanding section near the Zbojská Saddle goes up a slope with a 48 % gradient, so the cog-rail system was used here. It is still in place, but is not used by the powerful present-day engines. The cog-railway is a popular summer attraction. Part of this interesting technical work are is also two impressive viaducts Čertov and Pod Dielom.

## MURÁŇ (1)

This village is the gateway into the Muránska Planina National Park. It is situated on the southwest side of the plain in a beautiful location below the sharp Cigánka Peak with a ruin of Muránsky Castle. The village was founded in 1321 below the castle. Apart from farming and forest work its inhabitants once earned their bread by the production of the famous Muránská china and stoneware in a factory from 1823. A memorable battle took place near Muráň in February 1849; Slovakian rebels were defeated here and according to a legend the wounded survivors hid in the nearby Brestová Cave in the Hrdzavá Dolina Valley. The present-day Muráň boasts several vernacular buildings and it is the starting point for treks in the lovely Muránska Planina Plain during the summer.

## MURÁŇ CASTLE (2)

The infamous chapter of the history of Muráň Castle are the times of the rule of its castellan, M. Bašo. This dreaded robber knight tortured the surroundings with cruel pillaging. In the end the king sent an army to punish this self-made ruler in 1548 and after a long siege led

by M. of Salem the castle was finally conquered. Although Baš escaped through a hole, still visible in the eastern wall, he did not avoid punishment and died at the scaffold one year later. The castle had a famous inhabitant in the 17th century. It was Mária Séčiová (Széchy), who was called the Muránska Venus for her beauty. This granddaughter of the Head of Gemer County, T. Séči, managed to marry three important local lords and turned the castle into a grandiose seat with a rich social life. She bravely defended the castle following a suppression of the uprising led by her last husband in 1671, however she did not succeed. The castle burnt out in the 18th century and gradually fell to ruin.

## MURÁNSKA PLANINA (3)

This island with the best preserved natural environment in Slovakia lies between the Gemer, Malohont and Horehronie regions. Civilization has barely touched the poorly accessible terrain of plateaus and rocks of this plain. The Muránska Planina Protected Landscape Area was designated in 1976 to protect the rare natural wonders of this area and it became a National Park in 1997. The total

area of the strictly protected territory takes up 21,318 ha plus there is a protection strip of 21,698 ha. Muránská Planina is steep and rocky around its perimeter while the area inside boasts karst plateaus divided by valleys cutting deep into the limestone massif. This applies especially in the case of the wild Hrdzavá Dolina Valley, abundant with bizarre rocks. There are several karsts formations including sinkholes, chasms, abysses and caves. The longest karst system, Bobačka, is 3 km long and the deepest cave, Michňová, is 105 metres deep. Ice stays in the abysses all year round.

## STUD FARM VEĽKÁ LÚKA (4)

The wild landscape of Muránska Planina has been the home to horses since 1950. The stud farm in Veľká Lúka first started breeding the half-wild traditional Carpathian Huculs horse, which was brought here from an army stud farm in Prešova. However, the small tough horse did not fulfill the requirements of hard forest work and a new, so-called Slovakian Mountain Horse, began to be bred. Unfortunately the project was not successful so a different direction was taken, focusing this time

on the cross-breeding of the Hucul and Silesian Noriker horses. It resulted in the present-day Noriker of the Muráň type, accepted as a horse breed in 1995. To see these lovely horses grazing the mountain meadows of Muránska Planina is an unusual experience, but it requires some luck, as the herd moves constantly in search of the best pastures.

## CIGÁNKA (5)

The relatively large complex of Muráň Castle is accessible by a path from the tourist Zámok Chalet with a 200–year history. The best preserved part of this ruin is the entry gate that leads inside the much destroyed walls. A viewing point on the other side offers a breathtaking view of the southwestern scenery. A limestone rock called Cigánka (935 m) looms in the foreground; it is not accessible to the public. The name of the rock is associated with a legend about a beautiful gypsy girl (Cigánka) who married the captain of Muránsky Castle. Once, while her jealous husband was away, she joined a merry celebration with the castle sentry. Seeing this, her unexpectedly returning husband threw her down the rock.

## MANSION IN PREDNÁ HORA (6)

There is an elegant bulding in the style of a hunting chateau at the edge of Muránská Planina. Its history started with the daring plans of F. Cobrurg to restore Muránsky Castle. This young hussar officer became the Bulgarian Tsar in 1903 and kept visiting his possessions in the Horehronie Region where his family was active in iron production. However, squabbles with his brother Filip ended his original plans, so he bought a hunting chateau in Predná Hora in 1909 near Muránska Huť and rebuilt it into an elegant representative hunting seat. It was completed in 1914 and had a botanical garden, a heated pool and an original horologe. The dethroned Tsar Ferdinand I used the mansion until 1944. It now houses a drug addiction rehabilitation centre which has been successful for some time in helping people with alcoholism.

## VEĽKÁ STOŽKA AND MALÁ STOŽKA (7)

The deep valley of the Hronec Creek cuts into the Muránska Planina Plain at the north. A pair of rocky peaks, Veľká Stožka (1,297 m) and Malá Stožka (1,204 m), tower high above the bottom of the valley in its upper part. Both landmarks are best to look at from the viewing point near Skalná Gate below Nižná Kľaková. They are both Protected National Reserves, so there is no tourist trail to their rocky tops. The massif of Veľká Stožka is made mostly of limestone with karst formations. The slopes of the hill are covered with forests, mainly spruce and some relikt larch, Malá Stožka is limestone-dolomite with karst formations mainly in the northeastern slope.

## STOLICA (8)

This peak (1 476 m n. m.) is the highest in the Solické Vrchy Hills, Gemer Region as well as in the entire Slovakian Rudohorie Mountains. Its massif with a large round peak is from schist and granite. The meadows in its top part are slowly overgrowing with forests so the famous and splendid far-reaching views are disappearing. The Slaná River springs on its northern slope.

1

2

## SLOVAKIAN GRAMMAR SCHOOL IN REVÚCA (1)

Revúca was one of the main centres of the Slovakian national and cultural life in the second half of the 19th century, and it was the site of an important event in September 1862. One of the first three Slovakian grammar schools was opened in a Rococo mansion from the 18th century. It was managed by the local Evangelists and the opening celebration of the school was held in the local Evangelic church from the 18th century. The grammar school was the first complete Slovakian high school where lessons were taught in the Slovakian language; it began testing for 0-level exams in 1868. Several important personages of the Slovakian cultural and artistic community worked in the school: Štefan Marko Daxner, Ján Francisci, Samuel Ormis and Ivan Branislav Zoch. As the grammar school received no support from the state institutions, it was closed down in 1874.

## CHURCH OF ST. LAURENCE IN REVÚCA (2)

Revúca is the largest town in the valley of the Muráň River. In the past it prospered thanks to the mining, which soon started iron production and the town became the centre of the so-called Muránska Únia, a union of the iron traders of the

Gemer Region. Two high church towers are landmarks of the town. The tower nearer the centre belongs to the Church of St. Laurence, while the second one is a later addition of the Evangelic church. The Roman-Catholic church once had two towers, however one was demolished after a fire in 1892. The relatively new façade from the end of the 19th century hides a Neo-Gothic building from the second half of the 15th century. There are valuable desk paintings from the 15th century on the Pseudo Gothic main altar, depicting scenes from the life of St. Kvirin. One of the largest bells in Gemer also bears the name of this saint, venerated mainly in Bavaria. A legend says that it was brought to Revúca from a Gemer village. Another identical bell stayed in the original place and when one of the bells chimed, the other started too.

## CHURCH IN CHYŽNÉ (3)

This small village lies near Lubeník in the valley of the Muráň River. It is worthwhile to turn off the main road to see the local valuable Early Gothic church from the 13th century. The smallish Church of the Annunciation of the Virgin Mary is part of the interesting tourist Gothic Path that connects the most important medieval monuments of the Gemer and Spiš regions. The main reason for the significance of the church is its va-

luable medieval fresco painting, and the altar from the workshop of Master Pavel of Levoča. Chyžné also boasts an Evangelic church from 1886. The writer and poet S. Tomášik (1813 – 1887), famous for the text of the hymn *Hej, Slováci*, worked as a priest in the church.

### SMELTERY IN ČERVEŇANY (4)
The area of the Revúca Vrchovina Hills near the Ratková and Sirok was an important centre of iron ore mining and production. Several preserved technical monuments are reminiscent of the long passed glory of miners and iron workers. The most valuable is the blast furnace in Červeňany near Sirok, built together with a hammer mill in 1871. The blast furnace processed iron ore of the haematit type from the nearby mines in Železník, Dobšiná, Hrádok and Rožňava. The blast furnace is a part of the cultural tourism project together with other monuments of the iron tradition in the Gemer Region. This project is part of the globally focused European Iron Path.

### RATKOVÁ (5)
This town, situated in the valley of the Turiec River, was the centre of the Revúcka Vrchovina with a history of iron mining and production. It developed from the mining settlement from the 13th century and was the centre of craft and tra-

ditional markets. It boasted three blast furnaces and four iron hammer-mills in the 16th century and, although it burnt out in 1827, several valuable cultural and historical monuments have been preserved. They are located around the square, one of the most beautiful in Slovakia. The oldest monument is the Late Gothic Evangelic church from the beginning of the 16th century. Next to it is a belfry from the turn of the 18th century. Among the secular monuments are the Classicism Evangelic school and the town hall.

### CHURCH OF ST. MARGARITA ANTIOCH IN ŠIVETICE (6)
An interesting sacral building with an unusual round ground-plan stands at the cemetery in the village of Šivetice in the valley of Muráň. The Church of St Margita Antioch from the mid-13th century is the largest Romanesque rotunda in Slovakia. It was first thought to be a preserved apse of a Romanesque church. According to its patron it was probably founded by the Knight Hospitallers. The ancient brick building with an inner area of 11 metres has a painted apse. The untraditional façade has lizeny, the blind arcades. A detached Baroque brick belfry is next to the church. Šivetice also boast an Evangelic Tolerance church from 1785.

# EASTERN SLOVAKIA

Great diversity is typical in eastern Slovakia. The landscape and natural surroundings are very colourful, as well as some man-made features. The same can be said about the people, their dialect, culture and traditions. The highest peak in Slovakia, the Gerlachovský Štít Peak, lies in this area; however there is also the lowest point in the country, in the spot where the Bodrog River leaves the Slovakian territory. The Spiš Region is the richest area with regards to culture and ethnography, and not only within eastern Slovakia. It boasts three of the most popular national parks as well as numerous cultural and historical monuments, some of which are on the UNESCO World Cultural Heritage List. The pride of the landscape are Levoča, Kežmarok, Spišská Sobota, Spišský hrad, Spišská Kapitula and Žehra. The Šariš Region offers, apart from the historical towns of Bardejov and Prešov, the greatest valuable wooden churches, while Východný Gemer is the region of ancient churches and also boasts the impressive karst phenomenon, mainly the Slovenský Kras National Park. Its charming caves are also part of the exclusive UNESCO List. Košice will entice visitors with its historical centre and splendid square with scores of monuments with the grandiose Gothic Dóm of St. Elisabeth. Then there is Zemplín, the region of many faces. This remote area, which is the most eastern section of Slovakia, boasts wild virgin beech forests, plains and flood plain forests and swamps, as well as the 'Eastern Sea', the Zemplínska Šírava Lake.

# HIGH TATRAS AND BELIANSKE TATRAS

### KRIVÁŇ (1)

Despite its crooked upper part, Kriváň (2,494 m) is the most popular peak and the national symbol of Slovakians. There is a legend behind the origin of the distortion, according to which God asked an angel on the seventh day of the creation of the world to make the finishing touches on his work. So the angel put as much natural beauty as possible in his pockets and set about his task, dotting the beauty around the world. However, he did not notice the barrier of the Tatra peaks and his wing caught on the first mountain, bending it. In the confusion his pocket tore open and numerous magnificent meadows, forests, creeks, waterfalls and lakes fell down on the rocky Tatras, while marmots, chamois, bears and numerous other animals ran to find their home in the area. Thus the Tatras received more beauty than other mountain ranges. The peak that caused all this remained crooked and got the corresponding name, Kriváň (Crooked). The peak was popular with medieval miners, who searched for ores at its slopes, and it became very famous when the Saxon king Fridrich August II admired the view from its peak. One year later, a group of Slovakian patriots and national revivalists climbed Kriváň, starting an ongoing tradition of the August national climbs of Slovaks to Kriváň.

### PODBANSKÉ (2)

The name of this place implies that miners searched for ores as early as in the 15th century on the slopes and in the valleys of the Tatras. Traces of these activities are still apparent almost below the peak of Kriváň. Shepherds and forest workers came after miners. Shepherds loved the endless lush meadows, while the woodcutters set off in a different direction into the endless Tatras forests. The first tourist arrived in the 19th century. The first building of the future village of Podbanské, the Harmanova Horáreň Lodge from 1871, provided modest accommodation. The year 1970 was an important landmark in the history of this village. The road from Štrbské Pleso to Podbanské was extended to Liptovský Hrádok thanks to the famous World Ski Championship, thus helping Podbanské to develop into the busy present-day tourist centre. It is the popular gateway for treks to Kriváň, Kôprová Dolina and Tichá Dolina, and to the most eastern part of the area, the Western Tatras.

### VODOPÁD SKOK (3)

This waterfall is an easily accessible and attractive tourist destination in the Mlynická Dolina Valley. Its normal flowage of 60 l/s goes up to 800 l/s in the spring. During the flood threat in 1958, a huge mass of water gushed over the rock step with a flowage of 30,000 l/s. The typical feature of Skok is a gentle veil of mist hovering above the edge of the rocky step. Indeed, there is a legend behind the origin of the waterfall, which talks about unhappy lovers and a crying girl that walks around the valley in

search of her lover who never returned from a chamois hunt below Štrbský Štít Peak. Her tears are the rich source of the waterfall.

## KMEŤOV VODOPÁD (4)

Similar to other Tatras valleys the Kôprová Dolina was covered by an iceberg during the Ace Age. It was one of the largest icebergs (11 km long) and thus created a very deep valley. The side valleys eroded by smaller iceberg are shallower and open high above the bottom of the main valley. This applies also in case of the valley of Nefcerka set in the massif of Kriváň. The Nefcerský Creek has to manage more than 700 metres of high rocky step before it spills into the Kôprovský Creek, creating the 80-metre high Kmeťov Waterfall, the highest one in Slovakia. It has 30 levels and was named after a Slovakian botanist, Andrej Kmeť (1841 – 1908).

## FURKOTSKÁ DOLINA (5)

This valley in the western part of the High Tatras is, in a way, a twin of the neighbouring Mlynická Dolina. The Ridgeway of High Tatras over the Bystré Saddle (2,314 m) passes through both valleys. Furkotská Dolina is charming mainly thanks to its two large mountain lakes (tarns), Wahlenbergove Plesá, which almost fill up the valley. The landscape scenery near the Nižné Wahlenbergovo Pleso is especially charming. The Ostrá Veža Peak (2,129 m) is beautifully reflected on its dark-blue surface, creating thus a twin of the pyramid-shaped peak on the surface. The two splendid lakes in Furkotská Dolina are named after the significant Swedish scientist and traveller G. Wahlenberg, who earned this honour by his successful botanical research in the Tatras in 1813.

## MLYNICKÁ DOLINA (6)

You can admire this valley in its entire beauty from Štrbské Pleso. It lies between the forks of the Solísk and Bášt with the proud conically-shaped Štrbský Štít Peak (2,381 m) in its centre. The historian and scholar Matej Bel wrote about Mlynická Valley in the 18th century, calling it a garden of healing herbs planted by Mother Nature and a land with many mountain goats

(chamois) and marmots. The area was probably abundant with chamois as there are Kozie (Goat) Plesá and Capie (Billy-goat) pleso. The highest located tarn is the round Okrúhle Pleso. A tourist trail leads up Mlynická Dolina, and there are several rock steps before the Bystré Saddle (2,314 m); the Skok Waterfall on the Mlynica Stream gushes over one of them.

## TEMNOSMREČINSKÁ DOLINA (7)

The Kôprová Dolina Valley in the most western section of the High Tatras forks into two smaller valleys in its upper part. The more western is called the Temnosmrečinská Valley and was once overgrown with a thick spruce forest. It was a popular hunting (chamois) area in the past. A Polish poet, Nowicki, accompanied by the legendary mountain guide Bachled, counted 80 species of chamois in 1887. The valley is one of the quietest and most beautiful nooks in the High Tatras. A lonely tourist, who sometimes visits the valley and has to negotiate the rocky step with the 30-metre Vajanský Vodopád Waterfall, will be rewarded with a view of the remarkably beautiful natural landscape.

### ŠTRBSKÉ PLESO (1)

It is hard to believe that the local farmers once wanted to empty this tarn to turn it into meadows for their cattle. Fortunately, priorities have changed over the times, and today nobody would think of destroying such a jewel of the landscape. Štrbské Pleso lies at 1,346 m and is the second highest tarn in the Slovakian High Tatras. It covers just below 20 hectares. The birth of the Štrbské Pleso settlement reaches as far as 1871. The first swallow of the future most popular tourist centre in Slovakia was a tourist chalet built by the estate owner J. Seniváni (Szentiványi) of Liptovský Ján. The centre provides excellent conditions for downhill and cross-country skiing. There is a modern sport centre in the Mlynická Dolina with bridges and a popular piste on the slopes of Solisko. In the summer Štrbské Pleso becomes an important base for Ridgeway treks. The village is also an important climatic spa.

### POPRADSKÉ PLESO (2)

Carriages brought people to this tarn with typically greenish water in the 19th century and the journey was often accompanied by gypsy music. The tarn was originally called Rybie (Fish); its present-day name derives from the name of the Poprad Creek that flows out of it. There are no carriages any more; however its banks are swarmed during the tourist season. Many of those who walk the Tatranská Magistrála Trail from Štrbské Pleso or from the station of the Tatras electrical train make Popradské Pleso their destination. Apart from the lovely scenery, there are also tourist facilities in the mountain hotel at the west bank of the lake. Other tourists leave the tarn and continue up the Hincova Dolina Valley to the Veľké Hincovo Tarn or walk up numerous coiling serpentines into the Sedlo pod Ostrvou Saddle.

### SYMBOLICKÝ CINTORÍN (3)

You can honour the victims of the Tatras at this symbolical cemetery located in the shade of swiss pine grove below the western wall of Ostrva near Popradské Pleso. It was established upon the initiative of the academic painter O. Štáfl.

## VEĽKÉ HINCOVO PLESO (4)

People once believed that Tatras tarns were connected with the seas and even serious scientists explored this idea in the 18th century. Moreover, some allegedly witnessed the wreck of a sailing ship on the banks of Zelené Pleso. The truth is, indeed, that tarns were created by icebergs, which melted at the end of the last Ice Age. Water was retained due to moraines that created dams in the lower parts. Tarns in the upper sections remained in holes carved by the iceberg. A nice example of an iceberg lake is Veľké Hincovo Pleso in the Hincova Dolina Valley. It takes up over 20 hectares, being the largest natural tarn in the whole of Slovakia. There are even larger tarns at the Polish side of the Tatras. Veľké Hincovo is also the deepest tarn, being 53 metres deep in one place.

## SEDLO POD OSTRVOU (5)

The sight of the tourist trail coiling in the steep slope on the east side of Popradské Pleso may discourage some. But those who carry on and do the challenging trek will get a great reward as the Sedlo pod Ostrvou Saddle (1,966 m) offers a view of breathtaking scenery, one of the best in the area. The view of Mengusovská Dolina and its side valleys is magnificent. From the height of almost 500 m Popradské Pleso looks minuscule and the mountain hotel on its banks resembles a matchbox. This makes some of the peaks look even huger and more imposing, mainly the crown of the Tatras, the Vysoká Peak, which looms gracefully on the northern horizon. The ser-

pentines to Sedlo pod Ostrvou are part of the Tatranská Magistrála, a long-distance 70-kilometre trail that skirts the southern foothills of the Tatras.

## VYSOKÁ (6)

Kriváň is the national symbol of Slovakians; however Vysoká regularly ranks the position of the most beautiful mountain. It looms at 2,547 metres and is the 14th highest amongst the mountains in the Tatras. In fact it has two identical peaks, and moreover, it has smaller peaks at both sides, the Ťažký (until recently Český) peak at the west and Dračí at the east. The silhouette of four peaks resembles a crown, hence the nickname the 'Crown of Tatras'. The climb is very demanding and can only be carried out with a mountain guide. The famous mountain guide J. R. Dirčný was present during the first known climb to the peak on 3rd September 1874 when he accompanied M. Dechy.

## CHATA POD RYSMI (7)

The highest located tourist chalet in the entire Tatras is Chata pod Rysmi at 2,250 metres. It is only open during the summer tourist season as avalanches are a serious problem here and the chalet was badly damaged in the past. Plans for its relocation to a safer place located closer to the Rysy Peak are currently being considered. The chalet sits in a small hollow below the Váh Saddle and it is a pleasant oasis before the last section of the climb to Rysy; it takes about another hour to get to the top. Construction works on the chalet

started in 1933 and due to several problems – mainly snowstorms and stone avalanches – it was a difficult task. In any case, it was opened to tourists before the end of the season. It was an asylum for Polish climbers fleeing from the Germans during World War II.

## VIEW FROM RYSY (8)

Allegedly the leader of the Soviet proletariat, I. Lenin, climbed the peak (2,499 m) to see the view in August 1913. This founded a tradition 43 years later; there are annual mass climbs to the peak, which is becoming the most visited mountain in the entire Tatras. Only the Lomnický Štít Peak experiences more tourists, as there is a cable car to its top. Rysy are also the highest peak of Poland and, at the same time, the highest peak in the Tatras, which is accessible by a tourist trail. With regards to its height, it holds the 26th position. Its name of Rysy (Lynx) has nothing to do with the animal but with the dialect name for the lines that make its slopes rugged. The first person to climb the peak was E. Blásy (1840) accompanied by mountain guide J. R. Driečny sr. There are two trails to the peak, one from the Slovakian side and the other from the Polish side.

### GERLACHOVSKÝ ŠTÍT (1)

It was discovered only relatively recently that this peak (2,654 m) is the highest in the Tatras, as inhabitants of Liptov believed there was no higher mountain than Kriváň and those from Spiš insisted the highest was Lomnický Štít. It seems from the north that the peak of this mountain is the Ľadový Štít behind it, as there is no other visible peak around. However, the director of Coburg Forests, Ľ. Greiner, climbed the Lomnický Štít and measured the surrounding peaks, discovering with a surprise that the highest one is, indeed, Gerlachovský Štít. There is no tourist trail up to the peak and it can only be climbed with a mountain guide. The climb itself is not very demanding, the main problem is for inexperienced tourists to orientate themselves in the difficult terrain when the weather is bad, which is more than common here.

### TATRANSKÁ POLIANKA (2)

This is one of the oldest settlements at the southern foothills of the High Tatras. Three hotels, Mariana, Tusculum and Themis, were built here in 1888 and quickly became popular resting places for passengers of carriages operating on the newly opened Klotildina Path (present-day Cesta Slobody) between Smokovce and Štrbské Pleso. M. Guhr jr. (1873 – 1933) continued the commercial success of the hotel, building a sanatorium in Tatranská Polianka in 1902, which specialised in curing tuberculosis and asthma. One of the most famous patients of the spa was the Czech poet J. Wolker, who stayed here in November 1923. Unfortunately, despite the treatment, he died of illness in Prostejov in January 1924.

### VYŠNÉ HÁGY (3)

This village at the southern foothills of Gerlachovský Štít was founded upon the initiative of a squire named F. Mariáši (Máriássy) in 1890. His intention behind building a wooden house in the Northern style for twelve guests was to

offer cheaper yet quality services. Over time this village specialised in spa services. A tuberculosis sanatorium, then the largest in central Europe, was opened here in 1941. The modern eight-story building is 270 m long and accommodates 1,950 beds. It helps patients with respiratory diseases.

## VELICKÁ DOLINA (4)

The name of this valley is associated with its past, when it was part of the large area of the estate of the town of Veľká (present-day quarter of Poprad). This over 5 kilometre long ice valley between Gerlachovský Štít and the ridge of Velické Granáty Mountains has four levels. The terrace on the second step is considered the most beautiful part of the valley, and it is called Kvetnica (Flowery) for its abundant colourful fauna. The scholar and admirer of the Tatras D. Fröhlich called it the 'garden of spices' in the 17th century, pointing to the variety of medical plants that grow here. The famous Swedish botanist G. Wahlenberg went to see Kvetnica when he visited the Tatras in 1813. Imposing rocky towers and the wall of Velické Granáty create the eastern silhouette of Kvetnica. They are a site of the occurrence of Garnet specs, which attracted many miners and gold diggers in the past. A narrow gutter called Velická Próba starts at the other side of Kvetnica. It is the most popular trail to Gerlachovský Štít.

## SLIEZSKY DOM (5)

Sliezsky Dom (1,670 m) sits in a charming hollow on the lowest step of Velická Dolina. It is the largest tourist hotel in the upper area of the High Tatras. The terrace of the hotel offers views of magnificent scenery with the oblong Velické Pleso and huge rock step in the background with the white ribbon of the 15-metre Velický Waterfall. The first tourist chalet was built near Velické Pleso in 1871. A new chalet was built after it was destroyed by an avalanche and it was named after the

geographer Ján Hunfalvy from Veľký Slavkov. Another chalet was built in 1895, and Hynfalvyho Chalet was designated for mountain guides and servants accompanying rich tourists. As the new chalet was managed by the Silesian section of the Hungarian Carpathian Association, it was called Sliezsky Dom. The chalet was rebuilt many times, however it burnt down in November 1962. The present day Sliezsky Dom dates from 1968 and is a part of the tourist facilities on the Tatranská Magistrála Trail. It is the most popular starting point for climbs to the highest mountain in the Tatras, Gerlachovský Štít.

## VÝCHODNÁ VYSOKÁ (6)

Although it does not reach the heights of its neighbours, Východná Vysoká Peak (2,428 m) is one of the most popular thanks to its relatively easy access as well as remarkable location. It lies in the very heart of the High Tatras and is surrounded by charming natural beauty, typical for the alpine areas. A huge fork with the Bradavice and Slavkovský Štít peaks juts out from the junction peak in the main ridge of the High Tatras. The access to Východná Vysoká is along a tourist trail from the saddle Poľský Hrebeň (2,200 m). Tourists can also walk in the opposite direction along the popular Martinovka, a splendid climbing ridgeway that ends at the peak of Gerlachovský Štít.

### STARÝ SMOKOVEC (1)

People once visited these mineral springs at the foothills of the Slavkovský Štít Peak during the Petropavlovské Pilgrimages. However, this place has an even older traditional celebration that goes back to the times when local people celebrated an Old Slavic god called Zmok. Perhaps the name of this old pagan guardian of the waters and riches hidden in the earth's bowels gave name to four Tatras villages called Smokovce. However there are other explanations for the name of this village founded in 1793 near the spring. The present-day Starý Smokovec is the largest and most important village at the foothills of High Tatras and it is the administrative centre of the entire area.

### NOVÝ SMOKOVEC (2)

Starý Smokovec continues into the smaller Nový Smokovec at the west. This Tatras settlement from 1876 became the cradle of the climatic balneology. Doctor M. Szontagh started the idea of the balneology when he opened the first sanatorium built in the Swiss style. This pioneer doctor commenced several then unheard of experiments in Nový Smokovec. He left the sanatorium open during the winter in 1883, which was until then an untried method. The apprehensions about the cruel winter and snow storms were not fulfilled – quite the contrary. Tourists discovered the beauty of the winter Tatras and soon the winter season became commonplace in all Tatras villages.

### HREBIENOK (3)

This village is the advanced bastion of tourists that makes the access to the valleys of Studená Dolina and to Slavkovský Štít more convenient. Sitting at 1,285 metres, this tourist base (a skiing centre in the winter) on the Tatranská Magistrála Trail was built as part of the project of Studenopotocké Spa, which was initiated in 1883 and has never been completed. Hrebienok has been connected with Starý Smokovec by a cable car since 1908; it is 2,019 metres long and goes over an elevation of 354 metres. There is also a paved road which is a cycling paradise in the summer and a popular sledge track in the winter.

### SLAVKOVSKÝ ŠTÍT (4)

This majestic mountain (2,452 m) looming above Smokovce is easily recognisable thanks to its peculiarly round silhouette. The strange shape of the peak was associated with an earthquake that happened here on 6th August 1662. Allegedly, the earth's crust shook the peak with such vigour that its top fell off, crumbling into a pile of rocks. It was believed that the peak was originally higher by 200 metres and thus the highest in the Tatras. However, this theory has never been confirmed. A trail made in 1908 leads to the top of the mountain.

### REINEROVA CHATA (5)

This oldest mountain chalet from 1884 was almost demolished in the 1980s. The 'Rainerka' chalet provides for tourists trekking the Tatranská Magistrála Trail; its offer does not include accommodation and food services, however.

### VODOPÁDY STUDENÉHO POTOKA (6)

The striking cascade of the Vodopády Studeného Potoka Waterfalls lies in the spot where the Studená Dolina Valley meets with the Malá Studená Dolina Valley. The highest Obrovský Waterfall can be admired from a wooden bridge on the Tatranská Magistrála Trail. The white ruffled water of the Malý Studený Creek plunges 20 metres between two rocks. The lower Trojitý Waterfall has a more poetic name in Hungarian and German, 'Waterfall of Artists'. A further four waterfalls are below the confluence of the Veľký Studený and Malý Studený creeks. The highest is the cascade of the Malý Waterfall. The Skrytý Waterfall lies at 1,247. The bottom part of the Veľký Waterfall lies below it at 1,226 metres; most tourists usually gather here on the bank or small wooden bridge to admire the roaring water gushing over the 13-metre rock step. The cascaded Dlhý Waterfall lies exactly opposite the Bilíkova Chalet on Hrebeniek and can be reached by a yellow-marked trail from Tatranská Lesná.

1

## VEĽKÁ STUDENÁ DOLINA (1)

This over 7 kilometre long valley resembles a triangle on a map. Its very wide top section narrows down towards the bottom. The area between Východná Vysoká and Široká Veža in the wide amphitheatre of the upper part of the valley boasts a bizarre landscape of round hills with visible traces of the past iceberg activity. After the iceberg melted at the end of the Ice Age it left numerous tarns in the holes. The slopes of hills have rocks with lines that show the direction of the movement of the icebergs. There are 22 tarns in the valley, the largest group of these icebergs relics in Slovakia. The two remaining sides of the triangle-shaped Veľká Studená Valley create side forks with two mountains, Bradavica and Slavkovský Štít, which exceed the height of the Prostredný Hrot Peak. The two forks narrow down the valley. A tourist trail skirts the upper part of the valley. It forks out at the Zbojnícka Chalet; one branch climbs to the Priečne Sedlo Saddle and continues into the Malá Studená Valley, while the other leads into the Litvorová Dolina via the Prielom Saddle.

## ZBOJNÍCKA CHATA (2)

This chalet (1,960 m) lies in the wide amphitheatre of the upper part of Veľká Studená Dolina. Originally, it was a hunting lodge from 1907, which was later reconstructed for tourists. Cold air often gathers on the bottom of the valley and it made heating of the typically cold and moist interior of the cottage difficult. It gave this uncomfortable cottage the nickname Márnice (Mortuary); it had no official name at the time. However, members of the Club of Czechoslovakian Tourists managed to rebuild the chalet in 1924, making it more comfortable. They also employed a full-time manager of the chalet. It was open during the whole year in 1932-1933 and finally received its name. The mountain bearer and later successful chalet manager Zamkovský called it Zbojnícka Chalet, as features in the surroundings (Zbojnícke plesá, Zbojnícke sedlo a Zbojnícka kopa) bear a similar name. The chalet almost burned down in 1998. Fortunately it was repaired relatively quickly and it now provides complete services for tourists.

2

## MALÁ STUDENÁ DOLINA (3)

This valley is squeezed by the massifs of Lomnic-ký Štít and Prostredný Hrot. It is a typical Tatras valley created by a huge iceberg in the Ice Ages. It has typical high rocky steps, called *hangy*. The lower step (130 m) high lies below Zamkovské-ho Chalet; it is called Schodíky and there is the Obrovský Waterfall. The top step is in the upper section of the valley. It is even higher (200 m) and is called Jazerná Stena. It is a very deman-ding climb to its top, rewarded by refreshments in the Téryho Chalet above it. The upper part of the valley is a striking natural amphitheatre flanked by peaks that are amongst the highest in the entire mountain range. Apart from the huge Lomnický Štít there are the remarkable Veľký Ľadový and Ľadový peaks. Five tarns are on the bottom of the valley. The trail climbs up to the Sedielko at 2,372 metres, the highest tourist accessible saddle in the Tatras, and con-tinues past the Modré Pleso Tarn (2,190 m). This is the highest permanent tarn in the High Tatras.

## TÉRYHO CHALET (4)

There is no higher located chalet for tourists that is open during the winter season (2,015 m). The Chata pod Rysmi Chalet is even higher but it is only open during the summer. This stone cha-let in Malá Studená Dolina was built by a pio-neer of climbing in the Tatras, doctor E. Téry (1856 – 1917). This man, known in Banská Štiavnica as the 'doctor of the poor', also esta-blished the Tatras Association and as the hol-der of the exclusive right to built in Malá Stu-dená Dolina, he set about building a tourist chalet according to the design by G. Majunke. It was opened for the public on 21st August 1889. The location of the chalet is perfect. Not only is it located in one of the most beautiful valleys of the High Tatras, but its veranda also enables tourists to have tea while watching the mountaineers on the popular Žltá Wall that looms right above the chalet.

## ZAMKOVSKÉHO CHALET (5)

This chalet lies in the lower section of Malá Stu-dená Dolina and it is one of the newest and lowest chalets in the Tatras. It sits at 1,475 me-tres near the turn of of the Tatranská Magistrá-la Trail to Malá Studená Dolina. This wooden building was constructed in 1943 by the fa-mous Tatras mountaineer, mountain guide and manager of the Téryho Chalet, Š. Zamkovský (1908-1961). It was nationalised in 1951 and renamed as the Chata Kapitána Nálepku after the partisan leader who died in 1943 near the Ukrainian town of Ovruč. Zamkovský's grand-son received the chalet as a restitution (1992) and restored its original name. The rarity of this place is that it has a female manager, the only one among the male managers of the chalets in all of the Tatras.

### TATRANSKÁ LOMNICA (1)

This town at the foothills of Lomnický Štít developed as one of the last Tatras villages towards the end of the 19th century. At that time Starý Smokovec was 100 years old. Thanks to this, the development of Tatranská Lomnica was not spontaneous but rather followed an urban design with scores of maintained parks. If it wasn't for the cyclone in November 2004 the town would be nestled in lush greenery. The oldest building is the Lomnica Hotel from 1893. The largest and most luxurious is the Art Nouveau building of the Grandhotel Praha from 1906. The TANAP Museum from 1957 has its seat in Tatranská Lomnica.

### SKALNATÉ PLESO (2)

The cable car from Tatranská Lomnica is an attractive and also very comfortable way to Skalnaté Pleso Tarn, located 900 metres above the town. Its last stop is part of the Encián Hotel and also the base stop of the cable car to Lomnický Štít. The Skalnatá Chalet lies southward next to the Tatranská Magistrála Trail, while north of Encián is the observatory of the SAV Astronomical Institution with two domes. The view from Skalnaté Pleso is splendid, with the panorama of Popradská Kotlina and numerous mountains to the southeast; you can see as far as over 100 kilometres on a fine day. The view on the other side is also remarkable. Two peaks, Lomnický and Kežmarský, are reflected on the surface of the tarn.

### LOMNICKÝ ŠTÍT (3)

This peak (2,634 m) is the uncrowned king of the eastern part of the High Tatras. The first known climb to its peak was carried out by Doctor R. Townson in 1793 and was appropriately medialised. This English scientist and traveller described his experience in the book *Journey in Hungary*, published in London in 1797. Today, it is easy to get to the top of the peak. A lot of tourists use the cable car. Unless the peak is covered by thick fog, which happens very often, the view from the viewing terrace is breathtaking. The highest located workplace in Slovakia, the meteorological station, is located there.

### CABLE CAR TO LOMNICKÝ ŠTÍT (4)

The idea to build a cable car in the Tatras was born in 1895. The first section (not used at present) from Tatranská Lomnice to Skalnaté Pleso was constructed in 1937. The much more demanding section followed. The first passengers used the cable car from Skalnaté Pleso to the top of Tatranský Štít in 1940. The 1,870 metre cable car operates high above the Cmiter Hollow between Skalnaté Pleso and Lomnický Štít and manages an elevation of 856 metres. Only one support in the southern wall of the peak once held the cable car; however it is no longer needed following a complete reconstruction.

### LOMNICKÉ SEDLO (5)

The skiing season on the slopes below Lomnické Sedlo Saddle (2,190 m) starts rather late, as much snow must cover the rocky slopes, which are otherwise dangerous for skiers. However, the season lasts longer here, often until the end of May. Experts on winter sports consider the slope between Lomnické Sedlo and Skalnaté Pleso the top one in Slovakia. Its quality and technical demands are great, plus there is splendid natural scenery. Lomnické Sedlo is also interesting in the summer. The view from the cable car (from Lomnické Sedlo to Lomnický Štít) of Malá Studená Dolina is fantastic. There is a tourist trail from Lomnické Sedlo to the

nearby Veľká Lomnická Veža Peak (2,214 m) with views of the Tatras peaks and valleys from a slightly different angle.

### VEĽKÁ SVIŠŤOVKA (6)

Although this peak (2,038 m) is not amongst the Tatras greatest, it is very popular with tourists as it is easy to climb from the Tatranská Magistrála Trail and offers gorgeous views. Two different Tatras worlds can be seen from its top. Their different character is the result of the icebergs' locations in the Ice Ages. Although the Tatras were covered by ice, only valleys were covered by icebergs, while the outer slopes and highest peaks remained bare. The slopes of the mountain range descend sharply on the northern side into the Dolina Zeleného Plesa Valley with bizarre rocks. The Tatras landscape is very different on the other side. Unaffected by icebergs in the past, its shapes are mostly smooth and without any rock formations. The outer slopes of the mountain range are covered by huge eroded crusts created by the tectonic movement of the huge edge fault system on the southern edge of the Tatras.

## CHATA PRI ZELENOM PLESE (1)

This chalet (1,551 m) situated in a valley of the same name is known also by its older name, Brnčalova Chata or Brnčalka. It was named by A. Brnčal (1919-1950), a mountaineer instructor who died in the nearby Malá Zmrzlá Dolina Valley. A trip to the Zelené Pleso Tarn was a very challenging trek when the countess Laská of the Kežmarok Castle came here in the 16th century. The first tourist had none of the equipment that is now commonplace to present day visitors. A long time after the lady's memorable trek to Dolina Zeleného Potoka, there was nowhere to spend the night until the first wooden (Egidova) Chalet in 1876. When it burnt down later on, a new chalet was erected on the southern bank of Zelené Pleso, however it was also wooden and it too burnt down. Following that, the stone Fridrichova Chalet was built on the northern bank in 1897; it later underwent numerous reconstructions to become the present day chalet.

## JASTRABIA VEŽA (2)

The huge silhouette of the Jastrabia Veža Mountain (2,137 m) reflects on the greenish surface of Zelené Pleso. It is clad in legends. Allegedly a precious stone glittered on the top of the mountain in the past. Following numerous unsuccessful climbs, a young man finally reached the stone. When he took it into his hands wanting to bring it to his girlfriend, the guardian of the Tatras treasures shook the mountain, knocking the boy off the peak. He fell into the tarn below it still holding the diamond firmly in his fist. Since then, the greenish water of the lake has glittered from the diamond, and the tarn was named Zelené (Green). Allegedly, the unhappy man was the young count Š. Tököli (Thököly).

## DOLINA ZELENÉHO PLESA (3)

The Dolina Zeleného Plesa Valley is one of the forks of the large Dolina Kežmarskej Bielej Vody Valley. It was named after the splendid Zelené Pleso with the typically greenish colour of the water. The history of the tourism in the Tatras started in this valley, although the first events were not amongst the happiest. The first tourist undertaking was done by the countess Beáta Laská in 1565. The daring deed of the brave lady ended tragically, for her husband did not support her interest in tourism and imprisoned the unhappy lady in Kežmarok Castle. For a full six years her only joy was the view of the Tatras from two small windows. She left the castle in bad health and died shortly afterward in Košice.

## JAHŇACÍ ŠTÍT (4)

The rugged main ridge at the east ends with the Jahňací Štít (2,230 m), a great conically-shaped peak. Perhaps its name (Lamb) is associated with the herds of sheep from the Rakúsy and Spišská Belá that once grazed on its slopes. Or if not shepherds then maybe the poachers who chased young chamois named the mountain. Older sources also list a German name Gemsenspitze (Chamois). The summit of the mountain was probably first

reached by the above-mentioned poachers, however the first documented climb was executed by the English doctor R. Townson, who also climbed the more popular Lomnický Štít during his stay in the Tatras in 1793. Jahňací Štít is now one of the few tourist-accessible summits in the High Tatras. A tourist trail goes to its top from the Chata pri Zelenom Plese Chalet. The challenging climb is rewarded by a splendid panoramic view.

## DOLINA KEŽMARSKEJ BIELEJ VODY (5)

A large lowland area sprawls between the High Tatras and the Belianske Tatras. The Dolina Kežmarskej Bielej Vody Valley lies here. It was once a paradise for shepherds and gold diggers. This huge iceberg valley forks into three parts at its top section; Dolina Zeleného Plesa, Dolina Bielych Plies and Predné Meďodoly. A terrace with several smaller tarns lies above a rocky step with

the peculiar name of Jeruzalem. The largest tarn is Veľké Biele Pleso; the Kežmarská Chalet once was at its banks but it burnt down in 1974 and has not been restored. The Tatranská Magistrála Trail starts at Veľké Biele Pleso. It is the longest tourist trail in the Tatras. It is 65 km long and goes as far as the Jalovská Dolina Valley. Some sections of the trail have to be closed seasonally.

### BELIANSKA JASKYŇA (1)

This cave in the southern part of the Belianské Tatras was discovered by treasure seekers at the beginning of the 18th century. The desire to find gold also attracted M. Scholtz to come here. In the Kobylie Hill above the Tatranská Kotlina Hollow, he discovered a cave, soon called Hudobná Sieň, and engraved the date (1718) of his discovery on its wall. His discoveries were forgotten for some time until a forester named J. Husz and his companion J. Britz founded an opening between the fallen wood in August 1881. Thus the Belianska Cave was discovered and it was opened to the public the very next year. A section of 1,370 metres from the total length of its discovered 3,600 metres is accessible.

### DOLINA SIEDMICH PRAMEŇOV (2)

This smallish valley at the southeast of the Belianske Tatras is much different from other valleys due to its specific geologic formation and its relatively low location; even its highest sections are not above the upper border of forest. This valley is visited mainly by botanists and admirers of the flora. Rare species grow on the limestone bedrock well nested in this enclosed dale.

### ŽDIAR (3)

This interesting village below the Belianske Tatras developed differently than the villages at the southern foothills. It was not established as a tourist centre but rather settled by charcoal burners, farmers and shepherds. It is now a popular tourist centre, but mainly it boasts a Folk Architecture Monument Reserve. The church is made of brick; however other vernacular buildings are wooden.

### HAVRAN AND ŽDIARSKA VIDLA (4)

It would be difficult to imagine the village of Ždiar with its preserved wooden architecture devoid of the splendid silhouette of the Belianske Tatras in the background. The landmark of

this breathtaking scenery is the silhouette of the two highest peaks. When looking from the village, the left peak is called Ždiarska Vidla (2,142 m), while the slightly higher Havran (2,151 m) is to the left. Although these two peaks are lower than the mountains in the Tatras, they are similarly beautiful. While the High Tatras are formed mainly of granite and similar volcanic rocks, the Belianske Tatras are of schist and dolomite.

### MONKOVA DOLINA (5)
The Belianske Tatras are strictly protected and entry to this territory is fined. The only accessible part is along the trail from the Monkova Dolina Valley to the Kopské Sedlo Saddle. It is only open in the summer and can only be walked in one direction, from the bottom section to the top. Monkova Dolina is the most pronounced depression on the northern side of the Belianske Tatras. At places it resembles a narrow chasm with bizarre rocky shapes. A very attractive tourist section goes across a 140 metre high rocky step with cascades of waterfalls. There are six information stops on the six metre nature trail.

### TATRANSKÁ JAVORINA (6)
The history of this small village at the mouth of the Javorová Dolina Valley is closely connected with the count K. Kraft von Hohenlohe (1848 – 1926). This Prussian aristocrat came to the Tatras with great ideas, however his cultivating experiments were mostly unsuccessful. His grave is also in Javorina.

### JAVOROVÁ DOLINA (7)
Not many tourist visit this valley near Tatranská Javorina, as it is over 12 km long and also rather far from the busy tourist centres on the southern side of the High Tatras. Alpine stone pine was experimentally planted in this rather quiet valley in 1958. Maples were also prevalent in the valley as the wood of this tree was used in the local smeltery and gave the dale its name.

### BIELOVODSKÁ DOLINA (8)
The entry into this valley on the northern side of the High Tatras is near the Slovakian-Polish border crossing Lysá Poľana. The valley has several levels and it is the largest Tatras valley that was filled by the largest iceberg, 14 kilometres long and 330 metres thick. The valley has no competition with regards to the size and number of side valleys. Mainly on the Polish side it forks into huge branches with large lakes. One of them is the Dolina Rybiego Potoku Valley. The climb through Bielovodská Dolina takes about 5 hours. The trail goes over a splendid clear-cut area near the Biela Voda Lodge. From here it is a gentle climb to the last, much steeper section of the tour that starts at the highly positioned Litvorová Dolina Valley.

# SEVERNÝ SPIŠ

### ČERVENÝ KLÁŠTOR (1)
This monastery situated on the right bank of the Dunajec River is the gateway to the Peininský National Park. The entry into this ancient complex from the beginning of the 14th century is shaded by linden trees with patulous branches. According to strict ascetic rules, hermits of the Carthusian Order lived here in the ancient times. The community met only during prayer time. A new order came to the monastery in the 17th century, the Camaldolese Order. The life and mission of this order was different as they were much more forthcoming to the outside world. They were active in secular matters, focusing mainly on education and science. The pride of the monastery was the frater Cyprián (1724 – 1775), a man with many skills. He was called the 'doctor of a thousand sciences' for his universal interest in science, the 'master of a thousand crafts' for his skills and technical abilities' and also the 'flying monk' for, according to unconfirmed sources, his construction of a flying machine of an unknown construction and its successfully testing on a hill near the Tri Korúny locality. Cyprián is most famous for his unique herbarium, which included 272 flora species with names in Latin, Greek, German and the local mountain dialect. The monastery with the Church of St. Anton (14th century) was reconstructed and now houses the museum with historical, ethnographical and medical collections.

### CHASM ON DUNAJEC (2)
The wild Dunajec River created a bizarre chasm through the Pieniny Rocks. The 9-kilometre chasm full of breathtaking views is accessible by raft. The captain of the raft wears the traditional mountain costume and provides a lot of interesting information and legends about the surrounding rocks and peaks. The raft passes by the Jánošíkov Skok area. The legend has it that the legendary outlaw Jánošík picked his co-fighters here, taking on only those who could jump over the 12-metre wide river. The rocks called Sedem Mníchov (Seven Monks) were also inspiring for folk story-tellers.

### CHASM ON LESNICKÝ POTOK (3)
The small, interesting mountain village of Lesnica lies, as they say, right behind God's back. Its access road goes over a high mountain ridge and into a bizarre chasm at the end of the village with preserved folk architecture. The wild valley with picturesque terraced strips of fields narrows down to a chasm flanked by high limestone rocks. When looking from the village, the left rock is called Vylízana and the right one Osobitá. The karst stream Storočná Voda rises below Osobitá; it never freezes even during the winter; if you drink from it you will live to the age of 100. The chasm is 300 metres long and ends in the spot where Lesnický Potok empties into the Dunajec River.

### MALÉ PIENINY (4)
The name of the Malé (Small) Pieniny is a paradox as they are the highest in the entire range. The highest peak, Vysoké Skalky (1,050 m), is at the border range. A trek through Malé Pieniny is an unusual tourist experience. Long open sections leading across meadows provide remarkable views of the picturesque landscape of the Zamaguri Region. The scenery on the Polish side of the ridge is also lovely. Many parts of the ridge have limestone rocks; the conical rock called Rabšína is especially of interest. The western end of the ridge offers fantastic views of rock massifs with the Dunajec River coiling between them.

### HALIGOVSKÉ SKALY (5)
A mountain range with the huge wall of the Haligovské Skaly Rocks looms high above the Lipník Creek at the south edge of Pieniny. When observed from Haligovské, the massive limestone rocks are especially striking. A remarkable rock formation called Zbojnícka Brána is high in the limestone rocks. There is also the small Aksamitka Cave, not open to the public. With its 330 metre long corridors, it is the longest cave in the range. Its name is associated with the members of Bratríci active in this territory in the mid-15th century. P. Aksamit was a captain of the army of Ján Jiskra, which camped below Haligovské Skaly and pillaged the Spiš territory. According to a legend, Aksamit decided to repent of his sins towards the end of his life. He sat down in a cave and cried and all his tears turned into speleothems. Thus, Aksamitka received its cave formations as well as its name. An important archaeological finding was discovered in the cave in 1874 – a reindeer's horn, the first reliable evidence in that this place was settled in the Late Stone Age.

## OSTURŇA (1)

If you want to drive to this village you must go over two mountain ranges of the Spišská Magura Mountains. The remoteness of this place helped in the preservation of numerous original folk buildings that are part of the Folk Architecture Monument Reserve. Osturňa developed around 1590 during the Wallachian colonization on the thickly forested estate of Nedeca Castle in Poland; the urban character of the village, which spreads almost along the entire length of the valley of Ostrurnianský Creek, corresponds with this. The creek flows to Poland and under the name Kacwin empties into the Dunajec. It is over 7 km to walk from the beginning to the end of the village; it is one of the longest villages in Slovakia. There are several drying out natural lakes that were formed by landslides.

## JEZERSKÉ LAKE (2)

This remarkable lake is near the village of Jezersko with a popular ski centre. It was created by a huge landslide that fell down the slope of the valley at the northern side of Spišská Magura and dammed up the stream. The mountain people of the Zamagurie area tell several folk legends about this lake. The main character is a mysterious ghost that lives in the lake. One legend says that as a punishment for a shepherd who drowned two puppies the ghost created a lake to pay him back with the same destiny. Another story presents the lake ghost as an environmentalist who got angry when local millers used all the water from the Jezerské Lake for their millstreams and ordered them to give it back, or else he would flood the entire region.

## VYŠNÉ RUŽBACHY SPA (3)

The good influence of the mineral springs in Vyšné Ružbachy on the microclimate was known already to the prehistoric people; it is documented by archaeological findings in the local travertine quarries. The curative powers of the warm mineral water were discovered in the Middle Ages. The oldest written record about the spa was written by a captain of the Spiš castle in 1549 and the spa became popular with

the Polish and Hungarian aristocracy in the 19th century. Count A. Zamoyski bought and modernized the spa in 1882, however not much has been preserved from this period. The spa now consists mainly of modern pavilions from the second half of the 20th century. A nostalgic memory of the old 19th-century spa is the Biely Dom House. This attractive, white-travertine building in the Historicism Biedermeier style stands on a travertine knoll.

### MARIÁNSKE SQUARE IN PODOLÍNEC (4)

The ancient little town of Podolínec was designated a Monument Reserve in 1991. The centre of the town squeezed between the preserved town walls is the Mariánske Square surrounded by old burgher houses; many have preserved medieval cores. The Gothic church of the Assumption of the Virgin Mary from the end of the 13th century stands in the middle of the square. Its presbytery is decorated by valuable medieval murals from the 14th and 15th centuries. The Renaissance belfry at the church from 1659 houses Gothic bells from the 14th century. A town house on the site of a medieval castle on the southwest side of the square is remarkable.

### TRAVERTINES IN VYŠNÉ RUŽBACHY (5)

There are peculiar natural formations resembling craters in Vyšné Ružbachy, yet they have nothing in common with volcanoes or eruptions. They were developed by a lapse of travertine knolls that precipitated around the local mineral springs with a high content of calcium. There are four large and several smaller travertine cavities in the spa. The most famous one is called Kráter (Crater) and it is the largest travertine lake in Slovakia. Other craters are dry. The Kaplnkový Kráter, named after a small chapel at its edge, is noteworthy. It is the largest of its type in Slovakia. The Smerdžonk Kráter emits carbon dioxide and is called the Death Hole. The local travertine provides excellent material for sculptors and thus attracts artists from around the world who attend the local symposia.

### IZABELA THERMAL POOL IN VYŠNÉ RUŽBACHY (6)

The water from nine mineral springs is used in the spa of Vyšné Ružbachy. They provide 150 litres of water per second (19 – 22 degrees). Most of it is used for therapeutic purposes. The local thermal pool is called Izabela after the biggest spring that sources it, and it is rightfully considered one of the most beautiful pools in Slovakia. Its location as well as architecture is lovely. Outdoor pools, designed as a large quadrant with sides of 50 metres, are in the centre of the complex with a round grassy island with high trees in the middle.

### PIARIST MONASTERY AND CHURCH IN PODOLÍNEC (7)

Piarists came to Podolínec from Moravia during the turmoil of the Thirty Years' War. They supported education and founded a school. Thus Podolínec became an important cultural and educational centre (17th and 18th centuries) and got the nickname 'Athens below Poprad'. The central building of the monastery is the church, which is one of the most significant monuments in eastern Slovakia. There is a painting of St. Stanislaw, the bishop and martyr from Krakow, on the main altar by an unknown painter form 1688. The 1950s wrote a sad chapter in the history of the monastery, as priests from abolished monasteries were imprisoned here, including the Greek-Catholic priests who refused to convert to the Orthodox religion.

## NÁMESTIE SV. MIKULÁŠA
## IN STARÁ ĽUBOVŇA (1)

This ancient town was founded in the 13th century as the settlement below the Ľuvnianský Castle and was elevated to a free royal town by King Ľudovít I in 1364. Its peak period was after 1412 during the rule of a Polish mayor. He was responsible for administrating 16 wealthy towns in the Spiš Region that were given as a pledge to the Polish crown by the Hungarian King Sigismund. This enabled its inhabitants to sell their crafts, goods and services to participants of the diplomatic Polish-Hungarian meetings held in the office of the mayor. The present-day Stará Ľubovňa is the centre of northern Spiš and has a preserved historic core with several historic monuments. The rectangular Námestie Sv. Mikuláša was built in the centre of the town after a fire in 1556. The most significant secular building on the square

is the Renaissance arcaded Provinčný House. It was the seat of the administration of Spiš towns. The 1280-built Gothic Church of St. Nicholas is in the centre of the square.

## ĽUBOVNIANSKY CASTLE (2)

This massive castle from the end of the 13th century sits atop a towering limestone rock above the Poprad River. It was often visited by the crowned heads in the past, including the Hungarian kings Karol Róbert (1314), Sigismund of Luxemburg (1396 and 1420) and Ján Albrecht II (1449). The Hungarian empress Maria visited the castle in 1392 as well as the Polish rulers Vladislav II, Jan Kazimír and Jan Sobietsky, the great victor above the Ottoman Turks in a battle at Vienna. The count M. Beňanovský can be in a way counted amongst the crowned ones, for he became (although later) the king of Madagascar. Unfortunately he did

not visit Ľubovňa; he was held in the prison here and later escaped. At times royal insignia were stored in the castle. Polish crown jewels were hidden here from the Swedish army between 1655 and 1661. Even the present-day history of the castle boasts people related in some way to the royal families. The last lord of the castle, J. Zamoyski, married the princess Izabella, the neice of the Spanish king, in 1944.

## OPEN-AIR MUSEUM
## IN STARÁ ĽUBOVŇA (3)

This open-air museum was built as a replica of a settlement bellow Ľubovniansky Castle. It was opened to the public in 1984 as the Ethnographical exposition of the Ľubovnianske Museum. A visit to the museum is an excellent opportunity to learn about the life in the northern Spiš area towards the end of the 19th century and at the beginning of the 20th century. There are 23 ver-

nacular wooden buildings from the wider surroundings of Stará Ľubovňa, which document the folk architecture as well as the lifestyle of the region. There is a smithery, a mill, a gamekeeper's lodge and an old school. The most valuable building of the museum is the wooden Greek-Catholic Church of St. Michael, which was brought from the nearby village of Matysová. The church was built in 1833, however some icons in its interior date from the 17th century.

### ĽUBOVNIANSKE SPA (4)
This spa located in a side valley of the Ľubovnianka Stream was founded in the 19th century near four mineral springs with natural iron-carbonic water. The relatively cool mineral water (8 degrees) was initially used to cure illnesses of the digestive system, gynaecological diseases and blood circulation. The Amália and Alfréd springs were used for drinking while the Mária Spring was used for bath therapies. A mud wrap was also part of the offer. The spa was used mainly by patients from Budapest before World War I. The number of visitors decreased after the end of the monarchy and the spa started to decline. Its therapeutic purpose was overridden by recreation activities during the second half of the 20th century. A large advantage of the spa is its park area with exotic trees.

### LITMANOVÁ (5)
This Ruthenian village in the Ľubovnianska Vrchovina Hills became known among the public due to mass pilgrimages following an alleged appearance of the Virgin Mary in August 1990 in the spot called Zvir, located at the southern slope of the border Eliášovka Hill; its peak is the highest point of Ľubovnianska Vrchovina. The direct participants of the event were three small local children picking mushrooms in the forest. The visions were repeated until the 6th August 1995. Litmanová was swarmed by pilgrims mainly from northern Slovakia and southern Poland and the pilgrimages soon became mass events. Sometimes, over 100,000 worshippers gather near the wooden chapel at Zvir, making Litmanová the most visited village of northeast Slovakia.

### JARABINSKÝ CHASM (6)
A rocky range continues from Pieniny eastwards to neighbouring Ľubovnianska Vrchovina. The limestone rocks are not as imposing as in the chasm of the Dunajec River, however they brighten up the otherwise monotonous flysch landscape. Jarabinský Chasm is created by the Malý Lipník Creek, which cuts deep into a large massif near the mostly Ruhenian village of Jarabiná. This bizarre narrow chasm is approximately 200 metres long. The stream has formed huge potholes (called baďury) on five cascades. Some have a diameter of 5 metres and are 2 metres deep. It is rather challenging to walk through the chasm and you cannot avoid getting feet wet in the stream.

### WOODEN CHURCH IN HRANIČNÉ (7)
Most of the wooden churches at the northeast Slovakia belong to the Orthodox or Greek Catholic Church. However, the church in the village of Hraničné in Ľubovnianska Vrchovina belongs to the Roman Catholic religion. This splendid wooden sacral building was consecrated to the Immaculation of the Virgin Mary. It was built in 1785 and rebuilt several times. The interior boasts various styles, ranging from the Renaissance and Baroque sections from the parish church in Stará Ľubovňa to modern architecture.

## SOUTHERN SPIŠ

### NÁMESTIE SV. EGÍDIA IN POPRAD (1)

Poprad was developed by the merging of five historic towns of the Spiš Region and received the name of one of them. The medieval town could not quite compete with the much more powerful town of Spišská Sobota; however this was soon to be changed and Poprad developed into a powerful metropolis as its inhabitants were more flexible with regards to changes brought about by modern times. The historic Poprad developed around the Square of St. Egid, which has remained the busy centre; there is a Classicism Evangelic church (1829-1834) on its central square near the older Church of St. Egid.

### CHURCH OF ST. EGID IN POPRAD (2)

The central square of Poprad was named after the patron of the Church of St. Egid from the 13th century located in the centre of the square. The interior of the church is a remarkable gallery of medieval paintings from the 15th century. One of them depicts the panorama of the Tatras as part of the scenery of a Bible story about the Christ's resurrection. It is the oldest known painting of the Tatras. The church has a tall quadrant tower that creates a nice symbiosis with the Renaissance belfry (17th century) next to the church. Unfortunately, the original exterior graffiti and sculpture decoration has not been preserved.

## PODTATRANSKÉ MUSEUM IN POPRAD (3)

Poprad is called the gateway to the Tatras. A lot of visitors pass through its railway station and its airport. The town uses its advantageous location near the Tatras summits well and has been profiting from tourism since the 19th century. A rich inhabitant of the town, D. Husz (1813-1889), founded a brewery as well as the first tourist base of the town in 1868. It received his name, the Huszov Park. Not only was he a businessman, he was involved in the cultural and enlightenment process as well. He helped to support the Tatranské Museum that was established in 1882 in Veľká (now a quarter of Poprad). The Hungarian-Carpathian Association established the Carpathian Museum in a building on the Square of St. Egid in 1886. Both institutions merged in 1945, thus creating the present-day Podtatranské Museum located in the building of the former Karpatské Museum on the square. A part of the exposition of this museum, now one of the oldest n Slovakia, is located in Spišská Sobota.

## SPIŠSKÁ SOBOTA (4)

This was once one of the wealthiest towns in the Spiš Region. It was a thriving town in the Middle Ages with busy trade and crafts. However in the 19th century it was as if time stopped here; thanks to this, the attractive medieval character has remained preserved, and Spišská Sobota is now a town quarter of Poprad. It has exemplary restored cultural and his-

torical monuments that are protected in a Town Monument Reserve. The most valuable buildings are around the Sobotské Square. Rows of old burgher houses built over the span of the 15th, 16th and 17th centuries are nestled together to such extent that they could replace the town walls in the past. The wide overhanging roofs protrude into the square and have a similar function to arcades, to protect against the rain.

## CHURCH OF ST. GEORGE IN SPIŠSKÁ SOBOTA (5)

Apart from the town house and the Renaissance belfry there is also the Late Romanesque Church of St. George from the 13th century in the middle of the Sobotské Square in Spišská Sobota. The jewels of the church are five Gothic altars produced at the workshop of Master Pavol of Levoča at the beginning of the 16th century. The best art piece is the statue of St. George, depicting the traditional scene of his fight with the dragon, on the main altar from 1516.

## VEĽKÁ (6)

This was one of the five towns that formed the present-day Poprad; it is now one of its quarters. Its name is associated with the size of its area at the time when it was an independent town of the Spiš Region. Its lands reached as far as the Velická Dolina Valley in the Tatras. In the past it was famous for the blueprint and artistic wood-carving that is connected with the

traditional production of souvenirs. The historical core of Veľká is not that compact now. It was not even possible to maintain the original medieval square in its original shape, as it was very large. It seems that Veľká had to have everything huge, including the square. The monuments that are preserved are either solitary or smaller groups of buildings. The Evangelic church from 1817 is remarkable although it is not very old. It is amongst the largest Tolerance churches in Slovakia. The Roman-Catholic Church of St. John the Evangelist is much older; it dates from the 13th century.

### CHURCH OF ST. LADISLAW
### IN SPIŠSKÝ ŠTVRTOK (1)

The high, slim spire of the Church of St. Ladislaw in Spišský Štvrtok cannot be overlooked. It is one of the most beautiful landscape landmarks of the Spiš Region. Even from afar the church is splendid. The large sacral building is typical in Gothic architecture and it has preserved elements of Romanesque and Baroque styles. The burial chapel of the family of Zápoľský outside the church is one of the most splendid Gothic edifices in Slovakia. It was built in 1473 by the Head of the Spiš County Council and the Hungarian palatine Š. Zápoľský for his family. However when it was completed, the count, one of the most powerful contemporary people in the country, changed his mind and asked to be buried in a similar chapel in Spišská Kapitula instead. Next to the church with the chapel is an Early Baroque monastery built for the Minor Order in 1668.

### CHURCH OF ST. MARGARET
### IN MLYNICA (2)

This very valuable church stands in a village near Poprad. It dates from the 13th century and is one of the oldest churches in the region. The building itself is a valuable architectonic monument; however its interior is even more significant. The jewel of the church is a large altar that barely fits into the presbytery. It was created on the order of Margita, the daughter of the local feudal lord J. Thurzo I, between 1515 and 1520. It was produced by the workshop of

Master Pavol of Levoča. The top work of this greatest artist of the period is the wooden sculpture of the patron of the church. This wonderful statue depicts the saint with a mysterious smile, which could be justly called the 'Slovakian Mona Lisa'. St. Margaret holds a cross in her hand and her feet rest on a dragon. Mlynica also boasts an Evangelic church, however it no longer serves its original purpose as it was transformed into an original Museum of Historical Vehicles.

### CHURCH IN VEĽKÁ LOMNICA (3)

The route from Poprad to Kežmarok passes by the Church of St. Catherine from the 13th century in the village of Veľká. A significant discovery was made during the restoration works in the church in 1957 when extremely valuable murals from the 14th century were uncovered in the sacristy. An unknown painter created a remarkable work (1310 – 1320) depicting the scenes of the life of St. Ladislaw. The traditional topic of the victorious battle of this Hungarian King Ladislaw I (1040 – 1095) with Kunmáni in 1093 is commonplace in medieval paintings, yet the version in the church of St. Catherine is certainly one of the best.

### TRAVERTINES
### IN GÁNOVCE (4)

A stonemason discovered an unusual oval stone of unknown origin in a travertine knoll in Gánovce in 1926. It was stored in the depository of the National Museum in Prague for over

twenty years until the renowned expert on the prehistoric era, doctor E. Vlček, made an astonishing discovery. It was a piece of the skull of the prehistoric Neanderthal Man, one of the oldest inhabitants of prehistoric Slovakia. This man lived near the local thermal spring about 120,000 years ago. He drowned after being dazed by carbonate gasses emitting from the spring. A travertine hill piled up over the bodily remains of the Neanderthal Man later on. Calcareous sinter that got inside his skull congealed, thus creating its sinter cast piece.

### MANSION IN BETLANOVCE (5)

The Thurzo family from the smallish village of Betlanovce started as a lower aristocracy, however getting involved in trade they soon joined the wealthiest elite of the then Hungary. They established the family company near Levoča and soon merged with the Fugger family, setting up a significant company operating in mining, smelting and ore trading. Their Renaissance mansion is still to be seen in Betlanovce and it is considered a landmark in the architectural development in Slovakia. It is the first manor where architects restrained from building with the until then prevalent purpose of fortification, creating a dateless edifice without any fortification walls or bastions – an aristocratic residence and not a fortress. It was built by P. Faigel and his wife E. Bobstová (her mother was from the Thurzo family) between 1564 and 1568.

## KEŽMARSKÝ CASTLE (1)

The wealthy town of Kežmarok witnessed many wars and fights during the Middle Ages. Such was its conflict with the town of Levoča, that the period was called the Hundred Years' War in historical sources. Apart from ongoing fights the inhabitants of the town had to also endure the mutual grudge of the town and the lords of the Kežmarský Castle. The Gothic fortress in Kežmarok was built by I. and J. Zápoľskí in 1462. Its later owners, the Tököli (Thököly) family, gave it the present-day mostly Renaissance appearance. They transformed it into a town castle secluded behind the walls with gates and bastions. The nicely restored Kežmarský Castle is now used as a museum with interesting collections about the history of the town and the castle. Visitors can learn about the noble lady Beáta Laská who paid a very high price for her historically first tourist trip to the Tatras (see page 288). The Traditional Európske Ľudové Remeslo (European Folk Craft) festival takes place in Kežmarok annually in July. Some presentations of the rich program take place in the courtyard of the castle.

## CHURCH OF ST. CROSS
## IN KEŽMAROK (2)

Next to Levoča, Kežmarok boasts the largest and most unified collection of cultural and historical monuments in the Spiš Region and it was designated a Town Monument Reserve in 1950. The triangle-shaped historical core of the town lacks a larger square; it has a fork of two main streets. Inside the area bordered by these streets stands the Late Gothic Church of St. Cross, built on the site of an older Romanesque chapel in the 14th century. It is now the parish church of the Roman-Catholic religion. It was owned by the local Evangelists for some time in the 16th and 17th centuries and it is one of the largest hall churches in Slovakia. Wood-carved art pieces by artists from the workshop of Master Pavol of Levoča are on the main altar. A beautiful Renaissance graffiti-decorated belfry was built next to the church in 1568.

## TOWN HALL IN KEŽMAROK (3)

The busiest place in the centre of Kežmarok is the area around the town hall. The two main streets start here. The building is in the centre of a smallish Hlavné Square that narrows down into the Hradná Street, which goes up to Kežmarský Castle. The first Gothic edifice of the town hall was built here by master Juraj from Spišská Sobota in 1461 and burnt down in 1515. The mayor had a new seat for his office built later, this time in the then fashionable Renaissance style. Another story and a Baroque spire were added to the building in 1799. Later reconstructions (the last one was in 1922) did not seriously affect the appearance of the tower. It was important that this landmark of the town maintains a similar appearance to the tower of the monastery Church of St. Peter in Salzburg.

## EVANGELIC LYCEUM
## IN KEŽMAROK (4)

Many important personages worked in the Evangelic Lyceum in Kežmarok. The Classicism building hidden in the shade of a small park behind an Articular Evangelic church was built in 1776. Scores of Slovakian artists (Pavol Jozef Šafárik, Samo and Ján Chalupkovci, Janko Kráľ, Pavol Országh Hviezdoslav and Martin Rázus), as well as several great explorers and admires of the nearby nicely visible Tatras Mountains (David Fröhlich, Juraj Bucholtz jr., Juraj Bohuš etc.) either studied or taught at this institution. The library with 150 volumes is of special value.

## ARTICULAR CHURCH
## IN KEŽMAROK (5)

Upon the regulation of the 17th century the church of the Evangelists in Kežmarok had to stand outside the city, so it was built outside the southern town walls in 1717. This wooden Articular church is considered one of the most significant architectonic jewels in Slovakia. It has a Greek-cross-shaped ground-plan and it was built from the wood of yew and red spruce; no iron parts were used in the construction. The appearance of the façade corresponds with the principles of the vernacular architecture of the Spiš Region. The wooden walls are plastered white, however wood is visible on the shingle roof. The magnificent interior is also wooden. It houses an organ with wooden pipes, the oldest organ of this type in Slovakia.

**1**

**2**

## MUSEUM OF J. M. PETZVAL
## IN SPIŠSKÁ BELÁ (1)

The most famous native of the town of Spišská Belá is the significant inventor, mathematician and physician J. M. Petzval (1807-1891). He was born into the family of a Moravian teacher. After graduating from a technical university in Budapest he worked in Vienna and became one of the most significant scientists of the then Europe. Streets in several European cities bear his name and even one of the craters on the moon was named after this famous man. A museum devoted to his life and work is now in his native house. It has a collection of 600 valuable exhibits illustrating the history of the world photographic optics.

## CHURCH OF ST. ANTON PUSTOVNÍK
## IN SPIŠSKÁ BELÁ (2)

Spišská Belá was one of the wealthier towns in the Spiš Region in the Middle Ages thriving mainly thanks to craft and trade. The landmark of its central square is the Church of St. Anton Pustovník (the Hermit). Only the perimeter walls and west portal are preserved from this originally Late Romanesque building from around 1264. The interior of the church is mostly new, furnished in the Pseudo Historicism style. It once housed valuable painted desks of the original altar; however they became part of the collections of the Szépmüvészeti Museum in Budapest before World War I. A Renaissance belfry from the end of the 16th century is near the church.

3

## CHURCH IN STRÁŽKY (3)

The hero of the Ottomans war, M. Horváth-Stansith, settled on an empty estate in Strážky near Spišská Belá in 1556. This count of Croatian origins rebuilt the local Gothic castle into a grandiose Renaissance mansion. There was a Latin school for children from Hungarian aristocratic families in the mansion between 1588 and 1711; its teaching methods were very advanced for the time. Baron E. Medňanský (Mednyanszky) moved into the mansion in 1862 bringing his 10-year old son Ladislav with him; the boy later became a famous European painter. The splendid Renaissance mansion in Strážky nestled in an English-style park is now managed by the Slovakian National Gallery. There are also paintings by Medňanský done in a Impressionism-like style.

## CHURCH OF ST. ANNA AND BELFRY IN STRÁŽKY (4)

The Gothic Church of St. Anna from the turn of the 15th and 16th centuries stands opposite the Renaissance mansion in Strážky on the other side of the road. Its interior is adorned by valuable Late Gothic murals depicting a Passion cycle and three altars with wooden sculptures and desk paintings. This church originally housed two significant medieval art pieces (a sculpture of the Madonna and a statue of St. Andrew) that are now part of the Slovakian National Gallery in Bratislava. The church and the nearby Renaissance graffiti-decorated belfry are a National Cultural Monument.

4

## CHURCH OF ST. JAMES
## IN LEVOČA (1)

The grandiose and ostentatious appearance of the main Church of St. James corresponded with the statute of the wealthiest town that Levoča once had. The value of art pieces in the interior goes beyond the framework of the Spiš Region as well as Slovakia. The church was built on the site of an older sacral building from 1280 with only a part of the sacristy preserved. The Gothic three-nave cathedral was completed in 1400 and became an example for other churches even outside the borders of Spiš. The interior of the church is a unique museum of sacral art dating mainly from the Gothic period. The most significant jewel is the Late Gothic main Altar of St. James by Master Pavol of Levoče and there are further twelve valuable altars from the Gothic and Baroque periods. The baptismal font from 1380 is one of the oldest monuments and the murals depicting scenes from the legend about St. Dorothy and the cycle of Seven Deeds of Mercy and Seven Deadly Sins are also noteworthy. The church also houses a valuable collection of liturgical articles.

## ALTAR OF MASTER PAVOL
## OF LEVOČA (2)

The Late Gothic main altar of St. James is the highest of its type in the world (18.62 m). It was carved from linden wood between 1507 and 1517 in the workshop of Master Pavol of Levoča (1455 – 1540), who was considered one of the greatest artists in central Europe. Before coming to Levoča around 1500, he worked in prominent artistic workshops in Nuremberg and Krakow. His sculptures on the main altar, the Madonna with the child, St. James and St. John the Apostle, are the most splendid statues of this art piece. Allegedly one of the twelve apostles of this marvellous composition of the Last Supper on the altar bears the resemblance of Master Pavol. The author of the desk painting is believed to be Master Hans. Some of the paintings were based on woodcuts by Lucas Cranach. Some sculptures of the altar were presented at the EXPO '70 World Exhibition in Montreal, Canada.

## TOWN HALL IN LEVOČA (3)

Levoča boasts one of the most beautiful historical town halls in Slovakia. The splendid building is located in the centre of the Námestie Majstra Pavla Square next to the Church of St. James. The original Gothic house that stood here until 1550 was used by the town councillors. It was destroyed by a great fire that spread around most of the town together with a valuable town archive. Numerous significant documents about the history of the town turned to ashes, including the interesting details about a very venerated citizen of the town, Master Pavol of Levoča. Soon a new Renaissance town hall was built on the ruins and it became a jewel of the town. The original Renaissance elements have been preserved despite several later reconstructions and the building boasts two-story arcades, an audience hall with net vault, fragments of frescoes, a stone portal decorated with a painting of dolphins and a meeting room with a carved wooden ceiling. A remarkable art piece is the painting of the Meeting of the Town Council. The building served as the town hall until 1955, when the collections of the Spišské Museum were placed here.

## PILLORY IN LEVOČA (4)

The place of shame in Levoča was used for public pillory of less serious criminals. Today it is a part of the stage for a famous theatre show (Levočská Biela Panna) together with a balcony of the historical town hall. This show is very popular during the summer months. Its sad story takes the audience to the beginning of the 18th century, when Levoča was under the siege of the Emperor's army. After the main hero of the story, Júlia Géciová-Korponayová, said goodbye to her husband, who went to fight the army, she held a ball in her house. When dancing with the Levoča captain she stole a key from him that opened a secret gate and she let the enemy inside the town. The reason for her appealing deed was her love for an Emperor's officer. However, her lover soon rejected her and the young lady was put in jail at Červený Kameň Castle before she was taken to the town of Ráb (Győr) in Hungary and beheaded. However, her ghost came back to her native town and its inhabitants can see a sad lady wearing a white dress and walking on the walls of the castle – the White Lady of Levoča.

## VEĽKÝ ŽUPNÝ HOUSE IN LEVOČA (1)

For several centuries the seat of the Spiš County Council (Župa) was in Spiš Castle. From here the heirs of the function of the Head of the County Council from the wealthy Zápoľský, Thurzo and Čáki (Csáky) families ruled the rich Spiš Region. The highest office of the Spiš County Council moved into Levoča in the 16th century and had a new building seat constructed here between 1805 and 1831. The architect of this noble Empire edifice in the northwest corner of the Námestie Majstra Pavla Square was A. Povolný. At its time the building was one of the most grandiose seats of the county council in Hungary. Its appearance corresponded perfectly with the historical part of Levoča. The County Council remained in the building until 1922. It is called Veľký Župný House; there is also the Malý Župný House nearby. It was built in the Renaissance style on the square over the foundation of an older medieval edifice.

## HAINOV HOUSE IN LEVOČA (2)

The relatively large Hainov House is in the southwestern part of Námestie Majstra Pavla Square. It was built after a fire in 1550 on the site of an older medieval building. It was owned by the popular chronicle writer G. Hain in the 17th century and it thus received his name. A son of Hain bequeathed the house to the Evangelic Lyceum. Between 1844 and 1848 Slovakian students of the lyceum protested against a notice given to their teacher Ľudovít Štúr from the Bratislava Evangelic Lyceum. The revolutionary song *Nad Tatrou sa blýska,* which later became the national anthem of Slovakia, was allegedly first sung in the lyceum in Levoča. Hainov House now houses a museum with the exposition of the Spiš Museum in Levoča devoted to the art and culture in the Spiš Region. Valuable Renaissance murals were uncovered during a reconstruction of the building; they depict civil moralities.

## THURZOV HOUSE (3)

The graffiti-decorated façade of this house located on Námestie Majstra Pavla of Levoča is relatively young (1904). Its Neo Renaissance style matches the architectonic character of the town as Levoča is above all a Renaissance town. This building was erected after the great fire in 1550, which destroyed the historical Gothic Levoča. Currently the house is one of the more than 50 remarkable burgher and aristocratic houses on the central square of the town. Further dozens of burgher and craftsmen edifices are in the side streets; indeed many of them could be jewels of main squares in other towns. Arcades lined the entire central square until 1711; this Renaissance feature has only been preserved on the Hainov House and in the courtyard of Mariášiho (Mariássy) House and several other historical buildings.

## CHURCHES OF FRANCISCAN MINORITES IN LEVOČA (4)

The history as well as the present of Levoča is associated with the Franciscan Minorites (Friars Minor) Order. The old church of Minorites is located on Kláštorná Street. It is also called Gymnaziálny Church as a *gymnasium* (grammar school) was built next to it in 1915. It was built

at the beginning of the 14th century; the knight Donč financed the building in 1309. The church consecrated to St. Ladislaw is remarkable for its size; it is one of the largest sacral monuments in Slovakia. The new Minorites church stands near the Košická Gate. It dates from 1755 and it was built on the site of an older church, the oldest in the town, which was probably built by a Slavic settlement as early as in the 11th century. The church consecrated to the Holy Spirit is a remarkable Baroque monument with preserved original interior. The main altarpiece 'Visit of the Holy Spirit' is the work of J. Czauczik, a renowned painter of Levoča. This altar, painted in 1811, was his first grandiose work after he finished studying in Vienna. A monastery of the Minorites is adjacent to the church.

## TOWN FORTIFICATION IN LEVOČA (5)

The grand town of Levoča had to protect the possessions and lives of its rich aristocracy and burghers, so it was surrounded by an uninterrupted ring of massive town walls; they are preserved to a certain extent. The terrain enabled the building of the medieval town on a simple rectangular ground-plan. The construction of the fortification started as early as in the 13th century and was finally completed in 1410. Levoča received a fortification with a water moat, towers and bastions at several places. At the east the Menhardská and Košická Gate enabled access to the town, at the south was the Dolná Gate and at the west stood the Poľská Gate. Part of the southern fortification wall with the Dolná Gate was demolished in the 19th century. Only about four-fifths are preserved from the original 2.5 kilometre long walls The Košická Gate is now a restaurant and the polygonal bastion near the new monastery of the Minorites was reconstructed for the requirements of the Museum for the Blind. This unique museum is now a part of the Museum of Special Education, which is located in a burgher house at Námestie Majstra Pavla Square. The museum is the only one of its type in Slovakia.

## MARIÁNSKA HORA (6)

Levoča is amongst the most significant pilgrimage places in Europe, and it is in fact one of the oldest, as the tradition of Levoča's Marian Pilgrimages reaches back to the Middle Ages. The steps of thousands of pilgrims lead to Mariánska Hora, a hill that looms north of the town. A fortified settlement stood on its site as early as in the 13th century. It protected local people from the Tartar hordes. The pilgrimage chapel was also built in appreciation for the protection it provided. It was rebuilt into a smallish Gothic church later. A sculpture of the Virgin Mary was placed in the church and soon became the central symbol of the great Marian pilgrimages to Levoča. It was temporarily stored in the parish church in Levoča in the 18th century but was returned to Mariánska Hora in 1809. It now adorns the interior of the new Neo Gothic Church of the Visitation of the Virgin Mary that was ceremoniously consecrated by the Spiš Bishop J. Vojtaššák in 1922. The pilgrimages to Levoča were also mass events during the Communism era; they were a protest of Christian Slovakia against the forced atheistic ideology.

### SPIŠSKÝ CASTLE (1)

This castle was the ruling centre of the Spiš Region and the seat of the Head of the County Council for centuries. The construction of the medieval castle atop a large travertine hill started with the fortification walls from the 12th century. The castle underwent several reconstructions; each making it bigger and stronger. It is now one of the largest ruins in central Europe. The conical (Donjon) tower from the 13th century is the landmark of the castle. It belongs to the upper castle as does the originally Romanesque Palace of the Provost Matej. The palace was rebuilt by the Thurzo family into a luxurious Renaissance seat in the 17th century. The later Hungarian king, J. Zápoľský, was born in the second palace located in the upper castle. The area of the castle doubled during the 14th century. Members of the Bratríci Movement lead by J. Jiskra built the lower castle in the first half of the 15th century. The castle was destroyed by a fire in 1780 and started to fall apart. It is one of the UNESCO World Culture Monument Heritage listed monuments and now houses expositions of the Spišské Museum in Levoča with the collection related to the history of the castle, medieval weapons and feudal justice.

### SPIŠSKÉ PODHRADIE (2)

The heart of Spiš has always beat in the town of Spišské Podhradie and its surroundings. At the north of the town was Spišský Castle with the feudal rulers of the region. At the other side lay Spišská Kapitula Canonry, the seat of the religious authorities with provosts, bishops and capitularies. This specific position of the town greatly influenced the life of its inhabitants. Spišské Podhradie was a vassal town, yet it had certain privileges and developed and prospered well. Thus, it has preserved interesting cultural and historical monuments. The landmark of the town is the Church of the Birth of the Virgin Mary from the 13th century. It underwent numerous reconstructions, however it burnt down in 1794. The monastery of the Merciful Brothers was originally a medieval hospice of the Augustinian Order, which was rebuilt in the 17th century. The Classicism Evangelic church from 1818 houses an altar with a painting of Christ on the Olive Mount by J. Czauczik. The Renaissance town hall from the 16th century, Baroque Marian Column from 1726 and several burgher houses are also noteworthy.

### SPIŠSKÁ KAPITULA (3)

Although the canonry, the religious centre of Spiš, is a Town Monument Reserve, we could hardly call it a town as it is a very specific community with the main purpose of being the religious centre. Perhaps 'Slovakian Vatican' would be a more appropriate name. The first community was established here in the 11th century near a fortified Benedictine Monastery. It has not witnessed any significant changes from the time of the Middle Ages to the present day. It was surrounded by a stone fortification wall with two gates in the 13th century; the fortifications are fully preserved. The area inside the walls has never acquired a town-like character. It still resembles a medieval fortress; it is a specific priests' community with the area divided into narrow parcels of individual canonries. The picturesque houses of the canonries in the eastern

part of Spišská Kapitula are accessible from the only street in the town. There are two remarkable buildings; the Romanesque Cathedral of St. Martin from the 13th century and the old Bishop Palace from the same period.

## CATHEDRAL OF ST. MARTIN IN SPIŠSKÁ KAPITULA (4)

This grandiose cathedral is the most eastern European church consecrated to St. Martin, a very popular saint in eastern Europe. It could be said, with a slight exaggeration, that western culture ends here. The Romanesque church with Gothic elements was built between 1245 and 1275 as a tree-nave cathedral with two towers in its west facade. The interior boasts a lot of valuable art monuments. There is the rare Romanesque stone sculpture of a lion (Leo Albus) from the 13th century, one of the oldest in Slovakia. The unusual sacral mural from 1317 with the motif of the coronation of the Hungarian King Karol Róbert is also noteworthy. The main altar from the 15th century was reconstructed as part of the Gothic restoration of the church in the 19th century; however the side Gothic altars maintained their original appearance. The Gothic burial chapel of the Zápoľský family was added to the cathedral in 1493. It replaced an older chapel called Corporis Christi from 1382. It is reminiscent of the La Sainte-Chapelle in France.

## BISHOP'S PALACE IN SPIŠSKÁ KAPITULA (5)

The Spiš Canonry has been the religious centre of the Spiš Region since the end of the 12th century. It became the seat of the provost in 1198 and soon after the seat of the entire canonry. The Prepošstký Palace was built in 1281. The originally Romanesque building became the seat of the Spiš Bishop in 1776 and it has served its purpose ever since. However, it has been reconstructed several times in the Renaissance and Baroque styles. A French garden surrounded the Bishop's Palace in the past. Its entry tower from 1739 is preserved together with a smallish park; it is called the Hodinová (Clock) Tower.

## DREVENÍK (1)

This interesting hill near Spišský Castle is the largest travertine formation (609 m) in Slovakia. It was formed at the end of the Tertiary Era by the merging of several travertine knolls. Dreveník is a flat hill flanked by rocks, whose eroded edges crumbled into rock towers and depressions. The imaginative locals soon named the bizarre rock formation. One of the most beautiful valleys is called Peklo (Hell), while the 'stone town' at the eastern edge is called Kamenný Raj (Stone Paradise). Over time, the travertine transformed into a hard white rock with an attractive structure. Large quarries cut into the western edge of the massif; stone for building and decorative purposes was quarried here for centuries. This remarkable place is worth a visit.

## SIVÁ BRADA (2)

This round, smallish hill with the Baroque Chapel of St. Cross from 1675 atop it lies about 2.5 km west of Spišské Podhradie near the Hradská Road. It is a travertine knoll on a spot with mineral springs rich in calcium. According to historical sources the springs were already here in the 17th century. A bore (132 metres deep) was made at the north side of the hill in 1956. A geyser that appeared in it originally gushed three times a day for two minutes, with a height of up to 15 metres. However the geyser got weaker and finally vanished. Today there is only a small spring on Sivá Brada with gentle bubbling waters due to carbonic oxide emissions. It makes the mountain grow. This is an interesting example of a natural process.

5

### TOWN HALL IN SPIŠSKÉ VLACHY (3)

This small town on the left bank of the Hornád River was established on the site of a smaller Slavic settlement founded by colonists after the Tartar invasion. Their origins are unclear, but most likely they were stonemasons from northern Italy. The most beautiful building in the town is the former Gothic town hall from the 15th century located in the fork of two main streets. This building, called Ratuš or Turna, boasts a remarkable high tower. The town hall is partially used as a Catholic church. It houses an incomplete Gothic altar from the turn of the 15th century. The second landmark of the central square of the town is the originally Romanesque Church of St. John the Baptist form 1241, with a valuable crucifix from 1520 from the workshop of Master Pavol of Levoča.

### CHURCH AND ROTUNDA IN BIJACOVCE (4)

Apart from the mansion built by the family of Čáki (Csáky) towards the end of the 18th century after Spišský Castle burnt out, Bijanovice also boasts two sacral buildings – a Romanesque church and a Romanesque rotunda next to it. The ancient Church of All Saints from the 13th century was built as a Romanesque one-nave edifice and it has been preserved with some Gothic and Baroque adaptations. The interior is decorated with splendid murals from the 14th century. According to experts they are one of the most beautiful Gothic art pieces in Slovakia. Only a fragment of painted cycles depicting the apostles and the legend about St. Ladislaw are preserved. The Chapel of St. Kosmas and Damian from the first half of the 13th century is a Romanesque rotunda with a nice shingle roof.

### CHURCH OF HOLY SPIRIT IN ŽEHRA (5)

The feudal lord count Ján of Žehra received permission from the provost of the Spiš Region Matej to build a church in 1245. To carry out the deed, he invited experienced stonemasons who had worked at Spišský Castle. Beautiful local travertine was used as a building material as there was plenty available. The result of their work is splendid and the village of Žehra can boast a beautiful Church of the Holy Spirit; its architecture is a combination of two styles, the retreating Romanesque and upcoming Gothic. A tower with an onion-shaped roof was added to the older part of the church from the 13th century in 1769. It made the church atop a hill an impressive sight. The interior houses unique preserved murals that were created in several stages from the second half of the 13th century until the end of the 15th century.

## PROVINČNÝ HOUSE
## IN SPIŠSKÁ NOVÁ VES (1)

This town was included in the deposit that consisted of 16 towns in the Spiš Region and was given to the Polish king. Thus, the town was in a way without a proper ruler as it belonged to neither Hungary nor Poland. This wealthy mining town gradually advanced into one of the most important towns in the region and logically it received an important function. It became the seat of the Province of the Sixteen Towns in 1778. This powerful self-administration unit, created by Maria Theresa after the deposit was returned, moved into the Provinčný House, a reconstructed former town hall from the 13th century on the central square. Here the Hungarian King Vladislav I and Ján Jiskra of Brandýs signed a truce on the 1st September 1443. The original appearance of this building can be seen on one of the cartouches of the richly decorated Rococo façade. Six allegoric reliefs depict symbolical rules valid for the administrators of the office. Today there are collections of the Spišské Museum in the Provinčný House.

## REDUTA
## IN SPIŠSKÁ NOVÁ VES (2)

The centre of this town boasts buildings of various architectonic styles and ages that create a colourful and attractive environment. The Reduta building is no different. The former town hotel with a café and a theatre is an example of a nice Art Nouveau style. It was built between 1900 and 1905 in the eastern part of Radničné Square after a design by K. Gerster. The interior with murals by J. Hanula is as beautiful as the façade. Reduta is now the seat of the Spišské Theatre and it is the centre of the cultural and social life of the town; it has a concert hall and a café.

## PARISH CHURCH
## IN SPIŠSKÁ NOVÁ VES (3)

Names of streets and squares in the centre of this town are somehow different. The park with several buildings is called Radničné (Town Hall) Square, however the entire area with an uneven ground-plan is enclosed by two streets. The northern Letná (Summer) Street allows pedestrians to bathe in sunrays all day long. As the southern row of buildings create long shadows, the other street is called Zimná (Winter). The parish church in the centre is a landmark of the town. It has the highest church spire in Slovakia, its top looming to 86 metres. The Church of the Assumption of the Virgin Mary was built in the 14th century on the site of an original fortified Romanesque church. The courtyard of the church outside the city walls was the last hideout of the town's inhabitants. The southern Gothic portal of the church is noteworthy. The interior houses several valuable art pieces, among which are sculptures by Master Pavol of Levoča. A complete reconstruction of the church was carried out in 1954 and removed the Pseudo elements of different styles. Moreover, it uncovered precious murals from the 15th century.

## MANSION
### IN MARKUŠOVCE (1)

The grandiose mansion in Markušovce is rightfully considered an architectonic jewel. It was built by F. Mariáši (Máriássy), a member of a venerable aristocratic family, in 1643. It was a humanistic school for young feudal lords until 1663; the lessons were also taught in Slovakian. A reconstruction from 1773 left some basic architectonic elements of the former fortress. The tasteful Rococo decoration and the central spire greatly improved the appearance of the building. The mansion is now a museum that houses an exposition of the Spišské Museum with historical furniture.

## DARDANELY SUMMERHOUSE
### IN MARKUŠOVCE (2)

Wolfgang Mariáši (Máriássy) expected an important visit in his residence in 1778: the Emperor Joseph II. As he considered his new mansion unsatisfactory he started building a summer house in the French-style garden near the mansion with the vision of welcoming the ruler there. However the visit never happened so the Dardanely Summerhouse was not completed.

## ROCK MUSHROOM
### IN MARKUŠOVCE (3)

The Hornád River flows on the southern edge of the Hornádska Kotlina Hollow, cutting at places into the hard rocks at the end of the Slovenské Rudohorie Mountains. The river eroded several interesting geological and geomorphologic localities here. An area where the Mesozoic limestone is covered by the sea sediments from the Tertiary Era is visible right above Markušovce. This is called transgression by geologists. A remarkable rock formation was created downstream behind the meander of the valley on the basal Tertiary sea sediments. It is called Rock Mushroom and sits at a height of 50 metres above the river; it is about 8 metres high. The part that resembles the head of a mushroom is formed by more resistant sandstone and protects the lower conglomerate that formed the 'leg'. It is only a matter of time before this formation disappears.

## MARKUŠOVSKÝ CASTLE (4)

The lord of the estate of Markušovce demanded a permission from King Ladislav IV to build a castle, which became the seat of the Mariáši (Máriássy) family. This family was in constant argument with the town of Levoča. The squabbles climaxed in 1527 when inhabitants of Levoča attacked and conquered the castle; the reason behind the attack was their support of the future king Ferdinand Habsburg while the family of Mariáši stood by the interests of the unsuccessful candidate for the Hungarian Crown Š. Zápoľský. The castle was reconstructed in 11 years, however at that time the castles were being replaced by more popular mansions.

## PORÁČSKA DOLINA (5)

The eastern part of the Hnilecké Vrchy Hills is created by the karst Galmus Plain. The plateau, with numerous karst formations, is divided into two independent parts by the Poráčska Valley. The narrow central part of the valley (4 km) resembles a chasm. Both sides of the narrow bottom of the hollow are flanked by bizarre Červené Rocks, a Nature Reserve. A tourist trail skirts the bottom of the valley alongside the Poráčsky Creek connecting the villages of Poráč and Slovinky. From Poráče there is a splendid view of the valley and surrounding limestone peaks at the edge of Galmus. The landmark of the eastward view is the Skala Hill (1,014 m) known also as the Slovinská Rock. At the southern side of the valley is the eye-catching Biela Rock (926 m).

## COVERED WOODEN BRIDGE
### IN ŠTEFANSKÁ HUTA (6)

The Hornád River enters a chasm below the village of Klukava at the southeast of the Spiš Region. Part of the chasm was flooded by the Ružín Dam. The village of Štefanská Huta lies a bit above the narrowed part of the valley. There is an interesting wooden covered bridge from 1832 near the remains of an old copper smeltery from the 19th century. This pedestrian bridge over the Hornád was damaged and even taken apart numerous times, however it was restored and opened after the last reconstruction on 1st December 1985.

## PRIELOM HORNÁDU (1)

After the Hornád River leaves the Hornádska Kotlina Hollow near Podlesk it flows onto the territory of the Slovakian Paradise. The Prielom Hornádu Chasm starts here and there is the very attractive Chodník Horskej Služby Tourist Trail. The chasm ends after 16 kilometres and the Hornád returns into the Hornádska Hollow near the village of Smižany. The narrow chasm with a wide river was inaccessible in the past and to see it you would have to wait for winter and walk across the surface of the frozen river. Works on making the chasm accessible started in 1960, various technical aids were employed and the work was completed in 1974. The trail is secured by 7 iron bridges, 374 metres of chains, 164 iron steps, 15 supporting cramps and 85 metres of wooden bridges. The path is also a nature trail and is very popular. Sections with steep rock walls that must be climbed on steps directly over the river are the most interesting parts of the trail.

## TOMÁŠOVSKÝ VÝHĽAD (2)

By its chasm between Podlesok and Smižany the Hornád River cuts off the most northern section of the Slovakian Paradise. This geomorphologic process is called epigenesis. The northern edge of the mountain range became an isolated mountain crest that leads alongside the chasm of the Hornád. The ridge narrows down near Letanovský Mlyn into a saddle and it culminates at 667 metres at the Tomášovský Výhľad viewing point, which is a fascinating natural formation. It is a rock terrace surrounded by 142-metre high rock walls that drop down

into the chasm of Hornád. The beauty of this place is enhanced by the panorama of the Tatras summits in the background. This plan is certainly worth a visit.

### TIESŇAVA VEĽKÝ SOKOL (3)

In the past it was not at all commonplace to climb though the narrow chasms of the Slovakian Paradise as it is today. In fact, it was nearly impossible without technical aid. The first historically proved climbs that took place before World War I were challenging mountaineering tasks. The most zealous mountaineer and explorer of the chasms of the Slovakian Paradise was professor M. Roth (1841-1917), who taught at the grammar school in Spišská Nová Ves. Together with two similarly excited friends, he managed to climb the Veľký Sokol Chasm for the first time in 1898. Photographer V. Forsberg followed one month later, taking the first pictures of the chasms in the Slovakian Paradise. They woke up a great interest in the public. Veľký Sokol is the largest, longest and undoubtedly one of the most beautiful chasms in the Slovakian Paradise. It was opened for tourists in 1956. The climb starts at the Sokol Lodge and the demanding climb up the 6-kilometre long valley ends 350 metres higher at the plateau called Glac. The most beautiful section of the chasm is named after its explorer, Rothova Roklina. The chasm between the rock walls is only 1 meter wide in the spot called Kamenná Brána. This challenging walk is indeed a splendid experience.

### KLÁŠTORISKO (4)

One of the smaller karst plains of the Slovakian Paradise received its name from an ancient monastery with the Church of St. John the Baptist. This locality was once also called Skala Útočiska (Safe Haven), as it was a hiding place for the locals fleeing from the Tartars. The Carthusians chose this plateau in 1299 as the most suitable place for their monastery. The remote yet safe spot fulfilled their high requirements for the calm, undisturbed life strictly required by the order. However, their peace was disturbed by the frequent attacks of the members of Bratríci in the 15th century. The monks left Kláštorisko in 1543 and the monastery was left to dereliction. The first tourists came here towards the end of the 19th century, finding it a ruin. A gradual reconstruction of the monastery complex has been carried out since 1983. The ruins in the middle of a lush meadow now resemble the old abbeys on the British Islands. There is a tourist chalet at Kláštorisko with a crossroad of six tourist trails. One of them leads into the Kyseľ Chasm with the Obrovský Vodopád Waterfall.

### TIESŇAVA SUCHÁ BELÁ (5)

Suchá Belá is the most popular chasm as it is near the tourist basis in Podlesok at the northwest edge of the Slovakian Paradise. The first to climb the valley was a group led by M. Roth in 1900. The first winter climb was managed by another group led by A. Mervay ten years later. This pioneer event discovered the winter beauty of the chasm and the fantastic change of the

waterfalls into ice organs. The valley was opened to tourists in 1957. The 4-kilometre climb goes over an elevation of 400 metres. It starts at Podlesek and ends at the northern edge of the Glac Plain. The most beautiful part of the chasm is the area of the Misový Waterfalls, with the highest waterfall, the 15-metre high Okienkový Vodopád.

### KLÁŠTORSKÁ ROKLINA (6)

This gorge was opened to tourists in 1960 thanks to the uniquely constructed ropeway that enabled access to the mouth of the gorge. It is now possible to climb the gorge, in the same way as the others in the Slovakian Paradise, from the bottom to the top. Therefore tourists must walk a bit along the Chodník Horskej Služby Trail in the Prielom Hornádu Chasm. Kláštorská Roklina is relatively short, however very steep; the elevation of 250 metres is reached within 2 kilometres. Ladders, steps and chains help to climb the waterfalls: Vodopád objaviteľov, Vodopád Antona Straku, Dúhový vodopád, Kaskády Gusta Nedobrého, Malý vodopád, Machový vodopád and Kartuziánsky vodopád. The short but demanding climb ends on the Kláštorisko Plain, with a tourist chalet and the ruins of a medieval monastery. The gorge is a fascinating natural formation.

## MANSION IN JAKLOVCE (1)

A total of 106 houses in this village were flooded by the Ružín Dam, and the water got close to the mansion on a hilltop, taking thus a bit of its conspicuousness. This rather large mansion was built by the feudal lords of the Čáki (Czáky) family in the so-called Theresian Baroque in the second half of the 18th century. Initially, it was a one-story building with two wings and an L-shaped ground-plan. There once was a stud farm near the river, however it is not preserved. The Čákis rebuilt the mansion into the present-day appearance at the beginning of the 20th century, adding another story. The local Church of St. Anton Pustovník (the Hermit) is also noteworthy. It has preserved medieval murals and an ancient baptismal font from the 13th century.

## MINING MUSEUM IN GELNICA (2)

Gelnica was once one of the wealthiest towns of upper Hungary thanks to the rich deposits of gold, silver, iron and copper. Therefore local smelting and iron works soon started to develop. There were a large amount of workshops for the production of various iron products in the 19th century and it provided work for around 200 blacksmiths. The economy declined in the second half of the 19th century due to the exhaustion of the deposits and in the end the mining activities ended. A statue of a prying miner in the middle of the Banícke Square now commemorates the past fame of the town. A large building of the former town hall is at the northeast side of the square. It was built in the 18th century on the site of demolished Renaissance houses. Building material from the ruin of the medieval castle atop the town was used for its construction. The building with a high Baroque tower now houses the Mining Museum.

## GELNICKÝ CASTLE (3)

This castle from the 13th century was originally a town castle similar to castles in Kremnica and Banská Bystrica. First it belonged to the king who sent his administrator to look after the royal rights in the mining area of Gelnica. The Zápoľský family secured the town and the castle into hereditary possession in 1465 and was in permanent conflict with the inhabitants of the town. The new feudal lords of the 16th century became the Thurzo family, who got on better with the inhabitants, as they shared a common interest, profiting from the mining. The Kuruci army of Tököliho (Thököly) conquered the town and burnt the castle down. After the fire the inhabitants of the town took the walls of the castle apart and used it in the building of the town hall. The end of the castle was sped up by the tragic death of a young man, killed by a tumbled wall. The town council ordered a complete demolition of the medieval building, which is why not much has been preserved. However, it is worthwhile to climb up the hill, as it offers a pleasant view of the town.

## SMOLNÍK (4)

Smolník had a famous history of a wealthy town that prospered from the mining and copper and silver ore production. It was elevated to a free royal town as early as in 1327 and it also became the seat of the Mining Chamber. Its biggest economic boom was during the 18th century. Even the Emperor Joseph II visited the town in 1783, for at that time it was the largest town of the Spiš Region (according to a census of 1785, Smolník was larger then Spišská Nová Ves, Gelnica and Levoča). The economic decline of the 19th century affected Smolník as well as the entire region of the Hnilecká and Smolnícká Valleys. The copper mines and smelteries were closed. The last ore was loaded onto a mining carriage, which became the monument of this long past fame of the town. Some historical monuments in the town are reminiscent of its better times. The most interesting is the large historical building of the former Mining Chamber. The originally Renaissance building from 1872 was rebuilt into a tobacco factory; it still produces hand-made cigars.

## NÁLEPKOVO (5)

The railway connecting Červená Skala and Margecany meticulously follows the Hnilecká Valley. It does not swerve from the only larger Slovakian river, which flows away from the valleys and lowlands. Interestingly, that does not apply to the road, which stays in the valley until the village of Nálepkovo and then continues to Horehronie Region via the most northern route away from the main valley. Nálepkovo is the largest town in the upper part of Hnilecká Valley. Older inhabitants may remember it being called Vondrišel. It was a feudal town of the Máriáši (Mariássy) family from Markusovce. Its inhabitants mined the local iron and copper ores until 1969. Nálepkovo boasts a nicely maintained centre complemented by a modern belfry. There are three noteworthy monuments dating from the 18th century; the Baroque town hall and the Roman-Catholic Church of St. Štefan Kráľ, both with towers, and the towerless Evangelic church.

## UHORNÁ (6)

This interesting village with preserved folk architecture lies in the upper part of the Smolnícka Dolina Valley. It was founded later than the neighbouring Smolník, during the Wallachian colonization. As it was on the edge of the mining region its inhabitants earned their bread mainly by charcoal burning. It was needed by the iron and copper smelteries in the area. The inhabitants of Uhorná produced as well as transported the charcoal. They prospered reasonably also because they merged with the transporters association, which had regulations valid for the medieval roads. They developed their business further, transporting also iron products, local sheep cheese (bryndza), honey, pottery, cloth and Slivovitz to the lower lands. The road below Uhorná goes along a water reservoir of the same name, which was an important source for the Smolnícka Valley just as tajchy (lakes) were near Banská Štiavnica.

# VÝCHODNÝ GEMER

## NÁMESTIE BANÍKOV
## V ROŽŇAVE (1)

The name Rožňava derives from a German expression, Rosenau – a pink meadow. Roses once grew on the sunny hills around the town and rose (ruža) was also the name for pure ore. This town was completely devoted to mining, mainly the mining of iron ore. The peak period of local mines was during the 14th and 15th centuries and a short revival of the old fame occured in the second half of the 19th century. It is therefore no surprise that the centre of the town is the Námestie Baníkov (Miners) Square. The quadrant square developed in the 13th century and it has preserved historical buildings. The oldest burgher house dates from around 1500. The landmark of the town is a Renaissance town tower located in the middle of the square. It was built in 1654 near the old town hall, which was replaced by the Jesuit Church in 1687. The present-day Classicism town hall from 1711 stands on the western side of the square. Several small shops, which also existed in the Middle Ages, are below the tower with a splendid view of the town. The square is adorned by the Monument to Františka Hablwecová-Andrášiová, a highly venerated noble-minded lady who cared for the poor. It was built in 1905 from a public money collection, removed in 1953 and returned 20 years later. The central marble statue of Františka is the main art piece of the monument. A sculpture of a beggar and two children stands in front of it, representing those that she devoted her life to.

## BISHOPS CATHEDRAL
## AND RESIDENCE IN ROŽŇAVA (2)

An important chapter of history that reaches beyond the borders of the town happened here in 1707 when a council led by Francis II Rákoci (Rákoczi) was held here to decide about the dethroning of the Habsburg dynasty. Although the efforts failed, the ruling dynasty bestowed the privileges of the free bishop town on Rožňava and it became the seat of the bishop in 1776. The first bishop was the chancellor of the Trnava University Ján Galgóci who decided to reside in the Parish Church of the Assumption of the Virgin Mary. A medieval sacral building already existed here in 1304; it was rebuilt in the spirit of the Late Gothic style in the 15th and 16th centuries. A valuable desk painting of St. Anna from 1513 is preserved from this period. It depicts mining activities around the town. It is possibly the work of an artist from the workshop of Master Pavol of Levoča. The mostly Baroque furnishings date from the period when the church was transformed into the Bishop Cathedral. The Bishop's residency was built on the site of a demolished Jesuit monastery and school in the northeast corner of the square in 1778. The Baroque-Classicism palace houses a valuable library and a diocese archive. The visit by Pope John Paul II on the 13th September 2003 had great importance for the diocese as well as for the town.

## MINING MUSEUM IN ROŽŇAVA (3)

The interesting history of the museum in Rožňava goes as far back as 1907. The Regional Hungarian Mining and Smelting Association initiated the foundation of the mining and Smelting Museum of Gemer. The present-day main building of the museum was built three years later on Šafárikova Street. Expositions about mining, smelting and mineralogy were opened in the museum in 1912. The Town Museum of Rožňava was established in the same year and both institutions merged in 1940. A part of the collections was stolen during World War II and the museum was not reopened until 1956. Today the Mining Museum occupies several buildings. Its original building now houses an exhibition about the history of mining in the region. The part located on the premises of a brewery is especially interesting. It represents replicas of mining corridors with contemporary technology used for iron ore and magnesite mining. An exposition about the landscape of the Slovakian Paradise was placed in the former orphanage and the most beautiful and valuable art pieces are in an unusual exposition based inside the former Markova Fur Factory. This place is indeed worth a visit.

## MAUSOLEUM
## IN KRÁSNOHORSKÉ PODHRADIE (1)

Count Dionýz Andráši of Krásna Hôrka married the Viennese actress F. Hablawetzová in 1866 and the pair accepted the social restriction due to their uneven status. They lived abroad for a long time and were active in charitable deeds. When countess Františka died in Munich in 1902 her grieving husband decided to build her a luxurious mausoleum near Krásnohorské Podhradie. The architect of the splendid round Art Nouveau building was R. Brendl from Munich, the marble sarcophagus was made by a sculptor from the same city, M. Frick. The remnants of the countess were ceremoniously buried in the mausoleum exactly two years after her death and her husband soon followed; he died in Palermo in Sicily in 1913. The façade of the mausoleum is reminiscent of the famous Teodorichorovo Mausoleum built in the 6th century in Ravenna, Italy.

## KRÁSNA HÔRKA (2)

This castle from the 14th century on a limestone hill above Krásnohorské Podhradí was the centre of power in the Gemer Region in the past. It was a medieval Gothic castle of the powerful Bebekovci family. The equally important Andráši (Andrássy) family conver-

ted it into a Renaissance stronghold in the 16th century. This family came to Gemer from Transylvania and stayed for almost four centuries. The castle almost burnt down after being hit by lightning in 1817; fortunately the Andráši family invested in its restoration, planning to turn it into their family museum. The castle was repaired so well in 1817 that it is now one of the most beautiful and best preserved Slovakian castles. The museum in the castle is a very popular tourist destination. The glass sarcophagus with the mummified remnants of Žofia Seréďova (Serédyova) in a chapel is the most admired exhibit. The wife of the general of Kuruci Š. Andráši is a character in the Levočská Biela Pani by Jókai.

## SKALISKO (3)

Long, massive mountain ranges and valleys are typical for the landscape of the Volovské Vrchy Hills in the eastern part of the Slovakian Rudohorie Mountains. The highest hill of the range, Zlatý Stôl (1,322 m), lies in a side fork. It is not a very popular tourist destination as it is in a rather remote area. More people visit the massif of Volovec on the main forking range between the Hnilec and Slaná valleys. A rock called Skalisko (1,293 m) juts out from the high, wide mountain range. As this bizarre summit

rock is higher than its surroundings by approximately 10 metres, it is a great outlook point. It offers splendid views of the surrounding countryside.

## MANSION IN BETLIAR (4)

This small Gothic castle from the 15th century in Betliar has undergone a complicated building development that made it one of the most beautiful mansions in Slovakia. Its charming present-day appearance dates from 1880. E. Andráši (Andrássy, 1821-1891) had the mansion rebuilt in the style of the French romantic chateaus. He was called the Iron Count for his mining activities. He was an adventurous and artistic man and eagerly collected exotic and other art types. A similar person was his brother-in-law, the romantic 'daydreamer' J. F. Pálfi of Bojnice. Part of the collection is from Emanuel's journey to Africa and Asia. The Betiar Chateau houses a large amount of valuable furniture, china, porcelain, historical weapons, hunting trophies and a valuable collection of 500 paintings by prominent European and Hungarian masters. Some paintings were done by the count himself.

2

3

4

## PLEŠIVSKÁ PLANINA (1)

The Slovenský Kras National Park was designated to protect the largest karst territory in Slovakia. It is the karst of the plain type with plateaus, sinkholes and chasms. Two similar, yet in details different, plains of this territory are Plešivská Planina and Silická Planina. The Plešivská Plain spreads in the western part and it is an excellent example of the karst plain. The plateau is flanked by steep rocky slopes on all sides. Its surface is dotted with numerous karst formations. Although the rain water disappears underground and the plain is extremely dry, its large part is forested and the deforested parts resemble a savannah or a steppe. Numerous karst chasms and rifts are typical signs of this territory. They are mainly on the bottom of sinkholes that connect to vertical caves in the underground. The Diviačia Priepasť is the deepest chasm (122 m). The Zvonivá Diera Chasm is 100 metres deep and widens into a large cave dome in the bottom part that is decorated by a huge 26-metre stalagmite called Stlp hrôzy (Column of Dread). The entire area is a remarkable natukral wonder.

## CANYON OF THE SLANÁ RIVER (2)

The Slaná River leaves the Rožňavská Kotlina Hollow by an impressive canyon that separates the Silická and Plešivská plains. Both sides of the flat bottom of the valley are flanked by steep rocky slopes jutting up to over 400 metres. The splendid landscape of the canyon is spoilt by a huge scar of a limestone quarry. Its reddish wall stands exactly opposite the entry area into the Gombasecká Jaskyňa Cave. There is another, smaller gorge in the Slovakian Paradise created by the small Štítnik River in its western part. It lies between the Plešivská Plain and the Koniar Plain.

## SILICKÁ PLANINA (3)

This plain is the largest karst plain in Slovakia. It reaches onto the territory of Hungary and has an area of 132 km². The plateau is bound by a steep slope that plummets into Rožňovská Kotlina at the north. Its west side ends at the similarly steep slope of the canyon of the Slaná River. The plateau has numerous sinkholes. Brázda is the deepest from several karst chasms, it is 180.5 metres deep. The Silická Plain boasts the most beautiful area of grikes in the Slovakian Paradise. There is a rich cave world underneath the plain.

## JAŠTERIČIE JAZIERKO (4)

This small lake lies near the village of Silica on the Silická Plain. It is not a permanent lake, as it changes into a swamp and sometimes dries out during the dry season. Besides, the growing swamp vegetation is slowly causing it to disappear. Yet it is still the largest karst pond in Slovakia. It appeared on the bottom of a sinkhole blocked by earth that was created between porous limestone and impermeable schist. The Fabiánka Hill is also formed by schist; it lies east of the lake. Its round peak offers an impressive panoramic view. Surprisingly, on a fine day you can see as far as the Tatras summits. Being that Fabiánka is almost on the Hungarian border while the Tatras are on the Polish border, the view enables you to see the whole of Slovakia.

## KEČOVSKÉ ŠKRAPY (5)

Silická Plain is abundant with grike areas. These interesting karst formations consist of miniature rock shapes and forms called grikes (fissures). We are talking about formations that can be measured in centimetres and developed due to the influence of water on the surface of the limestone rock; water with organic material corrodes the limestone, etching small cavities and holes of various shapes, often quite bizarre. The density of grikes is higher in a badly cracked rock as water gets deeper into the rock through the fissures. Dominské grikes are near the Domica Cave, however are hidden in the vegetation, bushes and forest. More beautiful are the bare and thus well visible Kečovské grikes created on the rocky slope above the village of Kečovo.

## SILICKÁ ĽADNICA (6)

A visit to Silická Ľadnica on the plateau of Silická Planina will simply charm you. The surface of the karst plateau is as hot and dry as the sand in the Sahara Desert during the hot summer, yet there is a large hole in the forest that emits freezing air as if coming from an open fridge. It is a cave that can be entered via a rather large opening in a limestone rock wall resembling a tunnel entry. The opening was created on the broken edge of a sinkhole. Stairs will take you down to the viewing platform; the rest of the cave is not accessible. It is the lowest ice cave in Europe (503 m). The cave in the underground is connected with the Gombasecká Cave and is covered by a layer of ice throughout the year. Apart from ice, the cave is adorned by stalactites hanging down from the ceiling.

two men came across an underground hollow that was created in the Palaeozoic Era crystalline limestone. This in itself was a surprise; even more astonishing, however, was the discovery inside. This cave in the massif of the Hrádek Hill above the village of Ochtiná has specific and relatively rare aragonite decorations to an extent unsurpassed in the world. Aragonite is a particular type of crystallised calcite in the shape of slim, white needles. This process is only possible in stabile microclimatic conditions. Ochtinská Aragonitová Cave was opened to the public in 1972; the tour is 230 metres long.

### JASKYŇA DOMICA (4)

This cave with fantastic rich speleothem decoration ranks amongst the most beautiful in Slovakia. The entrance into the cave is on the Silická Plain near the border crossing to Hungary. The cave was known already to prehistoric people, and evidence of this is the discovery of the stone tip of a javelin about 35,000 years old. The modern discovery of the cave happened in 1926 and the first tourists could admire its beauty 6 years later. Domica is a part of the longest cave system of the Slovakian karst and is connected with the Hungarian cave system called Baradla. The total length of corridors is 22 kilometres; Domica is 5,368 metres long. When there is enough water, there is a nice 150-metre ride on the underground Styx River. Specific forms of the cave are bubny, peaks pagodas and onion-shaped stalactites. The Majkov Dome and Dome of Indian Pagodas are especially remarkable for their size and decoration. A visit to the Domica Cave is a lovely experience.

### DOBŠINSKÁ ĽADOVÁ JASKYŇA (1)

This cave is amongst the largest and most significant ice caves in the world. Its entrance is at less than 1,000 metres, while the renowned ice caves in Austria and Romania are situated in the much higher Alpine area. Dobšinská Ľadová was discovered by R. Ruffini and his friend in 1870 and it was opened to the public one year later. As the first in the world, the cave was lit by electricity in 1887. Another world first is summer ice skating, first organized in 1893. The cave developed towards the end of the Tertiary Era together with the neighbouring Stratenská Cave, which is one of the longest in Slovakia. After their connecting tunnel lapsed, it became an underground area with one entrance, which is the basic condition for ice creation. Cold air that flows through the entrance situated in the highest part of the cave pushes the warm air upwards. The temperature in the Malá Hall reaches 5 degrees below zero in the summer and heavy cold air remains in the bottom parts of the cave in the summer. There

are 110,132 m³ of ice in the cave; at places it is 25 metres thick.

### GOMBASECKÁ JASKYŇA (2)

The entry into this cave is from the canyon of the Slaná River at the western edge of the Silická Plain. It was discovered in 1951 by a group of speleologists from Rožňava, who entered the underground area via Čierná Vyvieračka Well. The first tourists visited the cave in 1955. Speleotherapy started here as the first in Slovakia in 1968. The Gombasecká Cave is a karst formation created by an underground river. The river bed of the Čierný Creek is in the lower of the two storys of the cave and it surfaces through Čierná Vyvieračka. Narrow hollow stalagmites are typical for its rich speleothem decoration.

### OCHTINSKÁ ARAGONITOVÁ
### JASKYŇA (3)

This cave was discovered by chance. During the tunnelling of an exploratory tunnel in 1954

4

## EVANGELIC CHURCH IN ŠTÍTNIK (1)

The village of Štítnik in the Gemer Region boasts a superb, large three-nave basilica with a history going back into the 13th century. The size of the village is associated with its past when it was a mining town with its own smelteries, which received the right to hold markets and other town privileges according to the Krupniské Law. The murals in the church created by the al fresco technique were done over the span of three centuries. When the church went to the Evangelists in the 17th century, the murals were covered by white plaster. They were gradually uncovered between 1874 and 1908. The paintings depict various religious themes and cover up to 220 m² of the internal walls of the church; the oldest date from the 14th century. They show the influence of Italian paintings of the time; perhaps they are the work of famous Italian fresco painters from the town of Lucca. The younger paintings from the 15th and 16th centuries bear signs of Czech and German influence. The oldest organ in Slovakia (1639) situated in the church is also remarkable.

## EVANGELIC CHURCH IN KOCEĽOVCE (2)

This village is an important stop on the Gemer branch of the tourist Gothic Path. The reason is the church from the 14th century with preserved

medieval paintings in the interior. The most valuable frescoes are in the polygonal presbytery with remarkable colourfulness. The light blue background is especially impressive; it is explained as the influence of the Siena painting that spread in this area during the reign of the Anjouovci family. The precious paintings done made between 1360 and 1380 in the workshop of a famous medieval artist known as the author of the Ochtinské presbytery. When the Evangelists owned the church in the 16th century they covered the murals with white plaster. They were uncovered during restoration works between 1894 and 1895.

## EVANGELIC CHURCH IN PLEŠIVEC (3)

This village at the southern foothills of the Slovakian Karst was favoured by the feudal lords of the Bebekovci, who built the Church of St. George here in 1320 to serve as their family and burial temple. Its interior was adorned by murals in the 14th century, fragments of which are preserved. A nice burial chapel built in the Late Gothic style was added to the north side of the church in the 16th century. It houses old tombstones of the members of the family of Bebekovci. There is a high Baroque-Classicism belfry from 1807, which is a landmark of Plešivec.

## HUSSITE CHURCH IN LÚČKA (4)

You can walk through the valley of the Čremošná Creek, which borders the Horný Vrch Plain in the Slovakian Karst at the north to the upper end of the Zádielská Chasm. It is worthwhile to stop in the village of Lúčka and admire the romantic ruin of an ancient church. It was built in the 13th century in a similar style to other medieval churches in the Gemer Region and surrounded by a stone defence wall with a sentry tower, used also as a belfry, in the 15th century. This transfor-

med the church into a fortress that was held by the Bratríci Movement of Jan Jiskra and therefore received the name Hussite Church. The fortress disappeared in 1605 and the Church of the Holy Spirit was left to become a ruin. A new church consecrated to the Holy Trinity was later built in the village. The third sacral building in the village is a modern church from 1993; its shape resembles a ship on the sea.

## NATIVE HOUSE OF ŠAFÁRIK IN KOBELIAROVO (5)

Even this remote village boasts a valuable church from the beginning of the 14th century. Like most of the churches in this area, it is Evangelical. The parish building is also remarkable. The famous Slovakian linguist and ethnographer P. J. Šafárik (1795 – 1861) was born in the building from the second half of the 18th century. After studying grammar schools in Rožňava, Dobšiná and Kežmarok he left for Jena to study philosophy, linguistics and history. He later worked in Prague as a renowned scientist and became a top Slavist. He did not accept the idea of Štúr about the formal Slovakian language but defended the idea of one common language for Czechs and Slovaks. There is a room devoted to the life and work of this great scholar in his native house in Kobeliarovo.

## PALCMANSKÁ MAŠA (1)

The village of Dedinky is the main tourist destination on the southern side of the Slovakian Paradise. It is on the northern bank of the Palcmanská Maša water reservoir created in 1956 on the Hnilec River (it is also called Hnilecká vodná nádrž). The 85-hectare lake is situated in a beautiful natural environment and is part of the first pumping electricity plant in Slovakia. Water from the reservoir flows though underground pipes below the Dobšinský Hill and propels the turbine of the water electricity plant 250 meters lower in the Vlčia Dolina Valley. The lake is used for recreation and water sports; however it is for those who are fitter, as the water is usually colder than in other lakes in Slovakia. Dedinky and the surrounding communities are bases for trekking and walking trips in the summer and skiing centres in the winter. It is the gateway into the southern part of the Slovakian Paradise.

## ZEJMARSKÁ ROKLINA (2)

There is only one chasm on the southern side of the Slovakian Paradise. It was opened to tourists in 1963 and as with other chasms and valleys you can only walk in one way, from the lower to the upper end. The entrance is near the village of Biela Voda and the upper part on the edge of the Gerava plateau is 240 metres higher. Zejmarská Roklina is remarkable for its bizarre rocks and cascades of waterfalls. The waterfalls were named after the anti-fascist fighter captain J. Nálepka. The chasm is a National Natural Monument.

## STRATENSKÁ DOLINA (3)

The landscape around the mountain village of Stratená is very attractive and picturesque. The Hnilec River cut its way through a canyon-like valley with numerous rocks above the village. It created a large meander in the Stratenský Kaňon Chasm. The road once copied the large curve of the valley, however a tunnel was built in the area in 1971 (342 metres long) so cars now avoid this romantic nook. A tourist trail turns northward roughly in the middle of the canyon. It leads to the Havrania Skala Rock (1,154 m); its peak is an important outlook point of the southern part of the Slovakian Paradise. South of the Stratenský Chasm is the Stratenská Jaskyňa Cave; it is not accessible. It is connected with another cave, named Psie Diery Cave, and the underground corridors of both caves are 22 kilometres long. The only longer caves in Slovakia are the Demänovské Jaskyne Caves in the Low Tatras.

## HNILECKÁ DOLINA (4)

This valley is one of the oldest in the Slovakian Carpathians. It was created in the upper Tertiary Era so it is over 25 million years old. The Hnilec River that flows on the bottom of the valley has a specific statute in Slovakia as it is the only larger river that never leaves the mountain territory. It rises on the slopes of the Kráľova Hoľa Mountain and after almost 90 kilometres, it empties into the Hornád River. The confluence now lies below the surface of the Ružín Dam. Hnilecká Dolina lies in a very attractive landscape of the Slovakian Rudohorie Mountains

with picturesque mountain villages. The villages of Stratená, Dedinky and Mlynky lie on its upper stream; they are now used mainly by tourists and for recreational purposes. Mlynky has been on the northern bank of the water reservoir Palcmanská Maša since its creation in 1956. A railway goes through the Hnilecká Valley; it was built in 1936 and connects Červená Skala and Margecany. The Hradská Road avoids the section between Mlynky and Nálepkovo, skirting instead the steep slopes on the left side of the valley.

## PRIELOM MURÁŇA (5)

Before the small Muráň River empties into the Slaná River it has to go though a narrow chasm in the Licinská Pahorkatina Hills in the most eastern part of the Rimanvská Kotlina Hollow. This narrow valley flanked by steep hills with a pronounced contour was created between the villages of Meliata and Bretka. It is cut into the hard limestone of the nearby Slovakian Karts. A tourist trail goes through the lower section of the chasm; it is a Protected Natural Monument. It offers a pleasant walk in the shade of the willow and alder trees that grow along the banks of the river. The surroundings of the chasm are interesting for their karst character, and there are two small caves, Horná Maškova and Peško. A visit to this lovely chasm is a pleasant experience.

# KOŠICKÝ REGION

### NATIONAL THEATRE IN KOŠICE (1)
The National Theatre in Košice was the last edifice to be built on the Hlavné Square in Košice in 1899. The remarkable and eclectic building is the work of A. Lang, who was considered one of the most talented European architects of his time. Born in Prague, he came to Košice after winning the prestigious international tender for the design of an art gallery in Budapest. He applied his knowledge of historical architectonic styles when working on the theatre building, which is considered his best work. He sensitively combined the elements of the Baroque and Art Nouveau styles. The faćade of the building is decorated by sculptures depicting scenes from mythology and the theatrical world. The richly figural and ornamental decorated interior has a stage in the shape of a lyre.

### CATHEDRAL OF ST. ELISABETH IN KOŠICE (2)
This grandiose cathedral consecrated to the patron of Hungary holds several primacies. It is the largest church in Slovakia and, at the same time, the most beautiful Gothic building in the country. Moreover, it is the most easterly located Gothic cathedral of the western type in Europe. The size of the church set in the middle of the spindle-shaped square is awe-inspiring. The construction of the five-nave cathedral was under royal control. It started in 1380 and, in fact, has never been finished. It has numerous original Gothic elements preserved despite later Neo-Gothic reconstructions. The most valuable item on the exterior is the northern portal; the gargoyles are also noteworthy. The main altar (1474-1477) with 48 desk paintings stands out in the interior. There is a crypt underneath the church, which is the last resting place of Francis II. Rákoci (1676-1735) and his loved ones. The leader of the last estate uprising was placed here with honours in 1906.

### ERBOVÝ MONUMENT IN KOŠICE (3)
This monument with a bronze statuette is in the southern part of the spindle-shaped Hlavné Square (also called Hlavná Street). It was erected to commemorate the blazon of the town, the oldest in Europe. The Hungarian King Ľudovít I bestowed the right to use the blazon on the town of Košice, confirming this by signing the Blazon Document on 7th May 1369. This day is now celebrated as the 'Day of the Town of Košice'. The final appearance of the blazon was determined by the fourth royal deed from 1502, signed by King Vladislav II. The monument was ceremoniously unveiled on 8th December 2002. Its author is the academic sculptor A. Račko, known also for the creation of the popular Maratónec Sculpture in Košice. The 310-metre high bronze statuette of the Erbový Monument depicts an angel with a shield, a helmet and a jewel. There are reliefs of old blazons of the town on the stone pedestal.

### URBANOVA TOWER IN KOŠICE (4)
This tower is also part of the monuments on the Hlavné Square in Košice. It is also called Červená (Red) Tower and dates from the 14th century when it was built as a detached Gothic belfry by the stonemasonry, which built the Cathedral of St. Elisabeth. It received a Renaissance appearance in 1628. It stood in a cemetery with defence walls until the 19th century. The tombstones from the cemetery were then incorporated into the wall of the Neo Renaissance arcaded corridor on the ground floor of the tower, thus creating a unique lapidary. The name of the tower is associated with the Bell of St. Urban, cast in 1557 from older bells that were damaged by a fire. The present-day bell in the tower is a copy of the original made in the ironworks in Košice. The original bell, destroyed by a fire in 1966, was pieced together from fragments; it is outside the tower.

### CHAPEL OF ST. MICHAEL IN KOŠICE (5)
South of the Cathedral of St. Elisabeth is a large Gothic chapel. Its remarkable length is 28 metres and it once served as an ossuary. It is consecrated to St. Michael the Archangel. The sculpture of the patron is placed above the entrance; he is depicted weighting the souls of the dead. The chapel was built in two stages. First the underground crypt was built in the 13th century, and the rest followed in the 14th century.

## RÁKOCIHO PALACE IN KOŠICE (1)

The Rákoci (Rákoczi) Palace stands in the northern part of the historical centre of Košice. It now houses the Slovakian Technical Museum. The building, with a nice Baroque-Classicism façade, is the result of the rebuilding of a Gothic burgher house from the 13th century. The reconstruction was carried out in 1653 and one year later the building became the seat of the County Council of Upper Hungary (Hornouhorský Generálny Kapitanát). The present-day name of the palace is associated with the leader of the estate uprising, Francis II Rákoci, who resided in the castle between 1706-1707 during the Krajinský Snem (National Assembly). The unique Slovakian Technical Museum has used the building since 1948. As the only one, this museum exhibits rare technical monuments and collections of utility art and has interesting expositions about mining, smeltering, engineering, art smithery, communication technology, chemistry, physics and astronomy.

## ČÁKIHO-DESSEWFFYHO PALACE IN KOŠICE (2)

This Classicism building stands on the western side of Hlavná Street. It was built in 1807 for the count A. Čáki (Csáky). His coat-of-arms with the cut-off head of a Tartar is in the tympanum above the balcony. The second coat-of-arms commemorates another owner of the house, the count Dessewffy. This typical town mansion hosted important personages of the time. The Russian Tsar Alexander I spent a night here on the 19th May 1821 and the Russian Grand Duke Constantine stayed here in the summer 1849. The palace was used by the Východoslovenská Gallery between 1966 and 1990 and it is now the seat of the Constitutional Court.

## SEMINARY CHURCH IN KOŠICE (3)

This Baroque jewel of Košice on the eastern side of Hlavná Street was originally built as a Gothic sacral building in the 15th century. It was then consecrated to St. Nicholas; however the patron of this church, the third largest in the town, is now St. Anthony of Padua. The church was owned by the Franciscan Order. It was built by the mansonry that built the cathedral in Košice. The landmark in the history of the church was a fire in 1556 after which the Franciscans left the church and the Royal Chamber gave it to the army, who used it for the storing of ammunition and as barracks. The Franciscans returned in 1671 and stayed for over a century. A reconstruction after another fire in 1775 resulted in the mostly Baroque appearance of today's church; mainly the front façade was restored in the pure Baroque style. When the cathedral in Košice was under reconstruction, this church took on the function of the Bishop Cathedral. The Seminary Church was visited by Pope John Paul II in 1995. The adjacent building is a Classicism monastery from the 17th century. It was a seminary for the priests until 1950 and gave the church its name.

## ŽUPNÝ HOUSE IN KOŠICE (4)

This Baroque-Classicism building near the Cathedral of St. Elisabeth once served as the seat of the County Council. It was built for the Abovská (Abovsko-Turnianska) County Council in 1779

and served its purpose until 1928. The relief of the coat-of-arms of the council adorns the tympanum in the upper part of the façade. The house was designed by the architect of the Emperor's Court Chamber in Bratislava, J. Langer, as a luxurious and stately town palace. It was rebuilt between 1888 and 1889. The Košický Governmental Program was declared in the representative hall of the Župný House on the 5th April 1945. It now houses the Východoslovenská Gallery of Július Jakoby.

## UNIVERSITY CHURCH IN KOŠICE (5)

The Jesuits built a monastery in Košice in 1654 and opened a Jesuit University in the building three years later. Its existence was confirmed by

the Golden Bull of the Emperor Leopold I. The grandiose edifice with two towers was built between 1671 and 1681 according to the Church of the Gesú in Rome. The town thus received a significant architectonic monument that blends elements of the Renaissance and Baroque styles. The richly decorated interior is mostly Baroque. The University Church is closely associated with famous martyrs of the town; it was built to commemorate them in the 17th century. The ceremonious canonizing of the three men who were murdered where the sacristy was built was carried out by Pope John Paul II on 2nd July 1995, 90 years after the blessing by Pope Pius X.

## DOMINICAN CHURCH AND MONASTERY IN KOŠICE (1)

The oldest sacral monument in Košice is away from the central square in the built-up area on the western side. The Dominican monastery was built around 1290 near the western fortification walls. The smallish Dominikánske Square is a busy market. The church of the monastery has one nave, a presbytery and a slim spire. The oldest element of the building is the large Romanesque nave dating from the oldest development stage of the building. The monastery and the church were damaged by a fire in 1556 to such an extent that the Dominicans left it as uninhabitable. However, they returned during the recatholisation. A Baroque renovation was carried out at the beginning of the 18th century. The present-day appearance of the complex is the result of a Neo Romanesque restoration in 1892. The 68-metre high tower, which is the highest tower in Košice, was added to the church in 1903. Outside the church is a copy of the Baroque Trinity Column from 1721.

## VÝCHODOSLOVENSKÉ MUSEUM IN KOŠICE (2)

The busy pedestrian zone leads onto the Námestie Maratónu Mieru Square at the north. The landmark of the square is the Renaissance Východoslovenské Museum, built between 1896 and 1899. It is one of the oldest and most significant museums in Slovakia. It was established in 1872 before the foundation of the Hornouhorský Muzeálny Spolok (Museum Association of Upper Hungary). The basis of the collections of the museum was a collection of art pieces, books, manuscripts and correspondence left to the museum by I. Henszlmann. There are 450,000 exhibits in the depository of the museum. The most popular exhibit is the famous Košice treasure. It consists of 2,920 gold coins, 3 gold medals and a gold chain over 2 metres long. The treasure was discovered during a reconstruction of the Rákóci Palace on Hlavná Street. The unique collection of golden coins comes from 81 European mints. A wooden church brought from Kožuchovce has adorned the courtyard of the museum since 1927.

## MARATÓNEC (3)

The most popular sporting event in Košice is the famous International Peace Marathon. It is the oldest in Europe and after the Boston Marathon the second oldest in the world. The competitors ran here as early as in 1924. The first winner was K. Halla, representing the then Czechoslovakia. The track record (2:12:35) was achieved by a Polish runner named Dobrzyňski in 2004. Such an important event is the marathon for Košice that its inhabitants built a monument to it on the Námestie Maratónu Square in 1959. The central part of the monument is the 320-centimetre high bronze statue of Maratónec (Marathon Runner), the work of a local sculptor named A. Račka. The statue of the naked runner stands on a granite pedestal with the names of all the past winners of the marathon.

## ČERMEĽSKÉ VALLEY (4)

Inhabitants of Košice enjoy their free time in this valley at the northwest edge of the town. This beautiful forested valley at the east of the Slovenské Rudohorie Mountains is a pleasant recreational zone landscaped as a forest-park. The popular Children's Railway has been operating in the valley since 1956. The rail is 6 km long and connects the suburb of Košice with the popular trip destination called Alpínka. Old narrow-gauge engines and carriages operate on the Children's Railway.

## HRADOVÁ (5)

The medieval ruins at the northern edge of Košice are called Hradová or Košický Castle. Its founder is believed to have been a palatine Omodej, an ally of M. Čáka, who led a war against the King Karol Róbert at the beginning of the 14th century. He tried to control the land from his castle built near the town of Košice, which supported the king. King Róbert gave the castle to his supporters, the Drugethov family, and it later went to the powerful Bebekovci, who squabbled constantly with the inhabitants of Košice. The free royal town of Košice received the castle in 1430, however it did not much care for the castle and left it to dereliction.

## MIKLUŠOVA PRISON (6)

The medieval appearance of this building in the eastern part of the historical centre of Košice attracts attention. It was rebuilt from two aristocratic houses from the 15th century. Originally, both buildings were used for habitation. Later on, a pottery workshop was opened here in the 16th century as well as a town prison with a tor-

ture room at the beginning of the 17th century. King Karol Róbert gave Košice the right to capital punishment, which the city had applied for almost 500 years before. The last execution took place in 1837, when Košice re-organised its jurisdiction and the prison became a part of a newly set town police. It ceased to serve its purpose in 1909 and it now houses the exposition of the Východoslovenské Museum, which documents the life of the inhabitants of Košice from the 13th to the 19th century. There is an interesting exposition underneath the museum associated with the original purpose of the building. Wax figures of the feared headsman Mikluš and his victims illustrate the cruel practices of medieval justice.

## JAKABOV PALACE IN KOŠICE (7)

Those who visit Košice by train or by bus will spot this remarkable house first. The building attracts attention with its romantic appearance inspired by the Gothic style. It was built in 1988 by A. Jakab as his private residence. He used stones left behind from the reconstruction of the Cathedral of St. Elisabeth in Košice. The attractive interior of the house is suitable for official events. President Beneš stayed here temporarily in May 1945.

## MANSION IN BUDIMÍR (1)

Two mansions are preserved on the right bank of the Torysa River in the Village of Budimír. The older is called Malý (Small) Mansion and dates from the 14th century. It houses the Hostinec u Floriána Restaurant. The younger Budimírsky Mansion is more interesting. Its attractive appearance is enhanced by the landscaped French-style garden; it houses a museum. It was built in the second half of the 18th century in the Classicism style, the prevalent architecture of aristocratic houses during the reign of the Empress Maria Theresa. It was owned by several lords, the last being the family of Ujháziov. There is an exhibition of the Východoslovenské Museum of clocks in the rooms furnished by historical furniture, paintings and accessories. Occasional exhibitions and classical concerts take place here as well.

## KOJŠOVSKÁ HOĽA (2)

The burly vault-shaped silhouette of this peak (1,246 m) stands out in the landscape, making it a landmark of the eastern part of the Slovenské Rudohorie Mountains. Its top section is somewhat rugged and it has steep forested slopes. It is formed of schist and sheets. A cable car goes to the top of Kojšovská Hoľa, starting at the springs of the Ida River. It is popular with skiers in the winter. Near the top station is a mountain chalet called Erica. A path from the chalet leads to the peak; a meteorological radiolocation observatory was built here in 1988. There is a panoramic view from the top of the mountain reaching as far as the Tatras Mountains, Košice, Prešov, Ukraine and Hungary.

## IZRA LAKE (3)

This splendid natural lake lies in the thick forested mountain range at the south of Slanské Vrchy Hills almost on the Hungarian border. It is surrounded by oak woods growing on the eastern slope of the Veľký Milič (900 m) Mountain. It was formed when the valley was blocked by a large landslide. An ancient Slavic legend talks about the proud princess Izra who had a castle built from boulders of salt. When Slav fighters came to conquer the castle, which shined like glass, rain helped them significantly, for the mass of melting salt mixed with earth and created a landslide, thus blocking the valley and creating a salt lake. It was named after the Avar princess who drowned in it. We shall not comment on the veracity of the story; however the water in the lake is not salty.

## HERLIANSKY GEYSER (4)

The Herliansky Geyser, located in the former spa town of Herľany at the eastern edge of the Košická Kotlina Hollow, is an attractive tourist destination. It is not a purely natural site, like the geysers in Greenland, as it was created by an artesian bore. The bore was done in the 1970s when a new source of mineral water for the growing spa was sought after. Water with a high gas content gushed out of the bore from a depth of 404.5 metres. Originally, the eruptions were more frequent and stronger; the present-day interval of the geyser is approximately 32 to 34 hours. Approximately 600 hecto-

litres of water gush for about 20 to 30 minutes to a maximum height of 15 metres. Information about this unique natural show is provided by the local post office.

## SLANEC CASTLE (5)

The village of Slanec lies in a strategically important point, in the place where the Slanské Hills descend steeply into a deep saddle, which enables an easy passage between Above and Zemplín and was protected by the medieval Slanec Castle from the 13th century. Apart from the historic path, the castle also guarded stored salt, which gave the name Slaný (Salty) to both the village and the castle. Its first owner was the Abov family, and the Drugeth family, an Italian aristocracy favoured by the King Karol Róbert, procured it in the 14th century. The remarkable cylindrical tower dates from this period. The emperor's army demolished the castle in 1679, for its owners supported the Tököli (Thököly) anti-Habsburg uprising. The Forgáč (Forgách) family, who owned the castle in the 19th century, tried to reconstruct it, copying the Andráši (Andrássy) family, who transformed Krásna Hôrka Castle into a family museum. However, the castle and the Classicism mansion in the village were destroyed during World War II.

## EVANGELIC CHURCH IN SVINICA (6)

Just before the ascent to the Dargovský Priesmyk Pass the road from Košice to Michalovce passes the village of Svinica, with a remarkable high quadrant tower of one of the oldest and best preserved medieval churches in eastern Slovakia. Fragments of medieval frescoes from the 14th and 15th centuries are preserved inside this sacral building from the 13th century, which is a blend of Romanesque and Gothic architecture. The church belonged to the Pauline Order in the Middle Ages; the order also built a monastery in the village. Historical sources from 1335 mention the priest Dominik in connection with the payment of the Pope Tithe. The cemetery that surrounds the church was used as early as in the 12th century; the evidence of this is discovered tombstones and various historical articles. Archaeologists unearthed the remains of a medieval settlement in the village. It had a manor from the 13th century and probably vanished in the 14th century.

## RUŽÍN WATER RESERVOIR (7)

When observed from the rocky peak of the Sivec Mountain in the Čierna Hora Mountains, the Ružín Dam resembles a long white snake coiling on a green carpet of thick forests. It fills a narrow valley of the Hornád River, creating undoubtedly one of the most beautiful sceneries in Slovakia. The dam, constructed between 1963 and 1973, was named after one of the flooded villages. As the dam (46 m high) was built in a narrow chasm, the length of the reservoir is 15 kilometres; the dam also affected the two right side tributaries of the Hornád, the Hnilec and Belá Rivers. The lake takes up 600 hectares and is 50 metres deep at its deepest point. The narrow ribbon of the lake copies the original meander of the Hornád. It coils around the forested hills of Čierna Hora with impressive rocks with numerous caves.

## HAMMER MILL IN MEDZEV (1)

The small town of Medzev was a famous centre of the smelting and iron production. Various tools of excellent quality were exported from Medzev almost throughout the world. They were produced in numerous local smitheries and hammer mills. There were 109 hammer mills and 198 smitheries in 1896. The best times of local iron production are long gone now, but work with iron was not completely finished. Several old hammer mills have been preserved and are protected as Technical Monuments. There is an interesting exposition in the Tischlerov Hammer Mill from the 19th century; it is a part of the Slovakian Technical Museum in Košice.

## JASOVSKÝ MONASTERY (2)

The village of Jasov on the border of the Slovakian Karst and Košická Kotlina Hollow boasts interesting natural and culture monuments. Apart from the Jasovská Cave, hidden in the imposing Jasovská Skala Rock, the Jasovský Monastery is also popular with tourists. The Baroque complex of the Premonstratensian Order is one of the largest architectonic jewels of Slovakia. Premonstratensians came to Jasov in the 12th century, before the Tartar invasion of Hungary. The monastery was repaired in 1255 after being damaged by the Tartars. It became a fortified Gothic castle and underwent significant building reconstruction over the span of the 15th and 17th centuries. After it was demolished in the mid-18th century, a new building was erected on the site. The present-day Baroque monastery with a church and a splendid French-style garden was completed in 1766, after the design of the contemporary prominent architect A. Pilgram. The monastery in Jasov is unique for its architecture, richly decorated interior and a valuable library. The preserved Baroque garden is one of the most beautiful in Slovakia.

## JASOVSKÁ JASKYŇA (5)

This cave located in the bowels of the Jasovská Rock, which looms above the village of Jasov, is accessible to the public. It was created by the underground section of the Bodva River at the northeast edge of the Jasovská Planina Plain. Its corridors, with a total length of 2,811 metres, are on five levels, spanning a height of about 50 metres. The cave was settled by the prehistoric people in the Palaeolithic Era; the locals knew about it at least as early as the early Middle Ages; the oldest known cave inscription in Slovakia from 1452 was discovered inside.

## CHURCH OF THE VIRGIN MARY IN MEDZEV (6)

The small town of Medzev in the southeast part of the Košická Kotlina Hollow is the result of a merger of several villages in 1960 – Nižný Medzev, Vyšný Medzev and Baňa Lucia. Two of the villages regained their independence in 1999 so the present-day Medzev is identical to the former Nižný Medzev. Mining and craft developed intensively in the past here with smelteries and ironworks that processed the local deposits of iron ore. The large Church of the Virgin Mary, in the middle of the well maintained central square, dates from the 15th century. Later Baroque reconstruction did not deprive this originally Gothic building of its ancient and attractive appearance. The inhabitants of the town speak a specific German, the so-called Mantácky dialect.

## ZÁDIELSKA CHASM (7)

The beauty of this chasm is charming; it is undoubtedly one of the most beautiful valleys in Slovakia. An interesting nature trail provides perfect information about it. Its first part climbs up a bizarre limestone chasm, at places 400 metres deep. In the middle, the path goes below a 105-metre high rock needle, appropriately called Cukrová Homoľa (Sugar Loaf). The trail turns right at the upper end of the Zádielska Chasm and climbs to the karst Zádielska Plain. The plateau with karst formations is surrounded by steep slopes that plummet into the chasm on the west side. The view from the eastern side of the valley shows the close relation of the extremely deep shape of the

valley with the microclimatic inversion that conditions the vegetation inversion. The valley has mainly Carpathian vegetation, while its slopes are overgrown by xerophilous Panonian vegetation.

## TURNIANSKY CASTLE (8)

The ruins of the caste are near the village of Turňa nad Bodvou, atop a symmetrical cone-shaped hill. It was built by Ján Turniansky in 1357 on the estate given to his predecessors for merits achieved in the anti-Tartar fights. After the family died out the castle often changed owners and suffered from numerous squabbles between aristocracies. The Ottoman threat started the reconstruction of the castle into a Renaissance fortress. However it was conquered by the Ottomans in 1652 and burnt down together with the settlement below the castle. Its fate was finally sealed when the Emperor's army demolished it during the Tököliho (Thököly) Uprising in 1685. The last inhabitable part of the castle burnt out in 1848.

## HÁJSKE WATERFALLS (3)

The Hájska Dolina Valley in the eastern part of the Slovakian Karst is a twin to the more attractive Zádielská Chasm. It is less popular, however also very interesting and pretty as it boasts unusual natural beauties. There are mineral springs with the Hájsky Creek creating waterfalls. A path climbs the valley to the village of Hačava with preserved folk architecture and splendid surroundings. The area with interesting natural formations is worth a visit.

## ŠTÓS SPA (4)

This spa is located relatively high above the former mining village of Štós on the upper stream of the Bodva River in the midst of the splendid landscape of the Volovské Vrchy Hills. It was founded in 1881 for hydrotherapy upon the initiative of the Štós Hydrotherapy Association, led by a burgher named M. Koporday. It now provides climatic therapy and speleotherapy in the nearby Jasovská Cave.

# ŠARIŠ

## CHURCH OF ST. NICOLAS
## IN PREŠOV (1)

The remarkable Church of St. Nicholas stands in the middle of the central square of Prešov. This parish church of the town is its oldest and largest sacral monument. Only two other churches in Slovakia, the Church of St. James in Levoča and the Cathedral of St. Martin in Bratislava, are larger. The construction works of this grandiose Gothic three-nave building started in the mid-14th century and it was completed in 1515. It underwent several renovations and its present-day appearance is the result of a massive restoration in the Gothic style carried out in 1904. The building has preserved many original Gothic elements, such as the net vaults, windows and portals. The main altar consecrated to the patron of the church is an interesting hybrid of various building styles; it harmonically incorporates elements of the Gothic, Renaissance and Baroque styles. The Gothic sculptures of angels from the beginning of the 16th century are most valuable; they are from the workshop of Master Pavol of Levoča.

## EVANGELIC CHURCH OF THE HOLY
## TRINITY IN PREŠOV (2)

The reformed religion held a very strong position in the Prešov of the 16th century; it had a lot of worshipers, whose church was built and maintained during the time of the Reformation. This was rather unusual in Slovakia, as during the times of the strong anti-Reformation, Evangelists either had older medieval churches or built modest buildings according to the strict rules of the Sopron Regulations of 1681. Moreover, they had to give up brick or stone churches in the period before the reign of Joseph II. The German Evangelists used the now vanished medieval Church of St. Ladislaw in the first half of the 17th

century, which made the Hungarian Evangelists demand their own church. Thus the new Evangelic church, now located in the centre of Prešov, was built next to the German church in 1642. Evangelists lost the church several times, however it was restored to them in 1783 and now serves the Evangelic religion.

## NEPTÚNOVA FOUNTAIN IN PREŠOV (3)

There are no buildings in the southern part of the central spindle-shaped square in Prešov; the most southern edifice is the Church of St. Nicholas. The area is maintained as a small park with the Neptúnova Fountain in the middle. It is the only preserved town water cistern, which provided water for the inhabitants of the town before the town water supply was constructed. There were ten similar cisterns around the town in the past. The sculpture decoration of this originally Renaissance fountain dates from a later period. It was financed by a Jewish trader, M. Holländer, at the beginning of the 19th century out of gratitude for having been granted permission to settle in the town.

## EVANGELIC COLLEGIUM
## IN PREŠOV (4)

Apart from two sacral and one secular building, there is also the former Evangelic Collegium on the central square in Prešov. This originally Renaissance edifice from the second half of the 17th century received its Classicism appearance during later reconstructions. It is an important site of the cultural history of the town. It was the seat of the famous collegium, a type of a higher school, founded in 1667 and it was influenced by the humanism of the Reformation Movement. Thanks to the collegium Prešov became an important cultural and educational centre with an appropriate nickname, 'Athens above Torysa'. Numerous fa-

mous personages studied here: J. M. Korabinský, M. M. Hodža, J. Botto, J. Francisci, L. Kossúth, J. Záborský, P. O. Hviezdoslav a J. Jesenský. The building of the former collegium is now the seat of the Bishopric Office of the Eastern District of the Evangelic Religion of the Augsburg Confession in Slovakia.

## MONUMENT TO VICTIMS OF THE
## CARAFFA'S BLOODY JUDGEMENT
## IN PREŠOV (5)

Prešov was an important bastion of reformed religions in Hungary in the 17th century and the centre of attention of the leaders of the estate anti-Hapsburg uprisings. Thus the town stood up to several attacks by the Emperor's army. The Tököli Uprising in 1687 had particularly cruel consequences. The hated emperor's general, A. Caraffa, imposed tough economic sanctions on the town and dealt with the rebels in an extremely cruel way. He held a court that sentenced 24 aristocrats and burghers of Prešov to death. This tragic event entered the Slovakian history as the 'Prešov Slaughter'. A monument to the victims of 'Craffa's Bloody Judgement' was placed on the northwest façade of the former Evangelic collegium in 1909. It bears the names of the beheaded men.

## SCULPTURE OF IMMACULATA
## IN PREŠOV (6)

The Baroque sculpture of Immaculata stands in the northern section of the central square. The 24 aristocrats and burghers of the town sentenced by the 'Caraffa's Bloody Judgement' were beheaded in this place in 1687. The construction of the Immaculata was initialised by the Jesuits in an effort to uproot the tradition of the veneration of the Protestant martyrs by the Marian symbolism.

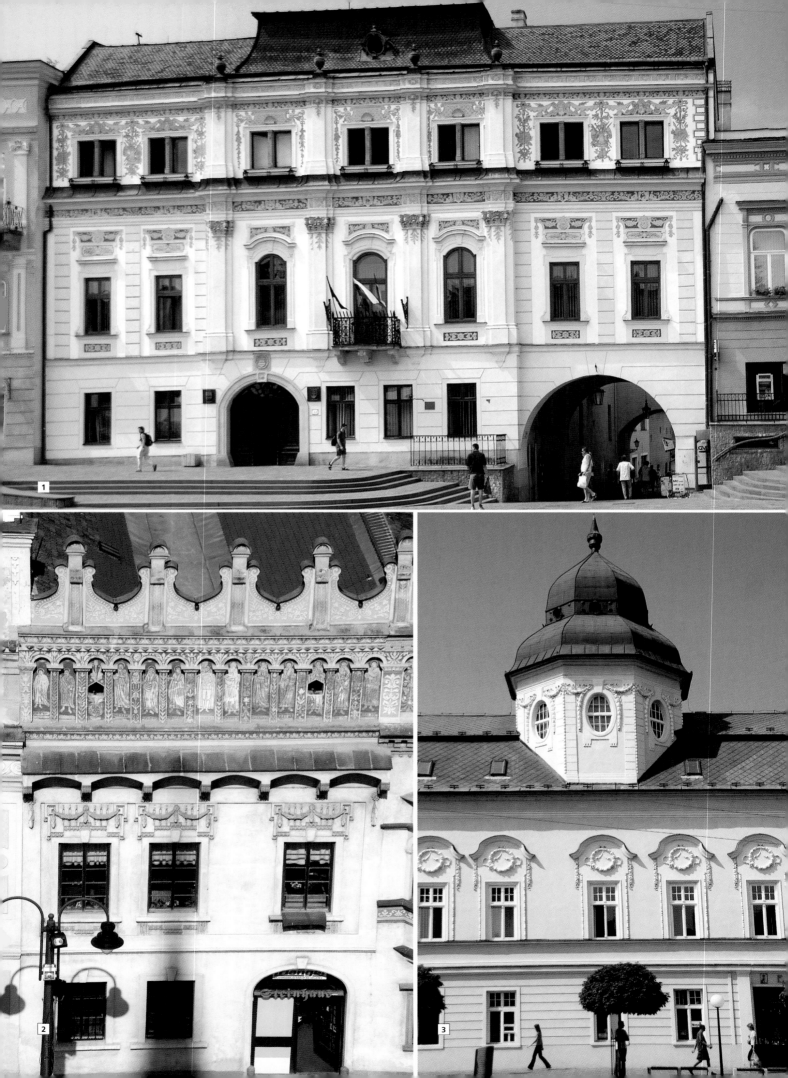

## TOWN HALL IN PREŠOV (1)

The town hall in Prešov is part of the built-up area in the west side of the central spindle-shaped square. There is a passage to the right part of the building that leads onto the side Floriánska Street. The building dates from 1520. Its original purpose was a town winery that was opened here for two centuries. The old town hall was originally on the square south of the Church of St. Nicholas. After the town council demolished it in the 17th century, it moved into the present-day building; it still resides here. The building received a Baroque appearance in the 18th century; it was partially altered during the last large reconstruction after a fire in 1887. Its dominant architectonic feature is the balcony. The *Slovenská Republika Rád* (Slovakian Republic of Councils) was declared from the balcony on 16th June 1919; it was a very short-lived communistic state based on the Russian Bolshevik Revolution. The entry from Floriánska Street leads into a small Wine Museum that built up on the old tradition. The exposition reminds us that the wealth and fame of the medieval Prešov came from the successful wine trade.

## RÁKOCIHO PALACE IN PREŠOV (2)

This building is on the eastern side of Hlavná Street and is a valuable architectonic monument; moreover it has an interesting history. A count of Transylvania called Žigmung Ráko-ci (Rákoczi) bought two medieval houses towards the end of the 16th century with a vision to rebuilt them into a luxurious town mansion with a splendid Renaissance faćade.

The original Renaissance graffiti decoration with floral motifs was restored during the reconstruction between 1951 and 1955. The history of the house is closely associated with the powerful Rákoczi family. Long negotiations between the representatives of Juraj I Rákoci and the Emperor Ferdinand II of Habsburg were held in the building in 1633, resulting in the Prešov Truce. Francis II Rákoczi, the leader of the anti-Habsburg uprising, was imprisoned in the palace in 1707. Presently it houses the Regional Museum in Prešov with rich ethnographic collections.

## GREEK-CATHOLIC BISHOP'S PALACE IN PREŠOV (3)

The Bishop's Palace is connected with the Greek-Catholic cathedral by a corridor with preserved Renaissance vaults. Originally a medieval hospice and alms-house stood on this site; it was rebuilt into a monastery by the Order of Franciscan Minorites. The army of Tököli expelled the monks from the town in 1682, however they returned four years later and soon started building a new monastery. As many others, the Order of Minorites was abolished, despite interventions by the Bishop of Jager with the Emperor Joseph II. The former building of the monastery was given to the Greek-Catholic Church in 1791. The worshipers of this religion were badly persecuted in 1950.

## ROMAN-CATHOLIC PARISH OF ST. NICHOLAS IN PREŠOV (4)

The building of the Roman-Catholic Parish of St. Nicholas on the west side of Hlavná Street

near the Church of St. Nicolas attracts attention. It was built at the beginning of the 17th century and later reconstructed several times. The white Rococo stucco ornaments stands out beautifully on the white plaster of the faćade. The typical sign of the Holy Trinity, God's eye in a triangle, stands out in the upper part. There is a relief portrait of the patron of the parish, St. Nicholas the Bishop, on the level of the first story.

## GREEK-CATHOLIC CATHEDRAL CHURCH OF ST. JOHN THE BAPTIST IN PREŠOV (5)

This cathedral church on Hlavná Street in Prešov witnessed a long and unsettled history. A town hospice with a Carmelite church was built on this site in 1429. The church went to the Slovakian Evangelists at the beginning of the Reformation Movement in the first half of the 17th century; however they lost it in 1673 when the building was given to the monks of the Minorites Order upon an order of the Emperor Leopold I. Both buildings were radically rebuilt in the Baroque style in 1754. The interior of the church was adorned with beautiful Rococo frescoes. It became a Greek-Catholic church in 1818 and was elevated to the cathedral church in relation with the establishment of the Greek-Catholic bishopric in Prešov in 1881. There are valuable relics in the cathedral next to the bishop's seat. A copy of the famous Turin Canvass was placed here on 17th November 2003. There are only four of these in the world – in Prešov, Turin, Jerusalem and Vilnius.

## BOSÁKOVA BANK (1)

This building at the northern edge of the historical centre of Prešov is a nice example of the Art Nouveau style. It was built between 1923 and 1924 and received its name after M. Bosák (1869-1937), a native of the nearby Okrúhle, who immigrated to the USA towards the end of the 19th century, where he worked his way up, becoming a prominent banker. His importance in the financial world is proved by the fact that his signature is on the ten-dollar note. He opened one of the branches of his America-Slovakian Bank in this building. It has remarkable roofed corner domes and a decorated faćade. It is adorned with sculptures symbolising the four seasons; other statues represent peace, abundance, charity and science.

## ORTHODOX CATHEDRAL
## CHURCH OF ST. ALEXANDER NEVSKY IN PREŠOV (2)

This Orthodox cathedral stands south of the centre of Prešov. The building, with impressive onion-shaped towers, was consecrated in 1950 and was to support the cathedral on Hlavná Street, which was taken from the Orthodox worshipers by the state force. It later became the cathedral church of the Orthodox religion in Czechoslovakia in 1969. It was reconstructed and enlarged in 2004 and a ceremonious consecration in the presence of the Washington Archbishop Herman, the Metropolita of Canada and the USA, followed. The relics of St. Alexej, the native of the Šariš Region and a great defender of the Orthodox religion in America, were placed in the church on this occasion. A monument to the victims of the famine in the Ukraine between 1932 and 1933 was unveiled in the church in 2006. At the same time, relics of the Archbishop Nikolaj, the Metropolita of the Orthodox Church in the Czech Republic and Slovakia, were placed in the church.

## CALVARY IN PREŠOV (3)

The Stations of the Cross are set in a nice place above the Torysa River on the western edge of the town on the side slope of the Šarišská Vrchovina Hills, and the site is a popular destination of the inhabitants of the town. The view of Prešov from the platform outside the church

is fascinating. The origins of the Calvary are narrowly connected with the Jesuits of Prešov; they fitted perfectly the recatholisation efforts of the strongly Protestant Prešov. The construction work started in 1720 and it was completed in 1769; however some stations were built in the 19th century. The whole complex of the Calvary consists of the Church of the Holy Cross, fourteen stations, the Chapel of the Holy Stairs, a catacomb and a cemetery. It is a very nice art piece that is rightfully considered the most beautiful Calvary in Slovakia (after the Calvary in Banska Štiavnica). The architectonic synthesis of the complex is enhanced by the red-coloured facades and roofs, which create a pleasant symbiosis with the surrounding greenery.

## CARAFFA'S PRISON IN PREŠOV (4)

The medieval appearance of the building behind the town hall on Floriánska Street differs significantly from the rest of the buildings. It is called Caraffa's Prison and is one of the few preserved Gothic monuments in the town. It was built in 1509 on the land of a councillor named P. Moler. Initially, it was used for the storing of wine barrels belonging to the town winery located in the next building (the present-day town hall). The ancient building received the name of the general A. Carraffa (1642-1693), who was behind the tragic 'Prešov Slaughter' and led the cruel court proceedings with the members of the Tököli Uprising in 1687. Paradoxically, despite the building being called a prison, Carraffa's victims were never held here. The interrogations and torture took place in the basement of the adjacent town hall and the prison was opened here much later, in the second half of the 19th century. Originally it was used for the storing of town measurements and weights and, for some time, it housed the town armoury.

## FRANCISCAN CHURCH AND MONASTERY IN PREŠOV (5)

The Carmelite Order arrived in Prešov in 1380 and built a church with a small monastery near the western fortification walls. The monks left the monastery during the Reformation in the 17th century and the Emperor Leopold I gave the monastery to the Franciscan Order from Nižná Šebestová in 1661. The architecture of the church consecrated to St. Joseph copied the Church of the Gesú in Rome. Further reconstructions at the beginning of the 18th century also affected the monastery, enhancing the Baroque architecture of the entire complex. The Altar of God's Heart in one of the side chapels in the interior of the church is noteworthy. It depicts an emblem associated with a legend about a stork and gold. During a hunt a flying stork dropped a piece of gold into the bosom of baron F. Klobušický. The count believed this to be a call for him to become the patron of the Franciscan Order.

## TOWN WALLS IN PREŠOV (6)

In the past Prešov earned its wealth by wine and salt trade and therefore needed the protection of solid fortifications. The town received the right to build town walls in 1374 from King Ľudovít I and the defence system was completed before the arrival of the Hussites in the first half of the 15th century. The quality of the walls was tested by the armies of the estate uprisings in the 16th century, while the Ottoman army never reached the fortification. Only fragments are preserved, as the defence system was demolished on the order of Maria Theresa in the last third of the 18th century. The solely preserved Floriánska Gate from the 15th century is west of the historical centre of the town. The Vodná Bastion from the 16th century stands in the northwest corner of the walls. It is also known as Kumšt, which is associated with its function as the town water works. It was furnished with ingenious hydraulic equipment for pumping water from the water moat; it functioned for almost 500 years. The Kováčska Bastion can be admired in the northern twist of the walls. The most preserved strip of walls is east of the historical centre; a path called Kmeťovo Stromoradie skirts this part of the walls.

## SOLIVAR (7)

Salt springs already existed at the foothills of the Slanské Vrchy Hills in the Middle Ages. The first salt was derived from the springs, however salt mining started here in 1572. German colonists, who were invited to do the work, founded a settlement called Soľná Baňa, which soon became the village of Solivar (it is now a quarter of Prešov). A new technology was required after the underground corridors of the mine were flooded in 1752. Soľná Baňa turned into an underground salt lake which required the application of until then unused technology. Salty water was pumped in leather bags by a horse or bull propelled pump, called 'gápeľ'. One of these historical pumps is above the Leopold Tunnel from the 19th century and it is accessible to the public. A salt storage room, a boiling room called František, water storages (čeretne), a clapper and the Chapel of St. Roch are also preserved. Salt water is now mined from bores situated on a hill east of Solivar. The present-day production capacity is almost 100,000 tons of salt per year.

## WOODEN CHURCH IN BREŽANY (1)

The wooden church in Brežany is separated from the largest concentration of the wooden sacral buildings in northeast Slovakia. Brežany is a small village in the Šarišská Vrchovina Hills northwest of Prešov. The church belongs to the Greek-Catholic religion and is consecrated to St. Lucas the Evangelist. It was built in 1727 on a small slope above the village in the middle of a cemetery. Its exterior and internal composition differ form other churches of the eastern religion. Its builders were probably inspired by a similar church in Trnové near Žilina. A wooden construction from spruce and fir wood was erected on a stone foundation wall. The church has a high shingle roof and a detached tower at its western side. The interior from the mid-18th century houses an iconostasis from 1782.

## ŠARIŠSKÝ CASTLE (2)

Despite being a ruin, this castle is still impressive due to its size. It was once one of the largest and most powerful castles in Hungary. Its size is documented by huge ruins and old paintings of the castle. It was built in the 13th century atop a volcanic hill, which, in contrast with other isolated hills around Prešov, has a plateau on the top. This predestined the hill to become the castle hill. Šarišský Castle was first a royal possession and a temporary seat of the ruler; however it was given as a permanent present to the Peréňi (Perény) family in the 15th century and as this family was the head of the county council, it became the seat of the council. However, the family took the 'wrong side' during the Battle at Moháč in 1526. In the fight over the Hungarian crown they supported J. Zápoľský, thus making their castle a target of the army of the Emperor Ferdinand. After it was conquered, the castle received a new owner. In 1660 during the time when it was owned by the Rákoczi family, a sudden gunpowder explosion blew up the building. Since then the castle has been a large ruin that offers splendid views of the picturesque landscape of the Šariš Region.

## KAPUŠIANSKY CASTLE (3)

The lords of this castle controlled the wide surroundings, as the view from the Zámčisko rock point at the eastern end of the volcanic range is far reaching. The castle was built on the site of an older building between 1410 and 1420, and it is a nice example of Gothic architecture. A Romanesque castle that once stood here was demolished after a battle near Rozhanovce in 1312 on the order of the King Karol Róbert. The first owner of the restored Kapušiansky Castle was Andrej de Koka; his ancestors acquired the name Kapyov. There were frequent fights over the castle and its defence was sometimes successful and sometimes not. The castle did not withstand the attack of the Bratríci movement, yet a bit later managed to hold up the army of the King Matthias Corvinus, and was finally conquered during the estate uprising by the army of Tököli and Rákoci rebels. It was demolished in 1709 and its fate was definitively sealed six years later when the County Council decided to demolish it.

## STRÁŽE (4)

Several isolated volcano-like hills jut out of the landscape around Prešov. The group of hills, which lies at the southeast part of the area between the Spiš and Šariš mountain ranges, is called Stráže and has, in fact, volcanic origins. The hills are formed by volcanic rocks produced by now extinct volcanoes of the Tertiary Era. Their activities ended millions of years ago and the rocks were consequently eroded by wind, water and other natural forces. The soft rock eroded away, leaving the persistent andesites that shaped the sharp hills. The hills that guard the landscape of the lower Šariš create a chain with the ruins of medieval castles on their tops.

Šarišský Castle lies at the west, while the opposite end is guarded by Kapušiansky Castle. In the middle of the chain are two huge conical hills; when looking from Prešov, Lysá Stráž (696 m) is to the left while to the right is the slightly higher Stráž Hill (740 m). Tourist trails lead to all four main hills.

## MONUMENT NEAR HANISKA (5)

The Furča hill above the village of Haniska near Prešov was once a battle site. One of the largest battles between the rebellious farmers and the army took place here during the memorable Farmer Uprising of Eastern Slovakia in 1831. The moment was erected in 1938.

## DUBNICKÉ OPAL MINES (6)

Dubnické opals are highly appreciated on international markets for their unique character. They are remarkable for their perfect colouring, the so-called opalescence. They come from the world-renowned site between the villages of Zlatá Baňa and Červenica in the Slanské Vrchy Hills near Prešov. The peak period of the opal mines was between 1845 and 1880 when a Viennese jeweller, S. Goldschmidt, and his descendants were renting the mines out. He managed to introduce the opals to the world markets, which was the cornerstone of their fame. The world's largest opal Harlekýn was exhibited in Vienna. The opal mines were closed down in 1922. A portal of the Josef Tunnel and several side entries into the underground corridors are preserved. A forest path leads to the portal of the Viliam Tunnel. A deposit of opals called Gizelina Chapel was discovered here in 1898; an unbelievable 200 kilograms of the precious stones were mined from this site.

## ŠARIŠSKÉ ROCKS (1)

The landscape south of the Čergov Mountains is unusually nice and picturesque. It owes its attractiveness to sharp limestone rocks which make the monotonous flysch landscape of the Spiš-Šariš area more interesting. The narrow strip of Šarišské Rocks is part of the rocks, which are the longest geological unit on the territory of Slovakia. They sprawl from the Záhorie Region at the west to Podhoroď on the border with Ukraine. The bizarre rocky peaks from Mesozoic limestone adorn the surroundings of the Šarišské Jastrabie and continue past Kyjov to

Kamenica; the ruins of Kamenický Castle loom atop one of the highest rocks here.

## NÁMESTIE SLOBODY SQUARE IN SABINOV (2)

Sabinov, which was once a free royal town, now boasts a compact historical core bounded by the remains of the medieval town fortification. The spindle-shaped Námestie Slobody Square is surrounded by old burgher houses. The landmark of the square is the parish Church of the Beheading of St. John the Baptist from the beginning of the 14th century. This original-

ly Gothic edifice received some Renaissance features during later reconstructions and was restored in the New Gothic style towards the end of the 19th century. The Renaissance reconstruction of the tower (1537-1557) is believed to have been carried out by a builder named Vincent of Dubrovnik. Copies of the original medieval paintings of the interior of the church are stored in Budapest. However, several valuable Gothic sculptures from the workshop of Master Pavol of Levoča have been preserved. Next to the parish church is the former Renaissance Evangelic lyceum from 1530. It was reconstructed for the requirements of the Piarist grammar school during the recatholisation.

## KAMENICKÝ CASTLE (3)

It is worthwhile to climb the steep hill above the village of Kamenica, although there is not much left of Kamenický Castle. However, the hardly visible ruins are set into an unusually pleasant landscape with numerous sharp limestone rocks. One of them is the hill with the castle, which was built in the 13th century in the royal hunting area. Its founder is believed to have been D. Tarczay, and his descendants owned the castle up to the 16th century. The last owner, A. Tarczay-Drugeth, participated in the movement against the Emperor Ferdinand I of Habsburg, so the castle was conquered and destroyed.

## MINČOL (4)

The Čergov Mountains are formed of flysch rocks and appear to be a massive wall. This compact mountain range is surrounded by steep slopes with wide and rather flat mountain ridges in its centre. The entire mountain massif culminates at the northeast where the Minčol Hill (1,157 m) juts out gently. The mountain meadows in the top area are part of the Čergovský Minčol National Nature Reserve. The lower sections of Minčol are overgrown with fir and oak forests. The view from the top is restricted. To see a panoramic view, tourists must descend lower to the hill with a cross.

## PLAVEČ CASTLE (5)

With regards to the historical border, the village of Plaveč belongs to Šariš, although it is now part of the Stará Ľubovňa district. Plaveč Castle was built towards the end of the 13th century as a sentry fortress on the border of Hungary and Poland. However, judging by the name it is not impossible that the castle is older, as some historians put the name in connection with the tribe of Plavci, known as guardians of the borders. Hungarian rulers placed them along the borders and rewarded them with various privileges during the 11th and 12th centuries. So perhaps Plavci built a stone sentry tower on the hilltop at this time. Plaveč got into the hands of the Horváth family in 1505, who later rebuilt it in the Renaissance style. Their descendant, Ferdinand, transformed the medieval castle into a luxurious aristocratic seat in the 17th century. The castle survived the estate uprising unscratched, however his fate was sealed by a fire in 1856, which destroyed it to such an extent that it was not worthy of repairs.

## MANSION IN FRIČOVCE (6)

This mansion was built between 1626 and 1630 for the aristocratic Berthoti family. The construction took a rather long time, for the builders were very focused on the quality of the building. The result was charming; the mansion with a rectangular ground-plan is complemented by a couple of square corner towers, and its front façade is topped by Renaissance attics. The mansion is unique thanks to the breathtaking graffiti decoration in a strip above the attic. Master M. Waxmann created a valuable artistic work here, which can be compared with a gallery. Graffiti depict various mythological and historical figures. Apart from antique gods, there is the Hussite leader Jan Žižka and others. The castle went to the Ghilláň family by a marriage in 1760; they carried out a large rebuilding in 1840, mainly in the interior.

## LAČNOVSKÝ CANYON (7)

The Lačnovský Creek springs in the flysch mountain range called Bachureň; however below the interesting village of Lačnov it flows onto the territory of the limestone massif, which is part of the Branisko Mountains. The different geological form remarkably changes the appearance of the valley. The large amphitheatre becomes a narrow chasm with scores of limestone rocks. The valley is erroneously called Lačnovský Canyon, as it would have to have a much wider bottom to qualify as a canyon. It would be better to call it Lačnovská Chasm. The Lačnovský Creek flows over rocky steps through this approximately 2-kilometre long chasm, creating nine smaller waterfalls. The slopes of the valley are dotted with bizarre rocks. The highest is the 60-metre high Mojžišov Stĺp Rock. The Kamenná Baba (Stone Crone) formation is to be seen in the Červené Rocks. According to a legend a nasty step-mother was turned to stone here.

## WOODEN CHURCH IN HERVARTOV (1)

The wooden church in the village of Hervartov at the northeast foothills of Čergov Mountains is the oldest in Slovakia. It was built as early as in the second half of the 15th century. It is rather different from the other wooden churches around Bardejov and Svidník. Its specific feature is that it belongs to the Roman-Catholic Church and is consecrated to St. Francis of Assisi. This makes its architecture as well as liturgy different from the Greek-Catholic and Orthodox churches. It has a two-part disposition, a nave and a presbytery, as well as a small sacristy and the ground floor area of the huge conical tower. The interior corresponds with the Roman-Catholic religion. Therefore there is no iconostas but rather a main altar with valuable Gothic paintings from the second half of the 15th century. The desk painting of the Last Supper from 1653 is also of high value. The original paintings by a painter named A. Haffčík from Bardejov, who also decorated the southern wall of the nave, were restored in 1970.

## WOODEN CHURCH IN LUKOV (2)

The peculiar name of this settlement, Venécia, which is a part of the village of Lukov at the northern foothills of the Čergov Mountains, is connected with Italian glassmakers who worked here in the past. The wooden church built on a rather steep slope above the village is one of the most beautiful and largest in Slovakia. Its attractive appearance was enhanced by a successful recent reconstruction. This particular and greatly impressive church consecrated to St. Cosmas and Damian was built between 1708 and 1709. It represents the transition of the architectonic church development, from the older more centralised churches to the newer sacral buildings with prolonged axis. A huge tower and three-story shingle roof are the landmarks of the exterior. The iconostasis is decorated by scores of icons mainly from the 18th century and by the gold plated richly carved 'tsar' door. The most valuable icon, the Last Judgement, from the end of the 16th century, is amongst the icons on the northern side of the nave.

## WOODEN CHURCH IN FRIČKA (3)

The village of Frička lies in a remote part of the upper Šariš area near the Polish border. The local wooden Church of St. Michael the Archangel stands in the centre of the village. Its present-day appearance dates from the beginning of the 19th century and it was rebuilt a couple of times. It is the most western sacral building of the so-called 'Lemkovský' type (Lemka is the Polish name for the Ruthenians). The church has a square sacristy, a square nave and the so-called 'babinec', the area designated for women. A huge tower occupies the west side of the church. One of the bells in the tower bears the date 1697. There are two unevenly sized small towers on the saddle shingle roof. The iconostasis has icons from the 19th century. The oldest (of St. Nicholas) was painted in 1830. The icon of the Protection of Mother of Jesus in the northern side of the nave dates from the end of the 18th century.

## WOODEN CHURCH IN KRIVÉ (4)

This wooden Church of St. Lucas the Evangelist was built in the village of Krivé near Bardejov in 1826 on the site of an older building. The church lies at the edge of the village in the cemetery. The external appearance of this Greek-Catholic church is rather specific. Its tower is disproportionately small compared to its rather large nave covered by shingle saddle roof. The modest exterior contrasts with the richly decorated interior. The iconostases from the 18th century are older than the church.

## WOODEN CHURCH IN JEDLINKA (5)

The road between Bardejov and Svidník goes by the small village of Jedlinka. The wooden Church of the Protection of the Holy Mother of God is visible from the road. The church belongs to the Greek-Catholic religion and was built in the middle of the village in 1763. Allegedly, it was brought from Poland. Its architecture corresponds with the so-called 'Lemkovsky' type of the wooden churches consisting of three parts. It is interesting however, that the 'babinec' (section for women only) of this church is the same size as the nave. The shingle roof and three differently sized towers also copy the three parts of the building. The

interior boasts a jewel, one of the most beautiful and most valuable Rococo iconostases in Slovakia from the second half of the 18th century. The oldest icons on the iconostasis date from 1715. The rarity of the church is service prayer books from the 17th century printed in the Cyrillic alphabet in Ľvov and bound in leather.

## WOODEN CHURCH IN KOŽANY (6)

The village of Kožany lies in the Ondavská Vrchovina Hills near the divide of the Topľa and Ondava rivers. It is worthwhile to visit this rather remote village to see the splendid wooden Church of the Meeting of the Lord with Simeon. Built towards the end of the 17th century, this rare building is one of the oldest in the northeast of Slovakia. It has a typical composition with the three parts of different sizes, starting with the highest 'babinec' to the sacristy. There are three bells in the tower, one of them from the Gothic period from 1406. Such a bell is unique in wooden churches of the Eastern religion. The interior of the church has remarkable and unique paintings and an especially valuable iconostasis richly decorated with Baroque carvings. It is probably from an older church from the 17th century.

## WOODEN CHURCH IN TROČANY (7)

To a layman the traditional churches of the Eastern Orthodox religion with three parts can seem to be very similar. However, the wooden Church of St. Lucas the Evangelist in Tročany is unmistakable for its specific appearance. Its typical sign is the pyramid-like tower finished off by a small conical spire. It stands at the cemetery in the middle of the village. An older church stood here in 1338 and another sacral edifice was built here later, so the present-day church from 1739 is the third one in the row. Its typical disposition with a wider nave stands on a cross-shaped ground-plan. There are icons from the 16th and 17th centuries. The icon depicting the patron of the church is from 1638, while the icon of the Crucifying at the top of the iconostasis is older by four years. The rarity of the church is a collection of service books from the 17th and 18th centuries, printed in the Cyrillic alphabet in Ľvov.

## RADNIČNÉ SQUARE
## IN BARDEJOV (1)

Bardejov is considered the most Gothic town in Slovakia. Yet, despite this 'medieval status', its historical core has a regular rectangular network of streets. The central Radničné Square also has a strictly geometrical ground-plan. This area of special historical and architectonical value has recently undergone a successful reconstruction. Its quality was rightfully appreciated by a prestigious European award in 1986: the Golden Medal of the ICOMOS Foundation by UNESCO. The historical Bardejov with its splendid Radničné Square is part of the UNESCO World Cultural Heritage List. The rectangular square has historical paving and boasts uninterrupted rows of ancient burgher houses with typical gable facades and arcades. The two most important buildings in the town, the Church of St. Egid and the historical town hall, are in the northern part of the square, while the southwestern section boasts a burgher house with massive arcades and graffiti-decorated facades. It houses an exposition of the Šarišské Museum that focuses on the landscape of northeastern Slovakia. The entry into the museum is from Rhódyho Street. The square is a pleasant as well as interesting sight.

## CHURCH OF ST. EGID
## IN BARDEJOV (2)

This grandiose church on the Randičné Square is the highest building in Bardejov and rates among the most remarkable Gothic monuments in Slovakia; it was designated a National Culture Monument in 1970. The construction works started at the beginning of the 15th century and it was probably erected on the site of an older Cistercian monastery. The church was built as a grandiose Gothic three-nave basilica and was finally completed by the construction of the vault of the main nave between 1513-1518. The Neo Gothic tower at the southwest corner of the church is 76 metres high. It has three bells on the fourth floor; the oldest is called Signum and dates from 1625. The terrace on the sixth floor is accessible to the public and offers nice views. The church has one of the most precious Gothic interiors in central Europe. It has a collection of 11 Late Gothic winged altars from between 1460 and 1520. The side altar of the Birth of Our Lord is considered the most significant; it is attributed to the royal workshop of Vít Štoss in Nuremberg. The Stolica Milosti (Seat of Mercy) sculpture on the Altar of St. Barbara was probably made in the workshop of Master Pavol of Levoča and is considered the peak woodcarving art piece in Slovakia;

it received great attention from experts as well as laymat at exhibitions held throughout the world.

## TOWN HALL IN BARDEJOV (3)

The splendid solitary building of the former town hall in the middle of the Radničné Square in Bardejov is an architectonic jewel that represents a symbiosis of the elements of the ending Gothic and starting Early Renaissance styles. It was built as one of the first buildings influenced by the Renaissance style, brought from beyond the Alps, in Slovakia between 1505 and 1511. The entire building is a valuable complex, however its numerous details – portals, Italian windows, a staircase, decorated gables and original murals – are especially precious. The building no longer serves its original purpose; it houses the valuable collections of the Šarišské Museum. There is an exposition about the history of Bardejov, mainly focusing on the golden period of the 15th and 16th centuries. The most valuable exhibits are the Altar of St. Nicholas from 1524, the Malá Kalvária (Small Calvary) sculpture by Master Pavol of Levoča from 1520, a valuable goblet by the goldsmith J. Siláši of Levoča from the 18th century, and a ring with jewels of Queen Elisabeth.

## GANTZUGHOF BURGHER HOUSE IN BARDEJOV (1)

One of the most valuable houses in Bardejov stands on the corner of the Radničné Square and Poštová Street. It is called Gantzughof and was built in the Gothic style and reconstructed in the Renaissance style in 1566. Several architectonic features are preserved from this period: the arcade, the painted wooden coffered ceiling in the Council Hall, portals, decorated gables and the staircase in the bay window. The façade of the building received a very impressive Rococo reconstruction in 1778. The building is now used by the Šarišské Museum, presenting a collection of icons. It has a complete Rococo iconostasis from 1766 from a wooden church that once was in the village of Zboj; it was moved to the open-air museum in Bardejovské Kúpele.

## TOWN FORTIFICATION IN BARDEJOV (2)

The historical centre of Bardejov has a regular network of streets and squares; however this cannot be said about its outskirts. A ring of town walls with a pear-shaped ground-plan has surrounded the town since the Middle Ages. It is the best preserved medieval fortification system in Slovakia. Apart from the walls, there are two gates with a barbican and nine bastions preserved. The Horná Gate with a stone bridge leads into the historical core from the south, while the northeast corner of the walls is guarded by the Dolná Gate with a barbican. In the eastern walls are the Veľká Bastion and Hrubá Bastion, and the Archívna Bastion stands in the park outside the northern walls. A square bastion is incorporated into the defence complex of the Horná Gate. The construction of the fortification walls started in the 14th century. The oldest written records about it date from 1352. The medieval walls were strengthened with new bastions in the 16th century.

## GOTHIC BURGHER HOUSE ON RADNIČNÉ SQUARE IN BARDEJOV (3)

The most interesting façade in the short southern row of houses on Radničné Square belongs to a burgher house, No. 26. The façade was adorned with splendid figural paintings and Rococo decoration in 1770. Other architectonic features show much older origins of the house. The windows suggest its once Renaissance appearance and the entry portal implies its medieval history at the time when Bardejov was a Gothic town.

## FRANCISCAN CHURCH AND MONASTERY IN BARDEJOV (4)

The medieval monastery of the Franciscan Order stands at the southwestern edge of the historical centre of Bardejov. A street called Ulica Františkánov leads to it from the Radničné Square. Data about its origins differ. Most often it is stated to have been founded in 1460. According to some sources, the Augustinians, who settled here before the Franciscans, built their monastery less then 100 years earlier. The Franciscan Church of St. John the Baptist is a Gothic monument although it received some Renaissance restorations. The Franciscans had a new vault built in their church and enlarged both the church and the monastery in 1685. The cloister with an interesting Renaissance cross vault dates from this period.

## HUMANISTIC GRAMMAR SCHOOL IN BARDEJOV (5)

Behind the Church of St. Egid in Bardejov is a remarkable historical edifice. It was probably built in the Middle Ages and, according to an archived document from 1435, it housed a parish school. It received a Renaissance appearance in 1538 and was rebuilt in the Classicism style in the 19th century. This fine building is noteworthy, as it once housed a humanistic school, which was the centre of culture and education with its influence reaching beyond the borders of the town and country in the 16th century. This institution was famous at its time. Renowned contemporary scholars worked in the school, for instance, a native of Bardejov named Leonard Stöckel, who was a pupil of and great admirer of Martin Luther. He was called the 'Hungarian Teacher'. The building now houses a music school.

## BARDEJOVSKÉ SPA (1)

This spa is an administrative part of Bardejov and lies less then 5 kilometres from its centre. The spa, located in the splendid natural environment at the edge of the Busov Mountains, was founded near 17 mineral springs. A record about the healing springs near Bardejov dates from 1247; it is written in a deed of the Hungarian King Bela IV. The first mostly wooden spa pavilions were built towards the 18th century and a brick inn was built near the springs by the Armenian traders at the end of the 18th century. The largest boom of the spa was during the 19th century. The contemporary, exclusive clientele proves the high quality and prestige of the spa. The most famous guest that underwent therapy in the spa was the Austrian Empress Elisabeth of Austria, the famous Sisi. The present-day spa has a collection of old and modern buildings situated in the oldest spa garden in Slovakia. The oldest building is the Astória Pavilion with elements of the Art Nouveau style. The busiest area of the spa is the modern spa colonnade. Bardejovské Kúpele specialises in the healing of the digestion system, unspecified respiratory diseases and occupational diseases. There is also a ski slope and a lift. The popularity of the spa is also enhanced by its well-maintained forest park.

## OPEN-AIR MUSEUM IN BARDEJOVSKÉ KÚPELE (2)

This museum in Bardejovské Kúpele was opened to the public in 1956 as the first open-air museum of folk architecture in Slovakia. The complex, which is on 1.5 hectares, includes 24 valuable buildings from the upper Šariš and upper Zemplín regions. The buildings represent the vernacular culture of the lifestyle of Slovakian and Ruthenian ethnic groups of these regions. There are log-built cabins, outbuildings and technical buildings. The sacral peasant architecture is represented by two churches. The first is the wooden Church of St. Nicholas (1775) that once stood in the village of Zboj, which represents the churches of the East Religion of the so-called 'lemkovské' types (Ruthenian style with several towers). The second church, also wooden, comes from the village of Mikulášov and stands outside the museum.

## MANSION IN HERTNÍK (3)

This Renaissance 16th-century mansion is in the village of Hertník at the eastern foothills of the Čergovo Mountains. The original building on this site was a small medieval castle, possibly built by the leader of the Bratríci Movement, Jan Jiskra of Brandýs. Allegedly, it belonged to the captain of the movement, J. Talafúz, and was a strategic point on the route between Prešov and Bardejov. The present-day mansion was built around 1563 when the local estate belonged to the rich Forgáč family of Gýmeš Castle near Nitra. The mansion was built as a stronghold with a rectangular ground-plan and four towers. Part of its original defence system was a water moat and a wall with bastions. According to a legend, a secret corridor led from the mansion to the local church, or perhaps ended at the nearby forest. Š. Forgáč (Forgách) gave the mansion, including the estate, to a German aristocrat, F. Leopold of Anhalt, in 1857. However, the new owner only used the mansion rarely, when hunting in the area.

## ZBOROV CASTLE (4)

A forested hill with a ruin atop looms above the village of Zborov north of Bardejov. It was built in the 13th century to protect the trade path from Bardejov to Poland. The local lords of the castle ruled the entire northern Šariš Region. Zborov remained Gothic until the 16th century when it was rebuilt into a massive Renaissance stronghold by its then owners, the wealthy Šeréď family. The Rácoczi family bought the castle and the estate in 1601, and the castle was to pay for the participation of its owners in the unsuccessful anti-Habsburg uprising in 1684, as the army of the Emperor conquered and demolished it. Moreover, the ruins were seriously damaged during the fights in 1914. The local cemetery gives evidence of these events.

## OPEN-AIR MUSEUM IN SVIDNÍK (1)

This Ukrainian Culture Museum was established in Svidník in 1956. Its most popular part was added in 1982; the open-air Ethnographical Exposition was built in the slope above the right bank of the Ondava River. This interesting complex takes up the rather large area of 10 hectares and presents the most typical monuments of the folk architecture of northeast Slovakia; the region of national minorities of the Ruthenians and Ukrainians with their particular language, culture and folk traditions. Vernacular buildings, barns, farms, granaries, haylofts, wells, a water-mill, a saw-mill, pubs and other peasant buildings have original folk furniture, farming equipment and other folk articles. The most admired building is the wooden Church of St. Paskareva from 1766, which was originally in the village of Nová Polianka.

## WOODEN CHURCH
## IN VYŠNÝ KOMÁRNIK (2)

This is one of the last villages before the border crossing to Poland, which is why its inhabitants suffered badly during the difficult times of the fights over the nearby Dukliansky Priesmyk Pass in the autumn 1944. The wooden Church of St. Cosmas and Damian was built in 1924 to replace an older church from the beginning of the 18th century, destroyed during World War I. It is the only building in northeastern Slovakia that combines modern architectonic elements while adhering to the basic principles of the traditional architecture of churches of the Eastern religion. The interior houses furnishings that allow for the local art Baroque-influenced form, however it also includes foreign styles, mostly influenced by the art of large Russian Orthodox churches.

## WOODEN CHURCH
## IN NIŽNÝ KOMÁRNIK (3)

The wooden Church of the Protection of the Blessed Mother of God is particular, as its owner is not anonymous. It was built in 1938 according to a design by V. Siczyňský, a renowned expert on folk architecture. A wooden church from the 18th century once stood nearby. Despite the location of Nižný Komárnik near the Dukliansky Priesmyk Pass, the church was not seriously damaged during the fights in the autumn of 1944, in contrast to the village below, which was completely burnt out. The log-built church is not paralleled anywhere else in Slovakia. From an architectonic point of view, it can be placed amongst the buildings of the 'Bokovský' type (featuring the saddle roof) built on the territory of the Carpathian Ruthenia. This type is closest to the Byzantine churches of the Eastern religion. The iconostasis from the beginning of the 18th century was brought from Trebišov. As it was built for another interior, the current position of icons differs from the original composition. The upper section of the iconostasis is significantly younger; it dates from the 20th century.

## ARMY MUSEUM IN SVIDNÍK (4)

A strange looking, modern building is set in a park west of the centre of Svidník. Its shape

resembles an anti-tank landmine, and this is no coincidence, as it houses the Army Museum. Svidník and its surroundings suffered badly during the two world wars. The town was close to the site of one of the largest battlefields of World War II in the autumn of 1944. It was part of the heavy fights over the Dukliansky Priesmyk Pass, which is how the Army Museum, opened in Svidník in 1965, received the name Dukelské Museum. It was opened on 4th October 1969 on the occasion of the 25th anniversary of the Dukla fights. The museum, which has an outdoor section as well, is managed by the Historical Army Institution in Bratislava. The military equipment from World War II is located in the park near the museum. The Monument to the Soviet Army is nearby. It was erected in 1954; there are the graves of about 9,000 soldiers of the Red Army who gave their lives in the Carpathian-Dukla Operation.

## DUKLIANSKY PRIESMYK (5)

Traces of the furious fights between the German Fascists and the Red Army in the autumn 1944 are still visible in the surroundings of the Dukliansky Priesmyk Pass. Even today grenades, ammunition and other army materials are sometimes found here. A large pieta site lies above Vyšný Komárnik near the border crossing to Poland. It is to commemorate the Carpathian-Dukla operation that cost the lives of over 60,000 Soviet and Czechoslovakian soldiers. The 28-metre monument with a bronze statue by Ján Kulich called *Žalujem (Indicting)* is a landmark of the area. The monument stands at a small army cemetery with 1,265 buried soldiers of the 1st Czechoslovakian Army Unit. The whole battlefield can be viewed from the outlook tower or from a trail that goes to the bunkers. The military equipment used in the battle is located in the surrounding landscape.

## ÚDOLIE SMRTI (6)

An unusual monument with two tanks stands slightly behind Svidník. The Soviet T34 tank in the victorious position over the German Panzer IV tank are the first exhibits of the Údolie Smrti (Death Valley). The name of the valley is very appropriate as many soldiers, who fought over every inch of land in the autumn of 1944, died here. After crossing Dukliansky Pass the Soviet 38th army met the fierce defence of the German 1st Tank Army near the villages of Vyšná Písaná, Nižná Písaná and Kapišová. The largest tank battle of the Carpathian-Duklian Operation took place here from 25th till 27th October 1944. Historical Soviet tanks were placed in the valley to commemorate the former battlefield; they form a tank platoon fighting formation.

named after the extremely hard fights that took place here during World War II. The view of the wooden Church of St. Paskareva at the edge of the village is very good as there is not much growth around. The church was believed to have been founded at the beginning of the 18th century (according to the date of 1705 on the wooden portal of 'babinec'), however it was discovered during an overhaul reconstruction that this date refers only to the portal and that most of the building was constructed in the 1930s. This is the only church in Slovakia with the ground-plan in the shape of the Greek Cross. The interior with the Baroque iconostasis comes from an older church. The painted wardrobe and chest from the 19th century illustrate the quality of the folk architecture.

## WOODEN CHURCH IN ŠEMETKOVCE (3)

This village lies in a rather remote place in the Ondavská Vrchovina Hills. A visit to it is worthwhile though, as it boasts the wooden Church of St. Michael the Archangel. The church from 1752 is near the cemetery, quite high above the village. Its architecture has the three-part disposition typical to the churches of the 'Lemkovský' type. The sacristy is small, much smaller than the nave and 'babinec' below the high, slim spire. The interior houses a Baroque iconostasis from the 18th century with icons from the 17th century.

## WOODEN CHURCH IN HUNKOVCE (4)

This village lies approximately mid-way between Svidník and Dukliansky Priesmyk Pass. The wooden Church of the Parting of the Holiest Mother of God is near the turn off to Korejovce. This church is set in the midst of a nice green cemetery and bears all the features of an Eastern religion sacral building. It has three parts and high, onion-shaped domes. Its specific feature is that the axis of the sanctuary leans slightly northwards; there are various explanations of this.

## WOODEN CHURCH IN LADOMÍROVÁ (1)

The wooden Church of St. Michael the Archangel in the village of Ladomírová is not visible from the main road from Svidník to the Dukliansky Priesmyk. The entry into the walled, shingle-covered church goes through a wooden gate with an onion-shaped roof. Apart from the church there is a detached wooden belfry and an old cemetery with nice wooden and iron crosses. The architecture and furnishings make the church in Ladomírová one of the most representative churches in Slovakia. It was built in 1742 and it is the most western building in the region that has been influenced by sacral architecture. It has the traditional three-part disposition and mainly Baroque furnishings from the second half of the 18th century.

## WOODEN CHURCH IN DOBROSLAVA (2)

The village of Dobroslava lies away from the main road in the Údolie Smrti (Death) Valley,

## WOODEN CHURCH IN KOREJOVCE (5)

If you want to visit the wooden Church of the Protection of the Holiest Mother of Jesus in Korejovce, you must turn westward in Korejovce. The church from the second half of the 18th century sits on a steep eastern slope above the village next to the cemetery. Most of the icons are from a vanished church in Krajná Bystrá. A detached wooden tower was added to the church in 1949. It houses three bells from the 18th and 19th centuries.

## WOODEN CHURCH IN KRAJNÉ ČIERNE (6)

The road to the village of Krajné Čierne turns off the main road from Svidník to Dukliansky Priesmyk. The first wooden church at the beginning of the valley is not very significant. However, the older wooden Church of St. Basil the Great at the other end of the village is noteworthy. It dates from 1730 and is enclosed by a wooden fence with a shingle covering and a wooden entry gate. It is a typical example of the eastern Carpathian churches of the 'Lemkovský' type with the three-part disposition. The specific feature of the exterior is the archaic ending of the roof; there are three pyramid-like domes instead of the usual onion-shaped ending. The icons inside show apparent features of western influence.

## WOODEN CHURCH IN BODRUŽAL (7)

The wooden Church of St. Nicholas is in the middle of the village of Bodružal. It is one of the oldest churches of the Eastern religion that dates from 1658. It is surrounded by a wooden fence with shingle roof and a wooden entry gate. The architectural features of the church correspond with the 'Lemkovský' type, however it has a specific construction disposition. The Baroque interior boasts plenty of gold, polychrome and silver furnishings. The iconostasis dates from 1794, yet some sections of the nave and sacristy decorations are older by 100 years. A mural from the 18th century was restored on the northern wall. The furnishings are Baroque and some icons of the iconostasis have atypical scenes from the lives of

simple folk in traditional costumes. The oldest icons on the walls of the nave likely date from an older, vanished church.

## WOODEN CHURCH IN PRÍKRA (8)

The village of Príkra is statistically the smallest village in Slovakia. It had only seven inhabitants according to a census carried out in 2001. Its church from 1777 is of interest.

## WOODEN CHURCH IN MIROĽA (9)

This village in the western part of the Laborecká Vrchovina Hills supposedly already had a wooden church in the 17th century; however it vanished together with the village after the Rákoczi anti-Habsburg Uprising at the beginning of the 18th century. The village was later restored and the present-day wooden Church of the Protection of the Holiest Mother of God was built in 1770.

# ZEMPLÍN

### STROPKOVSKÝ CHATEAU (1)
On the border of the Šariš and Zemplín regions in the town of Stropkov in the Ondava River valley once stood a medieval castle. It was founded by the Czudarovci family in 1245. It supposedly had a pentagonal ground-plan with the palace and chapel (perhaps even a church) enclosed by a ring of walls. The Bratríci Movement occupied the castle in the 15th century, and later the Polish army, which was chased out of Stropkov by the army of the King Matthias Corvinus, occupied it for a short time. The royal army once again occupied the castle in 1483 to prevent the pillaging of the lord of the castle, Mikuláš of Perín. The castle ceased to exists at the time of the estate uprisings; it was conquered together with the town by Imrich Tököli (Thököly) in 1686 and then by the Emperor's army, fighting against Francis II Rákoczi, in 1711. Consequently material from the castle was used in buildings in Stropkov. The castle palace was transformed into the present-day mansion, while the chapel became the presbytery of the today's parish church of Stropkov. The present-day appearance is the result of a reconstruction in 1811.

### WOODEN CHURCH IN POTOKY (2)
The only preserved wooden church in the Stropkov District is in the village of Potoky. It is consecrated to St. Paskareva. It is not the only one in the area, as another wooden church is to be found in Šemetkovice, which lies in the Svidník District and is only 10 km away. The wooden Church of St. Paskareva in Potoky was built on a gentle slope above the village next to the cemetery in 1773. It differs from other wooden churches of this area by its large western tower above the 'babinec'. A large part of the church covers the shingle roof. Murals are preserved in the interior. Apart from the ornamental decoration the nave also has figural paintings. The Baroque iconostasis dates from the same period as the church; according to experts the icons on it were influenced by folk architecture.

### MUSEUM OF MODERN ART OF A. WARHOL IN MEDZILABORCE (3)
This village is internationally renowned thanks to one man, whose parents were born in a nearby village. It started to profit from tourism after the establishment of the Museum of Modern Art of An-

dy Warhol. This unique museum devoted to the life and work of the renowned avant-garde artist was open in a rather unattractive building in 1991. Luckily its unappealing faćade was later improved by a series of colour portraits of Warhol. Moreover, a bus stop in the shape of the famous Campbell's Tomato Soup tin was constructed nearby. There is also an original fountain with a statue of Andy Warhol with an umbrella in the middle.

### HANUŠOVSKÝ ARCHED VIADUKT (4)

Trains go over the famous Hanušovský Arched Viaduct on the railway from Kapušian to Vranov nad Topľou right above the houses of the village of Hanušoviec nad Topľou. This 379.9-metre long railway viaduct was built in 1943 and allegedly it is still the longest bridge arched construction in central Europe. It was damaged by the partisans shortly after it was completed, however it was reconstructed after the war. It spans the valley at a height of up to 40 metres. The largest pillar of the bridge is 28 metres high.

### MANSION IN HANUŠOVCE NAD TOPĽOU (5)

The village of Hanušovce nad Topľou lies on the border of the lower Šariš and Zemplín regions and boasts a large mansion. However, it is not called Veľký (Large) Mansion for its size – the name simply differentiates it from another mansion in the town, the Malý (Small) mansion. Veľký Mansion was built by the Desswffy family at the turn of the 17th and 18th centuries and the family owned it until 1940. It is mainly a Renaissance mansion with some Baroque elements. The mansion is the seat of the Ethnographic Museum with historical, ethnographical and natural collections from the region.

### MONASTERY IN KRÁSNY BROD (6)

Approximately 40,000 colonists from the Ukraine Podolie, led by the priest Teodor Podoľskij, moved to this area pillaged by the Tartars in the 14th century. They founded a monastery in the village of Krásny Brod near Medzilaborce in the 15th century. According to a legend, they picked a spot where water from the local well restored sight to a blind man. The monastery of the Basilian Order became the spiritual centre of the Greek-Catholic religion in eastern Slovakia. It was burnt by the powerful Drugeth family in 1603; however the destroyed wooden building was replaced by a new one nine

years later. It was destroyed again during the Rákoczi Uprising in the 18th century and restored one more time by the monks from a monastery in Mukachevo. This time the monastery lasted until 1915, when it was seriously damaged in a cannonade of the Austria-Hungary army fighting against the local headquarters of the Russian army.

### VEĽKÁ DOMAŠA (7)

Eastern Slovakia has always suffered from a shortage of drinking water, so the Veľká Domaša Dam was built on the Ondava River in 1967. Its waters flooded six villages; only the Baroque Church of St. Steven the King from the village of Kelča remained on the left bank of the lake. The lake is 15 square kilometres, holds 185 million square metres of water and is 38 metres deep at its deepest point. The length of the dam is 14 kilometres. It was created as a drinking reservoir and boasts clean, clear water abundant with fish. This makes the lake, which enjoys pleasant weather with bathers and water sports enthusiasts.

## MANSION IN HUMENNÉ (1)

The originally French-Italian aristocratic Drugeth family came to Hungary in the 14th century with King Karol Róbert of Anjou and became one of the most powerful families in the country. The Head of the Zemplín County Council, Juraj III Drugeth from the Hummené branch of the family, held the largest estate in eastern Slovakia. He built a stately Renaissance mansion on the site of an original Gothic water castle in 1610. It was reconstructed after a fire in 1684 in the Baroque style, which was applied mainly to the splendid interiors. The present-day appearance of the mansion is the result of a reconstruction at the end of the 19th century. The original Renaissance appearance was replaced by a style that imitated the French Baroque chateaus. The reconstruction was initialized by A. Andráši (Andrássy), who also founded a nice park with a pond around the mansion. The mansion burnt out in 1945 and after a reconstruction became the seat of the Vihorlatské Museum, containing valuable historical and ethnographical collections. It also houses a unique exhibition about the history of the Roma people in Slovakia.

## OPEN-AIR MUSEUM IN HUMENNÉ (2)

An exposition of the folk architecture and lifestyle was opened north of the Humenné mansion's park in 1984. This open-air museum is part of the Vihorlatské Museum and boasts several valuable folk buildings from the upper Zemplín Region. The most popular is the wooden Church of St. Michael the Archangel from 1754. It comes from Nová Sedlice, the easternmost village of Slovakia.

It represents the 'Lemkovský' type of the sacral edifices of the Eastern religion; not even one nail was used in its construction. The church houses an iconostasis from the 18th century and there is a bell from 1811 in the tower. The open-air museum further boasts a smithery from Nechválova Polianka, a water mill from Vyšná Jablonka and several peasant houses and outbuildings.

### STATUE OF SOLDIER ŠVEJK IN HUMENNÉ (3)

The popular Czech writer J. Hašek sent the main character of his famous book, the good soldier Švejk, to fight for the Emperor and the country on the eastern front. He first went to Zemplín and Hališ in the neighbouring Poland. This inspired the inhabitants of the region to make an attractive tourist trail called 'In the footsteps of the good soldier Švejk'. It starts in Humenné; a statue of Švejk was unveiled at the local train station in 2000. From here the trail continues northwest, passing many army cemeteries from World War I. One of them is in the village of Radvaň nad Laborcom. There is a total of 32 cemeteries with 6,064 buried soldiers in the valley of Laborec. The valley ends at the Polish Sanoko, which has the famous hotel 'Pod Trzema Rózama'; the village also has a street named Ulička Dobrého Vojaka Švejka.

### JASENOV CASTLE (4)

The ruin of this castle sits relatively high above the village of the same name near Humenné. The castle was built on the forested hill at the northwest of the Vihrolatské Vrchy Hills in the 13th century. It came into the possession of the wealthy Drugeth family after the battle near Rozhanovce (victory of the family of Anjou) in 1312, and the family kept it until 1644. The original Gothic building was repeatedly reconstructed with the aim of strengthening mainly the fortification. Fake money was minted at the castle when it was owned by Gabriel Druheth. This stirred up the anger of the royal offices of Hungary as well as Poland, and they put the leader of the minting workshop, Master Mikuláš, in prison; he was beheaded on the main square in Prešov in 1551. The star-shaped fortification, popular in the 17th century, was added to the castle at the beginning of the 17th century. However, new bastions were not enough to defend it in 1644, when it was conquered and destroyed by the rebels of Juraj Rákoczi.

### BREKOV CASTLE (5)

The Laborec River turns southward below Humenné and enters the narrow Brekovská gate near Brekov. The ruins of the medieval Brekov Castle are atop a hill on the western side of the chasm. It was built toward the end of the 13th century on the site of a vanished Great Moravian hill fort. Like other castles in the area it was given to the Drugeth family after the battle at Rozhanovce in 1312 for their support of King Karol Róbert, and they owned it until 1698. For a short period between 1486 and 1488 it belonged to the Zápoľský family, who strengthened its fortification walls. The rebels of Juraj Rákoczi severely damaged the castle in 1644; however it was still partially inhabitable for about half of the century. It is now a romantic ruin with a nice view of the

surrounding countryside. It sits atop a limestone hill with karst formations.

### ČIČAVA CASTLE (6)

You will not find this castle near the village of Čičava, as it is about 5 km away from it, much nearer to the village of Sedliská (once called Podčičava). The ruins of the medieval castle sit atop a smallish hill above the right bank of the Ondava River. It was built in the 13th century on a large estate. Its important task was to protect a significant trade path below the castle. The castle was destroyed by the Emperor's army following the suppression of the Rákoczi Uprising in 1711; it has been a romantic ruin ever since. The castle is associated with the famous 'Čičavská Book', which listed the names of liars and their unbelievable lies and shams. A famous Slovakian saying is derived from this book: 'Such a lie should be written in the Čičavská Book.'

## STARINA WATER RESERVOIR (1)

The largest water reservoir in Slovakia was constructed in 1988 on the Cirocha River. It received the name of one of the seven flooded or relocated villages; in total 3,463 people had to be moved because of the dam. The construction works started in 1981 and water started to pour into the lake on 20th August 1987, after the 311-metre long and 50-metre high dam was completed. The reservoir holds almost 60 million square metres of drinking water and takes up an area of 281 hectares. The road from Stakčín to Nová Sedlica passes the village of Starina. There is an outlook tower above the dam that offers a nice view of the splendid lake situated in the Poloniny National Park. Several cemeteries dot the valleys above the lake. People from the flooded villages make nostalgic journeys to these places.

## SNINSKÉ LAKES (2)

These lakes are the best place to relax for the inhabitants of the village of Sniny. There are three swimming pools in this popular recreation area near the town. The local lake provides ideal conditions for water sports and fishing. The Sninský Kameň Peak makes a lovely reflection on the surface of the large lake sourced by the Bystrá Stream. This most popular hill in the Vihorlat Mountains has a rock at its top section; a nature trail that starts at Sninské Lakes goes over the viewing peak of Sninský Kameň and continues to the lake of Morské Oko.

## KREMENEC (3)

The borders of three countries, Slovakia, Poland and Ukraine, meet on top of this mountain (1,208 m). It is the highest peak of the Bukovské Vrchy Hills and the Slovakian part of the Eastern Carpathians and the easternmost point of the Slovak Republic (22° 34'). Some sources state its height as 1,221 metres, however this height belongs to a hill situated more to the east (outside the Slovakian territory). A tourist trail that starts at Nová Sedlica, the easternmost village in Slovakia, leads to the top of Kremenec. It cuts through the territory of the Stužica Forest. A granite triangle-shaped pylon was erected on Kremenec in 2000. On its sides are national symbols of the three neighbouring countries.

## HERCULES' FOUNTAIN IN SNINA (4)

There is a Classicism mansion dating from 1781 in the easternmost Slovakian district town of Snina. It was built by the countess Terézia van Dernáthová, the granddaughter of the last male descendant of the powerful aristocratic Drugeth family. Her sons later gave the mansion to the Rholovs, a wealthy banking and mining family, who transformed the mansion into a luxurious, breathtaking residence. The adjacent park was adorned by flowers imported from Holland and there was also a small zoo. Water to the Hercules' Fountain was provided by a special pipe system. The central statue of the legendary Hercules was cast in the ironwork in Zemplínske Hámre, which belonged to the family of Rholov, in 1814. The mythological hero on the fountain on the square is depicted as a stout warrior with a club in his hand, fighting a thee-headed dragon. It became the symbol of the town. The mansion is currently awaiting reconstruction.

## STUŽICA FOREST (5)

The greatest wealth of the Bukovské Vrchy Hills is its forests, and this was the main reason behind making this area the Poloniny National Park. Forests in the Stužica pri Novej Sedlici National Nature Reserve are preserved in their most natural form. They cover the spring area of the Stužická River, which flows in the direction of the Ukraine. The rare fir-oak forest in this remote area near the three boarders was designated as protected in the past, and it was added to the UNESCO Natural Heritage List in 2007. Stužica is amongst the most important forests in Slovakia. Original oaks, firs and mountain maples grow on a relatively large area on the territory, which has a large elevation difference. The firs in particular are remarkably large; some are 40 metres high with their trunks having a perimeter bigger than 160 cm. The oldest trees are over 300 years old. A nature trail goes through the forest to the nearby Kremenec Hill.

## WOODEN CHURCH IN TOPOĽ (1)

The village of Topoľ lies in the midst of the Bukovské Vrchy Hills in the valley of the Ulička River. The canon of the Greek-Catholic bishopric in Prešov and enlightened scientist, called Duchnovyč (1803-1865), was born here into the family of the local Greek-Catholic priest. A theatre in Prešov was named after this poet and Ruthenian national enlivener. The first wooden church in this village dated from the first half of the 17th century, however it was replaced by the present-day wooden Church of St. Michael the Archangel at the turn of the

17th century. A detached belfry was added in the mid-20th century. The architecture of the church is very specific, so it is not exactly possible to categorise it according to one of the basic types of churches of the Eastern religion. The landmark of the exterior is a large saddle shingle roof with a small spire. The interior keeps the three-part composition. The iconostasis from the 18th century shows the influence of the iconographical work of the artists from the Carpathian Ruthenia. It has a strict composition and typical Ruthenian depicting of the religious dogma and symbolism.

## WOODEN CHURCH IN ULIČSKÉ KRIVÉ (2)

This village set in the Bukovské Vrchy Hills is the third farthest village from Bratislava; only the neighbouring Zboj and Nová Sedlica are further. The first wooden church was built here in the 16th century and was replaced by the present-day Church of St. Michael the Archangel in 1728; it is one of the oldest in the region. The particularity of this building is the two-level shingle roof that covers all the three parts of the building, which is typical for the churches of the Eastern religion. The Baroque iconostasis dates from the beginning of the 18th century. The large icon of the Suffering of Jesus from 1834 is noteworthy. It is located on the side wall of the nave and consists of 15 smaller paintings.

## WOODEN CHURCH IN KALNÁ ROZTOKA (3)

This village lies on the southern edge of the Poloniny National Park. The wooden Church of St. John the Baptist from the end of the 18th century sits atop a hill above the village. It is enclosed by a wooden fence with a shingle roof. The detached wooden belfry is much younger than the church. This church is different, for it boasts white plastered exterior walls. The locals say this type of church is 'wearing a fur coat,' as the plaster protects it against the influences of weather. The polygonal sacristy in the three-part exterior is also to be found only in a few churches behind the Vihorlat Mountains. The interior is also plastered. The carved wooden iconostasis is quite valuable.

## WOODEN CHURCH IN RUSKÁ BYSTRÁ (4)

This village lies at the eastern edge of the Vihorlat Mountains away from the main road that connects Sniny and Sobraniec. The shade of patulous trees on the slope above the village hides the wooden Church of St. Nicholas the Bishop, from 1720. Its shape is relatively simple. It has the traditional three-part disposition consisting of the 'babinec', nave and polygonal sacristy, all covered by one shingle roof. The western side has a massive quadrant tower, while the spire at the other side of the roof above the sacristy is much smaller. The Baroque-Rococo interior dates from the same time as the church. The disposition of the iconostasis and the icons suggest that they were moved here from a different church.

## WOODEN CHURCH IN RUSKÝ POTOK (5)

This village lies in a remote side valley in the heart of Bukovské Vrchy. Tourists visit this place to see the wooden Church of St. Michael the Archangel built by the worshippers of the Greek-Catholic religion in 1740. The detached wooden belfry was added in 1956. This sacral construction of the 'Lemkovský' type was erected on a stone foundation. The polygonal shape of the sacristy is unusual for this type of church. The two-story shingle roof is a landmark of the exterior; an average-sized quadrant tower ended by an onion-shaped dome juts out of it. The iconostasis dates from the same time as the church. Liturgical books written in the Cyrillic alphabet and printed in the Ukraine are quite valuable.

## WOODEN CHURCH
## IN INOVCE (6)

This village lies at the northern foothills of the Popriečne massif in close vicinity of the Ukrainian borders. The wooden Church of St. Michael the Archangel sits in a rugged terrain. It is the youngest and one of the smallest churches beyond the Vihorlat Mountains. It was built in 1836 on a site with a beautiful view of the landscape. The perfect woodcraft work of the tree-part church is outstanding; the precisely laid shingle roof has impressive fillets at the edges. The spire is relatively small so it also has a detached wooden belfry. As the sacristy is very small, it was not possible to place the complete iconostasis from 1842 inside. The interior shows an apparent transition from the Baroque to the Classicism styles.

## WOODEN CHURCH
## IN HRABOVÁ ROZTOKA (7)

This village lies in a remote place on the northern side of Vihorlat. The wooden Church of St. Basil the Great is located relatively high above the village. Its position in the open space away from the territory of the village gives this monument an impressive appearance. It was built in the mid-18th century. It is enclosed, together with the cemetery, by a wooden fence with a shingle roof, and two wooden gates provide the entry. It is a building of the 'Lemkovský' type. It has a smallish tower above the 'babinec' and a small onion-shaped spire above the sacristy. The iconostasis from the 18th century was constructed according to the strict religious regulations, however as the nave is small, the top part of the icon was placed on the ceiling and the icons on the edge with figures of apostles are on the side walls.

## VINIANSKY CASTLE (1)

The ruins of this castle are atop a conical hill to the southwest of the Vihorlat Mountains. It was founded as a sentry castle in the 13th century on a trade path connecting the Potisie and southern Poland. According to the oldest record from 1249, it had the name of Winna and was owned by the lords of Michalovce for a long time. As it was shared amongst two aristocrats, Ondrej and Jako II, a rather detailed description of the then Gothic castle was recorded. It was seriously damaged during the battle between Hungary and Poland in 1466, yet it survived the damage. Its end came later though, when it was conquered by the Emperor's army in 1594. This was the beginning of its destruction, as its weakened defence system made the castle an easy task for the armies fighting in the estate uprisings. Following unsuccessful efforts to repair the castle, its lords moved into mansions in Vinné and Michalovce instead. The round Vinianske Jazero Lake lies east of the castle. It is used for recreational purposes.

## MORSKÉ OKO (2)

This splendid natural lake resembles a small blue spot on a crumpled green carpet when seen from the rock on the top of Sninský Kameň Hill. It lies in the midst of thick forests that cover most of the Vihorlat massif. As it is in a volcanic mountain range it was believed to have filled in a crater of an extinct volcano. However, its origins are different as it was created by a huge landslide off the eastern slope of Motrogon Mountain; the scar left by the separation of the huge mass of rocks is still visible. The 800-metre wide landslide blocked the Okna Valley, creating the lake with a surface of 7 hectares. Its dam was artificially raised in the 19th century, thus creating a lake with an area of 13.8 hectares. Morské Oko is the third largest natural lake in Slovakia; only three plesá (tarns) in the Tatras are larger. Five permanent and several temporary springs source the lake and water flows out of it into the Okna River. The lake is a valuable natural phenomenon protected as a National Nature Reserve.

## MANSION IN MICHALOVCE (3)

Michalovce is a metropolis of the Lower Zemplín Region and tourists use this pleasant town as the gateway to the nearby Zemplínska Šírava, the so-called Slovakian Riviera. However, if you stop in this town you should not miss the Zemplínske Museum. It is located in the mansion in Michalovce built in the 17th century near Laborec in the northern part of the town. A water castle once stood on this site; it was rebuilt into a Renaissance aristocratic seat and later reconstructed in the Baroque style. Its present-day mostly Classicism appearance dates from the first half of the 19th century. The collections of the museum include interesting archaeological exhibits, such as the valuable amphora from the Bronze Age. Golden bracelets are the oldest evidence of the gold processing in Slovakia. The ethnographical exposition exhibits the famous dark ceramics produced in the nearby Pozdišovec. There is a park around the mansion with the remains of a rotunda from the Great Moravian Empire.

## ZEMPLÍNSKA ŠÍRAVA (4)

The East Slovakian Sea or the Slovakian Riviera – these are the nicknames for Zemplínska Šírava, one of the key tourist destinations in eastern Slovakia. This second largest Slovakian water reservoir attracts tourists in the summer season with its pleasant climate. It has warm water due to its shallowness, being a maximum of 14 metres deep; this makes it similar to the Hungarian Balaton Lake. The lake was created in 1966 on the site of swamps called Podvihorlatské Blatá. The dam takes up an area of 330 square kilometres. The eastern part of the lake is a Protected Territory; about 100 species of water birds nest here. The tourism is concentrated mainly on the northern bank with the sunny slopes of Vihorlat. The main holiday resorts are Hôrka and Kaluža, while Biela Hora is the closest village to Michalovce. The southern bank has not been fully discovered yet and offers calmer holidays with fewer visitors.

## DARGOVSKÝ PRIESMYK (5)

The Slanské Vrchy Hill descends into the Dargovský Priesmyk Pass approximately in the centre of the range. The pass was named after the nearby village of Dargov. The pronounced depression between the massifs of Mošník and Bogota has always been used by a trade path that connected the Abov and Zemplín regions. It witnessed tragic events at the end of World War II during the fights between the German army and Red Army. The front stopped here for six long weeks at the turn of 1944 and 1945 with 20,000 soldiers meeting their death here. The fierce German defence was broken on 17th January 1945. The Monument to Victory, made from white marble, stands at the highest point in the road, which connects Košice and Michalovce.

## SNINSKÝ KAMEŇ (6)

According to a legend, the devil hauled a huge boulder along the Vihorlat. He planned to throw it into Morské Oko Lake and flood all the surrounding villages. He dragged it right to the top of the hill, however did not have enough strength to throw it down, so the boulder stayed there forever. The scientific explanation for the rocks on the top of Sninský Kameň (1,006 m) is rather less romantic. They are the remains of an andesite lava stream that erupted from a volcano in the Tertiary Era. A nature trail leads to the top of Sninský Kameň. It starts at Morské Oko, and the demanding climb is rewarded with a splendid panoramic view.

## MANSION IN TREBIŠOV (1)

Trebišov is the centre of farming south of Zemplín, with a well-developed food production industry. The appearance of this province town was marred by the construction of the unappealing concrete apartment blocks called 'paneláky' (typical for the Communism Era). One of the original preserved buildings is a Baroque-Classicism mansion. It was built for I. Čáki (Czáki) in 1786. The building renovations ordered by the count J. Andráši (Andrássy) in the second half of the 19th century altered the original appearance of the mansion. It has three wings on a U-shaped disposition. Two Baroque towers are placed in the divide of the wings. The back wings close up a courtyard that is adjacent to a French-style garden and an English-style park. The 62-hectare park was landscape on the territory of an original floodplain forest. The mansion now houses the Ethnographical Museum. Its expositions focus on the typical features of this rich lowland region. Its most popular section is the exposition devoted to Tokay wine making, with an archive and the opportunity to sample the delicious Tokay wines.

## MAUSOLEUM IN TREBIŠOV (2)

A remarkable Neo Gothic monument is reflected on the surface of a small pond in the large park in Trebišov. It is the mausoleum of the Andráši (Andrássy) family, which was built in 1893 to hold the body of the count J. Andráši (1823-1890). He came from the Betliar's branch of this rich Hungarian aristocracy. His father was a member of the Hungarian Assembly and his mother, born Sapáriová, was one of the richest women in Hungary thanks to inherited estates. Count Andráši succeeded as a politician and statesman. Together with F. Deák they prepared the concept of the Austro-Hungarian Compromise in 1867, and he was the first constitutional Hungarian minister at the time of the dual monarchy. The mausoleum was built according to the design by a German architect, A. Meining; the sarcophaguses of the count and his wife are the work of the sculptor J. Zala. They have a symbolical protector, a winged angel, and a sculpture of their kneeling daughter Helena is at the sarcophaguses. To the left is the tin coffin of their son.

## VEĽKÝ KAMENEC (3)

Conspicuous, isolated hills jut out from the monotonous lowlands of the Vychodoslovenská Nížina Plain. They are mostly formed by Tertiary volcanic rocks. Two such hills are near the village of Veľký Kamenec. The highest one is called Tarbucka and there are vineyards on its slopes. Sands that were blown up in an unusual place in the slope of the andesite hill are protected as a Nature Reserve. The smaller hill has the ruins of Veľký Kamenec Castle on its top. This landmark of the landscape is well visible on the bare hill. This locality was settled even before the existence of the castle; burial sites were uncovered in the surroundings, among others, dating from the Great Moravian period. The medieval castle was built in the 13th century following the Tartar invasion. It was occupied by the Bratríci Movement of J. Jiskra in 1451 and used as their base for pillaging attacks in the surroundings. The castle witnessed an important event in 1458, when Jan Jiskra and Ján Huňady signed a truce here. The castle was the seat of the powerful Šóšov family, who carried out a great reconstruction of the building; however as the feudal lord J. Šóša (Soós) participated in the Veseleni (Wesselényi) Uprising of 1672, the Emperor's army demolished his castle as revenge.

## MANSION
## IN STREDA NAD BODROGOM (4)

This village in the Zemplín Region sprawls on a flat piece of land near the lowest site in Slovakia. Extremely fruitful archaeological sites are to be found in the surroundings. A stone castle stood here in the Middle Ages. It was later demolished by the then feudal lord general Spork in 1670 and the present-day Renaissance mansion was built on its site in 1700. It is located in the middle of the village and its present-day appearance is the result of a reconstruction carried out in the 19th century. There is one more mansion in the village, from the 18th century, and yet another interesting building is a mansion from the 16th century in the village of Borša, the birthplace of Francis II Rákoczi (1676-1735). The famous leader of the last anti-Habsburg uprising was born here on 27th March 1676.

## TOKAY VINEYARDS (5)

Tokay wine is called the king of wines as well as the wine of the kings. At one time it could not be missing on the tables of many European rulers. The genuine Tokay can only come from one region in the world, which is shared between Slovakia and Hungary. The smaller, Slovakian, Tokay wine region spreads out on the southwestern slopes of the Zemplínske Vrchy Hills around the town of Nové Mesto. The vineyards take up an area of 1,000 hectares. Tokay wine is produced from the grapes of the Furmint, Lipovina and Yellow Muscat wine varieties. The real Tokay needs a dry autumn and tuff substrate. The most important condition is, however, the noble rot, a grey fungus called Botrytis cinerea, which grows on the so-called cibebach. These are in fact rotting berries which are picked in the late autumn and added to the wine. Cibéby give Tokay its unmistakable taste, bouquet and typical golden-yellow colour. A visit to this area gives you the opportunity to sample Tokay.

## LATORICKÝ FLOODPLAIN (1)

Since the oldest time people have fought an uneven struggle with water at the Východoslovenská Nížina Plain. Large rivers that collect waters from the slopes of the Eastern Carpathians spilt onto the wide plains. Many of areas thus became arable fields; however large territories still remain natural floodplains with abundant lush vegetation, swamps and a dense network of rivers and dead-end tributaries. The plains along the Latorica River are of the most value and were designated the Latorický Luh Protected Landscape Area in 1990. The entire natural area around the most natural river in Slovakia with numerous meanders is a territory of frequent floods that are essential for the occurrence of rare water and swamp biocenosis. In places, small hilltops jut out of this water world; they were created by sand dunes. Locals call them 'moľvy'.

## MONASTERY IN LELES (2)

Leles was an important site in the past. The local convent became the 'hodnverné' (authentic) place in the 13th century – a medieval type of notary office. It served eight Hungarian seats on the territory of the present-day Slovakia, Hungary, Ukraine and Romania and kept this important position until 1567. Thanks to this an archive was established in Leles, which became one of the most important historical sources of central European significance. Leles is now a smallish village that lies in the flatland part of the Východoslovenské Nížiny Plain near the village of Kráľovský Chlumec. The high church tower of the Premonstratensian priorate consecrated to the Holy Cross is visible from afar in this table-flat landscape. This oldest monastery in the Slovakian part of Zemplín was founded by the Bishop of Vacov Boleslav towards the end of the 12th century. The

original Romanesque building was destroyed by the Tartars. At its core the present-day monastery is a Gothic building. However, large reconstructions were carried out in the 18th century, when the monastery was enlarged and received its present-day Baroque appearance.

## TISA RIVER (3)

The Tisa, one of the largest central European rivers, skirts Slovakia only for five kilometres along its border. However even this small part of the river with sand banks and floodplain vegetation is very attractive and also suitable for swimming. The river, shared between Slovakian and Hungary, is accessible from the villages of Malé and Veľké Trakany near Čierna nad Tisou. A strip of a meandering dead-end tributary called Stará Tisa coils through this charming landscape. Previously it was the main riverbed that has been changing dynamically in the flat landscape. It often changed its flow and forked into side tributaries. These changes were brought about by active tectonic movements. The river flows through a depressed territory and compensates for this by deposits of a large amount of gravel and sand, especially in the spring.

## BODROG RIVER (4)

The Ondava and Latorica rivers of eastern Slovakia meet near the village of Zemplín. As the local people could not agree which river is the tributary and which the main flow, they decided to give the river below the confluence a new name, Bodrog. It flows for 15 kilometres across the territory of Slovakia and continues for a further 120 kilometres through Hungary before it empties into the Tisa River. The banks of the Slovakian Bodrog are different. The steep right bank skirts the southern edge of the Zemplínske Vrchy Hills with the famous Tokay vineyards. The left bank is low and, apart from isolated hills, flat. The Bodrog changed its route in the past, leaving several dead-end tributaries. One of them has developed into the Tajba Lake, known for the occurrence of the tortoise. The river is a natural obstacle in the territory, crossed only by two bridges, one pedestrian and one railway. Cruise ships are popular on the Hungarian section of the river and should soon start operating on the Slovakian part too.

## BRIDGE IN LELES (5)

A stone bridge is located west of the village of Leles near Kráľovský Chlmec. Its size does not correspond with the size of the river in this place; however there is a logical explanation for this. There are scores of shallow, longish depressions with a round shape. Apart from several dry holes most of them are swampy. The depressions are old, long ago dried out dead-end tributaries of the river, and although the nearest river is the Latorica, it is possible that these holes were created by the ever-changing Tisa River. Moreover, the man-made melioration systems influenced the changing of this river area to a large extent. The Bridge of St. Gotthard is a valuable Gothic monument, probably built in the 14th century. Its name dates from the beginning of the 18th century, when Czech monks stayed in the local monastery. The statue of St. Gotthard was removed from the bridge in 1948. The renowned poet S. Petőfi walked across this bridge on 10th July 1847 on his way from Széphalom to Užhorod. A reconstruction was completed in 1994; however this meant that the road traffic was redirected and the bridge now only serves pedestrians.

# LIST OF USED PHOTOGRAPHS

**Ján Lacika:** p. 8, 9; p. 10 (1, 4); p. 13 (2, 3, 4); p. 14 (1, 2); p. 15 (5, 6); p. 16 (1); p. 17 (2, 4); p. 18 (1, 2); p. 19 (3, 4, 5); p. 23 (4); p. 24 (2); p. 25 (4, 5); p. 27 (4); p. 28 (1, 2); p. 29 (3, 4, 5); p. 30 (2); p. 31 (3, 4, 5); p. 32 (1, 2); p. 33 (4, 5); p. 34 (2); p. 36 (1, 3); p. 37 (4); p. 39 (6); p. 40, 41; p. 43 (3, 4, 5); p. 44 (1, 2); p. 45 (3, 4); p. 46 (1, 2); p. 47 (3, 4, 5, 6); p. 48 (1, 2); p. 49 (3, 4); p. 50 (1, 2, 3); p. 51 (4, 5, 6); p. 53 (3); p. 60 (1, 2); p. 61 (4, 5); p. 62 (2, 3); p. 63 (7); p. 64 (3); p. 65 (5); p. 66 (2, 3); p. 69 (3, 4); p. 71 (3); p. 72 (1, 3); p. 73 (4); p. 74 (1, 2, 3); p. 75 (4, 5); p. 76 (1, 2); p. 77 (4, 6); p. 79 (5); p. 80 (1, 2, 3); p. 81 (4, 5, 6); p. 82 (1, 2, 3); p. 83 (5); p. 84 (1, 2, 3); p. 85 (4); p. 86 (1); p. 87 (4, 5, 6, 7); p. 88 (2, 3); p. 89 (4, 6); p. 91 (2, 5); p. 92 (1, 2, 3); p. 93 (4, 6); p. 94 (1, 2); p. 95 (4, 5); p. 96 (1, 3); p. 97 (4); p. 98 (1, 2); p. 99 (3, 4, 5, 6); p. 100 (1); p. 101 (3, 4); p. 102 (1); p. 103 (3, 4); p. 105 (5); p. 106 (1); p. 107 (5, 6); p. 108 (1, 2, 3); p. 109 (6); p. 111 (3, 4, 5, 6, 7); p. 112 (1, 2); p. 113 (4); p. 115 (3, 4, 5); p. 116 (1); p. 117 (4, 5); p. 118 (1); p. 119 (3); p. 121 (4); p. 123 (3, 4, 5); p. 124 (2); p. 125 (3, 4, 5, 6); p. 127 (3, 4); p. 128 (1); p. 129 (3); p. 130 (1); p. 131 (3, 5); p. 132 (1, 3); p. 134 (1, 2); p. 135 (4); p. 136, 137; p. 139 (2, 3, 4); p. 140 (1, 3, 4); p. 141 (2); p. 142 (1, 2); p. 143 (3, 4); p. 144 (1, 2); p. 145 (4); p. 146 (1, 2); p. 147 (3, 4); p. 148 (1, 2); p. 149 (3, 4); p. 151 (3, 4); p. 152 (1); p. 153 (3, 4); p. 154 (3); p. 155 (2, 4, 5); p. 157 (2, 3, 5); p. 158 (1, 2, 3); p. 159 (4, 6, 7); p. 160 (1); p. 161 (2, 3, 4); p. 162 (1, 2); p. 163 (3, 4, 5); p. 165 (4, 5); p. 166 (1, 2, 3); p. 167 (4, 5); p. 168 (1); p. 169 (4, 5, 6); p. 170 (1, 2); p. 171 (4); p. 172 (1); p. 173 (4, 5, 6, 7); p. 174 (1, 2, 3); p. 175 (4, 6); p. 176 (1, 2, 3, 4); p. 178 (1, 2); p. 179 (4, 5, 6); p. 180 (1, 2, 3); p. 181 (4, 5, 6); p. 182 (1, 2, 3); p. 183 (4); p. 184 (1, 2, 3); p. 185 (5, 6); p. 186 (1); p. 187 (4); p. 188 (3, 4); p. 190 (1, 2, 3); p. 191 (4); p. 193 (2, 4, 5, 6); p. 194 (1, 2, 3); p. 195 (5, 6); p. 196 (1, 2); p. 197 (3, 4, 5); p. 198 (1, 2); p. 199 (3, 4, 5); p. 200 (1); p. 202 (2, 3); p. 203 (5); p. 204 (1, 2, 3); p. 205 (5, 8); p. 206, 207; p. 208 (2, 3); p. 209 (4); p. 210 (1, 2); p. 211 (3, 4, 5, 6); p. 212 (1); p. 214 (3); p. 215 (4); p. 216 (1, 3); p. 217 (5, 7); p. 219 (6); p. 220 (1, 3); p. 221 (5); p. 222 (1, 2); p. 223 (3, 5, 6, 7); p. 224 (1, 2, 3); p. 225 (4, 5); p. 226 (2); p. 227 (4, 5); p. 228 (1); p. 229 (2); p. 230 (2, 3); p. 232 (1, 2); p. 233 (3); p. 234 (1, 2); p. 235 (3); p. 236 (1); p. 238 (1, 2); p. 239 (3, 4, 5); p. 240 (1, 2); p. 241 (4, 5, 6); p. 242 (1); p. 243 (5, 7); p. 244 (1); p. 245 (2, 5, 6); p. 246 (3); p. 247 (4); p. 248 (1, 3); p. 249 (4); p. 250 (2, 3); p. 251 (5); p. 253 (3, 5); p. 254 (1, 2, 3); p. 255 (6); p. 256 (1, 3); p. 257 (4, 6); p. 258 (1); p. 259 (3, 4, 5, 6); p. 260 (1, 2, 3); p. 261 (4, 5); p. 262 (1, 2); p. 263 (3, 4, 5); p. 264 (1, 2); p. 265 (3, 4, 5, 6); p. 266 (1, 2, 3); p. 267 (4, 5, 6, 7); p. 268 (1, 2); p. 269 (3, 4, 5); p. 270 (1, 2, 3, 4); p. 271 (5, 6, 7, 8); p. 272 (1, 2); p. 273 (3, 4, 5, 6); p. 274, 275; p. 276 (1, 2, 3); p. 277 (5, 6, 7); p. 278 (2); p. 279 (5, 6, 7); p. 280 (3); p. 282 (1, 2); p. 283 (3, 4, 5, 6); p. 284 (1, 2); p. 285 (3); p. 286 (1, 2); p. 287 (3, 4, 6); p. 289 (3, 5); p. 290 (1, 2, 3, 4); p. 290 (1, 2, 3, 4); p. 292 (1); p. 293 (3, 4, 5); p. 294 (1, 2, 3, 4); p. 295 (5, 6, 7); p. 296 (1, 2, 3); p. 297 (4, 5, 6, 7); p. 298 (1, 2); p. 299 (4, 5, 6); p. 300 (1); p. 301 (4, 5); p. 302 (2); p. 303 (3, 4, 5); p. 305 (3); p. 307 (3, 4); p. 308 (1, 2); p. 309 (4, 5, 6); p. 310 (1, 2); p. 311 (3, 4, 5); p. 312 (1, 2, 3, 4); p. 313 (5); p. 314 (1, 2); p. 315 (3); p. 316 (1, 2); p. 317 (3, 4, 5, 6); p. 318 (3); p. 319 (4, 5, 6); p. 320 (1, 2, 3); p. 321 (4, 5, 6); p. 322 (1); p. 323 (2, 3); p. 324 (1); p. 325 (3, 4); p. 326 (1, 2); p. 327 (3, 5); p. 330 (1, 2, 3); p. 331 (4, 5); p. 332 (1, 2); p. 333 (4, 5); p. 334 (3); p. 335 (4, 5); p. 336 (1, 2, 3, 4); p. 337 (5); p. 338 (1, 2, 3); p. 339 (4, 5, 6); p. 340 (1, 2); p. 341 (3, 4, 5, 6, 7); p. 342 (1, 2, 3, 4); p. 343 (6, 7); p. 344 (1, 2, 3); p. 345 (4, 5, 6); p. 346 (1, 2, 3); p. 347 (4, 5); p. 348 (1, 2, 3, 4); p. 349 (5, 6, 7); p. 350 (1, 2, 3); p. 351 (4, 5, 6); p. 352 (1, 2); p. 353 (3, 4, 5, 6, 7); p. 354 (1, 2); p. 355 (4, 5, 6, 7); p. 356 (1); p. 357 (3); p. 358 (1, 2); p. 359 (3, 4, 5); p. 360 (1, 2); p. 361 (3); p. 362 (1, 2); p. 363 (3, 4, 5, 6); p. 364 (1, 2, 3, 4); p. 365 (5, 6, 7, 8, 9); p. 366 (1, 2, 3); p. 367 (4, 5, 6, 7); p. 368 (1, 2, 3); p. 369 (4, 5, 6); p. 370 (2); p. 371 (3, 4, 5); p. 372 (1); p. 373 (3, 4, 5, 6, 7); p. 374 (2); p. 375 (3, 5); p. 376 (2); p. 377 (3, 4, 5); p. 378 (2); p. 379 (3, 4, 5)

**Jozef Lomnický:** s.10 (2, 3); p. 12 (1); p. 15 (3, 4); p. 17 (3, 5); p. 20 (1); p. 21 (2, 3, 4, 5); p. 22 (1); p. 23 (2, 3); p. 24 (1); p. 25 (3); p. 26 (1); p. 27 (3, 5); p. 30 (1); p. 33 (3); p. 34 (1); p. 35 (3, 4, 5); p. 36 (2); p. 37 (5); p. 38 (1, 2); p. 39 (3, 4, 5); p. 51 (7); p. 52 (1, 2); p. 53 (4, 5); p. 54 (1, 2); p. 55 (3, 4); p. 56 (1, 2); p. 57 (3, 4); p. 58 (1, 2, 3); p. 59 (4, 5); p. 60 (3); p. 61 (6); p. 62 (1); p. 63 (4, 5, 6); p. 64 (1, 2); p. 65 (4, 6); p. 66 (1); p. 67 (4, 5, 6, 7); p. 68 (1); p. 70 (2); p. 71 (4); p. 73 (2); p. 77 (3, 5); p. 78 (2, 3); p. 83 (4); p. 85 (5); p. 86 (2); p. 87 (3); p. 88 (1); p. 89 (5); p. 90 (1); p. 91 (3, 4); p. 93 (5); p. 94 (3); p. 96 (2); p. 101 (2); p. 105 (3, 4, 6); p. 106 (2, 3); p. 107 (4); p. 109 (4, 5); p. 110 (1, 2); p. 112 (3); p. 113 (5, 6, 7, 8); p. 114 (1); p. 115 (2); p. 116 (2); p. 117 (3); p. 118 (2); p. 119 (4, 5); p. 120 (1, 2, 3); p. 121 (5); p. 122 (1, 2); p. 124 (1); p. 126 (1, 2); p. 129 (2, 4, 5); p. 130 (2); p. 131 (4, 6); p. 132 (2, 4 ); p. 133 (5, 6, 7); p. 135 (5); p. 138 (1); p. 141 (5); p. 144 (3); p. 145 (5); p. 150 (1); p. 151 (2, 5); p. 153 (2); p. 154 (1); p. 157 (6); p. 159 (5); p. 164 (1, 2); p. 165 (6); p. 167 (6); p. 168 (2); p. 169 (3); p. 171 (5, 6); p. 229 (3); p. 230 (1); p. 231 (5, 6, 7); p. 236 (2); p. 237 (4); p. 240 (3); p. 242 (3); p. 245 (4); p. 246 (1, 2); p. 247 (5, 6); p. 248 (2); p. 250 (1); p. 251 (4); p. 252 (2); p. 253 (4); p. 255 (4); p. 258 (2); p. 325 (2); p. 327 (4, 6); p. 333 (3); p. 334 (1, 2); p. 339 (7); p. 343 (8); p. 370 (1); p. 372 (2); p. 374 (1); p. 375 (4, 6); p. 376 (1); p. 378 (1)

**Karol Demuth:** p. 42 (1, 2); p. 68 (2); p. 70 (1); p. 71 (5, 6); p. 78 (1); p. 79 (4, 6); p. 103 (2); p. 104 (1, 2); p. 135 (3); p. 156 (1); p. 157 (4); p. 165 (3); p. 169 (7); p. 170 (3); p. 171 (7); p. 172 (2); p. 173 (3); p. 175 (5); p. 177 (5); p. 179 (3); p. 181 (7); p. 185 (4); p. 186 (3); p. 187 (2, 5, 6); p. 188 (1, 2); p. 191 (5); p. 192 (1); p. 193 (3); p. 194 (4); p. 200 (4); p. 201 (5); p. 202 (1); p. 203 (4, 6); p. 204 (4); p. 205 (6); p. 208 (1); p. 212 (2); p. 213 (3, 4, 6, 7); p. 214 (1, 2); p. 215 (5); p. 216 (2); p. 217 (4, 6); p. 218 (1, 2); p. 219 (3, 4, 5); p. 220 (2); p. 221 (4, 6); p. 223 (4); p. 225 (6); p. 226 (1); p. 227 (3); p. 223 (4, 5); p. 231 (4); p. 233 (4); p. 237 (3); p. 239 (6); p. 242 (2); p. 243 (4, 6); p. 245 (3); p. 249 (5); p. 252 (1); p. 253 (6); p. 255 (5); p. 256 (2); p. 257 (5); p. 277 (4); p. 278 (1, 3, 4); p. 279 (8); p. 280 (1, 2); p. 281 (4, 5, 6); p. 285 (4, 5); p. 287 (5); p. 288 (1, 2); p. 289 (4); p. 291 (5, 6, 7, 8); p. 292 (2); p. 298 (3); p. 301 (2, 3); p. 302 (1); p. 304 (1, 2); p. 305 (4); p. 306 (1); p. 308 (3); p. 318 (1, 2); p. 354 (3); p. 357 (2); p. 361 (4)

**Michal Rengevič:** p. 200 (2); p. 205 (7); p. 213 (5); p. 328 (1, 2, 3); p. 329 (4); p. 343 (5)

**Karol Kállay:** p. 26 (2); p. 200 (3); p. 307 (2)

**Ladislav Sternmüller:** p. 27 (6)